Political Writings of Fr

Also by Frank Cameron
NIETZSCHE AND THE 'PROBLEM' OF MORALITY

Also by Don Dombowsky
NIETZSCHE'S MACHIAVELLIAN POLITICS

Political Writings of Friedrich Nietzsche

An Edited Anthology

Frank Cameron
Wilfrid Laurier University

and

Don Dombowsky
Bishop's University

palgrave
macmillan

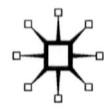

© Frank Cameron and Don Dombowsky 2008

All rights reserved. No reproduction, copy or transmission of this publication may be made without written permission.

No portion of this publication may be reproduced, copied or transmitted save with written permission or in accordance with the provisions of the Copyright, Designs and Patents Act 1988, or under the terms of any licence permitting limited copying issued by the Copyright Licensing Agency, Saffron House, 6-10 Kirby Street, London EC1N 8TS.

Any person who does any unauthorized act in relation to this publication may be liable to criminal prosecution and civil claims for damages.

The authors have asserted their rights to be identified as the authors of this work in accordance with the Copyright, Designs and Patents Act 1988.

First published 2008 by
PALGRAVE MACMILLAN

Palgrave Macmillan in the UK is an imprint of Macmillan Publishers Limited, registered in England, company number 785998, of Houndmills, Basingstoke, Hampshire RG21 6XS.

Palgrave Macmillan in the US is a division of St Martin's Press LLC, 175 Fifth Avenue, New York, NY 10010.

Palgrave Macmillan is the global academic imprint of the above companies and has companies and representatives throughout the world.

Palgrave® and Macmillan® are registered trademarks in the United States, the United Kingdom, Europe and other countries.

ISBN-13: 978-0-230-53772-9 hardback
ISBN-10: 0-230-53772-3 hardback
ISBN-13: 978-0-230-53773-6 paperback
ISBN-10: 0-230-53773-1 paperback

This book is printed on paper suitable for recycling and made from fully managed and sustained forest sources. Logging, pulping and manufacturing processes are expected to conform to the environmental regulations of the country of origin.

A catalogue record for this book is available from the British Library.

Library of Congress Cataloging-in-Publication Data

Nietzsche, Friedrich Wilhelm, 1844–1900.
  [Selections. English. 2008]
  Political writings of Friedrich Nietzsche : an edited anthology / Frank Cameron, Don Dombowsky.
    p. cm.
  Includes bibliographical references and index.
  ISBN-13: 978-0-230-53772-9 (hardback)
  ISBN-10: 0-230-53772-3 (hardback)
  ISBN-13: 978-0-230-53773-6 (pbk.)
  ISBN-10: 0-230-53773-1 (pbk.)
  1. Nietzsche, Friedrich Wilhelm, 1844–1900 – Political and social views.
  I. Cameron, Frank, 1969– II. Dombowsky, Don. III. Title.
JC233.N52A2513 2008
320.092—dc22   2008030126

10 9 8 7 6 5 4 3 2 1
17 16 15 14 13 12 11 10 09 08

Printed and bound in Great Britain by
CPI Antony Rowe, Chippenham and Eastbourne

*To the memory of my grandfather,
Frank Cameron Sr.,
who raised me, and filled my life with laughter, support,
encouragement, and most of all, love*

Contents

Acknowledgements ix
List of Abbreviations x

Introduction 1

1 Schulpforta, 1862 24
Preface 24
Napoleon III as President 26
Saint-Just 29
Two-poem cycle 'Two Kings' 30
  Louis the Sixteenth 30
  Louis the Fifteenth 30

2 Agonistic Politics, 1871–1874 31
Preface 31
The Greek State, 1871 38
On the Future of Our Educational Institutions,
  Third Lecture, February 27, 1872 46
Homer's Contest, 1872 52
Untimely Meditations 58
  David Strauss: the Confessor and the Writer, 1873 58
  Schopenhauer as Educator, 1874 61

3 The Free Spirit, 1878–1880 72
Preface 72
Human, All Too Human: A Book for Free Spirits, 1878 75
Miscellaneous Maxims and Opinions, 1879 100
The Wanderer and His Shadow, 1880 105

4 The Campaign against Morality, 1881–1885 116
Preface 116
Dawn: Thoughts on the Prejudices of Morality, 1881 119
The Gay Science, 1882 137
Thus Spoke Zarathustra: A Book for Everyone and
  No One, 1883–1885 151
  On the new idol 151
  On the rabble 153
  On the tarantulas 154
  On old and new tablets 156
Nachlass Fragments, 1883–1885 160

5 Aristocratic Radical, 1886–1887	**171**
Preface	171
Beyond Good and Evil: Prelude to a Philosophy of the Future, 1886	175
The Gay Science, Book V, 1887	212
On the Genealogy of Morals: A Polemical Tract, 1887	218
First Essay, Good and Evil, Good and Bad	218
Second Essay, Guilt, Bad Conscience and Related Matters	224
Third Essay, What Do Ascetic Ideals Mean?	230
Nachlass Fragments, 1885–1887	232
6 The Antichrist, 1888	**240**
Preface	240
Twilight of the Idols: Or How One Philosophises with a Hammer, 1888	243
Morality as Anti-Nature	243
The 'Improvers' of Mankind	244
What the Germans Lack	245
Skirmishes of an Untimely Man	248
The Antichrist: A Curse on Christianity, 1888	256
Ecce Homo: How One Becomes What One Is, 1888	270
Why I am so wise	270
Why I write such good books	272
The case of Wagner: A musician's problem	274
Why I am a destiny	275
Nachlass Fragments, 1887–1888	276
Notes	293
Primary and Secondary Historical Works	305
Selected Bibliography	309
Index	322

Acknowledgements

The editors express their appreciation to Nathalie Lachance, Ian Johnston and Jeff Mitscherling for their translations, and to James Retallack and Dan Mellamphy who served as consultants. We would also like to thank Walter de Gruyter for graciously granting us permission to translate contributions from Nietzsche's juvenilia ('Napoleon III as President', 'Saint Just', 'Two Kings: Louis the Sixteenth and Louis the Fifteenth') from *Nietzsche Werke: Kritische Gesamtausgabe. Nachgelassene Aufzeichnungen. Herbst 1858–Herbst 1862*, Herausgegeben von Johann Figl, Abt. 1, Bd. 2, Walter de Gruyter, 2000. We also owe thanks to the University of Nebraska Press for granting permission to reproduce selections from *Human, All Too Human: A Book for Free Spirits*, volume I; reprinted from *Human, All Too Human: A Book for Free Spirits* by Friedrich Nietzsche, translated by Marion Faber, with Stephen Lehmann, © 1984, 1986 by the University of Nebraska Press. Lastly, we would like to thank Bishop's University and Wilfrid Laurier University for contributing to the funding of this project.

List of Abbreviations

AC	*The Antichrist: A Curse on Christianity*
BGE	*Beyond Good and Evil: Prelude to a Philosophy of the Future*
BT	*The Birth of Tragedy Out of the Spirit of Music or: Hellenism and Pessimism*
CW	*The Case of Wagner: A Musician's Problem. Turinese Letter of May 1888*
D	*Dawn: Thoughts on the Prejudices of Morality*
EH	*Ecce Homo: How One Becomes What One Is*
GM	*On the Genealogy of Morals: A Polemical Tract*
HH; Vol. II: MM, WS	*Human, All Too Human: A Book for Free Spirits*. Vols. I and II (*Miscellaneous Maxims and Opinions* and *The Wanderer and His Shadow*)
GS	*The Gay Science*
KSA	*Kritische Studienausgabe*
KSB	*Sämtliche Briefe: Kritische Studienausgabe*
TI	*Twilight of the Idols: Or How One Philosophises with a Hammer*
UM	*Untimely Meditations*
UW	*Unpublished Writings from the period of Unfashionable Observations*
WP	*The Will to Power*
Z	*Thus Spoke Zarathustra: A Book for Everyone and No One*

Introduction

Friedrich Wilhelm Nietzsche was born in Röcken on October 15, 1844 and died in Weimar on August 25, 1900. He was named by his pious parents after the Prussian King Friedrich Wilhelm IV, with whom he shared a birthday. Nietzsche would also share with his father, Ludwig, a Lutheran pastor, a deep disdain for the 1848 liberal revolutions. Curtis Cate recalls, referring to the February Revolution in Paris and the uprisings it provoked in Germany, that 'when Ludwig Nietzsche read a newspaper account of how, to appease the noisy crowds milling around in front of his royal palace in Berlin, the Prussian monarch [Friedrich Wilhelm IV] had donned the red cockade of the revolutionaries, he broke down and wept.'[1]

Nietzsche came of age politically within the charged atmosphere of the Bismarckian era. As one commentator has written, 'Nietzsche's active career as a writer spans almost exactly the age of Bismarck'.[2] Nietzsche was neither a passive observer of nor indifferent to the political events of his day. He adopted a position on virtually every major political event that shaped his era, from the Schleswig-Holstein crisis of the 1860s to the rise of anti-Semitism and the 'Christian state' in the 1880s. But Nietzsche's political vision was also formed out of events that preceded him: the liberal revolutions of 1848–49, the German 'Wars of Liberation' of 1813–15 and the French Revolution of 1789,[3] all of which he opposed. In fact, he attributes much of his identity to events of the past: 'I should not be possible without a counter-type of race, without Germans...without Bismarck, without 1848, without "Wars of Liberation," without Kant, even without Luther. – The great crimes committed against culture by the Germans are justified in a *higher* economy of culture'.[4]

We do not accept the extreme view that Nietzsche's concern with culture was not also political, that 'the battleground was cultural, not political'.[5] We maintain that this distinction is erased symbolically for Nietzsche when he recounts the meeting between Goethe and Napoleon in Erfurt in 1808. In that meeting, between two posthumous representatives of the Renaissance, culture and politics come together and form a common anti-nationalistic

-democratic front against the legacy of the French Revolution and man Wars of Liberation.⁶

Nietzsche's nascent political views, expressed while he was a student at Schulpforta in the early 1860s and during Bismarck's ascent to power, were decisively monarchist, Prussian nationalist and anti-socialist. These political views would, with the exception of the latter, be relatively short-lived. Nietzsche's anti-socialism would persist and, arguably, compose the core of his politics. He consistently expressed outrage and fear over the strengthening organisation of the working class in Europe supported by the forces of the International. Apart from his early support for a National Liberal candidate in a *Landtag* election, Nietzsche's political thought was also anti-liberal. He referred to himself as anti-political, and this meant primarily that he was also anti-nationalist and anti-democratic.⁷ He saw a direct correlation between the transformation of the political order and cultural regeneration. His philosopher legislators, similar to Plato's, represent the coincidence of philosophy and political power. Nietzsche was not consistently anti-statist, nor did he perceive the 'new danger' merely in the 'secular state', for he was a severe opponent of the 'Christian state' as it developed in the 1880s. Nietzsche would come to reject constitutionalism, parliamentarianism, universal suffrage and eventually the nationalism championed by the liberals, but not out of loyalty towards the Prussian monarchy or conservative principles.

The Bismarckian system of government

According to the German historian Wolfgang Mommsen, 'It is almost universally agreed that Bismarck's policies were an attempt...to protect the existing social order against the stirrings of democracy, at whatever cost, and to crush all democratic aspirations at birth'.⁸ The Second German Empire (the *Kaiserreich*) was proclaimed on January 18, 1871; and on May 4, in the Hall of Mirrors at Versailles, King Wilhelm I was proclaimed Emperor of Germany. The Second *Reich* was founded on a 'revolution from above', which saw Bismarck, the 'White Revolutionary', imposing a policy of nationalism through an alliance with the National Liberals.

Bismarck's government has been characterised variously as 'a *semi-constitutional system with supplementary party-political features*';⁹ 'as a Bonapartist dictatorship...pseudo-constitutional..."Caesarist"'¹⁰ or 'at best autocracy based on consent'.¹¹ This last description has been disputed in our time, but it is generally accepted that Bismarck's aim was to promote conservative, feudal-military structures and authorities against democracy and parliamentarianism.¹² His true loyalties were to the *Junker* (aristocratic landowner) class. Bismarck's regime was described by Karl Marx in the *Gotha Programme* as 'a military despotism cloaked in parliamentary forms with a feudal ingredient and at the same time influenced by the bourgeoisie'.¹³

The new Germany was a federal entity unified by a new constitution. The constitution provided a foundation for progress in a democratic direction. Under the constitution there were three branches of government: the Executive, which was held by the Chancellor and the King of Prussia (as German Emperor), who had substantial powers, including control of the military; the Federal Council (*Bundesrat*), which represented the various states of the *Reich* possessing the power to revise the constitution; and the Parliament (*Reichstag*), elected by universal male suffrage and secret ballot, and whose consent was required for all legislation. While the *Reichstag* possessed significant power in theory, it nevertheless could be dissolved by the Kaiser on the advice of the Chancellor.[14] Bismarck intended parliament to be a passive body, giving the *Reich* a veneer of democracy. His strategy was to obstruct the revolutionary potential of social democratic forces in Germany and he thought that a strong authoritarian system, manipulating the *Reichstag* through controlled concessions, could achieve this. Bismarck's fear of these revolutionary forces was 'one of his reasons for refusing to grant even the moderate demands of the liberals for more parliamentary rights'. For Bismarck, 'every step in the direction of genuine mass participation in politics meant a strengthening of the revolutionary force which would first produce class and then Caesarist dictatorship'.[15] Ever since the Paris Commune of 1871, Bismarck had felt a profound hatred for socialists and anarchists, and he was determined to curtail their power.

Nietzsche's position towards Bismarck from 1866 to 1887 was quite positive as he shared similar anxieties, as well as a rejection of party politics, socialism and parliamentarianism. Nietzsche continued to express admiration for Bismarck while criticising democratic developments within the *Reich* until a final rupture in 1888.[16] Nietzsche, in effect, viewed Bismarck as a 'free spirit' implementing political policy in a play of forces. He recognised that Bismarck represented 'the *strong German type*. Harmlessly living among opposites, full of that supple kind of strength which cautiously avoids convictions and doctrines, by using the one as a weapon against the other and reserving absolute freedom for themselves.'[17] As a strategic and manipulative thinker, Bismarck had nearly mastered the *agon*. 'The conflict of opposed forces was for him the condition of human progress and hence an intentional part of "the divine plan".'[18] Like most of his contemporaries, Nietzsche saw Bismarck as a Machiavellian, referring in *The Gay Science* to 'Bismarck's Machiavellism...with *a* good conscience, his so-called "practical politics" in Germany'.[19] Peter Bergmann remarks that what 'seemed particularly "revolutionary" to Nietzsche was Bismarck's apparent scorn for the moral claims of the political', similar to his early admiration of Napoleon III.[20] Bismarck was a proponent of the politics of realism (*Realpolitik* – a term coined in 1854 by August Ludwig von Rochau).[21] Like Machiavelli, Bismarck considered the essence of politics to be power.[22] The state for him was primarily a device for governing, and its power but a means to concrete, practical ends. He believed that 'power takes precedence over law'.[23]

Nietzsche belongs to the historiography of those who see Bismarck's ruling strategy 'as a Bonapartist ruling strategy[24] – a combination of repression of opponents...concessions to progressive, liberal demands and diversion of domestic pressures into foreign adventures'. Such an interpretation views Bismarck as a Machiavellian 'master of *Realpolitik*'.[25] Nietzsche recognised that Bismarck's technique was one of 'negative integration', that Bismarck

> stylised internal conflicts so as to lead a majority of elements 'loyal to the Empire' against a minority of 'enemies of the Empire' (*Reichsfeinde*). The latter had to be made to appear a 'serious danger' without ever posing any real threat to the system. The various coalitions of groups loyal to the Empire were held together primarily by their enmity towards a common foe – on a negative basis.[26]

Nietzsche recognises these tactics in *Twilight of the Idols* as tactics used by virtually all political parties and by the new *Reich*.[27] Essentially, he rejected Bismarck because he was incapable of impeding the forces of democracy and the rise of organised labour.[28] He saw 'the German spirit' gradually 'making its transition, under the pompous pretence of founding a *Reich*, to a leveling mediocrity, democracy, and "modern ideas"!'[29] He did not reject Bismarck, as is often stated, strictly because of his *Machtpolitik* policies or his anti-Semitism.[30] It should be remembered that Bismarck involved Germans in wars on only three occasions, in 1864, 1866 and 1870,[31] and that by 1873 he had embraced a peaceful foreign policy initiated with the negotiation of the Three Emperors' League with Russia and Austria-Hungary.

Six major political parties sat in the *Reichstag* during the Bismarckian era. Among them were, first, the German Conservative Party: the most right-wing of the six which represented Prussian nationalism and the aristocratic *Junker* class. Federally, they were anti-nationalist and opposed to German unification. They also rejected the *Reichstag* because it was elected by universal male suffrage. Ludwig von Gerlach, a prominent conservative ideologue, wrote that the German Conservative Party 'was to be Christian, monarchist, agrarian, militarist and social, but above all independent, no Bismarckian party'.[32] Modern political anti-Semitism penetrated the German Conservative Party via both the 'Christian social' conservative followers of Adolf Stöcker and the Agrarian League.

Second was the Free Conservative Party: they represented industrialists and large commercial interests. The views of this party most closely resembled those of Bismarck. Its members supported German unification. The primary principles of conservative political philosophy were that 'the new *Reich* would derive its sovereignty not from abstract rational principles – such as the theory of "natural law" (or social contract theory) but from the principle of "the Christian State" which derived its authority and justification from the Lutheran doctrine of the state whose source was Luther's *Of Earthly Government* (1523)'.[33] Conservatives generally supported one national state under Prussian hegemony, placing the authority of the Church and the political and economic interests of the traditional, 'organic' social classes above the constitutional, parliamentary regime.

Third was the National Liberal Party: they were firm supporters of constitutional government, but not supporters of a parliamentary system on the British model. They represented the educated and wealthy middle class, supported national unification and favoured *laissez-faire* economics and secularisation. The National Liberals supported both the *Kulturkampf* and the anti-Socialist Laws, and became some of the most energetic promoters of German imperialism and colonial acquisitions.

Fourth was the Progressive Liberal Party: known as 'Manchester liberals', they followed the principles of classical liberalism and defended the increasing democratisation of the political system and the extension of the power of the *Reichstag*. (Secessionists split from the National Liberals in 1881 and merged with the Progressives in March 1884, forming the new German Free Thought Party, known as the 'Crown Prince's Party' because of its clear preference for the 'liberal' views of Crown Prince Friedrich.) The Progressive Party was in the vanguard of those forces opposed to the authoritarian rule of Bismarck.

Fifth was the Catholic Centre Party: founded in 1870 to defend the rights and interests of the Catholic minority within the new *Reich*. Their allegiance was to Rome. They were conservative in defence of tradition, monarchical authority and the hierarchical structure of society. Yet the Catholic Centre Party tended to be progressive in matters of social reform, for example, organising Christian trade unions and assisting the poor to raise their standard of living.[34] They were anti-capitalist and voted with Bismarck on his social insurance initiatives in the 1880s. Bismarck's severe measures against the Roman Catholic Church in the 1870s – the *Kulturkampf* – which attempted to reduce the Church's power over education and in society generally, turned the Catholic Centre Party against him.

Sixth was the Social Democratic Party: they supported the development of a parliamentary democracy and of democratic rights based on equality. Though many members supported revolution, the majority 'accepted the assumption that Social Democracy stood for parliamentarianism in both theory and practice'.[35] The Marxist SPD was founded in Gotha in 1875, a fusion of Ferdinand Lassalle's General German Workers' Association (formed 1863), which advocated state socialism, and August Bebel's and Wilhelm Liebknecht's Social Democratic Labour Party (formed 1869), which aspired to establish a classless communist society. They represented the workers of the rapidly expanding industrial regions. For these leaders, political democracy 'would have to become social democracy; it would have to encompass the economic and social interests of the working class'.[36] The SPD were anti-patriotic, pro-Commune, anti-Christian and anti-colonialist. The Catholic Centre Party and Social Democrats were Bismarck's principal opponents. Bismarck had not counted on the emergence of new parties such as the Catholic Centre or the Social Democrats, both of which began participating in imperial and Prussian elections in the early 1870s. He considered these parties, along with the left Progressive Liberal Party, enemies of the *Reich*.[37]

It is important to comment also on a dominant conservative newspaper of the era that exercised substantial influence on political issues: the *Kreuzzeitung* directed by Wilhelm von Hammerstein, to which Bismarck had early on contributed. Their manifesto stated the 'foremost duty to reconstruct with greater energy the [Christian] religious and ethical foundations of Germany ... to regard state sovereignty as a principle that emanates from a divine source'.[38] The *Kreuzzeitung* was elitist, believing that social classes should be incorporated into an order of hierarchical relationships. It was anti-socialist, anti-liberal, anti-capitalist and anti-Semitic. An opponent of the *Kulturkampf*, it defended church rights and cooperation between Protestant and Catholic conservatism.[39] It exercised a significant influence on the German Conservative Party and was closely connected with Stöcker's Christian Social movement.

If we were to regard Nietzsche as if he were the leader of a political party, and he does later in *Ecce Homo* invoke the 'New Party of Life',[40] where would he be situated on the political spectrum? Or, once situated, would his Dionysian philosophy undermine his political positions or would we recognise that he had always merely placed himself along political fault-lines? We suspend the idea that 'Nietzscheanism was not – nor could it have been – a separate political ideology backed by its own political party or movement.'[41] In order to begin to answer these questions, we have to understand where he stood with respect to the formative political events of the Bismarckian era. These include, among others, the Franco-Prussian war, the *Kulturkampf*, the anti-Socialist Laws, the 'Social Question' and anti-Semitism.

The 1860s: the Schleswig-Holstein Crisis; the Austro-Prussian War

Born in 1815, Otto von Bismarck was a descendent of a long line of Prussian *Junkers* who were accustomed to serving the Prussian monarchy, often through military service. Once, in a famous speech, Bismarck proclaimed that Germany should not look to the liberalism of Prussia but to her power, and that the great questions of the time could not be solved by speeches and majority votes – that was the great mistake of 1848 and 1849 – but by *blood and iron*.

The death of King Friedrich of Denmark in November 1863 occurred at a critical point in the complex Schleswig-Holstein affair and would provide

Bismarck with an opportunity to become involved in the era of blood and iron. The duchy of Holstein was part of the German Confederation and completely German, whereas Schleswig was a Danish fief and linguistically mixed between German, Danish and North Frisian. The Danish king served as duke of both duchies. In the autumn of 1863, Denmark violated the post-revolutionary settlement of 1852 when it adopted a new constitution that would integrate the duchy of Schleswig into the Danish kingdom. The Danish king died shortly thereafter without a male heir, which provoked disputes over the proper succession in the duchies as well as constitutional concerns involving the relations of the duchies to the Danish crown, to each other, and of Holstein to the German Confederation. Bismarck viewed the Schleswig-Holstein crisis as an occasion to increase Prussia's territorial advantage by annexing the two duchies, but he realised that there were important steps that needed to be taken along the way. To begin with, he persuaded Austria to form an alliance with Prussia and together demand that Denmark withdraw its constitution due to its violation of the London protocol of 1852. After Denmark refused, Prussian and Austrian troops entered Schleswig in January 1864, and on April 18, after storming the Düppel fortifications in Jutland, the joint army gained a decisive military victory. Within a few months, the Danes were defeated, the Treaty of Vienna was signed and the two duchies were ceded to Prussia and Austria under their joint administration. Bismarck's victory was greeted with great enthusiasm in Prussia and throughout Germany, including at Pforta, the famous boarding school where Nietzsche was a pupil.

Nietzsche was an enthusiastic observer of the Danish war and anticipated that he would be spending Christmas on the battlefield in Schleswig-Holstein. He explained to his family, 'To avoid [military service] would be difficult...moreover, I have little desire to do so.'[42] He had registered for military service in March 1864 during the conflict, but the war would conclude without his involvement. Following the news of the Prussian seizure at Düppel, Nietzsche expressed delight at the army's military victory.[43]

The Danish war had sown the seeds for a confrontation with Austria, for Bismarck realised that if Prussia were to emerge as a dominant power in Germany, Austria had to be defeated. Bismarck was also aware that a war between Prussia and Austria would dismantle the German Confederation and decide Germany's future. As part of his pre-war planning, Bismarck pursued efforts to secure foreign cooperation. Prussia received confirmation of Napoleon III's neutrality and entered into an alliance with Italy on April 8, 1866, which violated the terms of the German Confederation's constitution. This explicitly prohibited an alliance with a foreign power against one of its own members. Bismarck went on to deliver an ultimatum before the Diet demanding the unconditional acceptance of Prussia's plan for the reform of the German Confederation. This plan proposed the establishment of a democratically elected German parliament and was designed to isolate Austria from the southern German states. The plan was voted down on June 14, 1866, but this did not prevent Bismarck from declaring war. He sent troops into Hanover, Saxony and Hesse-Cassel and three weeks later, on July 3, the Prussians routed the Austrians at Königgrätz. Bismarck was now a national hero.

The terms of the peace treaty between Prussia and Austria, signed in Prague on August 23, 1866, resulted in Prussia's absolute ascendancy in northern Germany. Austria was forever vanquished from Germany, and gave Prussia its consent to organise northern Germany as it deemed fit. On July 3, 1866, the day before Berlin was informed of the Prussian military victory, *Landtag* elections had taken place in Prussia. The Liberals suffered severe losses, with the Progressive Party witnessing a sharp decline in its seats while the Conservatives benefited from a marked increase. The events of 1866 represented a revolution from above by the Prussian military monarchy which altered Europe's political landscape and Prussia's internal political developments.

Nietzsche followed the Austro-Prussian war with great interest, and from the moment it began, proudly declared himself to be 'a rabid Prussian'. After Prussian troops had occupied Leipzig, where Nietzsche was residing, he wrote an emotionally charged letter to his family commenting on the events: 'To found the unified German state in this revolutionary way is an audacity on Bismarck's part; courage and ruthless consistency he has, but he underestimates the moral forces among the people. Nonetheless, the latest moves are excellent; above all, he has known how to place a large, if not the largest, part of the guilt on Austria'.[44] These remarks not only express his Prussian patriotism, but also reveal his admiration for Bismarck's 'Machiavellian' statecraft.

The victory over Austria also relieved Nietzsche of any lingering doubts about Bismarck's 'audacious' game, and he confessed that it was 'a rare and quite new joy to feel for once entirely at one with the existing government'.[45] During this period, Nietzsche was critical of conservatism and the *Kreuzzeitung*, the principal organ of the extreme conservatives. Instead, his political allegiance was to a local group of Bismarckian liberals led by Gustav Freytag and Karl Biedermann, both of whom supported Heinrich von Treitschke's call for annexation. Nietzsche backed the Prussian annexation of Saxony which would eventually lead to the formation of the North German Confederation, claiming that it served best his 'own personal interests'.[46]

Bismarck spent the next few months preparing a new constitution for the North German Confederation; this was approved by the constituent *Reichstag* on April 16, 1867. German unification, however, would not be accomplished until the southern states joined the Confederation, and that prospect was unlikely without a war with France.

In 1870 the proposal for a Hohenzollern prince to ascend to the Spanish throne, which had become vacant after the 1868 revolution, precipitated a conflict between Prussia and France. The throne was offered to Prince Leopold of Hohenzollern who, after first declining, finally accepted on June 21, 1870, with the reluctant consent of King Wilhelm I. Napoleon III was greatly disturbed by these clandestine arrangements made by the House of Hohenzollern whom he had always treated with respect. France was opposed to her southern neighbour having a Hohenzollern on the throne. Napoleon III understood that a failure to respond to the candidature would lead to the end of his reign. France issued a stern warning to Prussia that it would not tolerate a foreign power placing one of its own princes on the Spanish throne as this would upset the balance of power. Up to this point, Bismarck had been a strong advocate of the candidature, perhaps with the intention of inviting a war with France. Bismarck would become outraged when Prince Leopold voluntarily resigned as it signalled a diplomatic victory for France. Napoleon III however did not treat the resignation as a victory, and ordered Count Benedetti, the French ambassador to Prussia, to demand from the Prussian king an apology and a guarantee that he would never again sanction Leopold's candidature. When Wilhelm I refused, it sparked hostilities between the two sides, with France declaring war on Prussia on July 19, 1870.

The 1870s: the Franco-Prussian War; the Paris Commune; *Kulturkampf*

The Franco-Prussian War was a conflict between France and Prussia, which was backed by the North German Confederation and the South German states of Baden, Württemberg and Bavaria. The military dominance of Prussian and German troops soon became evident and a German victory appeared imminent as early as mid-August, with the decisive defeat registered at Sedan on September 2, 1870.

The victory in the Battle of Sedan, and the capture of Napoleon III, did not seal the end of the war. On September 4, 1870, the Third Republic was declared in France, and French resistance continued under Adolphe Thiers, the head of the provisional government. It would take a further five months for the Prussian and German armies to defeat France, with the fall of Paris coming on January 28, 1871. A peace settlement, the Treaty of Frankfurt, was signed on May 10, 1871 amidst a civil war in France, the outcome not only of the war, but also of the uprising of the working class which led to the Paris Commune (a socialist government that ruled Paris for two months in the spring of 1871). Bebel referred to the Commune in his *Reichstag* speech of May 1871 as 'a small skirmish on the outposts' and defiantly asserted that 'the main events in Europe are still to come; before many decades the war cry of the Paris proletariat: War on the palaces, peace for the humble homes, death to poverty and idleness – this war-cry will be that of the whole proletariat of Europe'.[47]

The Paris Commune was the most significant event in the development of the European socialist movement in the nineteenth century. Bismarck's major confrontation with socialism had not yet transpired. For now, however, he had accomplished his aim of uniting Germany as a nation-state. The new *Reich* was a constitutional monarchy and Wilhelm I was given the imperial title of German Emperor.

At first, Nietzsche supported the war as a *contest* (or *agon*) between French and German culture, but later he observed with disgust the excessive German brutalities. For Nietzsche, the war was not really about culture, but about *conquest* bent on exacting national revenge.[48] (Helmuth von Moltke had, in fact privately called for a 'war of extermination' against France.)[49] In a letter to Gersdorff dated November 7, 1870, Nietzsche expressed his concerns: 'I am greatly worried about the immediate cultural future...Confidentially, I regard Prussia now as a power which is highly dangerous to culture.'[50] Nietzsche begins his essay on *David Strauss: the Confessor and the Writer* (1873) with a discussion of the consequences of the Prussian victory over France:

> But of all evil results due to the recent war with France, the most deplorable, perhaps, is that widespread and even universal error of public opinion...that German culture was also victorious in the struggle, and that it should now, therefore, be decked with garlands, as a fit recognition of such extraordinary events and successes. This delusion is pernicious in the highest degree...because it threatens to transform our struggle into a signal defeat: *into the defeat, if not the extirpation, of the German spirit for the benefit of the 'German Reich'.*[51]

His view that the German military victory resulted in a German cultural defeat, while not popular at the time,[52] was a recurring theme in his writings.[53] He also notes that Germany's military principles – 'discipline, scientific superiority among the leaders, unity and obedience among the led' – are entirely unrelated to culture. For Nietzsche, to possess political supremacy at the expense of cultural supremacy is a great disaster, and Germany needed to compensate for its political supremacy by putting its power to use. The state can utilise its power in a beneficial way by altering its aim. 'The task of the state is not to ensure that as many people as possible live well and ethically within it: the number is irrelevant: but rather to ensure that...it provides the basis for a *culture*...In a word: a nobler form of humanity is the aim of the state, its purpose lies outside of itself, it is merely the *means*.'[54] This indicates that Nietzsche is not consistently anti-statist and that he does not divorce culture from politics, since he assigns to the state the crucial task of overseeing the production of a nobler form of German culture.

The Paris Commune posed an additional threat to Nietzsche's task of cultural regeneration. For Nietzsche, this catastrophic proletarian insurrection betrayed the 'cultural barbarism of the lower classes'[55] and left him devastated. In a despairing letter to Gersdorff he wrote:

> When I heard of the fires in Paris, I felt for several days annihilated and was overwhelmed by fears and doubts; the entire scholarly, scientific, philosophical, and artistic existence seemed an absurdity, if a single day could wipe out the most glorious works of art, even whole periods of art; I clung with earnest conviction to the metaphysical value of art, which cannot exist for the sake of poor human beings but which has higher missions to fulfill.[56]

This event suddenly became more important than the war between nations. In the same letter he recognises that 'Over and above the struggle between nations the object of our terror was that international hydra-head, suddenly and so terrifyingly appearing as a sign of quite different struggles to come'.[57] Whereas Bebel indicated in his much-publicised speech that the proletariat would embrace the war-cry 'death to idleness', Nietzsche writes in 'The Greek State' that idleness is necessary for the development of culture.[58] It is evident that he is referring to the Commune when he writes in *The Birth of Tragedy*, 'There is nothing more terrible than a class of barbaric slaves who have learned to regard their existence as an injustice, and now prepare to avenge, not only themselves, but all generations',[59] utilising the word 'slaves' as an ideological and class code, and conveying the 'veiled warnings of the perils of proletarian revolution'.[60]

The first *Reichstag* of the new Empire was represented by the two liberal parties (the National Liberals who had collaborated with Bismarck, and the anti-Bismarckian Liberals, the Progressives), the two conservative parties, the Catholic Centre, and the socialists. This new Catholic Centre Party received approximately one fifth of the vote, enough to alert Bismarck and the Liberals to a potential threat. The Catholics were a large minority in a Protestant German state, and the Centre Party was formed to protect their interests. The problem was that Catholic interests were an object of concern for the state, which challenged the independence of the Church, its institutions and its role in education. The *Reich* denounced the Vatican Council's condemnation of the modern world in its *Syllabus of Errors*, and its proclamation of papal infallibility in 1870. These themes set the stage for a confrontation between the government and the Church. Tensions heightened when the Catholic Centre Party demanded that the Emperor assist in the restoration of the Papal States, and that special rights be entrenched in the constitution to protect Catholic rights. Bismarck provoked a conflict when he abolished the Catholic division in the Prussian Ministry of Culture in June 1871. What followed was a series of anti-Catholic legislation, beginning with the passage of the 'Pulpit Paragraph' at the end of 1871 which prohibited priests from using the pulpit for political ends.

The National Liberals joined forces with Bismarck in this 'cultural struggle' (*Kulturkampf*) against the Church (1871, 1878, 1887) as it was coined by Rudolf Virchow, one of the founders of the Progressive Party. The School Supervision Act of March 1872 denied Catholic priests the right to supervise religious teaching, and education was placed under the control of the state. In July 1872, the Jesuit Act prohibited any further Jesuit activity in Germany.

This legislation was followed by the Prussian May Laws of 1873, which introduced state supervision of the training of priests, who were now obliged to take a 'cultural exam' to determine their suitability for office. Severe penalties, such as heavy fines, imprisonment, the closure of seminaries and vetoing ecclesiastical appointments, were imposed on violators. These repressive measures only intensified after a failed assassination attempt on Bismarck in July 1874 by a Catholic cooper named Heinz Kullman. Although Bismarck suffered only a minor injury to his right hand, he wasted no time in blaming the Catholic Centre Party for influencing this would-be assassin.

Both liberal parties overwhelmingly supported these anti-Catholic measures, even though they violated freedom of speech and other liberal principles.[61] As the *Kulturkampf* persisted, the National Liberals became increasingly concerned with transforming the *Reich* from a constitutional state grounded in universal rational principles to a cultural state (*Kulturstaat*) rooted in historical national principles.[62]

Liberal leaders, then, did not perceive anti-Catholic legislation to be an infringement of basic freedoms since full freedom, they argued, was only possible when the historical national state exercised its sovereignty over the Church and established itself as the *Kulturstaat*.[63] The new German *Reich* considered itself the *Kulturstaat*, which meant that it assumed the role of guardian and promoter of 'culture', education and morals.[64]

During the early 1870s, Nietzsche was committed to the revitalisation of German culture, but he rejected the *Kulturstaat* as a means to the production of a nobler culture. In opposition to the cultural philistinism that he identifies with the *Kulturstaat*, Nietzsche argues that the state:

> must *employ* its power to achieve its lofty cultural aims. Secularisation to be combated. The struggle against the Catholic Church is an act of enlightenment, nothing loftier; and in the end it merely makes it disproportionately strong; which is wholly undesirable. Of course, in general it is correct. If only the state and the church would devour each other![65]

Although Nietzsche supported the *Kulturkampf* (the campaign against the Catholic Church) as essentially 'correct', he refused to side with the state (*Kulturstaat*), perhaps given his opposition to the state's encroachment on education, especially its democratisation (or universalisation) of education.

He also surmised that the *Kulturkampf* would generate the undesirable consequence of strengthening the Church,[66] an insight that proved to be prophetic.[67]

As Bismarck was forced to contend with a strengthened Centre Party, he had to abandon his alliance with the National Liberals, including their commitment to the liberal principle of free trade. By 1878 he realised that the *Kulturkampf* had not achieved its goals and began to repeal its laws after negotiations with Pope Leo XIII (certain laws were not repealed until 1887). On a pragmatic level, though, he now required the Centre Party to assist in his relentless struggle against the rising Social Democratic Party.

The 'liberal era' would start to unravel in the late 1870s and Bismarck became convinced of the necessity of moving Germany in a new political and economic direction. Some liberal parliamentarians fought the power of the executive, however this made Bismarck intent upon solving the financial woes of the *Reich* in a way that would not strengthen the budgetary powers of the *Reichstag*. His solution was to introduce a system of protective tariffs and state monopolies. In addition to generating revenue, these measures would benefit the economy and consequently curb the spread of social democracy, now considered by Bismarck to be a greater revolutionary threat than the Liberals. Bismarck's policies may have changed, but he never wavered from his long-term goal of creating a parliament of propertied men with loyal ties to the established order and dependent on the state. To accomplish these goals, he needed to remove the possibility of a liberal *Reichstag*. The 1877 elections did not produce a Liberal majority, but together the two Liberal parties retained the largest bloc of seats.

1878 and 1879: Bismarck's 'change of course'; anti-Socialist Laws; the social question (*Sozialpolitik*)

The *Reichstag* debates of February and March 1878 reinforced Bismarck's commitment to a shift in German politics since he did not have majority approval for his economic policies. In March 1878, he proceeded with his anti-liberal agenda when he forwarded to the *Bundesrat* his plan for fiscal reform and a tobacco monopoly. Bismarck's change of course had serious political implications: it signified his opposition to any further evolution in the direction of social democracy. He realised that this move would generate revenue without parliamentary obstruction, and could prove divisive given the deep-seated socioeconomic tensions within the Liberal movement. Bismarck also realised that the Liberals had always been divided over the dangers of revolution, and following an assassination attempt on Wilhelm I on May 11, he seized the opportunity to introduce legislation against the Social Democrats. The bill was rejected, but only eight days later a second and more serious assassination attempt on the Kaiser occurred. Bismarck blamed the Social Democratic Party although he knew better, and he immediately dissolved the *Reichstag*. 'Now I've got them,' he was reported to have claimed. 'The Social Democrats?' he was asked. 'No, the National Liberals!'[68] (The majority of the National Liberals refused to support Bismarck's legislation against the Social Democrats following the first assassination attempt on Wilhelm I.)

In the summer of 1878, Bismarck became involved in the election campaign. He exploited the public outrage over the Kaiser's injuries, manipulated the fear of revolution and threatened a *coup d'état* should all else fail. He went to exorbitant lengths to ensure a parliamentary majority for his policies. The results of the 1878 *Reichstag* elections confirmed the Liberals' decline and Bismarck's goal of procuring a conservative, political realignment. It also led to the swift passage of the anti-Socialist Laws on October 19, 1878 which the National Liberal left could not oppose due to pressures from the party's right wing. Bismarck had always despised socialism, but the anti-Socialist Laws were arguably the most repressive of his chancellorship. They banned all Social Democratic associations, meetings and newspapers, and nearly all unions, 'but permitted campaign activities before elections and the sending of SPD delegates to the *Reichstag*'.[69] Socialist agitators were arrested or expelled, and socialist clubs were forced to disband. Socialists would circumvent these laws by holding secret meetings, issuing new publications and creating new organisations. Bismarck, as Wehler writes, 'tried to make credible his claim that the fight against the Social Democrats was a case of "saving society from murderers and arsonists, in fact, from what took place under the Paris Commune". This meant that a "war of annihilation" was necessary against the Socialist Worker's Party'.[70]

The socialist controversy was simply a prelude to the government's effort to create a new political alignment. The government's protectionist economic reform was announced in December 1878, and despite opposition from liberal supporters of free trade, the tariff law was passed by a majority of Conservatives and Centrists on July 15, 1879. The Catholic Centre Party, an opponent of social democracy, liberalism, free trade and *laissez-faire*, was considered an ally for promoting Bismarck's political ends.

After 1878, the conservatives became the dominant political force in the *Reich*. The shift towards conservatism following the anti-Socialist Laws (1878) and the tariffs (1879) still did not give Bismarck a reliable majority in the *Reichstag*. The Centre Party supported the government's tariff policy, but on other political issues would occasionally join forces with the opposition (the Secessionists and the Progressive Party) to form a majority. Bismarck also had to contend with the strong gains made by the Socialists in the 1881 *Reichstag* elections. Socialist reform was a major threat that his repressive anti-socialist policy failed to curb. The Chancellor needed a new strategy to combat the socialist movement that would, at the same time, recognise workers' grievances about the existing economic structure. Bismarck embarked on a programme of 'practical Christianity'[71] or 'state socialism', which was announced on November 17, 1881 in the Imperial Message of Wilhelm I to the *Reichstag*. The Message 'recognised the obligation of the existing state to undertake measures for the improvement of the working classes',[72] and laws concerning health insurance and accident insurance were subsequently implemented in 1883 and 1884. They were a precursor to the present system of social security.

The issue of improving the lives of the working classes was a response to the German workers' movement which was largely allied with the Socialist International, the Paris Commune of 1871 and the fear of revolution that swept across Germany in its aftermath. The Paris Commune demanded that the social question be solved and it was debated throughout the 1870s and early 1880s. The social question 'signified the response to the workers' question, and involved legislation pertaining to the protection of wage earners and the "raising" of the working classes into the social and political order of the *Kaiserreich*',[73] which translated into increasing equality.

Nietzsche's views on the social question were expressed as early as 1862 when he began reading Theodor Mundt's *Geschichte der Gesellschaft* (1844), which examined socialist thought and its repercussions. Nietzsche wrote a detailed précis outlining Mundt's position on the social question. The précis reveals that Nietzsche displayed no socialist sympathies, and following the neoconservative Mundt, he denounces the communist attack on private property as undermining 'the essential essence of the human personality'.[74] In the early 1870s, Nietzsche criticised the democratisation of education in 'On the Future of Our Educational Institutions' (1872), his first public intervention on the social question, and in a notebook entry from 1873 rejected the idea of cooperatives, a component of liberal social reform, which offered the working class access to an organisation that would assist them in pooling their resources and providing the necessary education to enable them to overcome both their economic hardships and their spiritual isolation.[75]

In the past, Nietzsche had relied on Bismarck to serve as a bulwark against socialism, but he was dismayed by the concessions made to the working class in the Imperial Message, especially the conviction 'that the healing of social wrongs must be sought not only through the repression of social democratic excesses, but just as much by positively advancing the well-being of the workers'.[76]

Nietzsche also found the Kaiser's remark 'We are all workers' to be offensive since it failed to respect social hierarchy (or order of rank) and assigned to workers a dignity to which they are not entitled.[77] For Nietzsche, who expressed only contempt for socialism and the workers' movement, Bismarck's ensuing social security legislation was no more than misplaced (or unnecessary) sentimentalism. He made education free and compulsory and German social legislation became the most advanced in Europe. However, Bismarck's social security legislation failed in its attempt to wean the expanding working class away from the SPD. Bismarck was convinced that if workers were protected by the government, they would develop loyalties to the state and would not give a thought to revolution. His 'practical Christianity' was in accord with the Conservative agenda of upholding the Christian worldview, and its opposition to the non-Christian forces of socialism and 'Manchester' liberalism. Bismarck's strategy, however, backfired and in 1884 the Social Democrats again became a formidable force in the *Reichstag*.

In the summer of 1884, six months prior to the next *Reichstag* elections, the Secessionists and the Progressive Party merged to form a radical liberal party, the German Free Thought Party, popularly known as the 'Crown Prince's Party'. Bismarck was incensed by the emergence of this party for he anticipated that the Crown Prince would soon succeed his elderly father and would appoint members to his cabinet from this new party who would supplant him. The Crown Princess Victoria was British, and Bismarck feared that Germany would develop close relations with Britain once the Crown Prince ascended to the throne. Bismarck's pre-emptive strike against the 'German Gladstone Ministry', as he referred to it, came in the form of a new political project (colonialism) that would anger the anti-colonialist German Free Thought Party but would endear him to the upper middle classes, who would now be provided with an imperialistic warrior code. A colonial policy would potentially drive a wedge between the German Free Thought Party and the pro-colonialist Crown Prince.

The 1880s: Colonisation

Bismarck's decision to pursue an active colonial policy in the mid-1880s came as a surprise because he had always been wary of any involvement in the 'scramble for Africa' for fear of disturbing the balance of power in Europe. Although Germany's colonial experiment would be short-lived, support for imperial expansion had been voiced years before colonial policy actually came into effect.[78] Magnates of commerce and industry considered the acquisition of colonies indispensable for establishing stable markets and as a source of raw materials.[79] Moreover, Bismarck could capitalise on the colonial movement at the next election since members of pro-imperialist organisations included a strong contingent of National Liberals and Free Conservatives.

Bismarck served as host to an international conference held in Berlin from November 15, 1884 to February 26, 1885. The Berlin Conference featured representatives from every European country (except Switzerland) who gathered to decide the political partitioning of Africa. The Conference settled numerous colonial disputes especially over the Congo (which fell to the Belgians) and established anti-slavery provisions. Between 1884 and 1885 Germany acquired Togo, the Cameroons, German East Africa (present-day Tanzania) and South West Africa (present-day Namibia). By 1886, Bismarck abandoned his colonial ambitions and refocused his energies on Europe.

In terms of the results of the Berlin Conference, Nietzsche would have rejected the anti-slavery provisions since he did not support the 'abolition of slavery'.[80] And, in his later writings as part of his critique of the German spirit, Nietzsche comments on the colonisation of Africa: 'At this very moment...the German Kaiser calls it his "Christian duty" to liberate the slaves in Africa: among us other Europeans this would then simply be called "German"'.[81]

Nietzsche rejected German imperialism and the concept of the nation-state in favour of a unified Europe. He shared Bismarck's concern with becoming too close to the British and their parliamentary system. In a conversation with General von Schweinitz, Bismarck's eldest son, Herbert, offered a different account of Bismarck's unexpected endorsement of colonialism. 'When we entered upon a colonial policy, we had to reckon with a long reign of the Crown Prince. During this reign *English influence would have been dominant*. To prevent this, we had to embark on a colonial policy, because it was popular and conveniently adapted to *bring us into conflict with England at any given moment.*'[82]

Bismarck wanted to ensure that German and British relations remained adversarial in anticipation of the 'liberal' Crown Prince ascending to the throne. Although Nietzsche's political vision is not modelled after Bismarck's *Reich*, both regarded Britain as a formidable obstacle to the achievement of their respective political ends and recognised the need to confront it.[83]

Peter Bergmann remarks that it is no coincidence that 'Nietzsche embraced the concept of *grosse Politik* precisely at the moment when Germany was suddenly creating her own colonial empire...In the mid-eighties, Nietzsche, like his European contemporaries, turned outward onto what he saw as the coming struggle for "the mastery of the earth"'.[84] Nietzsche's idea of *grosse Politik* does not refer to the imperialistic ambitions of the German *Reich* but to a supra-nationalist imperialism. He had already in *Dawn*[85] supported a colonialism that would reduce social tensions and problems of domestic policy,[86] namely the worker question, and in *The Wanderer and His Shadow* imagined a global centre of power. There Nietzsche speaks of the 'good Europeans' whose 'great task' will be the 'guidance and guardianship of the universal world culture'.[87] During roughly the same period of German colonisation, in *Beyond Good and Evil* (1886), Nietzsche observes that the 'time for petty politics is past; the next century will bring the struggle for the dominion of the world – the *compulsion* to grand politics'.[88]

In 1886, Nietzsche became personally acquainted with colonialism through his sister and brother-in-law, Elisabeth and Bernhard Förster, founders of the Paraguayan colony of Nueva Germania. Nietzsche was neither a German nationalist (at this time) nor a supporter of Förster's colonial aspirations:

> About my sister's future, I have my own thoughts – that is to say, I do not think it would be a good thing for Dr. Förster to return to Paraguay.

Europe is not so small; and if one does not *want* to live in Germany (and in this I am like him), one still does not need to go so very far away. But of course I do not have his enthusiasm for 'things German,' and even less for keeping this 'glorious' race *pure*.[89]

The 1880s: Anti-Semitism; the Christian state

Nietzsche was not tolerant of Förster's anti-Semitism and the *'névrose nationale'*. The modern German anti-Semitic movement had experienced a revival from the late 1870s to the mid-1880s. The 1876 programme of the German Conservative Party, while not overtly addressing the 'Jewish question', emphasised the principle of Christian historical exclusiveness and promoted German nationalism, the Prussian monarchy and Lutheran Protestantism, and declared its opposition to the liberal democratic principle of civil equality (universal male suffrage). Modern Judaism was associated with the principles of classical liberalism, 'Manchester economics', and Jews were accused of dominating the press, education, parliament, morals, city life, music, German literature, and so on. This Jewish stereotype is captured in Konstantin Frantz's 1879 description of Berlin as a Jewish *Reich*:

> because one meets here in all areas of public life the arrogant Jew...the flea-market and marts-of-trade, and stock-market Jew, the Press, and literature Jew, the theatre and music Jew, the culture and humanity Jew, and – what is unique to Berlin – the city government Jew. Almost half of Berlin's city councilors...are Jews...and, hand in hand with their kept Press and stock-market, they actually control the whole city government.[90]

It was religion, in particular the ideal of the 'Christian state', that united Conservatives and anti-Semites and enabled them to cooperate in their campaign against industrialisation, secularisation, democratisation and the 'usurious' Jew. The 'Christian state' became an anti-liberal slogan that Conservatives used to show that the source of state sovereignty is not the sovereignty of the people or a social contract, but rooted in the principle of *civitas dei* as embodied in the person of the monarch.[91] Nietzsche, however, expresses contempt for the 'Christian state' insofar as 'the Church is still permitted to obtrude into all important experiences and main points of individual life'.[92] He is also critical of one of the leading proponents of the 'Christian state', Adolf Stöcker, whom he refers to as the 'court preacher *canaille*'.[93]

In 1878, Stöcker founded the Christian Social Workers' Party, whose primary objective was to draw the working classes away from socialism. After disappointing results in the 1878 elections, Stöcker turned to anti-Semitism to increase the party's popularity and dropped the word

'Workers' from the party's name. Stöcker's arguments against the Jews were essentially religious, social and ethical. Modern Jews were regarded as destroyers of ecclesiastical authority and of the traditional social order. For Stöcker, the only legitimate Christian solution to the 'Jewish question' was conversion since Christian redemption required the eventual disappearance of Judaism. Jews must decide to renounce their faith, forgo their separate identity and assimilate into the dominant society as German-Christian patriots – only then would they be accepted without prejudice.[94] In his September 19, 1879 speech, Stöcker not only emphasised the link between the 'Jewish question' and the 'social question', but also dissociated himself from all anti-Jewish views expressed in purely racial terms that negate the Christian worldview. He warned his listeners that 'a hatred against the Jews that is contrary to the gospels is beginning to flare up here and there'.[95] Following Uriel Tal, we can distinguish between two strands of modern anti-Semitism, 'Christian anti-Semitism' and 'anti-Christian anti-Semitism'.[96] As a progenitor of the German Christian heritage of the second *Reich*, Stöcker represents 'Christian anti-Semitism'. This type of anti-Semitism is a reflection of Christianity's anti-Jewish tradition. There is also a modern anti-Semitism that entails a repudiation of both Judaism *and* Christianity, and is called 'anti-Christian anti-Semitism' and 'refers to those movements, organisations and schools of thought whose antagonism to Jews and Judaism went hand in hand with their antagonism to monotheistic religion in general and to Christianity in particular'.[97] Eugen Dühring's racial anti-Semitism in the late 1870s asserted that hatred of the Jews should be understood as hatred of religion in general, in keeping with the tenets of anti-Christian anti-Semitism, but Dühring recommended a policy of planned breeding as a solution to the degenerate influence of both Judaism and Christianity. Other major proponents of anti-Christian racial anti-Semitism included Wilhelm Marr (who coined the term 'anti-Semitism' in the 1870s), Theodor Fritsch and Friedrich Lange, all of whom argued for the superiority of 'pre-Christian Germanism'.

Racial anti-Semitism did not emerge as a political force until the late 1880s, but its development owed much to the foundation of a new Anti-Semitic Centre in Leipzig in 1884 and to the creation of the *Antisemitische Correspondenz* in 1885. One name that was featured regularly in this new publication was 'Nietzsche'. After noting the 'comic fact' of his subterranean influence on all radical parties (Socialists, Nihilists, anti-Semites, Orthodox Christians and Wagnerians), Nietzsche comments specifically on his influence in anti-Semitic circles. He writes, 'In the *Antisemitische Correspondenz* (which is sent only privately through the mail, only to reliable "party members"), my name appears in almost every issue. The anti-Semites are smitten with Zarathustra, the divine man; there is a special anti-Semitic interpretation of it, which gave me a good laugh'.[98] A few months later, he was less amused when he wrote: 'I also do not like these latest speculators in idealism, the anti-Semites, who today roll their eyes in a Christian-Aryan-bourgeois manner'.[99] According to this, Nietzsche would be considered an opponent of Christian anti-Semitism, but he was also critical of Dühring's anti-Christian anti-Semitism, and both types he regarded as products of *ressentiment*.[100] As Nietzsche's critique of anti-Semitism pre-dates the influence of racial anti-Semitism as a dominant political force in the late 1880s, he does not draw a distinction between Christian anti-Semitism and racial anti-Semitism.

But Nietzsche does think in terms of the category of race. In *Human All-Too-Human* (1878), he acknowledges that within national states Jews have been used 'as scapegoats for every possible public and private misfortune', but if we set our sights on 'producing the strongest possible mixed European race, the Jew becomes as useful and desirable an ingredient as any other national quantity'. When he proceeds to describe the stock exchange Jew as perhaps 'the most repugnant invention of the whole human race', it is only to point out that every nation and every person has objectionable qualities, and it is unfair to expect the Jew to be an exception.[101]

In the 1880s Nietzsche intensifies his critical reaction to the anti-Semitism that has infected Germany. In *Beyond Good and Evil* he composes an indictment of the modern anti-Semitic movement in which he effectively undermines all popular Jewish stereotypes. To begin with, Nietzsche claims that the call to 'Let no more Jews come in!' is the rallying cry of a people whose instincts are 'feeble and uncertain'. He proceeds to state that the Jews are 'the strongest, toughest, and purest race at present living in Europe' and that anyone concerned with Europe's future must take them into account. In a deliberate attempt to offend anti-Semites, Nietzsche asserts that the Jews, 'if they were driven to it', could now have 'supremacy over Europe', but that 'they are *not* working and planning for that end is equally certain' (in other words, there was no Jewish conspiracy). Instead, he argues that the Jews want to be 'assimilated and absorbed by Europe' and suggests that even the officers of the nobility from the March Brandenburg would benefit from intermarriage with Jews – it would enrich them both financially and spiritually.[102] Nietzsche's solution is assimilation, but ultimately he is more concerned with the 'European problem' than the Jewish problem. The passage ends with Nietzsche articulating his fundamental concern: 'for I have already reached my *serious topic*, the "European problem," as I understand it, the breeding of a new ruling caste for Europe',[103] and towards that end Nietzsche recognises that Jews and Jewish finance capital will have a positive role to play in vanguard Europe.[104]

Aristocratic radical

Nietzsche accepted the description 'aristocratic radicalism' applied to his philosophy by Georg Brandes in 1887.[105] This appellation does not imply that he desired the conservation of the institution of the aristocracy (at most, certain of the aristocracy's codes and character traits). Nietzsche was 'radical' because he was an opponent of the existing political order and 'aristocratic' in claiming that society's goal should be the promotion of exemplary individuals. While he shared certain political positions with Bismarck and the various political parties, he was alienated from the left because of his anti-egalitarian sentiments and alienated from the right because of his anti-Christian stance and his opposition to anti-Semitism.

Nietzsche had some affinities with right-wing liberals, like Burckhardt, Treitschke and Sybel, who were concerned about the increasing political influence of the masses. With Burckhardt in particular, Nietzsche thought that such influence 'was detrimental to genuine individualism and fostered uniformity'.[106] As Roth writes, 'Liberalism was a major force of democratisation by advocating universal rights of man, but it did not favour a full-scale political mobilisation of the lower classes.'[107]

Consequently, Nietzsche was an opponent of universal suffrage supported by the Progressive (left-leaning) Liberals of his era but opposed by the National Liberal Party of which Treitschke was a member. Nietzsche shared the view of Treitschke and other right-wing liberals, that

> social reform was useless because it overlooked the essentially hierarchical nature of the social order.... [and] that social reform could [not] reduce the fundamental inequalities within society. [As Treitschke wrote in 'Socialism and Its Patrons']: 'class domination – or more accurately, the class order – is as necessary a part of society as the contrast between rulers and ruled is a natural part of the state'. It was unfortunate but nonetheless certain that the masses must labour so that a minority could engage in creative cultural and political activities.[108]

This is a notion of aristocracy that Nietzsche, inspired by Plato, advances in 'The Greek State' and well into his post-Zarathustran writings.

Still, Nietzsche's political principles do not conform to the basic principles of classical liberalism: natural law, rule of law, sovereignty of the people, equality of rights, welfare of all and the abolition of suffering, constitutional and parliamentary order, and distrust of personal authority.

If Nietzsche had been a liberal, then he should have supported those liberals in Germany who wanted to reform the government by making parliament stronger at the expense of the royal prerogative. Yet Nietzsche was anti-parliamentarian and considered himself 'anti-liberal to the point of malice'.[109] If we say that Nietzsche was a liberal engaged in an immanent critique of liberalism, then this means that his anti-parliamentarianism was nevertheless 'liberal' and that his 'malice' was an expression of a form of liberalism. If we read into Nietzsche even further and note his rejection of liberal institutions once they are achieved and his praise of the struggle for them, which is to say, 'war in favour of liberal institutions, which, as war, allows the illiberal instincts to subsist',[110] and if we think of 'illiberal' actions in the formation of liberal institutions to consist of actions like the anti-Socialist Laws and the *Kulturkampf* laws, then we have to conclude that Nietzsche's liberalism, given his implicit support of these laws, would assume 'illiberal' forms. If we take Nietzsche at face value, perhaps a more plausible conclusion would be that he was an opponent of liberalism, and at the very least did not wish to be read as a 'liberal'.[111] It is, however, arguable that his view of the state and his pronounced individualism are liberal in tenor.

Nietzsche's view of Bismarck is equally intriguing. His writings contain numerous references to the Chancellor and range in content from remarks on Bismarck's character to comments on his tactics and policies. These reflections reveal Nietzsche's evolving attitude towards Bismarck and can be said to be ambivalent in structure.

In the 1860s, Nietzsche had been a strong supporter of Bismarck. During the early 1870s, when the National Liberals made their peace with Bismarck, Nietzsche shed his National Liberal allegiance (particularly his support for German nationalism) and adopted a critical stance towards Bismarck's *Reich* for failing to advance the regeneration of German culture. In the late 1870s there was another convergence: Nietzsche was confident that Bismarck would suppress the socialist movement. For both Nietzsche and Bismarck, the Paris Commune had been a critical event. Both would recall Bebel's *Reichstag* speech of May, 1871 and the spectre it raised of a European proletarian insurrection. Bismarck considered the speech to be a 'ray of light' that alerted him to the socialist threat: 'From that moment on, I recognised in the social-democratic elements an enemy against which the state and the society finds itself in constant self-defence.'[112] In the 1880s, Nietzsche rejected Bismarck's social security legislation ('state socialism'), his 'practical Christianity' and his reconciliation with Rome[113] (i.e. the repeal of the *Kulturkampf* laws), yet still considered Bismarck to represent '*the strong German type*'.[114] This ambivalence may indicate that Nietzsche had maintained the hope that Bismarck, like that superior artist of government Napoleon, would be able to control the contradictions (the *agon* between social forces) through his 'practical politics', his various manipulations and concessions. But he could not stem the tide and was finally overwhelmed by social democratic interests. For Nietzsche, Bismarck commandeered the petty politics of nationalism and is one of the Germans who, in the process, destroyed any prospect of a venerable European culture.

Nietzsche's political thought confronted the living political forces and power structures of the Bismarckian era. It defined itself on a path of resistance with an obligation to rule. Nietzsche's philosophy of the future is formless without the concept of grand politics and the legislation of political values, energised by the danger scented at every turn, the climate of destabilisation and the prospect of future wars. Nietzsche's revaluation of all values was conceived in a society where power relations were changing drastically and transforming the ideas of rights and justice. His political thought constitutes a direct encounter with these changes, at once fearful and violent, affirmative and delimited by anarchic spaces.

1
Schulpforta, 1862

Preface

On October 5, 1858, Nietzsche entered the prestigious Pforta boarding school (*Schulpforta*) after receiving a scholarship from the city of Naumburg. The *Gymnasium* provided Germany's best classical education and could boast of such alumni as Leopold von Ranke and Friedrich Klopstock, and the precursors of German nationalism, Novalis and Johann Fichte.

A year earlier, King Friedrich Wilhelm IV, advocate of a 'Christian state', became insane after suffering a stroke. His brother Wilhelm was appointed regent and assumed control of the government in 1858, acceding to the throne on Friedrich's death in 1861 as Wilhelm I. The 'New Era' was welcomed at Pforta, which experienced a festive resurgence of the secular, liberal ideals of 1848 and the vision of a unitary, constitutional German state. When Nietzsche entered Pforta, German nationalist sentiment was at its height. The Rector, Carl Peter, and most of Nietzsche's professors were 'classical liberals' and proponents of cultural nationalism.

In the summer of 1860, Nietzsche and two classmates, Wilhelm Pinder and Gustav Krug, formed a literary and musical society which they called 'Germania'. It was in this context that Nietzsche presented an essay in January 1862, which provoked a harsh reaction from Pinder and Krug. It was entitled 'Napoleon III as President'.[1]

In this essay, Nietzsche defends the *coup d'état* of December 2, 1851 which subverted the Second French Republic and inaugurated the dictatorship of Napoleon III, who proclaimed himself Emperor in 1852. Nietzsche celebrates Napoleon III as a political genius, one who 'is governed by other and higher laws than the ordinary person' and whose genius can be recognised by his 'success'. Nietzsche did not wish to evaluate Napoleon III from the standpoint of traditional morality. Instead, his glowing admiration for the Emperor owes much to his 'daring *coups d'état*' which made his own sovereign will 'seem like the will of the entire nation'. In this early essay, Nietzsche is endorsing a political realism (*Realpolitik*) which justifies the extra-legal acts of the political genius. At about the same time Nietzsche was studying *The Prince* in his Italian class, which may explain the essay's Machiavellian perspective.

1862 was also the year Bismarck was appointed Prussian Premier and Minister for Foreign Affairs, and provoked a constitutional crisis over plans for military expansion. Nietzsche was pro-Prussian during this period: he wrote poems favouring German unification, participated in patriotic festivals anticipating national rebirth and attended nationalist student fraternity (*Burschenschaften*) meetings. His generation identified with the students of the era of the German Wars of Liberation, the seminal event for the German nationalist tradition. Why, then, does a Prussian patriot write a pro-Napoleonic piece in an anti-Napoleonic, anti-French period? Even though the essay was written some months before Bismarck's nomination, it may be read as supporting in principle Bismarck's later anti-constitutional manoeuvres and his arguably Bonapartist regime, which combined absolutism, militarism and plebiscitary consent and, at least between 1862 and 1866, contempt for parliament. Was Bonapartist autocracy Nietzsche's ideal for Germany?

Nietzsche had also just completed a study by T. H. Barrau of the French Revolution, the principal point of reference in nineteenth-century politics, which could very well have inspired his poems about Saint-Just (an unrelenting apologist of the Reign of Terror of 1793–94), and Louis XV and XVI. In his poem about Saint-Just from August 11, 1862, Nietzsche offers a negative appraisal of the radical revolutionary. Saint-Just is described as 'torn by torment, as if an evil spell had a hold over his heart'. Insofar as this remark is suggestive of the hate-filled resentment of the French revolutionaries, it seems to anticipate Nietzsche's later account of the French Revolution as representative of slave morality.

In his poems on the two kings, Nietzsche pays homage to Louis XVI and XV, quite out of step with 'satanic Saint-Just'. In contrast to the resentment-riddled Saint-Just and the 'muffled malice' of the people, Nietzsche portrays Louis XVI as showing no signs of resentment as he sits 'atop the guillotine's throne' awaiting his execution. Instead, the French Catholic monarch prays for forgiveness for the revolutionaries whose throne is violence and death. An ironic inversion occurs in the last line of the poem where the 'sans-culotte' is identified with Jesus Christ, the one who speaks in the poem, 'freedom's greatest son', pronouncing the king 'pious' and peaceful and, by inference, truly Christian as he communicates the Christian message of mercy and forgiveness. It is ironic for two reasons: because the spokesman of the sans-culottes, Jacques Réne Hébert, led a vitriolic de-Christianisation campaign during the Revolution, and because the sans-culottes, allied with the Jacobins, instigated and stoked the Reign of Terror. The sans-culottes, like Christ, may have spoken for the lowest classes in society, the proletariat, but, unlike Christ, the *true* sans-culotte, they propagated a doctrine of extreme violence. Through this inversion, Nietzsche appears to be saying that the true doctrine of freedom for the people lies in Christianity (and Christian monarchy), not in revolution. If Nietzsche was experiencing doubts about Christianity during this period, it is not evident in this poem.

The poem on Louis XV is written *in memoriam*. It depicts the rapid and secret conveyance of the king's body to its tomb and projects a fascination for the power and sacred status of the monarchy.

Although a mere sampling from Nietzsche's *Jugendschriften*, these Germania contributions from 1862 display his early royalist sympathies for both hereditary and elected monarchy (i.e. the democratic Caesarism of Napoleon III) and a clear disdain for the republican ideals defended by the French revolutionaries.

Napoleon III as President

The genius is governed by other and higher laws than the ordinary person, laws that often seem to contradict the general principles of morality and law, even though they are the same when perceived from the broadest points of view. This phenomenon is the final link in a chain. Just as that genius constitutes the culmination of natural and spiritual harmony, from which the ability of man degrades itself to the near-bestial coarseness of savage peoples, so is this seeming contradiction of the principles of genius with the general principles only the utmost point of a gradual extension, proceeding in parallel with the advances of the spiritual development of man. This entire perception, moreover, rests on a general principle – that everything that confronts man can be perceived only from the point of view of his spiritual ability. Thus, for man everything is really only appearance; something naturally must be truth; the knowledge of it is for us only presumption.

On this initially announced observation is grounded also the justification of the principle that seizing a government, which was previously in unworthy hands, is irreproachable if it is secured by a sovereign of genius and undertaken for the welfare of the people. The genius is recognised by his success; for he carries within himself a guaranteed certainty of auspicious success. The chosen path only bears witness to a refined spirit. The main condition is agreeing to the will of the people; every government that is not to carry within itself the seeds of its own destruction can be traced back to the people. The will of the people makes the ruler; the prototype of a free state is for this reason a presidency determined by the people amidst representatives of the people. Without the will of the people, a regime is insecure and exposed to the vengeance of the awakening spirit of the people. Since the people hold within themselves great restraint and are very dependent on the power of the everyday and the legitimate, and since they hold with ineradicable certainty such superstitious prejudices as the significance of individual names and days, an upstart is obliged to fulfil all of these conditions. Now we see how Napoleon III, at first derided as incapable, climbs with certain steps, firm as iron, from one rank to another, ascending to ever higher echelons of power, marching forward with such cheerful certainty of fortunate success and such unbelievable restraint that his most daring *coups* seem to be the will of the entire nation. When we finally see how he realises the goal of his efforts and actually lives up to the expectations tied to his rise, how he makes his people happy and prosperous, and his army glorious, and how he raises France to a unique status among the nations, must we not properly judge this man as a sovereign of genius, however much German hatred of the French wants to see in him only a sly dog?

Allow me briefly to sketch the most important period in this man's life and his presidency. – Napoleon was in London. From there he surveyed the latest events and their consequences: the victory of Cavaignac over the socialists and with that the victory of the principle of monarchy over the Republic, the longing of all higher classes for a lasting peace, the reciprocal fallings out and contestations of the heads of the Republic, Blanqui, Louis Blanc, Ledru-Rollin, their self-caused fall, the gradual retreat of Cavaignac and Lamartine, finally the efforts of Thiers and other schemers to step to the forefront of the events. Elected to the general assembly by five *departements*, Napoleon appeared in Paris and proceeded with a short speech, almost a mockery to all the newspapers, which portrayed him as entirely incapable and limited, but at the same time a hope to the army, the peasants of France, who attached the highest expectations to his name. The draft of the constitution is finished: a very dependent president will stand at the head of the government. Napoleon's candidature, disputed by the deputy Thomas on October 25, is defended by Napoleon the next day with the beautiful words: 'France sees in my name a guarantee for the strengthening of society. What is more necessary than a government that no longer brushes aside the evils but heals them? Someone is setting snares for me but I will avoid them and earn the respect of this magnanimous nation.' The powerful parties of schemers of the time of Louis-Philippe already entered his following, with Thiers at their head albeit for unworthy reasons; also many generals, such as Bugeaud and Girardin joined him out of envy and jealousy of Cavaignac. He even didn't fail to make himself friendly to the Church with a letter, a fact that raised concerns for Cavaignac. And these were not unfounded. On December 10, some 5,470,000 votes for Napoleon sprang from the ballot boxes. The measures of the new president, his choice of ministers, the suppression of clubs, the partial dissolution of the mobile Guard, the dispatch of Marshal Oudinot in order to reinstall the Pope in Rome, the response to Ledru-Rollin's personal attacks against him, the quick resolution of unrest in the National Guard caused by the new legislative assembly, the suppression of the Republican press and finally round trips in Ham, Tours, Angers and Rouen, all bearing witness to a fine, careful and moderate intellect, increased his power, secured his independence from the shifting corpse of the legislative assembly and drew to him as adherents the younger and older Orleanists. The army's loyalty and confidence in him increased due to his enormous military banquets, which he, like Caesar, defrayed from the significant salary of 2,160,000 Fr. Further tours allowed him to witness the increased peace and prosperity of France, the beneficial results of his government. It was in Cannes where he said: 'Now that prosperity has returned, it would be sacrilegious to change the existing state again. If stormy times were to return and the people wanted to impose a new burden on the head of the government, it would be sacrilegious to withdraw from the same.' The endeavour to make his presidency lasting is unmistakable. In September he tried, by means of glowing reviews in Versailles, to secure the loyalty of his army in order to have a secure background for his more clearly emerging intentions. The dismissal of Changarnier, the last foothold of the Republic, and various changes of ministers were the forerunners of a bold *coup d'état*. His bill for the revision of the constitution, i.e. the restoration of the Empire, was rejected twice in quick succession; the subversive intrigues of the Chamber became more dangerous. On the eve of December 2, the anniversary of the Empire of 1804, all the heads of the opposing party – in particular, Cavaignac, Lamoricière, Changarnier, Thiers, Victor Hugo, Eugene Sue – were arrested and brought to Château Ham. On the big placards that announced his act to the Parisian people, it said among other things: 'Things could not go on like that. The National Assembly, instead of enacting laws for the common good, subverted and attacked the power bestowed to me by the people. As the chosen one, the one chosen by 6 million people, I have destroyed their intrigues. If the people are not content with that, then they can elect someone else. But if they give me their confidence, they will also give me the means to accomplish my great mission.' A national referendum would decide. An enormous majority of votes decided in his favour, and elected him president for a period of ten years, and assigned to him a Senate. The army, whom he called the elite of the nation, was enchanted by him and all his plans. The resistance, consisting of 252 deputies who wanted to remove the President and hand over supreme command of the army to Oudinot, was broken by armed force. A violent revolt of the democrats in the departments of Cher, Allier and Nièvre was quickly overcome. When Laroche informed him on the eve of the year 1852 of the success at the poll, with almost eight million votes, he said: 'France has recognised that I deviated from the path of legality only in order to enter the path of law. If I congratulate myself for such astonishing approval by the people, it is not out of pride, but because I have faith in my power to act as is fitting for the head of such a great nation.'

The release of his enemies, the new constitution – according to which he held all power, while at his side stood a privy council, a council of Notables and a powerless legislative body – the confiscation of properties of the house of Orleans, the abolition of the previously existing academic freedom and the appointment of its loudest detractors, the new nobility and an exceptionally bright Napoleon festival, all of these were indications of his power and omens of the Empire. A new tour through the South of France afforded him the opportunity to explore the mood of these *departements* and to enhance his popularity. In Lyons he unveiled the equestrian statue of Napoleon, the 'most legitimate ruler of France', in Bordeaux he spoke those proud words: '*l'empire c'est la paix*! When France is at peace, so is the rest of the world.' Upon his return to Paris, he found the city decked out in holiday mood: everywhere emblems of the Emperor, everywhere the cheering '*vive l'empereur*!' But he wanted to take this little step on legal ground. On November 4 the restoration of the Empire was to be discussed. A national referendum would decide. The question was put in such a way that the former governments were taken as illegitimate: Would the nation want to transfer the hereditary empire, as it had existed under Napoleon I and by whose abdication then went to Napoleon II, to Napoleon III? The splendid result, an electoral majority of six million, thoroughly entitled him, on that historic December 2, to proclaim himself Emperor.

Translated by Frank Cameron and Jeff Mitscherling

Saint-Just

You know the man, wan and wiry:
Onto the shoulders falls lightly
The black hair, long and slick,
The glances he casts are a wonder,
So odd and deep, torn by torment,
As if an evil spell had a hold over his heart.
And what the eye cries and feels
Blazes as a stream of flames,
And glows, a frightful sacrificial fire,
In the proud dome of his words,
Faintly at first, from afar, a timid
Touch of light spilling onto walls,
Until, in a crude crimson glimmer,
Everything everywhere flows into one another
And wildly wastes away, limbs distorted,
In the wink of a witch's dance.
You stand stiff and follow from afar
Into the abyss, he calls: you must!
The stars above you are already slipping away:
You are in step with satanic Saint-Just.

Two-poem cycle 'Two Kings'

Louis the Sixteenth

>They led you out,
>Refused to heed your word of peace,
>Waved the flags, beat the drums.
>All around stood the folk, with muffled malice,
>Saw you and stayed still,
>As you uttered the words
>The caring words atop the guillotine's throne.
>For the sins of others has been shed
>Your pious blood, the executioner's scorn,
>And, dying, your word rang out,
>That you forgive and have mercy for
>The people of the revolution.
>Thus spoke freedom's greatest son,
>The sans-culotte Jesus Christ.

Louis the Fifteenth

>The storm rages with all its might,
>A train roars in the middle of the night.
>A train of horsemen, 'round whom lightning blazes,
>Before them a carriage, loaded with death.
>The horses are dashing, the sparks are flying,
>The thunders are rolling, the bolts are flashing.
>Afar a sigh, all around the scent of a grave,
>And nightly ghosts spin in the air.
>The horsemen shiver: in the light dimly
>The Higher Law grins down grimly.
>The wanderer crosses himself, falls upon his knees:
>'Where to – the procession?' 'To Saint-Denys!'

Translated by Nathalie Lachance

2
Agonistic Politics, 1871–1874

Preface

In November 1863, during Nietzsche's final year at Pforta, the Danish *Rigsraad* (Federal Council) passed a new constitution which incorporated the duchy of Schleswig into the Danish kingdom, but in the process violated the Treaty and Protocol of London (1852). Instead of striving to defuse this international crisis, Bismarck was eager to exercise his military power in order to satisfy his main objective: the annexation of Schleswig and Holstein. When Denmark refused to rescind the new constitution, the Austro-Prussian army invaded Schleswig in January 1864. In March 1864, Nietzsche had registered for the military, and was notified that his one-year service would commence no later than October 1, 1867. News of the decisive military victory over the Danes on April 18, with the seizure of the Düppel fortifications, was greeted with much enthusiasm in Prussia and was cause for celebration at Pforta. The war concluded without Nietzsche's participation, but he was particularly impressed by 'the fatherland's army for its glorious deeds'.[1]

In October 1864, Nietzsche entered Bonn University to study theology and classical philology. During his first week there, he surveyed the various fraternities before joining the anti-Napoleonic, Franconia *Burschenschaft*, founded in 1815 by young soldiers who had just returned from the Wars of Liberation. Nietzsche's membership ended not long after the fraternity decided to change its colours to the democratic black, red and gold, as the fraternity sought German unification on a popular basis. He left deriding Franconia's 'capacity for political judgement'[2] and their claim to represent 'the future of Germany, the seedbed of German parliaments'.[3]

While at Bonn, Nietzsche attended the right-wing liberal Heinrich von Sybel's lectures on 'Politics' and identified with the new 'national liberalism'. Sybel rejected the revolutionary principles of 1848 and opposed the introduction of universal male suffrage and parliamentary institutions, a rejection shared by his colleague Heinrich von Treitschke and the young Nietzsche, who thought Sybel's lectures were the best he had heard.[4]

Nietzsche was also inspired by Bonn's pre-eminent classical philologists, Friedrich Ritschl and Otto Jahn, but he had to witness their academic rivalry escalate into a 'philological war' that eventually led to Ritschl's defection to Leipzig, where he was accompanied by a number of students, including Nietzsche. When Nietzsche enrolled at Leipzig University, geopolitical tensions between Austria and Prussia were increasing, and war seemed imminent. Nietzsche declared his desire to fight in the impending war, believing that it was 'dishonourable to sit at home when the fatherland is beginning to struggle for life and death'.[5]

On June 15, 1866, the Prussian army invaded Saxony, Hanover and Hesse, and within a few weeks Nietzsche was expressing his admiration for Bismarck's *Realpolitik*. However, he was sceptical that Bismarck could succeed in uniting Germany by force, suspicious that Bismarck was underestimating 'the moral strength of the people'. But Nietzsche's political allegiance was not in question when in a letter he called himself a 'rabid Prussian' (*enragirter Preusse*).[6]

The Prussian army's defeat of the Austrians at Sadowa on July 3, 1866 quelled any reservations Nietzsche had regarding Bismarck. With Prussia victorious, he was so optimistic as to concede that 'In the last fifty years we have never been so close to the fulfilment of our German hopes. I am beginning gradually to understand that there was probably no softer alternative to a horrific war of annihilation'. It is 'a rare and...new pleasure to feel totally in accord with the existing government'. Nietzsche's scepticism had been allayed by Bismarck's 'success'. This 'time success is there: the achievement is a great one'.[7]

Nietzsche experienced at first-hand, however, that the entire nation was not in a celebratory mood when he returned to Leipzig to find the city decked out in the white and green of Saxony and the democratic black, red and gold. Nietzsche, a Prussian supporter, living in occupied Leipzig, did not hide his support for the Bismarckian liberals, led by von Treitschke, and their call for the Prussian annexation of Saxony, which served his 'own personal interests'.[8] He became actively involved in the local election for the constituent *Reichstag* of the North German Confederation, campaigning strongly for the Bismarckian Saxon National Liberal candidate, Stephani. In effect, the election became a plebiscite on whether the new nationalistic Bismarckian state would be chosen over the forces of particularism. In the end, the Lassallean candidate, Würkert (who, according to Nietzsche, spoke on behalf of the 'most impotent and unreal things' as a 'European workers' state')[9] and Wuttke ('the imperial weasel', representing the *Volkspartie*, comprised of 'fanatical Prussian-haters',[10] those who oppose Prussian hegemony, and emphasise democratic political goals) joined forces to help elect Wächter, the champion of Saxon particularism. Nietzsche's postwar jubilation was partially deflated by Stephani's disappointing electoral defeat and also by the political process in general, with candidates canvassing for votes by any means possible. It would be the first and last time that Nietzsche would be involved in a political campaign. Nevertheless, he was consoled by the fact that the victory of Saxon particularism in the local election did not prevent the *Reichstag*, on April 16, 1867, from approving the constitution that Bismarck had drafted in the autumn of 1866, which founded the new North German Confederation, thereby satisfying Bismarck's goals of perpetuating the Prussian military monarchy and, consequently, his own power.

With his October 1867 deadline for military service fast approaching, Nietzsche travelled to Berlin to enlist in one of the Royal Guard Regiments, but was informed that they were no longer accepting one-year 'volunteers'. Instead, he registered for the Naumburg detachment of the (Mounted) Field Artillery Regiment. In mid-March 1868, while training on horseback, Nietzsche was involved in a serious accident that effectively put an end to his military career. Having been declared 'temporarily unfit for military service', he returned to civilian life on his twenty-fourth birthday, October 15, 1868. He spent most of that year concentrating on his philological projects at Leipzig, but politics was very much on his mind. In a letter to Gersdorff, he mentions having read J. E. Jörg's, *History of Social-Political Parties in Germany* (1867) and expresses his admiration for Bismarck: 'Bismarck gives me great pleasure. I read his speeches as if I were drinking heavy wine.'[11]

In 1869, Nietzsche was appointed professor of classical philology at Basel University during a period in which he was under the spell of Arthur Schopenhauer and enjoying a burgeoning friendship with Richard Wagner. In the spring of 1870, Nietzsche was championing Wagner's programme of German cultural renewal and would continue to do so until the mid-1870s. This vision of the rebirth of tragic culture was curtailed by the outbreak of the Franco-Prussian War in the summer of 1870. Nietzsche perceived the war in agonistic terms as a contest between French and German culture. A French victory would mean the unwanted dissemination of French cultural influences in Germany and threaten Wagner's cultural reformation. Nietzsche, now a Swiss citizen, requested leave of absence from the university so that he could, as he put it, fling the 'tiny mite' of his personal capacities into 'the Fatherland's alms box',[12] thereby satisfying his *German* duty. The city's educational board granted him temporary leave of absence with the following condition: that his military service would be restricted, out of respect for Swiss neutrality, to the medical care of the wounded.

By October, Nietzsche's opinion of the war had changed considerably. The destruction horrified him. The German victory was one-sided, excessively violent and only benefited the state, 'money-making' and Prussian militarism, leaving Nietzsche disillusioned over the war's consequences for culture. He expressed these concerns in a letter written to Gersdorff dated November 7, 1870: 'I am terribly concerned about the impending state of culture. If only we do not have to pay too dearly for the tremendous national success in an area in which I, for one, do not want to face any loss. Between you and me, I now consider Prussia a power that is extremely dangerous for culture.'[13] The new *Reich* won a military victory, but it was not the victory of German culture. The horrors of war did not lead Nietzsche to denounce war or militarism as such, but rather hegemonic wars of extermination (such as Helmuth von Moltke had fought against the French). Instead, inspired by the Ancient Greeks, he defended an agonistic, anti-hegemonic conception of war that would benefit culture.

The idea that war functions as a life force appears in the original draft for *The Birth of Tragedy*, but Nietzsche chose to omit lengthy passages discussing war and slavery in Greece, and opted instead to rework these passages into a preface for a work he planned called 'The Greek State'. This early, unpublished essay was written in January 1871 and contains the most detailed treatment of Nietzsche's early political views, some of which owe an intellectual debt to Jacob Burckhardt's discussion of the agonistic culture of the Ancient Greek *polis* and his critique of the modern state. In this essay, Nietzsche praises the Ancient Greek *polis* for its hierarchical structure and its capacity to generate cultural excellence through the exploitation of slave labour. Similar sentiments are echoed for contemporary Europe: 'In order that there may be a broad, deep and fertile soil for the development of art, the overwhelming majority must, in the service of a minority, be slavishly subjected to life's struggle.' This minority is identified as a group of elite individuals possessing artistic genius, and the role of the state is to produce and protect these exemplary individuals within a caste-like society. 'We moderns' fail to acknowledge the 'cruel-sounding truth that slavery belongs to the essence of a culture', and instead cling to the spurious ideals of the French Enlightenment and Revolution that have been inherited and nourished by Communists, Socialists and 'Liberals' – i.e. universal suffrage, equal rights for all, fundamental rights of man, 'dignity of work' and the 'dignity of man'. Today, the state does not serve as a means to culture, but is reduced to a means for furthering the interests of the egoistic individual. Nietzsche offers war as a cure for the state's decline into liberalism since war indicates that the state is not a protective institution for self-seeking individuals, but rather speaks to a higher ideal for those driven by a love of 'fatherland and prince'.

In Nietzsche's pyramidal social structure, the slaves would neither benefit from nor participate in the cultural achievements of the artistic geniuses. Their existence matters only to the extent that they threaten the artistic accomplishments of 'a small number of Olympian men', otherwise, 'if culture really rested upon the will of the people', we would witness the 'cry of pity' of the oppressed masses 'tearing down the walls of culture'. This description is a response to a nexus of events which culminated in the Paris Commune, an extremely distressing event for Nietzsche. In May 1871, Thiers's soldiers were trying to contain the uprising of the Commune during the infamous

'Week of Blood' as European newspapers reported that the Communards were committing acts of vandalism and arson, and that their most defiant act – later determined to be an exaggeration – was setting the Louvre on fire, destroying its valuable artworks. When word of the Louvre's destruction reached Nietzsche he was so devastated that he had to cancel his class, and proclaimed: 'This is the worst day of my life.'[14] He later wrote: 'When I heard of the fires in Paris, I felt for several days annihilated and was overwhelmed by fears and doubts'.[15] He was aware of the German workers' movement from his years in Leipzig, was witness to the massive strikes in Basel, home of a large and militant urban proletariat, and always viewed these revolutionary movements with contempt. Furthermore, Nietzsche was certainly not impressed by August Bebel's parliamentary speech of May 1871 defending the Commune and predicting that the main event was still to come.

'The Greek State' marks Nietzsche's decisive break with the 'white race of Liberals' and their philosophy of state which he will subsequently challenge for its cultural imperialism and educational policies.

Many themes expressed in 'The Greek State' are revisited in his five public lectures 'On the Future of Our Educational Institutions' delivered at Basel University in 1872. Nietzsche had previously pondered 'a new principle of education'[16] and, as early as 1866, he promised to 'expose' the 'organisation of schools...in public'.[17] In these lectures he criticises the German education system and its democratisation. These lectures reveal his plans for educational reform, an outlook that is informed by his commitment to hierarchy ('in the kingdom of the intellect'), 'the servitude of the masses', their 'instinct of loyalty to the rule of genius' and a disdain for the *Kulturstaat* (the idea that the state should be involved in promoting education and morals among its citizens). In this chapter, we include Nietzsche's third public lecture delivered on February 27, 1872. After expressing the Schopenhauerian notion that geniuses are rare, Nietzsche announces the danger of popular education, claiming that the emancipation of the masses from the rule of the great individual would result in a 'saturnalia of barbarism'. At the same time, he criticises the *Kulturstaat*, specifically, the state's 'barbaric' effort to view itself as a 'mystogogue of culture', as promoting universal state education so that the state becomes recognised as the 'highest goal'. Nietzsche perceived the state's emphasis on the education of the masses as a great danger because it would inevitably dilute the overall quality of German education. The true aim, he contends, cannot be the education of the masses, but rather the education of the select few – those who are destined for great things. Today, however, the aristocratic nature of true education is feared and the masses aim to alienate individual great human beings, which amounts to undermining the 'hierarchy in the kingdom of the intellect'. Even middle-class liberals were now expressing fears that broadening the educational base could subvert the social order. In any case, Nietzsche's preferred model is that of the Ancient Greek state, which did not equate culture with what is 'directly useful to the state'.

In 'Homer's Contest' (1872), Nietzsche's thoughts focus on the relationship between war and culture. He explains that the Greeks possessed 'a trait of cruelty, of tiger-like pleasure in destruction', a truth that is easily discernible on reading the Homeric epics. In Homer's *Iliad*, the reader can look into the 'abysses of hatred', for example, when Achilles drags the corpse of Hector through the city on a chariot to display his heroism. But Nietzsche draws on Hesiod's *Works and Days*, the Greeks' first didactic poem, to show that Greek culture succeeded at sublimating their cruelty through contest (*agon*) in all spheres of life (politics, social life and art). Hesiod's poem describes two Eris goddesses, one promoting 'evil war and feuding' and the other who channels these destructive tendencies productively by inciting individuals to compete rather than kill. This second Eris 'urges even the unskilled man to work, and if one who lacks property sees another who is rich, then he hastens to sow and plant in similar fashion and to put his house in order'. This agonistic feature of Ancient Greek culture allowed Nietzsche to view war not as a means of conquest, but as a contest intended to preserve and promote culture.

The first of Nietzsche's *Untimely Meditations* was a polemic against 'David Strauss, the Confessor and the Writer' (1873). This essay is an attack on 'cultural Philistinism' and singles out for critique, although the real target is the *Kulturstaat*, David Friedrich Strauss, who had arrogantly glorified the Prussian victory over France. In the opening section, Nietzsche argues that the Prussian victory over France does not signal a victory for German culture. Instead, the military victory represents 'the defeat, if not the extirpation, of the German spirit for the benefit of the "German *Reich*"'. The fact that the German military could boast of 'the moral qualities of severe discipline, of more placid obedience' has nothing at all to do with culture. In the *Nachlass* from 1874, Nietzsche recognises that German culture was not victorious over French culture 'since we are just as dependent on it as we were before, and no changes have been wrought in French culture itself'.[18] Nietzsche saw the Franco-Prussian war and the rise of the German empire, proclaimed in 1871, as a threat to German identity: 'We are getting a German empire at precisely that time when we are on the verge of ceasing to be Germans....I no longer have the courage to claim one simple characteristic as especially German.'[19]

In 'Schopenhauer as Educator' (1874), the third of the *Untimely Meditations*, Nietzsche continues his assault on the contemporary world, including, but not limited to, the idolators of the new German *Reich*. The fundamental task for a healthy educational system is to focus on the production of geniuses, but this noble ambition is thwarted by the selfishness of the modern state whose concerns are limited to the production of useful, law-abiding, money-making citizens. The issues of slavery, hierarchy and exemplary individuals recur in this essay as Nietzsche reinforces his view of what society should consider its aim. He writes: 'Mankind must toil unceasingly to bring forth individual great men – this and nothing else is its task.'

Not to be overlooked when assessing Nietzsche's early political thou is the *Kulturkampf* against the Catholic Church, led by Bismarck and t National Liberals, which began at the end of 1871. The Catholic Centre Party was founded in December 1870 and sought to secure Catholic interests within the new *Reich*. Bismarck treated the Catholic Centre Party, as he would later treat the socialists, as *Reichsfeinde* (enemies of the *Reich*) and throughout the early 1870s passed anti-Catholic legislation. For instance, priests could be prosecuted for making statements undermining public order and they could no longer supervise religious teaching. The most severe measures were enacted in the Prussian May laws of 1873. From now on, the state would supervise the training of priests, and priests would have to pass a 'cultural exam' to assess their suitability for office. The state authorities had to be notified of all ecclesiastical appointments and they had the power to veto any appointments. There were harsh penalties for failing to adhere to these laws. Nietzsche's early political thought emerged within the charged atmosphere of the *Kulturkampf*, but did he support Bismarck's anti-Catholic measures and defend a secular state? It is clear from a note written in 1874 that while he did not challenge the measures, he did recognise that the *Kulturkampf* would make Catholic interests even stronger: German culture 'must *employ* its power to achieve its lofty cultural aims. Secularisation to be combated. The struggle against the Catholic Church is an act of enlightenment, nothing loftier; and in the end it merely makes it disproportionately strong: which is wholly undesirable. Of course, in general it is correct. If only the state and the churches would devour each other!'[20] So it may be argued that Nietzsche supported the *Kulturkampf* in principle, but not from any loyalty to the modern state, and not from any sympathy for secularism.

A transition transpires in Nietzsche's political thought between his university years (1864–68), throughout which he betrays Prussian nationalist sympathies (supporting both Bismarck and the National Liberals), and the period of his early writings, both published and unpublished (1871–74), during which he reassesses the relationship between war and culture through the lens of agonism and becomes critical of the new German *Reich* for its power politics, which he considers a threat to the development of culture. Relying now on the model of the Ancient Greeks, Nietzsche affirms an anti-democratic, hierarchical society that includes slavery as a means for producing rare instances of artistic genius while denouncing egalitarian, socialist and liberal ideals.

Both 'The Greek State' and 'On the Future of our Educational Institutions' may be read as a veiled warning against a democratic (or socialist) revolution in Germany. Thus it cannot be merely hegemonic power politics that disturbs Nietzsche. There must be developments occurring within Germany which disturb him equally. When Nietzsche warned his friend Rohde to leave 'that fatal anti-cultural Prussia', it was not only because power politics was emerging there, but also 'slaves and priests', democrats (socialists)

who would soon 'darken the whole of Germany with their
he savage war between Prussia and France, it is not even
which vexes him, for in 1871 he finds its 'heroic' and
...fresh and vigorous...full of old Germanic health' and sees
...it as something that can be built on for a *'German* mission' not yet
dead. He sees, too, that there is an 'inward difference' between the Germans and the French, and he is 'in better heart than ever, for not everything has been ruined by French-Jewish superficiality'. Was that what almost won over German culture? The war between France and Germany, however, was not the main 'object of [his] terror', but rather 'that international hydra-head, suddenly and so terrifyingly appearing as a sign of quite different struggles to come.... we would agree that precisely in that phenomenon does our modern life.... show the enormous degree to which our world has been damaged, and that, with all our past behind us, we are all of us responsible for such terror coming to light ...'[22] In Nietzsche's mind, the event of the Paris Commune and international socialism (the 'international hydra-head') represents the struggle to come, the social question, and within Germany that means, for Nietzsche, resistance to any social democratic initiatives: 'I consider a representational constitution to be superfluous in Prussia: indeed, to be infinitely detrimental'.[23]

The Greek State, 1871

Preface

We moderns have an advantage over the Greeks with two concepts, which are given as a consolation as it were to a world behaving thoroughly slavishly and yet at the same time anxiously eschewing the word 'slave': we speak of the 'dignity of man' and of the 'dignity of work'. Everything is at pains to miserably perpetuate a miserable existence; this awful need compels man to exhausting work; he – or more correctly the human intellect – seduced by the 'will', now occasionally marvels at work as something dignified. However, in order that work might have a claim on titles of honour, it would be necessary above all that existence itself, to which work after all is only a painful means, should have more dignity and value than it appears to have had up to the present, to serious-minded philosophies and religions. What else may we find in the toil of all the millions but the drive to exist at any price, the same all-powerful drive by which stunted plants stretch their roots into arid rocks!

Out of this awful struggle for existence only those individuals can emerge who are, at once, again occupied with the noble illusions of artistic culture, lest they should arrive at practical pessimism which nature abhors as truly unnatural. In the modern world which, compared with the Greek, usually creates only freaks and centaurs, in which the individual, like that fabulous creature in the beginning of Horace's *Ars Poetica*, is a colourful patchwork, the craving of the struggle for existence and of the need for art arise often at the same time in the same man: out of this unnatural amalgamation has originated the need to excuse and to consecrate that first craving before this need for art. Therefore we believe in the 'dignity of man' and the 'dignity of work'.

The Greeks did not require such conceptual hallucinations, for among them the idea that work is a disgrace is expressed with startling frankness; and another piece of wisdom, more hidden and rarely expressed, but everywhere alive, added that the human thing also was a disgraceful and pathetic nothing, and the 'dream of a shadow'. Work is a disgrace because existence has no value in itself; but even if this very existence shines forth in the alluring embellishment of artistic illusions and really seems to have a value in itself, then that pronouncement is still valid that work is a disgrace indeed, as it is impossible for man, fighting for sheer survival, to be an *artist*. In modern times it is not the man in need of art but the slave who determines general views, the slave who according to his nature must give deceptive names to all the circumstances of his life in order to be able to live. Such phantoms as the dignity of man, the dignity of work, are the needy products of a slavery that hides from itself. Woeful time, in which the slave requires such conceptions, in which he is incited to think about and beyond himself! Cursed seducers, who have destroyed the slave's state of innocence by the fruit of the tree of knowledge! Now the slave must scrape through from one day to the next with such sheer lies recognisable to anyone with deeper insight, such as the alleged 'equal rights of all' or the so-called 'fundamental rights of man', of man as such, or such as the 'dignity of work'. Indeed he is not to understand at what stage and at what height one can start talking about 'dignity', namely, at the point, where the individual completely transcends himself and no longer has to produce and to work in order to preserve his individual existence.

And even upon this height of 'work' the Greek at times is overcome by a feeling that resembles shame. Plutarch, with ancient Greek instinct, once said that no youth of noble birth, on beholding the Zeus in Pisa, would have the desire to become himself a Phidias, or on seeing the Hera in Argos, to become himself a Polyklet; and just as little would he wish to be Anacreon, Philetas or Archilochus, however much he might revel in their poetry. To the Greek artistic creativity falls just as much under the undignified conception of work as any ignoble craft. But if the compelling force of the artistic impulse operates in him, then he *must* create and submit himself to that hardship of work. And as a father admires the beauty and the gift of his child but thinks of the act of procreation with embarrassed reluctance, so it was with the Greek. The joyful astonishment at the beautiful has not blinded him as to its origin which appeared to him, like all becoming in nature, to be a tremendous hardship, a forcing of itself into existence. That feeling by which the process of procreation is considered as something shameful, to be hidden, although by it man serves a higher purpose than his individual preservation, the same feeling veiled also the origin of the great works of art, in spite of the fact that through them a higher form of existence is inaugurated, just as through that other act comes a new generation. *Shame* seems therefore to occur where man is merely a tool of infinitely greater manifestations of will than he is permitted to consider himself to be in the isolated shape of the individual.

Now we have the general concept with which to categorise the feelings which the Greeks had with regard to work and slavery. Both were considered by them as a necessary disgrace, of which one feels *ashamed*, both as a disgrace and as a necessity. In this feeling of shame is hidden the unconscious realisation that the real aim *needs* those conditions, but that in that *need* lies the fearful and beast-of-prey-like quality of this Sphinx which is nature, which in the glorification of the artistically free life of culture so beautifully stretches forth her virginal body. Culture, which is chiefly a real need for art, rests upon a terrible basis: the latter however makes itself known in the sensation of a shame, which dawns upon one. In order that there may be a broad, deep and fertile soil for the development of art, the overwhelming majority must, in the service of a minority, be slavishly subjected to life's struggle, thus *exceeding* what their own wants necessitate. At their cost, through their extra work, that privileged class is to be relieved from the struggle for existence, in order to create and to satisfy a new world of want.

Accordingly we must accept this cruel-sounding truth that *slavery belongs to the essence of a culture*; a truth of course, which leaves no doubt as to the absolute value of existence. *This truth* is the vulture that gnaws at the liver of the Promethean promoter of culture. The misery of toiling men must still increase in order to make the production of the world of art possible to a small number of Olympian men. Here is to be found the source of that secret wrath nourished at all times by Communists and Socialists, and also by their paler descendants, the white race of 'Liberals', not only against the arts, but also against classical antiquity. If culture really was left to the discretion of a people, if here inexorable powers did not rule, powers which are law and restraint to the individual, then the contempt for culture, the glorification of a poorness in spirit, the iconoclastic annihilation of artistic claims would be *more* than an insurrection of the oppressed masses against drone-like individuals: it would be the cry of pity tearing down the walls of culture; the desire for justice, for equal suffering, would swamp all other ideas. In fact, an exuberant degree of pity has once for a short time opened, here and there, all the flood gates of culture-life; a rainbow of pitying love and of peace appeared with the first radiant rise of Christianity and beneath it was born Christianity's most beautiful fruit, the Gospel of St John. But there are also instances to show that powerful religions for long periods petrify a given degree of culture, and cut off with inexorable sickle everything that still wants to grow strongly and luxuriantly. For it is not to be forgotten that the same cruelty, which we found in the essence of every culture, lies also in the essence of every powerful religion and in general in the nature of *power*, which is always evil; so that we shall understand it just as well, when a culture breaks down a too highly piled bulwark of religious claims with a cry for liberty, or at least justice. That which in this sorry scheme of things wants to live, that is, must live, is at the bottom of its nature the image of the primal-pain and primal-contradiction, and must therefore strike our eyes – 'organs made for this world and earth' – as an insatiable craving for existence and as an eternal self-contradiction, within the form of time, therefore as *becoming*. Every moment devours the preceding one, every birth is the death of innumerable beings; procreation, living, murdering, are one. Therefore we may compare this grand culture with a blood-stained victor, who in his triumphal procession drags along the defeated chained to his chariot as slaves, slaves whom a beneficent power has so blinded that, almost crushed by the wheels of the chariot, they nevertheless still exclaim: 'Dignity of work!' 'Dignity of man!' The voluptuous Cleopatra-culture throws ever again the most priceless pearls into her golden goblet: these pearls are the tears of pity for the misery of the slave. Out of the pampering of modern man arose the enormous social distress of the present time, not out of the true and deep compassion for that misery; and if it should be true that the Greeks perished through their slavery, then another fact is much more certain, that we shall perish through the *lack* of slavery. Slavery did not appear in any way objectionable, much less abominable, either to early Christianity or to the Germanic tribes. What an uplifting effect on us has the contemplation of the medieval serf, with his inwardly strong and tender legal and ethical relationship to the man of higher rank, with the profound fencing in of his narrow existence – how elevating! – and how reproachful!

He who cannot reflect upon the position of affairs in society without melancholy, who has learnt to conceive of it as the continual painful birth of those who are set apart, the men of culture, in whose service everything else must be sacrificed, will no longer be deceived by that false glamour, which the moderns have spread over the origin and meaning of the state. For what can the state mean to us, if not the means by which that social-process described previously is to get underway and to be guaranteed in its unimpeded continuance? Be the sociable instinct in individual man as strong as it may, it is only the iron clamp of the state that constrains the large masses upon one another in such a fashion that a chemical separation of society, with its new pyramidal superstructure, is *bound* to take place. But what is the origin of this sudden power of the state, whose aim lies far beyond the insight and egoism of the individual? How did the slave, the blind mole of culture, *originate*? The Greeks in their instinct relating to the law of peoples have betrayed it to us, in an instinct, which even in the ripest fullness of their civilisation and humanity never ceased to utter as out of a brazen mouth such words as: 'to the victor belongs the vanquished, with wife and child, goods and blood. Power gives the first *right*, and there is no right, which at bottom is not presumption, usurpation, violence'.

Here again we see with what pitiless inflexibility nature, in order to arrive at society, forges for herself the cruel tool of the state – namely, the *conqueror* with the iron hand, who is nothing but the objectification of the instinct indicated. By the indefinable greatness and power of such conquerors the spectator feels that they are only the means of an intention manifesting itself through them and yet hiding itself from them. The weaker forces attach themselves to them with such mysterious speed, and transform themselves so wonderfully, in the sudden swelling of that violent avalanche, under the charm of that creative kernel, into an affinity hitherto not existing, as if a supernatural will were emanating from them.

Now when we see how little the vanquished trouble themselves after a short time about the dreadful origin of the state, so that history informs us of no kind of events worse than the origins of those sudden, violent, bloody and, at least in *one* point, inexplicable usurpations: when hearts involuntarily go out towards the magic of the developing state with the presentiment of an invisibly deep intention, where the calculating intellect is enabled to see an addition of forces only; when now even the state is viewed with fervour as the goal and ultimate aim of the sacrifices and duties of the individual: then out of all that speaks the enormous necessity of the state, without which nature might not succeed in achieving, through society, her salvation in appearance, in the mirror of the genius. What discernments does the instinctive pleasure in the state not overcome! One would indeed feel inclined to think that a person who looks into the origin of the state will henceforth seek his salvation at an awful distance from it; and where can one not see the monuments of its formation, devastated lands, destroyed cities, savaged men, consuming hatred of peoples! The state, of ignominious birth, for the majority of men a continually flowing source of toil, at frequently recurring periods the consuming torch of humankind – and yet a word, at which we forget ourselves, a battle cry, which has filled men with enthusiasm for innumerable truly heroic deeds, perhaps the highest and most venerable object for the blind and egoistic mass which only in the tremendous moments of state-life has the strange expression of greatness on its face!

We have, however, to consider the Greeks, with regard to the unique zenith of their art, as the 'political men in themselves', and certainly history knows of no second instance of such an awesome release of the political passion, such an unconditional sacrifice of all other interests in the service of this state-instinct; at best one might distinguish the men of the Renaissance in Italy with a similar title for like reasons and by way of comparison. So overloaded is that passion among the Greeks that it begins ever anew to rage against itself and to sink its teeth into its own flesh. This bloody jealousy of city against city, of party against party, this murderous greed of those petty wars, the tiger-like triumph over the corpse of the slain enemy, in short, the incessant renewal of those Trojan scenes of struggle and horror, in the spectacle of which, as a genuine Hellene, Homer stands before us absorbed with delight – what does this naïve barbarism of the Greek state indicate, and what is its excuse before the tribunal of eternal justice? The state appears before it proudly and calmly, and by the hand it leads the exquisitely blooming woman: Greek society. For this Helen, the state waged those wars – and what grey-bearded judge could here condemn? Under this mysterious connection which we here divine between state and art, political greed and artistic creation, battlefield and work of art, we understand by the state, as already remarked, only the iron clamp producing society by force; whereas without the state, in the natural *bellum omnium contra omnes* society cannot strike root at all on a larger scale and beyond the sphere of the family. Now, after states have been established almost everywhere, that bent of the *bellum omnium contra omnes* concentrates itself from time to time into a terrible gathering of war clouds between peoples and discharges itself as it were in rare but so much the more violent thunders and lightning flashes. But in consequence of the effect of that *bellum* – an effect which is turned inwards and compressed – society is given time during the intervals to germinate and turn green everywhere, as soon as warmer days come, to let the shining blossoms of genius sprout forth.

With regard to the political world of the Hellenes, I will not hide those phenomena of the present in which I believe I detect dangerous atrophies of the political sphere equally critical for art and society. If there should exist men, who as it were through birth are placed outside the popular and state instincts, who thus have to esteem the state only insofar as they conceive that it coincides with their own interest, then such men will necessarily imagine as the ultimate national aim the most undisturbed co-existence possible of great political communities, in which *they* might be permitted to pursue their own purposes without restriction. With this in mind they will promote that policy which will best allow this; whereas it is unthinkable that they, against their intentions, guided perhaps by an unconscious instinct, should sacrifice themselves to the state purpose, unthinkable because they lack that very instinct. All other citizens of the state are in the dark about what nature intends for them with her state instinct, and they follow blindly; only those who stand outside this instinct know what *they* want from the state and what the state should grant them. Therefore it is almost unavoidable that such men should gain great influence on the state because they are allowed to consider it as a *means*, whereas all the others under the sway of the unconscious intentions of the state are themselves only means for the fulfilment of the state purpose. In order now to attain, through the medium of the state, the highest furtherance of their selfish aims, it is above all necessary, that the state be wholly freed from those terrible, unpredictable outbreaks of war so that it may be used rationally;

and thereby they strive, as consciously as possible, for a condition of things in which war is an impossibility. For that purpose the thing to do is first to curtail and to weaken the specific political impulses and through the establishment of large *equipoised* state bodies and the mutual safeguarding of them to make the successful result of an aggressive war and consequently war itself the greatest improbability; as on the other hand they will endeavour to wrest the question of war and peace from the decision of individual rulers, in order to be able rather to appeal to the egoism of the masses or their representatives; for which purpose they again need slowly to dissolve the monarchic instincts of the peoples. This purpose they attain best through the most general dissemination of the liberal optimistic world view, which has its roots in the ideals of the French Enlightenment and the French Revolution, i.e. in a wholly un-Germanic, genuinely neo-Latin, shallow and unmetaphysical philosophy. I cannot help seeing in the prevailing international movements of the present day, and the simultaneous spread of universal suffrage, the effects of the *fear of war* above everything else, I cannot help seeing behind these movements those truly international, homeless, financial recluses, as the really alarmed, who, with their natural lack of the state instinct, have learned to abuse politics as a means of the stock exchange, and state and society as an apparatus for their own enrichment. The only remedy against the threatened deviation of the state tendency towards money matters from this side is war and once again war, in the emotions of which it at least becomes obvious, that the state is not founded upon the fear of the war-demon, as a protective institution for egoistic individuals, but that rather, in the love for fatherland and prince, it produces an ethical impulse, indicative of a much higher destiny. If I therefore designate as a dangerous and characteristic sign of the present political situation the application of revolutionary thoughts in the service of a selfish, stateless money-aristocracy, if at the same time I conceive of the enormous dissemination of liberal optimism as the result of modern financial affairs fallen into strange hands, and if I imagine all evils of social conditions together with the necessary decay of the arts to have either sprouted from that root or grown together with it, one will have to pardon my occasionally chanting a paean on war. Horribly clangs its silvery bow; and although it comes along like the night, war is nevertheless Apollo, the true divinity for consecrating and purifying the state. First of all, however, as is said in the beginning of the *Iliad*, he lets fly his arrow on the mules and dogs. Then he strikes the men themselves, and everywhere pyres break into flames. Be it then pronounced that war is just as much a necessity for the state as the slave is for society, and who can avoid this verdict if he honestly asks himself about the causes of the never equalled Greek artistic perfection?

He who contemplates war and its uniformed potential, the *military profession*, with respect to the hitherto described nature of the state, must arrive at the conviction, that through war and in the military profession is placed before our eyes a type, or even perhaps the *archetype of the state*. Here we see as the most general effect of the war tendency, an immediate division and decomposition of the chaotic masses into *military castes*, out of which rises, pyramid-shaped, on an exceedingly broad base of slaves, the edifice of the 'martial society'. The unconscious purpose of the whole movement constrains every individual under its yoke, and produces also in heterogeneous natures, as it were, a chemical transformation of their qualities until they are brought into affinity with that purpose. In the higher castes one perceives already a little more of what in this internal process is basically involved, namely the creation of the *military genius* – with whom we have become acquainted as the original founder of the state. In the case of many states, as, for example, in the Lycurgian constitution of Sparta, one can distinctly perceive the imprint of that fundamental idea of the state, that of the creation of the military genius. If we now imagine the original military state in its greatest activity, at its proper 'work', and if we fix our glance upon the whole technique of war, we cannot avoid correcting our notions picked up from everywhere, of 'dignity of man' and 'dignity of work' by the question, whether the idea of dignity is applicable also to work, which has as its purpose the destruction of the 'dignified' man, as well as to the man who is entrusted with that 'dignified work', or whether in this warlike task of the state those mutually contradictory ideas do not offset one another. I should like to think the warlike man to be a *means* of the military genius and his work again only a tool in the hands of that same genius; and not to him, as absolute man and non-genius, but to him as a means of the genius – who can choose his tool's destruction as means to the martial artwork – to him is due a degree of dignity, of that dignity namely, *to have been deemed worthy of being a means of the genius*. But what is shown here in a single instance is valid in the most general sense; every human being, with his total activity, only has dignity insofar as he is a tool of the genius, consciously or unconsciously; from this we may immediately deduce the ethical conclusion, that 'man in himself', the absolute man, possesses neither dignity, nor rights, nor duties; only as a wholly determined being serving unconscious purposes can man excuse his existence.

Plato's perfect state is according to these considerations certainly something still greater than even the warm-blooded among his admirers believe, not to mention the superior smirk with which our 'historically' educated refuse such a fruit of antiquity. The proper aim of the state, the Olympian existence and ever-renewed procreation and preparation of the genius, – compared with which all other things are only tools, expedients and factors towards realisation – is here discovered with a poetic intuition and harshly described. Plato saw through the awfully devastated Herma of the contemporary state-life and perceived even then something divine in its interior. He *believed* that one might be able to take out this divine image and that the grim and barbarically distorted exterior did not belong to the essence of the

state: the whole fervour and sublimity of his political passion threw itself upon this belief, upon that desire – and in the flames of this fire he perished. That in his perfect state he did not place at the head the genius, in its most general sense, but only the genius of wisdom and of knowledge, that he altogether excluded artistic geniuses from his state, that was a rigid consequence of the Socratic judgement on art, which Plato, struggling against himself, had made his own. This more external, almost incidental gap must not prevent our recognising in the total conception of the Platonic state the wonderfully great hieroglyph of a profound *esoteric doctrine of the connection between state and genius* eternally needing to be interpreted. We have said in this preface what we believed we could fathom of this secret script.
Translated by M. Mügge with modifications – Nathalie Lachance

On the Future of Our Educational Institutions, Third Lecture, February 27, 1872

...Both the philosopher and his companion sat silent, sunk in deep dejection: the peculiarly critical state of that important educational institution, the German public school, lay upon their souls like a heavy burden...

...These two worthy men saw clearly, by the system of instruction in vogue, that the time was not yet ripe for a higher culture, a culture founded upon that of the ancients...that the most beneficial of those forces which have come down to us from classical antiquity are not yet known in our public schools: forces which would train students for the struggle against the barbarism of the present age, and which will perhaps once more transform the public schools into the arsenals and workshops of this struggle.

...

'...There may be a few people, hopelessly unfamiliar with pedagogical matters, who believe that our present profusion of public schools and teachers, which is manifestly out of all proportion, can be changed into a real profusion, an *ubertas ingenii*, merely by a few rules and regulations, and without any reduction in the number of these institutions. But we may surely be unanimous in recognising that by the very nature of things only an exceedingly small number of people are destined for a true course of education, and that a much smaller number of higher educational establishments would suffice for their further development, but that, in view of the present large numbers of educational institutions, those for whom in general such institutions ought only to be established must feel themselves to be the least facilitated in their progress.

'The same holds good in regard to teachers. It is precisely the best teachers – those who, generally speaking, judged by a high standard, are worthy of this honourable name – who are now perhaps the least fitted, in view of the present standing of our public schools, for the education of these unselected youths...but who must rather, to a certain extent, keep hidden from them the best they could give: and, on the other hand, by far the larger number of these teachers feel themselves quite at home in these institutions, as their moderate abilities stand in a kind of harmonious relationship to the dullness of their pupils. It is from this majority that we hear the ever-resounding call for the establishment of new public schools and higher educational institutions: we are living in an age which, by ringing the changes on its deafening and continual cry, would certainly give one the impression that there was an unprecedented thirst for culture which eagerly sought to be quenched. But it is just at this point that one should learn to hear aright: it is here, without being disconcerted by the thundering noise of the education-mongers, that we must confront those who talk so tirelessly about the educational necessities of their time. Then we should meet with a strange disillusionment, one which we, my good friend, have often met with: those blatant heralds of educational needs, when examined at close quarters, are suddenly seen to be transformed into zealous...fanatical opponents of true culture, *i.e.* all those who hold fast to the aristocratic nature of the mind; for, at bottom, they regard as their goal the emancipation of the masses from the mastery of the great few; they seek to overthrow the most sacred hierarchy in the kingdom of the intellect – the servitude of the masses, their submissive obedience, their instinct of loyalty to the rule of genius.

'I have long accustomed myself to look with caution upon those who are ardent in the cause of the so-called "education of the people" in the common meaning of the phrase; since for the most part they desire for themselves, consciously or unconsciously, absolutely unlimited freedom, which must inevitably degenerate into something resembling the saturnalia of barbaric times, and which the sacred hierarchy of nature will never grant them. They were born to serve and to obey; and every moment in which their limping or crawling or broken-winded thoughts are at work shows us clearly out of which clay nature moulded them and what trademark she branded thereon. The education of the masses cannot, therefore, be our aim, but rather the education of a few men selected for great and lasting works. We well know that a just posterity judges the collective intellectual state of a time only by those few great and lonely figures of the period, and gives its decision in accordance with the manner in which they are recognised, encouraged and honoured, or, on the other hand, in which they are snubbed, elbowed aside and kept down. What is called the "education of the masses" cannot be accomplished except with difficulty; and even if a system of universal compulsory education be applied, they can only be reached outwardly: those individual lower levels where, generally speaking, the masses come into contact with culture, where the people nourishes its religious instinct, where it poetises its mythological images, where it keeps up its faith in its customs, privileges, native soil, and language – all these levels can scarcely be reached by direct means, and in any case only by violent demolition. ...

...we know the aim of those who profess to satisfy excessive educational requirements by means of an extraordinary increase in the number of education institutions and the conceited tribe of teachers originated thereby. These very people, using these very means, are fighting against the natural hierarchy in the realm of the intellect, and destroying the roots of all those noble and sublime plastic forces which have their material origin in the unconsciousness of the people, and which fittingly terminate in the procreation of genius and its due guidance and proper training. It is only in the simile of the mother that we can grasp the meaning and the responsibility of the true education of the people in respect to genius: its real origin is not to be found in such education; it has, so to speak, only a metaphysical source, a metaphysical home. But for the genius to make his appearance; for him to emerge from among the people; to portray the reflected picture, as it were, the dazzling brilliancy of the peculiar colours of this people; to depict the noble destiny of a people in the similitude of an individual in a work which will last for all time, thereby making his nation itself eternal, and redeeming it from the ever-shifting element of transient things: all this is possible for the genius only when he has been brought up and come to maturity in the tender care of the culture of a people; whilst, on the other hand, without this sheltering home, the genius will not, generally speaking, be able to rise to the height of his eternal flight...

'...I fully understand what you have said about the surplus of public schools and the corresponding surplus of higher grade teachers; and in this regard I myself have collected some information which assures me that the educational tendency of the public school *must* right itself by this very surplus of teachers who have really nothing at all to do with education, and who are called into existence and pursue this path solely because there is a demand for them. Every man who, in an unexpected moment of enlightenment, has convinced himself of the singularity and inaccessibility of Hellenic antiquity, and has warded off this conviction after an exhausting struggle – every such man knows that the door leading to this enlightenment will never remain open to all comers; and he deems it absurd, yea disgraceful, to use the Greeks as he would any other tool he employs when following his profession or earning his living, shamelessly fumbling with coarse hands amidst the relics of these holy men.'

...

'...The public schools may still be seats of learning: not, however of *the* learning which, as it were, is only the natural and involuntary auxiliary of a culture that is directed towards the noblest ends; but rather of that culture which might be compared to the hypertrophical swelling of an unhealthy body. The public schools are certainly the seats of this obesity, if, indeed, they have not degenerated into the abodes of that elegant barbarism which is boasted of as being "German culture of the present!"'

'But', asked the other, 'what is to become of that large body of teachers who have not been endowed with a true gift for culture, and who set up as teachers merely to gain a livelihood from the profession, because there is a demand for them, because a superfluity of schools brings with it a superfluity of teachers? Where shall they go when antiquity peremptorily orders them to withdraw? Must they not be sacrificed to those powers of the present who, day after day, call out to them from the never-ending columns of the press: "We are culture! We are education! We are at the zenith! We are the apexes of the pyramids! We are the aims of universal history!" – when they hear the seductive promises, when the shameful signs of non-culture, the plebeian publicity of the so-called "interests of culture" are extolled for their benefit in magazines and newspapers as an entirely new and the best possible, full-grown form of culture! Whither shall the poor fellows fly when they feel the presentiment that these promises are not true – where but to the most obtuse, sterile scientificality, that here the shriek of culture may no longer be audible to them? Pursued in this way, must they not end, like the ostrich, by burying their heads in the sand? Is it not a real happiness for them, buried as they are among dialects, etymologies and conjectures, to lead a life like that of the ants, even though they are miles removed from true culture, if only they can close their ears tightly and be deaf to the voice of the "elegant" culture of the time.'

'You are right, my friend', said the philosopher, 'but whence comes the urgent necessity for a surplus of schools for culture, which further gives rise to the necessity for a surplus of teachers? – when we so clearly see that the demand for a surplus springs from a sphere which is hostile to culture, and that the consequences of this surplus only lead to non-culture. Indeed, we can discuss this dire necessity only in so far as the modern state is willing to discuss these things with us, and is prepared to follow up its demands by force: which phenomenon certainly makes the same impression upon most people as if they were addressed by the eternal law of things. For the rest, a "culture-state", to use the current expression, which makes such demands, is rather a novelty, and has only come to a "self-understanding" within the last half-century, i.e. in a period when (to use the favourite popular word) so many "self-understood" things came into being, but which are in themselves not "self-understood" at all. This right to higher education has been taken so seriously by the most powerful of modern states – Prussia – that the objectionable principle it has adopted, taken in connection with the well-known daring and hardihood of this state, is seen to have a menacing and dangerous consequence for the true German spirit; for we see endeavours being made in this quarter to raise the public school, formally systematised, up to the so-called "level of the time". Here is to be found all that mechanism by means of which as many scholars as possible are urged on to take up courses of public school training: here, indeed, the state has its most powerful inducement – the concession of certain privileges respecting military service, with the natural consequence that, according to the unprejudiced evidence of statistical officials, by this, and by this only, can we explain the universal congestion of all Prussian public schools, and the urgent and continual need for new ones. What more can the state do for a surplus of educational institutions than bring all the higher and the majority of the lower civil service appointments, the right of entry to the universities, and even the most influential military posts into close connection with the public school: and all this in a country where both universal military service and the highest offices of the state unconsciously attract all gifted natures to them. The public school is here looked upon as an honourable aim, and everyone who feels himself urged on to the sphere of government will be found on his way to it. This is a new and quite original occurrence: the state assumes the attitude of a mystogogue of culture, and, whilst it promotes its own ends, it obliges every one of its servants not to appear in its presence without the torch of universal state education in their hands, by the flickering light of which they may again recognise the state as the highest goal, as the reward of all their strivings after education.

'Now this last phenomenon should indeed surprise them; it should remind them of that allied, slowly understood tendency of a philosophy which was formerly promoted for reasons of state, namely, the tendency of the Hegelian philosophy: yea, it would perhaps be no exaggeration to say that, in the subordination of all strivings after education to reasons of state, Prussia has appropriated, with success, the principle and the useful heirloom of the Hegelian philosophy, whose apotheosis of the state in *this* subordination certainly reaches its height.'

'But', said the philosopher's companion, 'what purposes can the state have in view with such a strange aim? For that it has some state objects in view is seen in the manner in which the conditions of Prussian schools are admired by, meditated upon, and occasionally imitated by other states. These other states obviously presuppose something here that, if adopted, would tend towards the maintenance and power of the state, like our well-known and popular conscription. Where everyone proudly wears his soldier's uniform at regular intervals, where almost everyone has absorbed a uniform type of national culture through the public schools, enthusiastic hyperboles may well be uttered concerning the systems employed in former times, and a form of state omnipotence which was attained only in antiquity, and which almost every young man, by both instinct and training, thinks it is the crowning glory and highest aim of human beings to reach.'

'Such a comparison', said the philosopher, 'would be quite hyperbolic, and would not hobble along on one leg only. For, indeed, the ancient state emphatically did not share the utilitarian point of view of recognising as culture only what was directly useful to the state itself, and was far from wishing to destroy those impulses which did not seem to be immediately applicable. For this very reason the profound Greek had for the state that strong feeling of admiration and thankfulness which is so distasteful to modern men; because he clearly recognised not only that without such state protection the germs of his culture could not develop, but also that all his inimitable and perennial culture had flourished so luxuriantly under the wise and careful guardianship of the protection afforded by the state. The state was for his culture not a supervisor, regulator and watchman, but a vigorous and muscular companion and friend, ready for war, who accompanied his noble, admired and, as it were, ethereal friend through disagreeable realty, earning his thanks thereby. This, however, does not happen when a modern state lays claim to such hearty gratitude because it renders such chivalrous service to German culture and art; for in this regard its past is a ignominious as its present, as a proof of which we have but to think of the manner in which the memory of our great poets and artists is celebrated in German cities, and how the highest objects of these German masters are supported on the part of the state.

'There must therefore be peculiar circumstances surrounding both this purpose towards which the state is tending, and which always promotes what is here called "education"; and surrounding likewise the culture thus promoted, which subordinates itself to this purpose of the state. With the real German spirit and the education derived therefrom, such as I have slowly outlined for you, this purpose of the state is at war, covertly or openly: *the spirit of education*, which is welcomed and encouraged with such interest by the state, and owing to which the schools of this country are so much admired abroad, must accordingly originate in a sphere that never comes into contact with this true German spirit: with that spirit which speaks to us so wondrously from the inner heart of the German Reformation, German music and German philosophy, and which, like a noble exile, is regarded with such indifference and scorn by the luxurious education afforded by the state. This spirit is a stranger: it passes by in solitary sadness, and far away from it the censer of pseudo-culture is swung backwards and forwards, which, amidst the acclamations of "educated" teachers and journalists, arrogates to itself its name and privileges, and metes out insulting treatment to the word "German". Why does the state require that surplus of educational institutions, of teachers? Why this education of the masses on such an extended scale? Because the true German spirit is hated, because the aristocratic nature of true culture is feared, because the people endeavour in this way to drive single great individuals into self-exile, so that the claims of the masses to education may be, so to speak, planted down and carefully tended, in order that the many may in this way endeavour to escape the rigid and strict discipline of the few great leaders, so that the masses may be persuaded that they can easily find the path for themselves – following the guiding star of the state!

'A new phenomenon! The state as the guiding star of culture! In the meantime one thing consoles me: This German spirit, which people are combating so much, and for which they have substituted a gaudily attired *locum tenens*, this spirit is brave: it will fight and redeem itself into a purer age, noble, as it is now, and victorious, as it one day will be, it will always preserve in its mind a certain pitiful toleration of the state, if the latter, hard-pressed in the hour of extremity, secures such a pseudo-culture as its associate. For what, after all, do we know about the difficult task of governing men, i.e. to keep law, order, quietness, and peace among millions of boundlessly egoistical, unjust, unreasonable, dishonourable, envious, malignant, and hence very narrow-minded and perverse human beings; and thus to protect the few things that the state has conquered for itself against covetous neighbours and jealous robbers? Such a hard-pressed state holds out its arms to any associate, grasps at any straw; and when such an associate does introduce himself with flowery eloquence, when he adjudges the state, as Hegel did, to be an "absolutely complete ethical organism", the be all and end all of everyone's education, and goes on to indicate how he himself can best promote the interests of the state – who will be surprised if, without further parley, the state falls upon his neck and cries aloud in a barbaric voice of full conviction: "Yes! Thou art education! Thou art indeed culture!"'

Translated by J. M. Kennedy with modifications

Homer's Contest, 1872

When one speaks of *humanity*, the underlying notion is that humanity is that which *separates* and distinguishes man from nature. But such a distinction does not in reality exist: the 'natural' qualities and the properly called 'human' ones have grown up inseparably together. Man in his highest and noblest powers is nature and bears in himself her uncanny dual character. His abilities generally considered dreadful and inhuman are perhaps indeed the fertile soil, from which alone can grow forth all humanity in emotions, actions and works.

Thus the Greeks, the most humane people of ancient times, have in themselves a trait of cruelty, of tiger-like pleasure in destruction: a trait, which in the grotesquely enlarged image of the Hellene, in Alexander the Great, is very visible, which, however, in their whole history, as well as in their mythology, must terrify us who meet them with the softish concept of modern humanity. When Alexander has the feet of Batis, the brave defender of Gaza, bored through, and binds his living body to his chariot in order to drag him around exposed to the scorn of his own soldiers: that is a sickening caricature of Achilles, who at night desecrates Hector's corpse by dragging it around in a similar fashion; but even this trait has for us something offensive and horrific about it. It gives us a look into the abysses of hatred. With the same sensation we observe the bloody and insatiable self-laceration of two Greek parties, as for example in the Corcyrean revolution. When the victor, in a battle between cities, according to the *rights* of war, executes the whole male population and sells all the women and children into slavery, we see, in the sanction of such a right, that the Greek deemed it a serious necessity to allow his hatred to break forth unimpeded; in such moments the compressed and swollen feeling relieved itself; the tiger bounced forth, a voluptuous cruelty shone out of its fearful eye. Why did the Greek sculptor repeatedly have to represent war and battles in innumerable repetitions, extended human bodies, their sinews tightened with hatred or the arrogance of triumph, fighters wounded and writhing with pain, the dying with the last rattle in their throat? Why did the whole Greek world exult over the battle scenes of the *Iliad*? I am afraid we do not understand them enough in a 'Greek' way, and that we would even shudder if we ever did understand them in a Greek way.

But what lies, as the mother-womb of the Hellenic, *behind* the Homeric world? In the *latter*, by the extreme artistic precision, the calm and purity of the lines we are already lifted far above the purely material fusion: its colours, by an artistic deception, appear lighter, milder, warmer; its people, in this coloured, warm illumination, appear better and more likable – but where do we look if, no longer guided and protected by Homer's hand, we step backwards into the pre-Homeric world? Only into night and horror, into the products of a fantasy accustomed to the horrible. What earthly existence is reflected in the loathsome, fearful Theogonistic myths: a life ruled over only by the *children of the night*, by strife, lust, deception, age and death. Let us imagine the suffocating atmosphere of Hesiod's poem, still thickened and darkened and without all the mitigations and purifications, which poured over Hellas from Delphi and the numerous seats of the gods: let us mix this thickened Bœotian air with the grim voluptuousness of the Etruscans; then such a reality would *extort* from us a world of myths within which Uranus, Kronos and Zeus and the struggles of the Titans would appear as a relief; combat in this brooding atmosphere is salvation and safety, the cruelty of victory is the summit of life's glories. And just as in truth the concept of Greek law developed from *murder* and atonement for murder, so also nobler civilisation takes her first wreath of victory from the altar of atonement for murder. Behind that bloody age stretches a wave-furrow deep into Hellenic history. The names of Orpheus, of Musaeus and their cults indicate to what consequences the uninterrupted sight of a world of warfare and cruelty led – to the loathing of existence, to the conception of this existence as a punishment to be borne to the end, to the belief in the identity of existence and indebtedness. But these particular conclusions are not specifically Hellenic: through them, Greece comes into contact with India and the Orient generally. The Hellenic genius had ready yet another answer to the question: 'what does a life of fighting and of victory want?' and gives this answer in the whole breadth of Greek history.

In order to understand it we must start from the fact that the Greek genius admitted the existing fearful impulse, terrible as it was, and deemed it *justified*; whereas in the Orphic phase of thought was contained the belief that life with such an impulse at its root would not be worth living. Strife and the pleasure of victory were acknowledged: and nothing separates the Greek world more from ours than the resultant *colouring* of some ethical concepts, e.g. of *Eris* and *envy*.

When the traveller Pausanius visited the Helicon during his wanderings through Greece, an ancient copy of the first didactic poem of the Greeks, Hesiod's *Works and Days*, was shown to him, inscribed upon lead plates and severely damaged by time and weather. But he still recognised this much, that in contrast to the usual copies, it had not at its head that little hymn to Zeus, but began at once with the declaration: 'There are *two* Eris-goddesses on earth.' This is one of the most remarkable Hellenic ideas and worthy to be impressed on the newcomer immediately at the entrance gate of Greek ethics. 'One should praise the one Eris just as one should blame the other, if one uses one's reason. For these two goddesses have quite different dispositions. For the one, the cruel one, furthers evil war and feuding! No mortal likes her, but under the yoke of need one pays honour to the burdensome Eris, according to the decree of the immortals. She, as the elder, gave birth to black night; but Zeus, the high-ruling one, placed the other Eris on the roots of the earth and among men as a much better one. She urges even the unskilled man to work, and if one who lacks property sees another who is rich, then he hastens to sow and plant in similar fashion and to put his house in order; the neighbour competes with the neighbour who strives after fortune. This Eris is good for men. The potters also have a grudge against the potters, the carpenters against the carpenters; beggars envy beggars, and singers envy singers.'

The two last verses about *odium figulinum* appear to our scholars to be incomprehensible in this place. In their judgement the predicates: 'grudge' and 'envy' fit only the nature of the bad Eris, and for this reason they do not hesitate to designate these verses as spurious or thrown by chance into this place. For that judgement however a system of ethics other than the Hellenic must have inspired these scholars unawares: for in these verses to the good Eris Aristotle finds no offence. And not only Aristotle but the whole of Greek antiquity thinks of grudge and envy otherwise than we do and agrees with Hesiod, who first designates as a wicked one that Eris who leads men against one another to a hostile war of extermination, and secondly praises another Eris as the good one, who as jealousy, grudge and envy incites men to deeds but not to deeds of annihilation but to deeds of *contest*. The Greek is *envious* and conceives of this quality not as a blemish, but as the effect of a *benevolent* deity. What a gulf of ethical judgement between him and us! Because he is envious he also feels, with every superfluity of honour, riches, splendour and fortune, the envious eye of a god resting on him, and he fears this envy; in this case the god reminds him of the transitoriness of the human lot, he dreads his very happiness and, sacrificing the best of it, he bows before the divine envy. This idea does not estrange him from his gods: on the contrary, their significance is expressed by the thought that man, whose soul burns with jealousy of every other living being, *never* has the right to compete with them. In Thamyris' fight with the Muses, Marsyas' with Apollo, in the heart-moving fate of Niobe appears the terrible opposition of the two forces, who must never fight with one another, man and god.

However, the greater and more sublime a Greek is, the brighter bursts out of him the flame of ambition, devouring everybody who runs with him on the same track. Aristotle once made a list of such hostile contests on a grand scale: among them is the most striking instance of how even a dead person can still incite a living one to consuming jealousy. Indeed, that is how Aristotle describes the relationship of the Kolophonian Xenophanes to Homer. We do not understand the strength of this attack on the national hero of poetry if we do not imagine, as later on also with Plato, the root of this attack to be the ardent desire to step into the place of the fallen poet and to inherit his fame. Every great Hellene passes on the torch of the contest; at every great virtue a new light is kindled. If the young Themistocles could not sleep at the thought of Miltiades' laurels, so his early awakened urge released itself only in the long rivalry with Aristides, when he developed that remarkable, purely instinctive genius for political action which Thucydides describes for us. How characteristic are both question and answer, when a notable opponent of Pericles is asked, whether he or Pericles is the best wrestler in the city, and answers: 'Even if I throw him down he denies that he has fallen, attains his purpose and convinces those who saw him fall.'

If we want to see that sentiment unashamed in its naive expressions, the sentiment as to the necessity of contest, lest the state's welfare be threatened, we should think about the original meaning of *ostracism*: as for example the Ephesians pronounced it at the banishment of Hermodor. 'Among us nobody shall be the best; if however someone is the best, then let him be so elsewhere and among others.' Why should not someone be the best? Because with that the contest would dry up, and the eternal life basis of the Hellenic state would be endangered. Later, ostracism receives quite another position with regard to the contest: it is applied when the danger becomes obvious that one of the great competing politicians and party leaders feels himself urged on in the heat of battle towards harmful and destructive measures and dangerous *coups d'état*. The original function of this peculiar institution, however, is not that of a safety valve but that of a stimulant. The preeminent individual was to be removed in order to renew the tournament of forces: a thought which is hostile to the 'exclusivity' of genius in the modern sense, but which assumes that in the natural order of things there are always *several* geniuses which incite one another to action, as much also as they hold one another within the limits of moderation. That is the kernel of the Hellenic idea of competition: it abominates a monopoly of predominance and fears its dangers; it desires as a *preventive* against the genius – a second genius.

Hellenic popular pedagogy demands that every talent must develop through struggle: whereas modern educators fear nothing more than the unchaining of so-called ambition. Here one fears selfishness as the 'evil in itself' – with the exception of the Jesuits, who, with regard to this, agree with the Ancients and who, possibly for that reason, are the most effective educators of our time. They seem to believe that selfishness, i.e. the individual element is only the most powerful *agens*, but that it obtains its character as 'good' and 'evil' essentially from the aims towards which it strives. To the Ancients, however, the aim of agonistic education was the well-being of the whole, of state society. For example, every Athenian was to develop himself, through the contest, to the extent that it should be of the highest service to Athens and should do the least harm. It was not unmeasured and immeasurable as modern ambition generally is: the youth thought of the good of his native city when he competed with others in running, throwing or singing; it was its glory that he wanted to increase with his own; it was to his city's gods that he dedicated the wreaths which the umpires set upon his head in honour. From childhood, every Greek felt the burning desire within him to be an instrument of bringing salvation to his city in the contest between cities: in this, his selfishness was kindled into flame, as well as curbed and restricted. For that reason, the individuals in antiquity were freer, because their aims were nearer and more tangible. Modern man, on the contrary, is everywhere hampered by infinity, like the fleet-footed Achilles in the parable of Zeno of Elea: infinity impedes him, he does not even overtake the tortoise.

But as the youths to be educated were brought up competing against one another, so their educators were in turn in rivalry with each other. Distrustfully jealous, the great musical masters, Pindar and Simonides took their places next to each other; in contest the sophist, the higher teacher of antiquity met his fellow sophist; even the most common kind of instruction, through the drama, was imparted to the people only under the form of an enormous wrestling of the great musical and dramatic artists. How wonderful! 'Even the artist has a grudge against the artist!' And the modern man dislikes in an artist nothing so much as the personal impulse to battle, whereas the Greek recognises the artist *only in such a personal struggle*. Where the modern suspects the weakness of the work of art, there the Hellene seeks the source of its highest strength! What, for example, is of special artistic importance in Plato's dialogues is usually the result of a competition with the art of the orators, the sophists, the dramatists of his time, invented deliberately in order that at the end he could say: 'Behold, I can also do what my great rivals can; yes, I can do it even better than they. No Protagoras has written such beautiful myths as mine, no dramatist such a spirited and fascinating whole as the *Symposium*, no orator has composed such an oration as I present in the *Gorgias* – and now I reject all that together and condemn all imitative art! Only the contest made me a poet, a sophist, an orator!' What a problem reveals itself there before us when we ask about the relationship of the contest to the conception of the work of art! –

On the other hand, if we remove the contest from Greek life, then we look at once into the pre-Homeric abyss of horrible savagery of hatred and pleasure in destruction. Sadly, this phenomenon showed itself frequently when a great personality was, owing to an enormously brilliant deed, suddenly withdrawn from the contest and became *hors de concours* according to his and his fellow citizens' judgement. Almost without exception the effect is terrible; and if we usually draw the conclusion from these effects that the Greek was unable to bear fame and fortune, then we should say more exactly that he was unable to bear fame without further struggle, and fortune at the end of the contest. There is no more distinct instance than the fate of Miltiades. Placed upon a solitary height and lifted far above every fellow competitor through his incomparable success at Marathon: he feels a base thirsting for revenge awaken within himself against a citizen of Para, with whom he had been at enmity long ago. To satisfy his desire, he misuses his reputation, the state's money and civic honour and disgraces himself. Conscious of his failure he resorts to unworthy machinations. He forms a clandestine and godless connection with Timo, priestess of Demeter, and enters at night the sacred temple from which every man was excluded. After he has jumped over the wall and is approaching the shrine of the goddess, the dreadful horror of a panic-stricken terror suddenly seizes him: almost collapsing and unconscious, he feels himself driven back and, jumping back over the wall, he falls down paralysed and severely injured. The siege must be lifted, the people's court awaits him, and a disgraceful death impresses its seal upon a glorious heroic career to darken it for all posterity. After the battle of Marathon he became the victim of the envy of the gods. And this divine envy flares up when it sees a man without rival, on the solitary height of fame. He now has beside him only the gods – and therefore he has them against him. But these entice him into an act of hubris, and he collapses under it.

Let us also mention that just as Miltiades perishes so the noblest Greek states perish when they, by merit and fortune, have arrived from the racecourse at the temple of Nike. Both Athens, which had destroyed the independence of her allies and avenged with severity the rebellions of her subjected foes, and Sparta, which, after the battle of Aegospotamoi, used her preponderance over Hellas in a still harsher and crueller fashion, both these, as in the case of Miltiades, brought about their own ruin through acts of hubris. This proves that without envy, jealousy, and ambition in the contest, the Hellenic state, like the Hellenic man, degenerates. It becomes evil and cruel, thirsting for revenge and godless; in short, it becomes 'pre-Homeric' – and then it needs only a panic-stricken terror to bring about its fall and to crush it. Sparta and Athens surrender to the Persians like Themistocles and Alcibiades did; they betray the Hellenic after they have given up the noblest Hellenic principle, the contest: and Alexander, the coarsened copy and abbreviation of Greek history, now invents the common Hellene, and so-called 'Hellenism'.

Translated by M. Mügge with modifications – Nathalie Lachance

Untimely Meditations

David Strauss: the Confessor and the Writer, 1873

1

Public opinion in Germany seems strictly to forbid any allusion to the evil and dangerous consequences of a war, more particularly when the war in question has been a victorious one. Those writers, therefore, command a more ready attention who, regarding this public opinion as final, proceed to vie with each other in their exultant praise of the war and of the powerful influences it has brought to bear upon morality, culture and art. Yet it must be confessed that a great victory is a great danger. Human nature bears a triumph less easily than a defeat; indeed, it might even be urged that it is simpler to gain a victory of this sort than to turn it to such account that it may not ultimately prove a serious rout. But of all evil results due to the recent war with France, the most deplorable, perhaps, is that widespread and even universal error of public opinion and of all who think publicly that German culture was also victorious in the struggle, and that it should now, therefore, be decked with garlands as a fit recognition of such extraordinary events and successes. This delusion is pernicious in the highest degree: not because it is a delusion – for there are errors which are both salutary and productive – but because it threatens to transform our victory into a signal defeat: *into the defeat, if not the extirpation, of the German spirit for the benefit of the 'German Reich'*.

Even supposing that the fight had been between the two cultures, the standard for the value of the victor would still be a very relative one and, in any case, would certainly not justify such exaggerated triumph or self-glorification. For, in the first place, it would be necessary to ascertain the value of the conquered culture. This might be very little; in which case even if the victory had involved the most glorious display of arms, it would still offer no warrant for ecstatic triumphs. Even so, however, there can be no question, in our case, of the victory of German culture; and for the simple reason that French culture remains as heretofore, and that we depend upon it as heretofore. Our culture played no part even in our success in arms. Harsh military discipline, natural bravery and sustaining power, superior leadership, unity and obedience among the rank and file – in short, factors which have nothing to do with culture – were instrumental in enabling us to conquer an opponent in whom the most essential of these factors were absent. The only wonder is that precisely what is now called 'culture' in Germany did not prove an obstacle to the military operations which seemed vitally necessary to a great victory – perhaps, though, this was only owing to the fact that this 'thing' which calls itself 'culture' saw its advantage, for once, in keeping in the background. If, however, it be permitted to grow and spread, if it be pampered by the flattering and nonsensical assurance that it has been victorious, then, as I have said, it will have the power to extirpate the German spirit – and, when that is done, who knows whether there will still be anything to be made out of the surviving German body!

Provided it were possible to direct that calm and tenacious bravery which the German opposed to the pathetic and spontaneous fury of the French, against the inward enemy, against the highly suspicious and, at all events, alien 'cultivation' which, owing to a dangerous misunderstanding, is called 'culture' in Germany, then all hope of a really genuine German 'culture', the reverse of that 'cultivation', would not be entirely lost. For the Germans have never lacked clear-sighted and heroic leaders, though these, often enough, probably, have lacked Germans. But whether it be possible to turn German bravery in a new direction seems to me to become ever more and more doubtful; for I realise how fully convinced everyone is that such a struggle and such bravery are no longer requisite; on the contrary, that most things are regulated as satisfactorily as they possibly can be – or, at all events, that everything of moment has long ago been discovered and accomplished: in a word, that the best seed of culture is already sown everywhere and is now either shooting up its fresh green blades, or, here and there, even bursting forth into luxuriant blossom. In this sphere not only happiness but ecstasy reigns supreme. I am conscious of this ecstasy and happiness, in the ineffable, truculent assurance of German journalists and manufacturers of novels, tragedies, poems and histories: for it must be clear that these people belong to one category which seems to have conspired to improve the leisure and ruminative hours – that is to say, 'the cultural moments' – of the modern man, by bewildering him with their printed paper. Since the war, all is happiness, dignity and self-consciousness in this merry throng. After the stunning successes of German culture, it regards itself not only as approved and sanctioned, but almost as sacrosanct. It therefore speaks with gravity, affects to apostrophise the German people and publishes complete works in the manner of the classics; nor does it shrink from proclaiming in those journals which are open to it some few of its adherents as new German classical writers and model authors. It might be supposed that the dangers of such an *abuse of success* would be recognised by the more thoughtful and enlightened among cultivated Germans; or, at least, that these would feel how painful is the comedy that is being enacted around them: for what in truth could be more embarrassing than the sight of a cripple strutting like a cock before a mirror and exchanging complacent glances with his reflection! But the scholar caste willingly allows things to remain as they are and are too concerned with their own affairs to busy themselves with the care of the German spirit. Moreover, the units of this caste are too thoroughly convinced that their own scholarship is the ripest and most perfect fruit of the age, indeed, of all ages, to see any necessity for a care of German culture in general; since, insofar as they and the legion of their brethren are concerned, preoccupations of this order have everywhere been, so to speak, surpassed. The more conscientious observer, more particularly if he is a foreigner, cannot help noticing that no great disparity exists between that which the German scholar regards as his culture and that other triumphant culture of the new German classics, save in respect of the quantum of knowledge: wherever the question is one not of knowledge and information, but of art and ability – wherever, that is to say, life bears witness to the culture – there is now only one German culture: and is it this that is supposed to have triumphed over France?

The contention appears to be altogether too preposterous. It was solely to the more extensive knowledge of German officers, to the superior training of their soldiers and to their more scientific military strategy that all impartial judges, and even the French nation, in the end ascribed the victory. Hence, if it be intended to regard German erudition as a thing apart, in what sense can German culture be said to have conquered? In none whatsoever; for the moral qualities of severe discipline, of more unquestioning obedience, have nothing in common with culture: these were characteristic of the Macedonian army, for instance, despite the fact that the Greek soldiers were infinitely more cultivated. To speak of German scholarship and culture as having conquered, therefore, can only be the outcome of a misapprehension, probably resulting from the circumstance that every precise notion of culture has now vanished from Germany.

Culture is, above all, the unity of artistic style in every expression of the life of a people. Abundant knowledge and learning, however, are not essential to it, nor are they a mark of its existence; and, at a pinch, they might coexist much more harmoniously with the very opposite of culture – with barbarism: that is to say, with a complete absence of style, or with a riotous jumble of all styles.

But it is precisely amid this riotous jumble that the German of today subsists; and the serious problem to be solved is how, with all his learning, he can possibly avoid noticing it; how, into the bargain, he can rejoice with all his heart in his present 'culture'? For everything conduces to open his eyes for him – every glance he casts at his clothes, his room, his house; every walk he takes through the streets of his town; every visit he pays to his art dealers and to his trader in the articles of fashion. In his social intercourse he ought to realise the origin of his manners and movements; in the heart of our art institutions, the pleasures of our concerts, theatres and museums, he ought to become apprised of the super- and juxtaposition of all imaginable styles. The German heaps up around him the forms, colours, products and curiosities of all ages and zones, and thereby succeeds in producing that garish newness, as of a country fair, which his scholars then proceed to contemplate and to define as 'modernism *per se*'; and there he remains, squatting peacefully, in the midst of this conflict of styles. But with this kind of culture, which is, at bottom, nothing more or less than a phlegmatic insensibility to real culture, men cannot vanquish an enemy, least of all an enemy like the French, who, whatever their worth may be, do actually possess a genuine and productive culture, and whom, up to the present, we have systematically copied, though in the majority of cases without skill.

Even supposing we had really ceased copying them, it would still not mean that we had overcome them, but merely that we had lifted their yoke from our necks. Not before we have succeeded in imposing an original German culture upon them can there be any question of the triumph of German culture. Meanwhile, let us not forget that in all matters of form we are, and must be, just as dependent upon Paris now as we were before the war; for up to the present there has been no such thing as an original German culture.

We all ought to have become aware of this of our own accord. Besides, one of the few who had the right to speak to Germans in terms of reproach publicly drew attention to the fact. 'We Germans are of yesterday', Goethe once said to Eckermann. 'True, for the last hundred years we have diligently cultivated ourselves, but a few centuries may yet have to run their course before our fellow-countrymen become permeated with sufficient intellectuality and higher culture to have it said of them, it is a long time *since they were barbarians*.'

Translated by A. Ludovici with modifications

Schopenhauer as Educator, 1874

4

The last hint may well remain obscure for a time: I have something easier to explain, namely how Schopenhauer can help us to educate ourselves *against* our age, since we have the advantage of really knowing our age, through him – if it be an advantage! It may no longer be possible in a couple of centuries. I sometimes amuse myself with the idea that men may soon grow tired of books and their authors, and the savant of tomorrow come to leave directions in his will that his body be burned in the midst of his books, including of course his own writings. And in the gradual clearing of the forests, might not our libraries be very reasonably used for straw and brushwood? Most books are born from the smoke and vapour of the brain: and to vapour and smoke may they well return. For having no fire within themselves, they shall be visited with fire. And possibly to a later century our own may count as a *saeculum obscurum*, because our productions raised the temperature of the furnace more and more continuously than ever before. We are anyway happy that we can learn to know our time; and if there be any sense in busying ourselves with our time at all, we may as well do it as thoroughly as we can, so that no one may have any doubt about it: the possibility of this we owe to Schopenhauer.

Our happiness would of course be infinitely greater if our inquiry showed that nothing as hopeful and splendid as our present epoch had ever existed. There are simple people in some corner of the earth today, perhaps in Germany, who are disposed to believe in all seriousness that the world was put right two years ago, and that all stern and gloomy views of life are now contradicted by 'facts'. The founding of the new German *Reich* is, to them, the decisive blow that annihilates all the 'pessimistic' philosophisers – no doubt of it. To judge the philosopher's significance in our time as an educator, we must oppose a widespread view like this, especially common in our universities. We must say that it is a scandal that such nauseating, idolatrous flattery should be uttered by a herd of so-called reflective and honourable men; it is a proof that we no longer see how far the seriousness of philosophy is removed from that of a newspaper. Such men have lost the last vestige of feeling, not only for philosophy, but also for religion, and have put in its place a spirit not so much of optimism as of journalism, the evil spirit that broods over the day and the daily paper. Every philosophy that believes the problem of existence is touched on, or even solved, by a political event is a sham. There have been innumerable states founded since the beginning of the world; that is an old story. How should a political innovation manage once and for all to make a contented race of the inhabitants of this earth? If anyone believes in his heart that this is possible, he should report himself to our authorities: he really deserves to be Professor of Philosophy in a German university, like Harms in Berlin, Jürgen Meyer in Bonn and Carrière in Munich.

We are feeling the consequences of the doctrine, preached lately from all the rooftops, that the state is the highest end of man and there is no higher duty than to serve it: I regard this not as a relapse into paganism, but into stupidity. A man who thinks state service to be his highest duty very possibly knows no higher one; yet there are both men and duties in a region beyond – and one of these duties, that seems to me at least of higher value than state service, is to destroy stupidity in all its forms, and this particular stupidity among them. That is why I am concerned with a class of men whose teleological conceptions extend further than the well-being of a state, I mean with philosophers, and only with them in their relation to the world of culture, which is again almost independent of the welfare of a state. Of the many links that make up the twisted chain of humanity, some are made of gold and others of pewter.

How does the philosopher of our time regard culture? Quite differently, I assure you, from the professors who are so satisfied with their new state. He seems to see the symptoms of an absolute uprooting of culture in the increasing rush and hurry of life, and the decay of all reflection and simplicity. The waters of religion are ebbing and leaving swamps or stagnant pools: the nations are pulling apart in enmity again, and long to tear each other to pieces. The sciences, blindly driven along, on a *laissez-faire* system, without a common standard, are splitting up and losing hold of every firm principle. The educated classes and states are being swept along in the contemptible money economy. Never was the world more worldly, never more impoverished in goodness and love. Men of learning are no longer beacons or sanctuaries in the midst of this turmoil of worldliness; they themselves are daily becoming more restless, thoughtless, loveless. Everything bows before the coming barbarism, art and science included. The educated men have degenerated into the greatest enemies of education, for they will deny the universal sickness and hinder the physician. They become peevish, these poor nerveless creatures, if one speaks of their weakness and combats the shameful spirit of lies in them.

...

It may be one-sided to insist only on the blurred lines and the dull colours in the picture of modern life: yet the other side is no more encouraging, it is only more disturbing. There is certainly strength there, enormous strength; but it is wild, primitive and merciless. One looks on with a chill expectancy, as though into the cauldron of a witch's kitchen: at any moment there may arise sparks and vapour, to herald some fearful apparition. For a century we have been ready for a world-shaking convulsion; and though we have lately been trying to set the constitutive power of the so-called national state against the great modern tendency to volcanic destructiveness, it will only be, for a long time yet, an aggravation of the universal unrest that looms over us. We need not be deceived by individuals behaving as if they knew nothing of all this anxiety: their own restlessness shows how well they know it. They think more exclusively of themselves than men ever thought before; they plant and build for their little day, and the pursuit of happiness is never greater than when the quarry must be caught today or tomorrow: the next day perhaps there will be no more hunting. We live in the age of atoms, of atomistic chaos. The opposing forces were practically held together in the Middle Ages by the Church, and in some measure assimilated by the strong pressure which she exerted. When the common tie broke and the pressure relaxed, they rose once more against each other. The Reformation taught that many things were *adiaphora*, domains that needed no guidance from religion: this was the price paid for its own existence. Christianity paid a similar one to guard itself against the far more religious antiquity: and laid the seeds of discord at once. Everything on earth nowadays is directed by the crudest and most evil forces, the egoism of the money-makers and the military despots. The state in their hands makes a good show of reorganising everything and of becoming the bond that unites the warring elements; in other words, it wishes for the same idolatry from mankind as they showed to the Church. ...

6

It is sometimes harder to agree to a thing than to understand it; many will feel this when they consider the proposition: 'Mankind must toil unceasingly to bring forth individual great men – this and nothing else is its task.' One would like to apply to society and its ends a fact that holds universally in the animal and vegetable world: where progress depends only on the higher individual types, which are rarer, yet more persistent, complex and productive. But traditional notions of what the end of society is absolutely bar the way. We can easily understand how in the natural world, where one species passes at some point into a higher one, the aim of their evolution cannot be held to lie in the high level attained by the mass, or in the latest types developed, but rather in what seem accidental beings produced at random by favourable circumstances. It should be just as easy to understand that it is the duty of mankind to provide the circumstances favourable to the birth of the new redeemer, simply because men can have a consciousness of their object. But there is always something to prevent them. They find their ultimate aim in the happiness of all, or the greatest number, or in the expansion of a great commonwealth. A man will very readily decide to sacrifice his life for the state; he will be much slower to respond if an individual, and not a state, asks for the sacrifice. It seems to be out of reason that one man should exist for the sake of another: 'Let it be rather for the sake of every other, or, at any rate, of as many as possible!' O upright judge! As if it were more in reason to let the majority decide a question of value and significance! For the problem is: 'In what way may your life, the individual life, retain the highest value and the deepest significance? And how may it least be squandered?' Only by your living for the good of the rarest and most valuable types, not for that of the majority, who are the most worthless types, taken as individuals. This way of thinking should be implanted and fostered in every young man's mind: he should regard himself both as a failure of nature's handiwork and a testimony to her larger ideas. 'She has succeeded badly', he should say; 'but I will do honour to her great idea by being a means to its better success.'

With these thoughts he will enter the circle of culture, which is the child of every individual's self-knowledge and dissatisfaction. He will approach and say out loud: 'I see something above me, higher: and more human than I: let all help me to reach it, as I will help all who know and suffer as I do, that the man may arise at last who feels his knowledge and love, vision and power, to be complete and boundless, who in his universality is one with nature, the critic and judge of existence.' It is difficult to give anyone this courageous self-consciousness, because it is impossible to teach love; from love alone the soul gains, not only the clear vision that leads to self-contempt, but also the desire to look to a higher self which is yet hidden, and strive upward to it with all its strength. And so he who rests his hope on a future great man receives his first 'initiation into culture'. The sign of this is shame or vexation at one's self, a hatred of one's own narrowness, a sympathy with the genius that ever raises its head again from our misty wastes, a feeling for all that is struggling into life, the conviction that nature must be helped in her hour of need to press forward to the man, however ill she seem to prosper, whatever success may attend her marvellous forms and projects: so that the men with whom we live are like the debris of some precious sculptures, which cry out: 'Come and help us! Put us together, for we long to become complete.'

I called this inward condition the 'first initiation into culture'. I have now to describe the effects of the 'second initiation', a task of greater difficulty. It is the passage from the inner life to the criticism of the outer life; the eye must be directed to find in the great world of action the desire for culture that is known from the immediate experience of the individual; who must use his own strivings and aspirations as the alphabet to interpret those of humanity. He cannot rest here either, but must go higher. Culture demands from him not only that inner experience, not only the criticism of the outer world surrounding him, but action too to crown them all, the fight for culture against the influences and conventions and institutions where he cannot find his own aim: the production of genius.

Anyone who can reach the second step will see *how extremely rare and imperceptible the knowledge of that end is*, though all men busy themselves with culture and expend vast labour in her service. He asks himself in amazement, 'Is such knowledge perhaps completely unnecessary? Can nature be said to attain her end, if men have a false idea of the aim of their own labour?' And anyone who thinks a great deal of nature's unconscious adaptation of means to ends will probably answer immediately: 'Yes, men may think and speak what they like about their ultimate end, their blind instinct will tell them the right road.' It requires some experience of life to be able to contradict this: but let a man be convinced of the real aim of culture, the production of the true man and nothing else; let him consider that amid all the pageantry and ostentation of culture at the present time the conditions for his production are nothing but a continual 'battle of the beasts': and he will see that there is great need for a conscious will to take the place of that blind instinct. There is another reason also: to prevent the possibility of turning this obscure impulse to quite different ends, in a direction where our highest aim can no longer be attained. For we must beware of a certain kind of misapplied and parasitical culture; the powers at present most active in its propagation have other casts of thought that prevent their relation to culture from being pure and disinterested.

The first of these is the greed of the money-makers, which needs the help of culture, and helps her in return, though at the price of prescribing her ends and limits. And their favourite proposition is: as much knowledge and education as possible; therefore, as much demand as possible, therefore, as much production as possible, therefore, as much happiness and profit as possible – this is the seductive formula. Its preachers would define education as the insight that makes man through and through a child of his age in his desires and their satisfaction and gives him command over the best means of making money. Its aim would be to make current men, in the same sense as one speaks of the currency in money; and in their view, the more current men there are, the happier the people. The object of modern educational systems is therefore to make each man as current as his nature will allow him, and to give him the opportunity for the greatest amount of happiness and profit that can be gained from his particular stock of knowledge. He is required to have just so much idea of his own value, through his general education, as to know what he can ask of life; and he is assured that a natural and necessary connection between 'intelligence and property' not only exists, but is also a *moral* necessity. All education is detested that makes for loneliness, and has an aim above money-making, and requires a long time: men look askance on such serious education as mere 'refined egoism' or 'immoral cultural Epicureanism'. The converse of course holds, according to the ordinary morality, that education must be soon over to allow the pursuit of money to be soon begun, and should be just thorough enough to allow of much money being made. The amount of education is determined by commercial interests. In short, 'man has a necessary claim to worldly happiness; only for that reason is education necessary'.

There is, secondly, the greed of the state, which requires the greatest possible breadth and universality of culture, and has the most effective weapons to carry out its wishes. If it be firmly enough established not only to initiate but control education and bear its whole weight, such breadth will merely profit the competition of the state with other states. A 'cultural state' generally implies, at the present time, the task of setting free the spiritual forces of a generation just so far as they may be of use to the existing institutions: as a mountain stream is split up by embankments and channels, and its diminished power made to drive mill-wheels, its full strength being more dangerous than useful to the mills. And thus setting free comes to mean instead enchaining. Compare, for example, what the greed of the state has done for Christianity. Christianity is one of the purest manifestations of the impulse towards culture and the production of the saint; but being used in countless ways to turn the mills of the state authorities, it gradually became sick at heart, hypocritical and degenerate, and antagonistic to its original aim. Its last phase, the German Reformation, would have been nothing but a sudden flickering of its dying flame, had it not taken new strength and light from the clash and conflagration of states.

In the third place, culture will be favoured by all those people who know their own character to be offensive or tiresome and wish to draw a veil of so-called 'good form' over them. Words, gestures, dress, etiquette and such external things are meant to produce a false impression, the inner side to be judged from the outer. I sometimes think that modern men are eternally bored with each other and look to the arts to make them interesting. They let their artists make savoury and inviting dishes of them; they steep themselves in the spices of the East and West, and have a very interesting aroma after it all. They are ready to suit all palates: and everyone will be served, whether he wants something with a good or bad taste, something sublime or coarse, Greek or Chinese, tragedy or lewd drama. The most celebrated chefs among the moderns who wish to interest and be interested at any price are the French; the worst are the Germans. This is really more comforting for the latter, and we have no reason to mind the French despising us for our want of interest, elegance and politeness, and being reminded of the Indian who wanted a ring through his nose and demanded to be tattooed.

And here I must digress a little. Many things in Germany have evidently been altered since the late war with France, and new requirements for German culture brought over. The war was for many their first venture into the more elegant half of the world: and what an admirable simplicity the conqueror shows in not scorning to learn something of culture from the conquered! The applied arts especially will be reformed to emulate our more refined neighbours, the German house furnished like the French, a 'sound taste' applied to the German language by means of an academy on the French model, to shake off the doubtful influence of Goethe – this is the judgement of our new Berlin academician, Dubois-Reymond. Our theatres have been gradually moving, in a dignified way, towards the same goal, even the elegant German savant is now discovered: and we must now expect everything that does not conform to this law of elegance, our music, tragedy and philosophy to be thrust aside as un-German. But there would be no need to raise a finger for German culture, did German culture, which the Germans have yet to find, mean nothing but the little amenities that make life more decorative, including the arts of the dancing master and the upholsterer, or were they merely interested in academic rules of language and a general atmosphere of politeness. The late war and the self-comparison with the French do not seem to have aroused any further desires, and I suspect that the German has a strong wish for the moment to be free of the old obligations laid on him by his wonderful gifts of seriousness and profundity. He would much rather play the buffoon and the monkey, and learn the arts that make life amusing. But the German spirit cannot be more dishonoured than by being treated as wax for any elegant mould.

And if, unfortunately, a good many Germans will allow themselves to be thus moulded, one must continually say to them, until they finally listen: 'The old German way is no longer yours: it was hard, rough, and full of resistance; but it is still the most valuable material, one which only the greatest modellers can work with, for they alone are worthy to use it. What you have in you now is a soft pulpy stuff; make what you will out of it, elegant dolls and interesting idols – Richard Wagner's phrase will still hold good, "The German is awkward and ungainly when he wishes to be polite; he is high above all others, when he begins to take fire".' All the elegant people have reason to beware of this German fire; it may one day devour them with all their wax dolls and idols. – The prevailing love of 'good form' in Germany may have a deeper cause in the breathless seizing at what the moment can give, the haste that plucks the fruit too green, the race and the struggle that cut the furrows in men's brows and stamp the same mark on all their actions. As if there were a poison in them that would not let them breathe, they rush about in disorder, anxious slaves of the moment, opinion and fashion: they see too well their want of dignity and fitness, and need a false elegance to hide their galloping consumption. The fashionable desire of 'good form' is bound up with a loathing of man's inner nature: the one is to conceal, the other to be concealed. Education means now the concealment of man's misery and wickedness, his wild beast quarrels, his incessant greed, his shamelessness in fruition. In pointing out the absence of a German culture, I have often had the reproach flung at me: 'This absence is quite natural, for the Germans have been too poor and modest up to now. Once rich and conscious of themselves, our people will have a culture too.' Faith may often produce happiness, yet *this* particular faith makes me unhappy, for I feel that the culture whose future raises such hopes – the culture of riches, politeness, and elegant concealments – is the bitterest foe of that German culture in which I believe. Everyone who has to live among Germans suffers from the dreadful greyness and apathy of their lives, their formlessness, torpor and clumsiness, still more their envy, secretiveness and impurity: he is troubled by their innate love of the false and the ignoble, their wretched mimicry and translation of a good foreign thing into a bad German one. But now that the feverish unrest, the quest of gain and success, the intense prizing of the moment, is added to it all, it makes one furious to think that all this sickness can never be cured, but only painted over, by such a 'culture of the interesting form'. And this among a people that has produced Schopenhauer and Wagner! And will produce others, unless we are blindly deceiving ourselves; for should not their very existence be a guarantee that such forces are even now potential in the German spirit? Or will they be exceptions, the last inheritors of the qualities that were once called German? I can see nothing to help me here, and return to my main argument again, from which my doubts and anxieties have made me digress. I have not yet enumerated all the forces that help culture without recognising its end, the production of genius. Three have been named; the greed of the money-makers, of the state, and of those who draw the cloak of 'good form' over them. There is fourthly the greed of science, and the peculiar nature of her servants, the learned.

Science has the same relation to wisdom as current morality to holiness; she is cold and dry, loveless, and ignorant of any deep feeling of dissatisfaction and yearning. She injures her servants in helping herself, for she impresses her own character on them and dries up their humanity. As long as we actually mean by culture the progress of science, she will pass by the great suffering man and harden her heart, for science only sees the problems of knowledge, and suffering is something alien and unintelligible to her world, though no less a problem for that!

If one accustoms himself to put down every experience in a dialectical form of question and answer, and translate it into the language of 'pure reason', he will soon wither up and rattle his bones like a skeleton. We all know it: and why is it that the young do not shudder at these skeletons of men, but give themselves blindly to science without motive or measure? It cannot be the so-called 'impulse to truth': for how could there be an impulse towards a pure, cold and objectless knowledge? The unprejudiced eye can see the real driving forces only too plainly. The vivisection of the professor has much to recommend it, as he himself is accustomed to finger and analyse all things, even the worthiest! To speak honestly, the savant is a complex of very various impulses and attractive forces, he is a base metal throughout. Take first a strong and increasing desire for intellectual adventure, the attraction of the new and rare as against the old and tedious. Add to that a certain joy in nosing the trail of dialectic, and beating the cover where the old fox, Thought, lies hidden; the desire is not so much for truth as the chase of truth, and the chief pleasure is in surrounding and artistically killing it. Add thirdly a love of contradiction whereby the personality is able to assert itself against all others; the battle's the thing, and the personal victory its aim, truth only its pretext. The impulse to discover particular 'truths' plays a great part in the professor, coming from his submission to definite ruling persons, classes, opinions, churches, governments, for he feels it a profit to himself to bring truth to their side. ...

In fact, all these considerations go to prove that the aim of culture is most unknown precisely where the interest in it seems liveliest. The state may trumpet as it will its services to culture, it merely helps culture in order to help itself, and does not comprehend an aim that stands higher than its own well-being or even existence. What the money-makers in their continual demand for education merely wish for is money. When the pioneers of 'good form' pretend to be the real helpers of culture, imagining that all art, for example, is merely to serve their own needs, they are clearly affirming themselves in affirming culture. Of the savant enough has already been said. All four are zealously thinking how they can benefit *themselves* with the help of culture, but have no thoughts at all when their own interests are not engaged. And so they have done nothing to improve the conditions for the birth of genius in modern times; and the opposition to original men has grown so far that no Socrates could ever live among us, and certainly could never reach the age of seventy.

I remember saying in the third chapter that our whole modern world was not so stable that one could prophesy an eternal life to its conception of culture. It is likely that the next millennium may reach two or three new ideas that might well make the hair of our present generation stand on end. The belief in the metaphysical significance of culture would not be such a horrifying thing, but its effects on educational methods might be so.

It requires a totally new attitude of mind to be able to look away from the present educational institutions to the strangely different ones that will be necessary for the second or third generation. At present the labours of higher education produce merely the savant or the official or the business man or the philistine or, more commonly, a mixture of all four; and the future institutions will have a harder task – not in itself harder, as it is really more natural, and so easier; and further, could anything be harder than to make a youth into a savant against nature, as now happens? But the difficulty lies in unlearning what we know and setting up a new aim; it will be an endless trouble to change the fundamental idea of our present educational system that has its roots in the Middle Ages and regards the medieval savant as the ideal type of culture. It is already time to put these objects before us; for some generation must begin the battle, of which a later generation will reap the victory. The solitary man who has understood the new fundamental idea of culture is at the parting of the ways; on the one he will be welcomed by his age, laurels and rewards will be his, powerful parties will uphold him, he will have as many in sympathy behind him as in front, and when the leader speaks the word of deliverance, it will echo through all the ranks. The first duty is to 'fight in line', the second to treat as enemies all who will not 'fall in'. On the other way he will find fewer companions; it is steeper and more tortuous. The travellers on the first road laugh at him, as his way is the more troublesome and dangerous; and they try to entice him over. If the two ways cross, he is ill-treated, cast aside or left alone. What significance has any particular form of culture for these several travellers? The enormous crowd that press to their end on the first road, understand by it the laws and institutions that enable them to go forward in regular fashion and rule out all the solitary and obstinate people who look towards higher and remoter objects. To the small company on the other road it has quite a different office: they wish to guard themselves, by means of a strong organisation, from being swept away by the crowd, to prevent their individual members from fainting on the way or turning in spirit from their great task. These solitary men must finish their work; that is why they should all hold together; and those who have their part in the scheme will take thought to prepare themselves with ever-increasing purity of aim for the birth of the genius and ensure that the time be ripe for him. Many are destined to help on the labour, even among the second-rate talents, and it is only in submission to such a destiny that they can feel they are living for a duty, and have a meaning and an object in their lives. But at present these talents are being turned from the road their instinct has chosen by the seductive tones of the 'fashionable culture' that plays on their selfish side, their vanities and weaknesses; and the *Zeitgeist* ever whispers in their ears its flattering counsel: 'Follow me and go not thither! There you are only servants and tools, overshadowed by higher natures with no scope for your own, drawn by threads, hung with fetters, slaves and automatons. With me you may enjoy your true personality, and be masters, your talents may shine with their own light, and yourselves stand in the front ranks with an immense following round you; and the acclamation of public opinion will rejoice you more than a wandering breath of approval sent down from the cold ethereal heights of genius.' Even the best are ensnared by such allurements, and the ultimate difference comes not so much from the rarity and power of their talent, as the influence of a certain heroic disposition at the base of them, and an inner feeling of kinship with genius. For there are men who feel it as their own misery when they see the genius in painful toil and struggle, in danger of self-destruction, or neglected by the short-sighted greed of the state, the superficiality of the money-makers, and the cold arrogance of the professors: and so I hope there may be some who understand what I mean by my sketch of Schopenhauer's destiny and to what end Schopenhauer can really educate.

Translated by Adrian Collins with modifications

3
The Free Spirit, 1878–1880

Preface

Bismarck would begin to relax the *Kulturkampf* laws in 1878, with Nietzsche prophesying the consignment of the Catholic Church to 'the shadows of oblivion'.[1] In *Human, All Too Human*, two volumes of aphorisms published in 1878 and 1879 and dedicated to Voltaire, Nietzsche alters his philosophical orientation by writing as a rationalist promoting the ideals of the Enlightenment. This new Nietzsche is anti-nationalist and cosmopolitan, projecting a 'universal world culture' under the 'guidance and guardianship' of the 'good Europeans', whose task will be to 'work actively on the merging of nations' in order to produce 'the strongest possible mixed European race', including the Jews.[2] *Human, All Too Human* was written in 1876 'in the midst of the *Bayreuther Festspiele*', at a time when his friendship with Wagner was drawing to a dramatic conclusion due to the composer's anti-Semitism, Christianity and commitment to German cultural nationalism. Moreover, Nietzsche no longer greeted Wagner's programme of cultural renewal, with which he had allied himself in the early 1870s, with the same enthusiasm. The Bayreuth Festival had dispelled any hope for a revitalisation of the Dionysian spirit.

This break with Wagner and the Wagnerian movement explains Nietzsche's description of *Human, All Too Human* as 'the monument of a crisis' and a victory of sorts: 'here I liberated myself from what in my nature did not belong to me'.[3] In this book, Nietzsche identifies himself as a free spirit, one who symbolises independence and sovereignty, and adopts an attitude of scepticism towards all habitual evaluations and perspectives. The free spirit's intellectual liberation is marked by approval of the critical processes of reason and science, and a repudiation of faith. The emancipation that Nietzsche sought aimed at self-conquest and self-discovery, but he was careful to point out in *The Wanderer and His Shadow* (1880) that this inward turn was not to be interpreted as a rejection of all social and political matters: 'We withdraw into concealment: but not out of any kind of personal ill-humour, as though the political and social situation of the present day were not good enough for us, but because through our withdrawal we want to economise and assemble forces of which culture will *later* have great need, and more so if this present remains *this* present and as such fulfils *its* task.'[4] The free spirit is precisely the individual who in the 'present day' will prepare the ground for a reversal of values. As the 'problem' of the free spirits is 'order of rank', the vertical reconfiguration of the Dionysian, a reversal of values must anticipate a new philosophy of 'right' and 'power'.[5]

Nietzsche now promotes the Enlightenment, but an Enlightenment that would sever Europe's historical ties to the French Revolution, since true Enlightenment 'is essentially foreign to the Revolution', which 'became flesh and spirit...in Rousseau'. With the violence of the French Revolution, Nietzsche explains, the Enlightenment itself became violent and thus its 'danger' became 'almost greater than its useful quality of liberation and illumination.... Whoever grasps this will also know from what confusion it has to be extricated, from what impurities to be cleansed, so as then to *continue* the work of the Enlightenment *in himself*, and to strangle the Revolution at birth and nullify its effects.'[6] Nietzsche interprets Rousseau as a theorist of revolutionary violence and thus a deviation in Enlightenment philosophy, and recommends Voltaire, whom he recognises as a spiritual precursor,[7] and his Enlightenment of '*progressive development*'[8] as a corrective. In the context of 1878–80, the inherited 'confusion' and 'impurities' of the Enlightenment reside in the doctrine of socialist revolution, growing in the aftermath of the Paris Commune.

The socialist revolutionary threat is a salient theme in Nietzsche's writings; but it is only one path of his thought that advises against it the 'progressive development' Voltaire inspires. A more subtle way is revealed in his affirmation of the Renaissance, which he considers to be 'the Golden Age of this millennium'.[9] The Renaissance provides Nietzsche with an ethical model of resistance spun out of the dynamics of a Machiavellian turn which places the analysis of power and political tactics at the centre of his efforts. When Nietzsche expresses hope for a '*new Renaissance*' it has political implications. Obviously, his vision excludes socialism, but it also excludes the 'neurotic', 'cultivated classes of European countries',[10] yet welcomes the invisible church of the '*oligarchs of the spirit*', who, in spite of their 'spatial and political separation...grasp their hands in the struggle as much against the ochlocratic nature of...superficial culture as against the occasional attempts to set up a tyranny with the help of mass manipulation'.[11]

October 1878 saw the enactment of Germany's anti-Socialist Laws.[12] In *Human, All Too Human*, Nietzsche views socialism as a 'reactionary' form of despotism that strives for the 'destruction of the individual....it needs the most submissive subjugation of all citizens to the absolute state', and he associates its existence with 'extreme terrorism'.[13] It seems doubtful that he 'was anxious to dissociate himself from reactionaries who were manipulating the fear of socialism',[14] for his own published writing on socialism nourishes that fear. Socialism, Nietzsche says, 'secretly prepares for reigns of terror, and drives the word "justice" like a nail into the heads of the semi-educated masses, to rob them completely of their reason.... and to give them a good conscience for the evil game that they are supposed to play. – Socialism can serve as a rather brutal and forceful way to teach the danger of all accumulations of state power.' Against this potential accumulation of state power, Nietzsche, in a liberal register, calls for ' *"as little state as possible"* '.[15] He recognises that the socialist speaks for the 'subjugated caste' (i.e. the working class) and puts into question the socialist labour theory of value,[16] the demand for equality of rights,[17] the 'desire to produce the good life for the greatest number'[18] and even the abolition of slavery.[19]

In 1879, Nietzsche describes socialism as an 'epidemic' and wonders who can 'arrest' it. But he believes that the 'wealthy bourgeois' of Germany, who call themselves 'liberals', are largely to blame for causing it to spread, for socialism is motivated by an 'envy' that continues to be provoked by 'lavish' consumption. The 'only remedy against socialism', then, is to 'live in moderation... to prevent as far as possible all lavish display, and to aid the state as far as possible in its taxing of all... luxuries'.[20] Note that Nietzsche's 'remedy' does not include banning the Socialist Party.

Thus it is not certain that Nietzsche accepted the anti-Socialist Laws, but it is also not certain that he was critical of them either.[21] Up to this point, it may be said that he is a tacit supporter of the anti-Socialist Laws who harbours, in principle, lingering doubts that those very laws may strengthen socialism.[22]

In 1880, however, Nietzsche's perspective changes. He is now convinced that democracy alone will gain the advantage from the exploitation of the fear of socialism by the 'political powers': 'for *all* parties are now compelled to flatter the "people" and grant them facilities and liberties of all kinds, with the result that the people finally become omnipotent'. Secondly, he thinks what is more likely is the growth of a middle class, with 'great majorities in their parliaments', who will '*forget* socialism.... like a disease that has been overcome', simply because the people will never accept the socialist doctrine of the abolition of property.[23]

To claim that Nietzsche is pro-democratic during this period (1878–80) may be simplistic given that he denigrates majorities and their capacity to reason and puts into question the principle of equality, the rule of law, party organisation, parliamentary representation and universal suffrage, all of which would be axiomatic to a true democrat. In addition, Nietzsche supports a caste system, which he thinks will better serve the creation of 'higher culture',[24] does not think democracy produces the 'individual' (crucial to his elitist way of thinking) but rather the 'private person',[25] and, in spite of his rationalistic denial of faith, is hesitant to relinquish the sacralised state, suggesting that state legitimacy requires a non-secular basis.[26] In 1880,

Nietzsche conceives of a future democracy which notably denies 'political suffrage' to certain social classes and suppresses 'party organisation'.[27]

It may be more accurate to claim that during this period Nietzsche supports Bismarck's democracy – 'the constitutional form as a compromise between government and people', not as 'an organ of the people' – against the much more dangerous threat of a socialist state that would remove any hopes for the creation of 'genius'. Nietzsche rejects the 'latest concept' (democracy as 'an organ of the people') for the Bismarckian 'compromise' or *Realpolitik*.[28] Typical of this period, he recommends 'slow evolution'[29] and a gradual transformation,[30] an emphasis which displays his anxiety about a revolution from below.

But Nietzsche arguably has doubts about Bismarck's compromises, if we take the following quotation to include Bismarck:[31] 'political parties today have in common a demagogic character and the intention of influencing the masses; because of this intention, all of them are obliged to transform their principles into great *al fresco* stupidities'.[32] Nevertheless, for Nietzsche, it is important that 'one...adapt to the new conditions',[33] to the 'democratisation of Europe', which is 'irresistible'.[34] But precisely how, then, does Nietzsche begin to adapt to this *fait accompli*? His strategy is to approach this ineluctable democratisation as merely a link in the evolutionary chain of the modern era that will allow for the 'intellectual preparation of the highest artist in horticulture, who can apply himself to his real [future] task when the other is fully accomplished!' In short, Nietzsche defends democracy not as an end, but as a *means*, even if modern workers 'loudly proclaim that the wall and the fence'(by which he means democracy) 'are already the end and the final goal'.[35] Evidently, democracy is not the *ultima ratio* of the higher culture that Nietzsche aims to promote.

Human, All Too Human: A Book for Free Spirits, 1878

25

Private morality, world morality. – Since man no longer believes that a god is guiding the destinies of the world as a whole, or that, despite all apparent twists, the path of mankind is leading somewhere glorious, men must set themselves ecumenical goals, embracing the whole earth. The older morality, namely Kant's, demands from the individual those actions that one desires from all men – a nice, naïve idea, as if everyone without further ado would know which manner of action would benefit the whole of mankind, that is, which actions were desirable at all. It is a theory like that of free trade, which assumes that a general harmony would *have* to result of itself, according to innate laws of melioration. Perhaps a future survey of the needs of mankind will reveal it to be thoroughly undesirable that all men act identically; rather, in the interest of ecumenical goals, for whole stretches of human time special tasks, perhaps in some circumstances even evil tasks, would have to be set. – In any event, if mankind is to keep from destroying itself by such a conscious overall government, we must discover first a *knowledge of the preconditions of culture*, a knowledge surpassing all previous knowledge, as a scientific standard for ecumenical goals. This is the enormous task of the great minds of the next century.

45

Double prehistory of good and evil. – The concept of good and evil has a double prehistory: namely, *first* of all, in the soul of the ruling clans and castes. The man who has the power to requite goodness with goodness, evil with evil, and really does practise requital by being grateful and vengeful, is called 'good'. The man who is unpowerful and cannot requite is taken for bad. As a good man one belongs to the 'good', a community that has a communal feeling, because all the individuals are entwined together by their feeling for requital. As a bad man one belongs to the 'bad', to a mass of abject, powerless men who have no communal feeling. The good men are a caste; the bad men are a multitude, like specks of dust. Good and bad are for a time equivalent to noble and base, master and slave. Conversely, one does not regard the enemy as evil: he can requite. In Homer, both the Trojan and the Greek are good. Not the man who inflicts harm on us, but the man who is contemptible, is bad. In the community of the good, goodness is hereditary; it is impossible for a bad man to grow out of such good soil. Should one of the good men nevertheless do something unworthy of good men, one resorts to excuses; one blames God, for example, saying that he struck the good man with blindness and madness. – *Then*, in the souls of oppressed, powerless men, every *other* man is taken for hostile, inconsiderate, exploitative, cruel, sly, whether he be noble or base. Evil is their epithet for man, indeed for every possible living being, even, for example, for a god; 'human', 'divine' mean the same as 'devilish', 'evil'. Signs of goodness, helpfulness, pity are taken anxiously for malice, the prelude to a terrible outcome, bewilderment and deception, in short, for refined evil. With such a state of mind in the individual, a community can scarcely come about at all, or at most in the crudest form; so that wherever this concept of good and evil predominates, the downfall of individuals, their clans and races, is near at hand. – Our present morality has grown up on the ground of the *ruling* clans and castes.

92

Origin of justice. – Justice (fairness) originates among approximately *equal powers*, as Thucydides (in the horrifying conversation between the Athenian and Melian envoys) rightly understood. When there is no clearly recognisable supreme power and a battle would lead to fruitless and mutual injury, one begins to think of reaching an understanding and negotiating the claims on both sides: the initial character of justice is *exchange*. Each satisfies the other in that each gets what he values more than the other. Each man gives the other what he wants, to keep henceforth, and receives in turn that which he wishes. Thus, justice is requital and exchange on the assumption of approximately equal positions of strength. For this reason revenge belongs initially to the realm of justice: it is an exchange. Likewise gratitude. – Justice naturally goes back to the viewpoint of an insightful self-preservation, that is, to the egoism of this consideration: 'Why should I uselessly injure myself and perhaps not reach my goal anyway?' – So much about the origin of justice. Because men, in line with their intellectual habits, have forgotten the original purpose of so-called just, fair actions, and particularly because children have been taught for centuries to admire and imitate such actions, it has gradually come to appear that a just action is a selfless one. The high esteem of these actions rests upon this appearance, an esteem which, like all estimations, is also always in a state of growth: for men strive after, imitate, and reproduce with their own sacrifices that which is highly esteemed, and it grows because its worth is increased by the worth of the effort and exertion made by each individual. – How slight the morality of the world would seem without forgetfulness! A poet could say that God had stationed forgetfulness as a guardian at the door to the temple of human dignity.

93

The right of the weaker. – If one party, a city under siege, for example, submits under certain conditions to a greater power, its reciprocal condition is that this first party can destroy itself, burn the city, and thus make the power suffer a great loss. Thus there is a kind of *equalisation*, on the basis of which rights can be established. Preservation is to the enemy's advantage. –

Rights exist between slaves and masters to the same extent, exactly insofar as the possession of his slave is profitable and important to the master. The *right* originally extends *as far as* the one *appears* to the other to be valuable, essential, permanent, invincible, and the like. In this regard even the weaker of the two has rights, though they are more modest. Thus the famous dictum '*unusquisque tantum juris habet, quantum potentia valet*' (or, more exactly, '*quantum potentia valere creditur*').

99

Innocence of so-called evil actions. – All 'evil' actions are motivated by the drive for preservation, or, more exactly, by the individual's intention to gain pleasure and avoid unpleasure; thus they are motivated, but they are not evil. 'Giving pain in and of itself' *does not exist*, except in the brain of philosophers, nor does 'giving pleasure in and of itself' (pity, in the Schopenhauerian sense). In conditions *preceding* organised states, we kill any being, be it ape or man, that wants to take a fruit from a tree before we do, just when we are hungry and running up to the tree. We would treat the animal the same way today if we were hiking through inhospitable territory. – Those evil actions which outrage us most today are based on the error that the man who harms us has free will, that is, he had the *choice* not to do this bad thing to us. This belief in his choice arouses hatred, thirst for revenge, spite, the whole deterioration of our imagination; whereas we get much less angry at an animal because we consider it irresponsible. To do harm not out of a drive for preservation, but for requital – that is the result of an erroneous judgement, and is therefore likewise innocent. The individual can, in conditions preceding the organised state, treat others harshly and cruelly to *intimidate* them, to secure his existence through such intimidating demonstrations of his power. This is how the brutal, powerful man acts, the original founder of a state, who subjects to himself those who are weaker. He has the right to do it, just as the state now assumes the right. Or rather, there is no right that can prevent it. The ground for all morality can only be prepared when a greater individual or collective individual, as, for example, society or the state, subjects the individuals in it, that is, when it draws them out of their isolatedness and integrates them into a union. *Compulsion* precedes morality; indeed, for a time morality itself is compulsion, to which others acquiesce to avoid unpleasure. Later it becomes custom, and still later free obedience, and finally almost instinct: then it is coupled to pleasure, like all habitual and natural things – and is now called *virtue*.

224

Ennoblement through degeneration. – History teaches us that that part of a people maintains itself best whose members generally share a vital public spirit, due to the similarity of their long-standing, incontrovertible principles, that is, of their common faith. In their case, good, sound custom strengthens them; they are taught to subordinate the individual, and their character is given solidity, at first innately and later through education. The danger in these strong communities, founded on similar, steadfast individual members, is an increasing, inherited stupidity, which follows all stability like a shadow. In such communities, *spiritual progress* depends on those individuals who are less bound, much less certain, and morally weaker; they are men who try new things, and many different things. Because of their weakness, countless such men are destroyed without having much visible effect; but in general, especially if they have descendants, they loosen things up and, from time to time, inflict a wound on the stable element of a community. Precisely at this wounded, weakened place, the common body is *inoculated*, so to speak, with something new; however, the community's overall strength has to be sufficient to take this new thing into its bloodstream and assimilate it. Wherever progress is to ensue, deviating natures are of greatest importance. Every progress of the whole must be preceded by a partial weakening. The strongest natures *retain* the type, the weaker ones help to *advance* it. – Something similar also happens in the individual. There is rarely a degeneration, a truncation, or even a vice or any physical or moral loss without an advantage somewhere else. In a warlike and restless clan, for example, the sicklier man may have occasion to be alone, and may therefore become quieter and wiser; the one-eyed man will have one eye the stronger; the blind man will see deeper inwardly and certainly hear better. To this extent, the famous theory of the survival of the fittest does not seem to me to be the only viewpoint from which to explain the progress of strengthening of a man or of a race. Rather, two things must coincide: first of all, stable power must increase through minds bound in faith and communal feeling; and secondly, it must be possible to attain higher goals when degenerating natures partially weaken or wound the stable power; it is precisely the weaker nature, as the more delicate and free, that makes progress possible at all. If a people starts to crumble and grow weak at some one place, but is still strong and healthy in general, it can accept being infected with something new and can incorporate it to its advantage. The task of education is to make the individual so steadfast and sure that, as a whole being, he can no longer be diverted from his path. But then the educator must wound him, or use the wounds that fate delivers; when pain and need have come about in this way, something new and noble can also be inoculated into the wounded places. His whole nature will take it in, and show the ennoblement later in its fruits. – Regarding the state, Machiavelli says that 'the form of governments is of very slight importance, although semi-educated people think otherwise. The great goal of politics should be *permanence*, which outweighs anything else, being much more valuable than freedom.' Only when permanence is securely established and guaranteed is there any possibility of constant development and ennobling inoculation, which, to be sure, will usually be opposed by the dangerous companion of all permanence: authority.

225

The free spirit a relative concept. – A man is called a free spirit if he thinks otherwise than would be expected, based on his origin, environment, class and position, or based on prevailing contemporary views. He is the exception: fettered spirits are the rule; the latter reproach him that his free principles have their origin either in a need to be noticed, or else may even lead one to suspect him of free actions, that is, actions that are irreconcilable with bound morality. Sometimes it is also said that certain free principles derive from perverseness and eccentricity; but this is only the voice of malice, which does not, itself, believe what it says, but only wants to hurt: for the free spirit generally has proof of his greater kindness and sharp intellect written so legibly on his face that fettered spirits understand it well enough. But the two other derivations of free-thinking are meant honestly; and many free spirits do indeed come into being in one or the other of these ways. But the tenets they arrive at thereby could still be more true and reliable than the tenets of fettered spirits. In the knowledge of truth, what matters is *having* it, not what made one seek it or how one found it. If the free spirits are right, the fettered spirits are wrong, whether or not the former arrived at truth out of immorality and the others have kept clinging to untruth out of morality. – Incidentally, it is not part of the nature of the free spirit that his views are more correct, but rather that he has released himself from tradition, be it successfully or unsuccessfully. Usually, however, he has truth, or at least the spirit of the search for truth, on his side: he demands reasons, while others demand faith.

227

Reason or unreason deduced from the consequences. – All states and social arrangements – class, marriage, education, law – acquire strength and permanence solely because of the faith of fettered spirits in them; they exist, then, in the absence of reasons, or at least in the resistance to asking for reasons. That is something fettered spirits do not want to admit, and they probably feel that it is a *pudendum*. Christianity, which was very innocent in its intellectual ideas, perceived nothing of this *pudendum*; it demanded faith and nothing but faith, and passionately rejected the desire for reasons; it pointed to the successful result of faith: you'll soon discover the advantage of faith, it suggested, you'll be blessed because of it. The state, in fact, does the same thing, and each father raises his son in the same way: just take this to be true, he says, you'll discover how good it feels. But this means that the *truth* of an opinion should be proved by its personal *benefit*; the usefulness of a teaching should guarantee its intellectual certainty and substantiation. This is as if the defendant were to say in court: my defender is telling the whole truth, for just see what happens as a result of his plea: I am acquitted. – Because fettered spirits hold principles for the sake of their usefulness, they also assume that the free spirit is likewise seeking his benefit with his views, holding for true only that which benefits him. But since he seems to find useful the opposite of what his countrymen or people of his class do, they assume that his principles are dangerous to them; they say or feel, he must not be right, for he is harmful to us.

235

Genius and ideal state in contradiction. – Socialists desire to produce a good life for the greatest number. If the enduring homeland of this good life, the perfect state, were really achieved, it would destroy the earth from which a man of great intellect or any powerful individual grows: I mean great energy. When this state is achieved, mankind would have become too feeble to produce genius any longer. Should we not therefore wish that life retain its violent character, and that wild strengths and energies be called forth over and over again? Now, a warm, sympathetic heart desires precisely the *elimination* of that violent and wild character, and the warmest heart one can imagine would yearn for it most passionately; though this same passion would have had its fire, its warmth, even its existence from that wild and violent character of life. The warmest heart, then, desires the elimination of its rationale and its own destruction; that is, it wants something illogical; it is not intelligent. The highest intelligence and the warmest heart cannot coexist in one person, and a wise man who passes judgement on life also places himself above kindness, considering it only as something to be evaluated along with everything else in the sum of life. The wise man must oppose the extravagant wishes of unintelligent kindness, because he cares about the survival of his type and the eventual genesis of the highest intellect. At least he will not further the establishment of the 'perfect state' if there is room there only for feeble individuals. Christ, on the other hand, whom we like to imagine as having the warmest of hearts, furthered men's stupidity, took the side of the intellectually weak and kept the greatest intellect from being produced: and this was consistent. We can predict that his opposite, the absolute wise man, will just as necessarily prevent the production of a Christ. – The state is a clever institution for protecting individuals from one another; if one goes too far in ennobling it, the individual is ultimately weakened by it, even dissolved – and thus the original purpose of the state is most thoroughly thwarted.

237

Renaissance and Reformation. – The Italian Renaissance contained within itself all the positive forces to which we owe modern culture: namely, liberation of thought, disdain for authority, the triumph of education over the arrogance of lineage, enthusiasm for science and men's scientific past, the unshackling of the individual, an ardour for veracity and aversion to appearance and mere effect (which ardour blazed forth in a whole abundance of artistic natures who, with the highest moral purity, demanded perfection in their works and nothing but perfection). Yes, the Renaissance had positive forces which *up to now* have not yet again become so powerful in our modern culture. Despite all its flaws and vices, it was the Golden Age of this millennium. By contrast, the German Reformation stands out as an energetic protest of backward minds that had not yet had their fill of the medieval worldview and perceived the signs of its dissolution, the extraordinary shallowness and externalisation of religious life, not with appropriate rejoicing, but with deep displeasure. With their northern strength and obstinacy, they set men back, forced the Counter-Reformation, that is, a defensive Catholic Christianity, with the violence of a state of siege, delaying the complete awakening and rule of the sciences for two or three centuries, as well as making impossible, perhaps forever, the complete fusion of the ancient and modern spirit. The great task of the Renaissance could not be carried to its completion; this was hindered by the protest of the now backward German character (which in the Middle Ages had had enough sense to redeem itself by climbing over the Alps again and again). The fact that

Luther survived at that time and that his protest gathered strength lay in the coincidence of an extraordinary political configuration: the Emperor protected him in order to use his innovation to apply pressure against the Pope, and likewise the Pope secretly favoured him in order to use the imperial Protestant princes as a counterweight against the Emperor. Without this strange concert of intent, Luther would have been burned like Huss – and the dawn of the Enlightenment would have risen a bit earlier, perhaps, and with a splendour more beautiful than we can now even imagine.

241

Genius of culture. – If one were to dream up a genius of culture, what would be his nature? He uses lies, power, the most inconsiderate self-interest so confidently as his tools that he could only be called an evil, demonic creature; but his goals, which shine through here and there, are great and good. He is a centaur, half-animal, half-human, and even has angel's wings attached to his head.

244

In the neighbourhood of madness. – The sum of feelings, knowledge, experiences, that is, the whole burden of culture, has grown so great that the general danger is an over-stimulation of nervous and mental powers; the cultivated classes of European countries are altogether neurotic, and almost everyone of their great families has, in one of its branches, moved close to madness. It is true that we can now approach health in all kinds of ways, but in the main we still need a decrease of emotional tension, of the oppressive cultural burden, a decrease that, even if it must be bought with serious losses, does give us room for the great hope of a *new Renaissance*. We owe to Christianity, to the philosophers, poets and musicians, a superabundance of deeply agitated feelings; to keep these from engulfing us we must conjure up the spirit of science, which makes us somewhat colder and more sceptical on the whole, and cools down particularly the hot flow of belief in ultimate truths, which Christianity, especially, has made so wild.

261

Tyrants of the spirit. – The life of the Greeks shines bright only when the ray of myth falls on it; otherwise it is gloomy. Now, the Greek philosophers rob themselves of precisely this mythology; is it not as if they wanted to move out of the sunlight into the shadows, the gloom? But no plant wants to avoid light: actually, those philosophers were only seeking a *brighter* sun; mythology was not pure or brilliant enough for them. They found the light they sought in their knowledge, in what each of them called his 'truth'. But knowledge shone ever brighter at that time; it was still young and still knew too little of all the difficulties and dangers of its ways; it could still hope to reach the midpoint of all being in a single bound, and from there solve the riddle of the world. These philosophers had a firm belief in themselves and in their 'truth', and with it they overcame all their neighbours and predecessors; each of them was a combative and violent *tyrant*. Perhaps the happiness of believing oneself in possession of the truth was never greater in the world, but neither was the harshness, arrogance, tyranny, and evil of such a belief. They were tyrants, which is what every Greek wanted to be, and which each one was if he was *able*. Perhaps only Solon is an exception; in his poetry he tells how he despised personal tyranny. But he did it out of love for his work, for his lawgiving; and to be a lawgiver is a sublimated form of tyranny. Parmenides, too, gave laws, probably Pythagoras and Empedocles as well; Anaximander founded a city. Plato was the incarnate wish to become the greatest philosophical lawgiver and founding father of a state; he seems to have suffered terribly that his nature was not fulfilled, and towards the end his soul became full of the blackest bile. The more Greek philosophy lost power, the more it suffered inwardly because of this bile and need to slander. When various sects finally fought for their truths in the streets, the souls of all these suitors of truth were completely clogged with jealousy and venom; the tyrannical element raged like a poison in their bodies. These many petty tyrants would have liked to devour one another raw; there was not a spark of love left in them, and all too little joy in their own knowledge. – The tenet that tyrants are usually murdered and that their descendants live briefly is also generally true of the tyrants of the spirit. Their history is short, violent; their influence breaks off suddenly. One can say of almost all great Hellenes that they seem to have come too late, thus Aeschylus, Pindar, Demosthenes, Thucydides; one generation follows them – and then it is always over forever. That is the turbulent and uncanny thing about Greek history. These days, of course, we admire the gospel of the tortoise. To think historically these days almost means to imply that history was always made according to the principle, 'As little as possible in the longest time possible!' Alas, Greek history goes so quickly! Never has life been lived so prodigally, so immoderately. I cannot convince myself that the history of the Greeks took that *natural* course for which it is so famous. They were much too diversely gifted to be *gradual* in a step-by-step manner, like the tortoise racing with Achilles, and that is what is called natural development. With the Greeks, things go forward swiftly, but also as swiftly downwards; the movement of the whole mechanism is so intensified that a single stone, thrown into its wheels, makes it burst. Such a stone was Socrates, for example; in one night, the development of philosophical science, until then so wonderfully regular but, of course, all too swift, was destroyed. It is no idle question to wonder whether Plato, if he had stayed free of the Socratic spell, might not have found an even higher type of the philosophical man, now lost to us forever. We look into the ages before him as into a sculptor's workshop, full of such types. The sixth and fifth centuries, however, seem to promise even more and greater things than they produced; but it remained at promises and declarations. And yet there is hardly a heavier loss than the loss of a type, the loss of a new, previously undiscovered, supreme *possibility of philosophical life*. Even of the older types, most have been handed down to us inadequately; it seems to me extraordinarily difficult to see any philosopher from Thales to Democritus clearly; but the man who is successful in recreating these figures strolls among creatures of the mightiest and purest type. Of course, this ability is rare; even the later Greeks who studied the older philosophers did not have it. Aristotle particularly seems not to have his eyes in his head when he is faced with them. And so it seems as if these marvellous philosophers had lived in vain, or even as if they had only been meant to prepare the ground for the combative and garrulous hordes of the Socratic schools. As we said, there is a gap here, a break in development; some great misfortune must have occurred, and the sole statue in which we might have recognised the sense and purpose of that great creative preparatory exercise must have broken or been unsuccessful. What actually happened has remained forever a secret of the workshop. –

What took place with the Greeks – that each great thinker, believing he possessed absolute truth, became a tyrant, so that Greek intellectual history has had the violent, rash and dangerous character evident in its political history – was not exhausted with them. Many similar things have come to pass right up to the most recent times, although gradually less often, and rarely now with the Greek philosophers' pure, naïve conscience. For the opposite doctrine and scepticism have, on the whole, too powerful and loud a voice. The period of the spiritual tyrants is over. In the domain of higher culture there will of course always have to be an authority – but from now on this authority lies in the hands of the *oligarchs of the spirit*. Despite all spatial and political separation, they form a coherent society, whose members *recognise* and *acknowledge* each other, whatever favourable or unfavourable estimations may circulate due to public opinion and the judgements of the newspaper and magazine writers. The spiritual superiority which formerly caused division and enmity now tends to *bind*: how could individuals assert themselves and swim through life along their own way, against all currents, if they did not see their like living here and there under the same circumstances and grasp their hands in the struggle as much against the ochlocratic nature of superficial minds and superficial culture as against the occasional attempts to set up a tyranny with the help of mass manipulation? Oligarchs need each other; they are their own best friends; they understand their insignias – but nevertheless each of them is free; he fights and conquers in his *own* place and would rather perish than submit.

438

Permission to speak. – Political parties today have in common a demagogic character and the intention of influencing the masses; because of this intention, all of them are obliged to transform their principles into great *alfresco* stupidities and paint them that way on the wall. Nothing more can be changed about this, indeed, it is superfluous even to lift a finger against it; for what Voltaire says applies here: '*Quand la populace se mêle de raisonner, tout est perdu.*' Now that this has happened, one must adapt to the new conditions, as one adapts when an earthquake has moved the old limits and outlines of the land, and changed the value of property. Moreover, if the business of all politics is to make life tolerable for the greatest number, this greatest number may also determine what they understand by a tolerable life; if they think their intellect capable of finding the right means to this goal, what good would it do to doubt it? They simply want to be the architects of their own fortune and misfortune; and if this feeling of self-determination, this pride in the five or six concepts their heads contain and can bring to light does indeed make their life so agreeable that they gladly bear the fatal consequences of their narrowness, then there is little to object to, provided that their narrowness does not go so far as to demand that *everything* should become politics in their sense, and that *everyone* should live and act according to their standard. For, first of all, some people must be allowed, now more than ever, to keep out of politics and stand aside a little; the pleasure of self-determination is driving these people too, and there may even be a little pride involved in being silent when too many, or only many, are speaking. Second, one must overlook it if these few do not take the happiness of the many, whether defined as peoples or classes of population, so seriously, and are now and then guilty of an ironic attitude; for them, seriousness lies elsewhere; they have a different concept of happiness; their goal cannot be embraced by any clumsy hand with just five fingers. Finally – and certainly this is hardest to grant them, but must also be granted – they too have an occasional moment when they emerge from their silent isolation and test the power of their lungs again; then they call to each other, like men lost in a forest, to make themselves known and encourage each other; of course, when they do, various things are heard that sound bad to ears not meant to hear them. – Soon afterwards, it is quiet in the forest again, so quiet that one can again hear clearly the buzzing, humming and fluttering of the innumerable insects that live in, above and below it.

439

Culture and caste. – A higher culture can come into being only where there are two castes of society: the working caste and the idle caste, capable of true leisure; or, to express it more emphatically, the caste of forced labour and the caste of free labour. The distribution of happiness is not a crucial factor when it is a matter of engendering a higher culture, but the caste of the idle is in fact the more capable of suffering and does suffer more; its contentment in existence is slighter; its task greater. Now, if there should be an exchange between the two castes, so that duller, less spiritual individuals and families from the higher caste are demoted into the lower, and, conversely, the freer people from that caste gain admission to the higher: then a condition has been achieved beyond which only the open sea of indefinite desires is still visible. – Thus the fading voice of the old era speaks to us; but where are the ears left to hear it?

440

Of blood. – Men and women of blood have an advantage over others, giving them an indubitable claim to higher esteem, because they possess two arts, increasingly heightened through inheritance: the art of being able to command, and the art of proud obedience. – Now, wherever commanding is part of the daily routine (as in the great world of big business and industry), something similar to those generations 'of blood' comes into being, but they lack the noble bearing in obedience, which the former inherited from feudal conditions and which will no longer grow in our cultural climate.

441

Subordination. – The subordination that is valued so highly in military and bureaucratic states will soon become as unbelievable to us as the secret tactics of the Jesuits have already become; and when this subordination is no longer possible, it will no longer be possible to achieve a number of its most astonishing consequences and the world will be the poorer. Subordination must vanish, for its basis is vanishing: belief in absolute authority, in ultimate truth; even in military states physical coercion is not sufficient to produce subordination; rather it requires an inherited adoration of princeliness, as of something superhuman. – In *freer* situations, one subordinates himself only on conditions, as a consequence of a mutual contract, that is, without any prejudice to self-interest.

442

Conscript army. – The greatest disadvantage of the conscript army, now so widely acclaimed, consists in the squandering of men of the highest civilisation; they exist at all only when every circumstance is favourable – how sparingly and anxiously one should deal with them, since it requires great periods of time to create the chance conditions for the production of such delicately organised brains! But just as the Greeks wallowed in Greek blood, so Europeans are now wallowing in European blood: and, in fact, it is the men of highest culture who are always sacrificed in the relatively greatest number, the men who guarantee an abundant and good posterity; for these men stand as commanders in the front lines of a battle, and moreover, because of their greater ambition, expose themselves most to dangers. – Today, when quite different and higher tasks are set than *patria* and *honour*, crude Roman patriotism is either something dishonest or a sign of backwardness.

444

War. – One can say against war that it makes the victor stupid and the vanquished malicious. In favour of war, one can say that it barbarises through both these effects and thus makes man more natural; war is the sleep or wintertime of culture: man emerges from it with more strength, both for the good and for the evil.

446

A question of power, not justice. – For men who always consider the higher usefulness of a matter, socialism, if it *really* is the uprising against their oppressors of people oppressed and kept down for thousands of years, poses no problem of *justice* (with the ludicrous, weak question: 'How far *should* one yield to its demands?'), but only a problem of *power* ('To what extent *can* one use its demands?'). So it is like a natural power, steam, for example, which is either forced by man, as a god of machines, into his service, or, when there are flaws in the machine, that is, errors of human calculation in its construction, wrecks itself and the human with it. To solve that question of power, one must know how strong socialism is, and in which of its modifications it can still be used as a mighty lever within the current political power game; in some circumstances one would even have to do everything possible to strengthen it. With every great force – even the most dangerous – humanity must think how to make it into a tool of its own intentions. – Socialism gains a right only when the two powers, the representatives of the old and new, seem to have come to war, but then both parties prudently calculate how they may preserve themselves to best advantage, and this results in their desire for a treaty. No justice without a treaty. Until now, however, there has been neither war in the indicated territory nor treaties, and thus no rights, no 'ought' either.

448

Complaining too loudly. – When the description of an emergency (the crimes of an administration, or bribery and favouritism in political or scholarly corporations, for example) is greatly exaggerated, it does of course have less of an effect on insightful people, but it has all the greater effect on the uninsightful (who would have remained indifferent to a careful, measured presentation). But since the uninsightful are considerably in the majority and harbour within themselves greater strength of will and a more vehement desire for action, the exaggeration will lead to investigations, punishments, promises and reorganisations. – To that extent, it is useful to exaggerate when describing emergencies.

450

New and old concept of government. – To differentiate between government and people, as if two separate spheres of power, one stronger and higher, the other weaker and lower, were negotiating and coming to agreement, is a bit of inherited political sensibility that still accords exactly with the historical establishment of the power relationship in *most* states. When, for example, Bismarck describes the constitutional form as a compromise between government and people, he is speaking according to a principle that has its reason in history (which is, of course, also the source for that portion of unreason, without which nothing human can exist). By contrast, we are now supposed to learn – according to a principle that has sprung from the *head* alone, and is supposed to *make* history – that government is nothing but an organ of the people, and not a provident, honourable 'above' in relationship to a habitually humble 'below'. Before one accepts this formulation of the concept of government, which is as yet unhistorical and arbitrary, if more logical, we might consider the consequences: for the relationship between people and government is the strongest model relationship, according to which the interactions between teacher and pupil, head of the house and servants, father and family, commander-in-chief and soldier, master and apprentice, are automatically patterned. All these relationships are now being slightly transformed under the influence of the prevailing constitutional form of government; they are *becoming* compromises. But how will they have to reverse and displace themselves, changing name and nature, when that very newest concept of government has captured everyone's mind! But it will probably take another century for that. In this regard, there is nothing to wish for *more* than caution and slow development.

451

Justice as a party's lure. – Noble (if not exactly very insightful) representatives of the ruling class may well vow to treat people as equals and grant them equal rights. To that extent, a socialistic way of thought, based on *justice*, is possible; but, as we said, only within the ruling class, which in this case *practises* justice by its sacrifices and renunciations. On the other hand, to *demand* equality of rights, as do the socialists of the subjugated caste, never results from justice but rather covetousness. If one shows the beast bloody pieces of meat close by and then withdraws them again until it finally roars, do you think this roar means justice?

452

Possession and justice. – When socialists prove that the distribution of wealth in present-day society is the consequence of countless injustices and atrocities, rejecting *in summa* the obligation towards anything so unjustly established, they are seeing one particular thing only. The whole past of the old culture is built on violence, slavery, deception, error; but we, the heirs of all these conditions, indeed the convergence of that whole past, cannot decree ourselves away, and cannot want to remove one particular part. The unjust frame of mind lies in the souls of the 'have-nots' too; they are no better than the 'haves' and have no special moral privilege, for at some point their forefathers were 'haves' too. We do not need forcible new distributions of property, but rather gradual transformations of attitude; justice must become greater in everyone, and the violent instinct weaker.

453

The helmsman of passions. – The statesman creates public passions in order to profit from the counter-passion they awaken. To take an example: a German statesman knows well that the Catholic Church will never have the same plans as Russia, indeed that it would much rather ally itself with the Turks than with Russia; he likewise knows that Germany is greatly threatened by the danger of an alliance of France with Russia. Now, if he can succeed in making France the hearth and home of the Catholic Church, he will have eliminated this danger for a long time to come. Thus he has an interest in showing hatred towards the Catholics and, by hostilities of all kinds, transforming believers in the Pope's authority into a passionate political power that is inimical to German politics and must naturally merge with France as Germany's adversary. He aims as necessarily at the Catholicisation of France, as Mirabeau saw the salvation of his fatherland in its de-Catholicisation. – Thus, one state desires to cloud millions of minds in another state in order to derive its benefit from this clouding. This is the same attitude that supports the neighbouring states' republican form of government – '*le désorde organisé*', as Mérimée says – for the sole reason that it assumes it will make the people weaker, more divided, and less able to wage war.

454

Dangerous subversive spirits. – One can divide those who are intent on overthrowing society into the ones who want to gain something for themselves and the ones who want to gain it for their children and grandchildren. The latter are the more dangerous; for they have faith and the good conscience of selflessness. The others can be diverted: the ruling society is still rich and clever enough for that. Danger begins when goals become impersonal; revolutionaries whose interest is impersonal may regard all defenders of the existing order as having a personal interest and may therefore feel superior to them.

455

Political value of paternity. – If a man has no sons, he has no full right to speak about the needs of a single matter of state. He has to have risked with the others what is most precious to him; only then is he bound firmly to the state. One must consider the happiness of one's descendants, and so, above all, have descendants, in order to take a proper, natural part in all institutions and their transformation. The development of higher morality depends on a man's having sons: this makes him unselfish or, more exactly, it expands his selfishness over time and allows him seriously to pursue goals beyond his individual lifetime.

457

Slaves and workers. – That we lay more value on satisfying our vanity than on all other comforts (security, shelter, pleasure of all kinds) is revealed to a ludicrous degree by the fact that (except for political reasons) everyone desires the abolition of slavery and utterly abhors bringing men into this state: while each of us must admit that slaves live more securely and happily than the modern worker in all regards, and that slave labour is very little labour compared to that of the 'worker'. One protests in the name of human dignity, but expressed more plainly, that is that good old vanity, which experiences Not-being-equal-to or Publicly-being-esteemed-lower as the harshest fate. The cynic thinks differently about the matter because he scorns honour – and so for a time Diogenes was a slave and a tutor.

458

Guiding minds and their tools. – We see that great statesmen, and in general all those who must use many men to execute their plans, proceed now in one way, now in another: either they choose very subtly and carefully the men who suit their plans and then give them relatively great freedom, knowing that the nature of these select men is driving them exactly to where they themselves wish to have them; or else they choose badly, indeed, take whatever falls into their hands, but then model each piece of clay into something fit for their purposes. This last sort is the more violent; they also desire more submissive tools; their knowledge of human psychology is usually much less, their disdain for humans greater than among the first-named minds; but the machine that they construct usually works better than the machine from the workshops of the former.

459

Arbitrary law necessary. – Lawyers argue whether that law which is most thoroughly thought out or that which is easiest to understand should prevail in a people. The first type, whose greatest model is Roman law, seems incomprehensible to the layman and therefore no expression of his sense of justice. Popular laws, like the Germanic, for example, were crude, superstitious, illogical, in part silly, but they reflected quite specific inherited native customs and feelings. – But when law is no longer a tradition, as in our case, it can only be *commanded* or forced; none of us has a traditional sense of justice any longer; therefore, we must content ourselves with *arbitrary laws*, which express the necessity of *having to have* a law. Then, the most logical law is the most acceptable because it is the *most impartial*, even admitting that, in the relationship of crime and punishment, the smallest unit of measure is always set arbitrarily.

460

The great man of the masses. – It is easy to give the recipe for what the masses call a great man. By all means, supply them with something that they find very pleasant, or, first, put the idea into their heads that this or that would be very pleasant, and then give it to them. But on no account immediately: let it rather be won with great exertion, or let it seem so. The masses must have the impression that a mighty, indeed invincible, strength of will is present; at least it must seem to be there. Everyone admires a strong will because no one has it, and everyone tells himself that, if he had it, there would be no more limits for him and his egoism. Now, if it appears that this strong will is producing something very pleasant for the masses, instead of listening to its own covetous desires, then everyone admires it all the more and congratulates himself. For the rest, let him have all the characteristics of the masses: the less they are ashamed before him, the more popular he is. So, let him be violent, envious, exploitative, scheming, fawning, grovelling, puffed up or, according to the circumstances, all of the above.

462

My utopia. – In a better social order, the hard work and misery of life will be allotted to the man who suffers least from it, that is, to the dullest man, and so on step by step upwards to the man who is most sensitive to the highest, most sublimated kind of suffering, and therefore suffers even when life is most greatly eased.

463

A delusion in the theory of subversion. – There are political and social visionaries who hotly and eloquently demand the overthrow of all orders in the belief that the proudest temple of fair humanity would then immediately rise up on its own. In these dangerous dreams there is still the echo of Rousseau's superstition, which believes in a wondrous, innate but, as it were, *repressed* goodness of human nature, and attributes all the blame for that repression to the institutions of culture, in society, state and education. Unfortunately, we know from historical experience that every such overthrow once more resurrects the wildest energies, the long since buried horrors and extravagances of most distant times. An overthrow can well be a source of energy in an exhausted human race, but it can never be an organiser, architect artist, perfecter of the human character. – It is not *Voltaire's* temperate nature, inclined to organising, cleansing and restructuring, but rather *Rousseau's* passionate idiocies and half-truths that have awakened the optimistic spirit of revolution, counter to which I shout: '*Ecrasez l'infame!*' Because of him, *the spirit of the Enlightenment and of progressive development* has been scared off for a long time to come: let us see – each one for himself – whether it is not possible to call it back again!

Resurrection of the spirit. – On its political sickbed a people usually regenerates itself and finds its spirit again, which had been lost gradually in the seeking and claiming of power. Culture owes its highest achievements to politically weakened times.

468

Innocent corruption. – In all institutions that do not feel the keen wind of public criticism (as, for example, in scholarly organisations and senates), an innocent corruption grows up, like a mushroom.

472

Religion and government. – As long as the state, or more precisely the government, knows that it is appointed as trustee on behalf of a group of people in their minority, and for their sake considers the question whether religion is to be preserved or eliminated, it will most probably always decide to preserve religion. For religion appeases the individual soul in times of loss, privation, fear or mistrust, that is, when government feels itself unable to do anything directly to alleviate the private man's inner suffering; even during universal, inevitable and initially unpreventable misfortunes (famines, financial crises, wars), religion gives the masses a calm, patient and trusting bearing. Wherever the necessary or coincidental failings of a state government, or the dangerous consequences of dynastic interests catch the eye of a man of insight and make him recalcitrant, the uninsightful will think they are seeing the finger of God and will submit patiently to the directives from *above* (in which concept, divine and human ways of government are usually merged). Thus the citizens' inner peace and a continuity of development will be preserved. Religion protects and seals the power that lies in the unity of popular sentiment, in identical opinions and goals for all, discounting those rare cases when a priesthood and the state power cannot agree about the price and engage in battle. Usually, the state will know how to win the priests over, because it needs their most private, secret education of souls and knows how to appreciate servants who seem outwardly to represent a quite different interest. Without the help of priests no power can become 'legitimate': even now, as Napoleon understood. – Thus, absolute tutelary government and the careful preservation of religion necessarily go together. It is to be presumed that ruling persons and classes will be enlightened about the benefit provided them by religion and thus feel somewhat superior to it, in that they are using it as a tool: and this is the origin of free-thinking. – But what if a quite different view of the concept of government, as it is taught in *democratic* states, begins to prevail? If one sees in government nothing but the instrument of popular will, no Above in contrast to a Below, but solely a function of the single sovereign, the people? Then the government can only take the same position towards religion that the people hold; any spread of enlightenment will have to reverberate right into its representatives; it will not be so easy to use or exploit religious energies and comforts for state purposes (unless powerful party leaders occasionally exert an influence similar to that of enlightened despotism). But if the state may no longer draw any use from religion itself, or if the people think so variously about religious matters that the government cannot take uniform, unified measures regarding religion, then the necessary alternative will appear to be to treat religion as a private matter and consign it to the conscience and habits of each individual. At the very first, the result is that religious feeling appears to be strengthened, to the extent that hidden or repressed stirrings of it, which the state had unwittingly or deliberately stifled, now break out and exceed all limits; later, it turns out that religion is overrun with sects and that an abundance of dragon's teeth had been sown at the moment when religion was made a private matter. Finally, the sight of the strife and the hostile exposure of all the weaknesses of religious confessions allow no other alternative but that every superior and more gifted man makes irreligiosity his private concern. Then this attitude also prevails in the minds of those who govern, and gives, almost against their will, an anti-religious character to the measures they take. As soon as this happens, the people who are still moved by religion, and who used to adore the state as something half-divine or wholly divine, develop an attitude decidedly *hostile to the state*; they attack government measures, try to impede, cross, disturb as much as they can, and because their opposition is so heated, they drive the other party, the irreligious one, into an almost fanatical enthusiasm *for* the state; also contributing secretly to this is the fact that, since they parted from religion, the non-religious have had a feeling of emptiness and are provisionally trying to create a substitute, a kind of fulfilment, through devotion to the state. After these transitional struggles, which may last a long time, it is finally decided whether the religious parties are still strong enough to resurrect an old state of affairs and turn the clock back: in which case, the state inevitably falls into the hands of enlightened despotism (perhaps less enlightened and more fearful than before) – or whether the non-religious parties prevail, undermining and finally thwarting the propagation of their opponents for a few generations, perhaps by means of schools and education. Yet their enthusiasm for the state will also diminish then. It becomes clearer and clearer that when religious adoration, which makes the state into a *mysterium*, a transcendent institution, is shaken, so is the reverent and pious relationship to the state. Henceforth, individuals see only the side of it that can be helpful or harmful to them; they press forward with all the means in their power to get an influence over it. But soon this competition becomes too great; men and parties switch too quickly; too impetuously, they throw each other down from the mountain, after they have scarcely arrived at the top. There is no guarantee that any measure a government puts through will endure; people shy away from undertakings that would have to grow quietly over decades or centuries in order to produce ripe fruit. No longer does anyone feel an obligation towards a law, other than to bow instantaneously to the power that introduced it; at once, however, people begin to undermine it with a new power, a new majority yet to be formed. Finally – one can state it with certainty – the distrust of anything that governs, the insight into the uselessness and irritation of these short-lived struggles, must urge men to a quite new decision: the abolition of the concept of the state, the end of the antithesis 'private and public'. Step by step, private companies incorporate state businesses; even the most stubborn vestige of the old work of governing (for example, that activity which is supposed to secure private parties against other private parties) will ultimately be taken care of by private contractors. Neglect, decline and the *death of the state*, the unleashing of the private person (I am careful not to say 'of the individual'), this is the result of the democratic concept of the state; this is its mission. If it has fulfilled its task (which, like everything human, includes much reason and unreason), if all the relapses of the old illness have been overcome, then a new leaf in the storybook of humanity will be turned; on it one will read all sorts of strange histories and perhaps some good things as well. – To recapitulate briefly, the interests of tutelary government and the interests of religion go hand in hand, so that if the latter begins to die out, the foundation of the state will also be shaken. The belief in a divine order of political affairs, in a *mysterium* in the existence of the state, has a religious origin; if religion disappears, the state will inevitably lose its old veil of Isis and no longer inspire awe. The sovereignty of the people, seen closely, serves to scare off even the last vestige of magic and superstition contained in these feelings; modern democracy is the historical form of the *decline of the state*. – But the prospect resulting from this certain decline is not an unhappy one in every respect: of all their qualities, men's cleverness and selfishness are the best developed; when the state no longer satisfies the demands of these energies, chaos will be the last thing to occur. Rather, an invention even more expedient than the state will triumph over the state. Mankind has already seen many an organisational power die out, for example, associations by sex, which for thousands of years were much more powerful than the family, indeed held sway and organised society long before the family existed. We ourselves are witnessing how the significant legal and political idea of the family, which once ruled as far as Roman culture reached, is growing ever fainter and feebler. Thus a later generation will also see the state become meaningless in certain stretches of the earth – an idea that many men today can hardly contemplate without fear and abhorrence. To be sure, to *work* on the spread and realisation of this idea is something else again: one must have a very arrogant opinion of his own reason and only a superficial understanding of history to set his hand to the plough right now – while there is still no one who can show us the seeds that are to be scattered afterwards on the ravaged earth. So let us trust to 'men's cleverness and selfishness' that the state will still endure for a good while, and that the destructive efforts of overzealous and rash pretenders to knowledge will be repulsed!

473

Socialism in respect to its means. – Socialism is the visionary younger brother of an almost decrepit despotism, whose heir it aspires to be. Thus its efforts are reactionary in the deepest sense. For it desires a wealth of executive power, as only despotism had it; indeed, it outdoes everything in the past by striving for the downright destruction of the individual, which it sees as an unjustified luxury of nature, and which it intends to improve into an expedient *organ of the community*. Socialism crops up in the vicinity of all excessive displays of power because of its relation to it, like the typical old socialist Plato, at the court of the Sicilian tyrant; it desires (and in certain circumstances, furthers) the Caesarean power state of this century, because, as we said, it would like to be its heir. But even this inheritance would not suffice for its purposes; it needs the most submissive subjugation of all citizens to the absolute state, the like of which has never existed. And since it cannot even rely any longer on the old religious piety towards the state, having rather always to work automatically to eliminate piety – because it works on the elimination of all existing *states* – socialism can only hope to exist here and there for short periods of time by means of the most extreme terrorism. Therefore, it secretly prepares for reigns of terror and drives the word 'justice' like a nail into the heads of the semi-educated masses, to rob them completely of their reason (after this reason has already suffered a great deal from its semi-education) and to give them a good conscience for the evil game that they are supposed to play. – Socialism can serve as a rather brutal and forceful way to teach the danger of all accumulations of state power, and to that extent instil one with distrust of the state itself. When its rough voice chimes in with the battle-cry *'as much state as possible'*, it will at first make the cry noisier than ever; but soon the opposite cry will be heard with strength the greater: *'as little state as possible'*.

474

The development of the spirit, feared by the state. – Like every organisational political power, the Greek *polis* spurned and distrusted the increase of culture among its citizens; its powerful natural impulse was to do almost nothing but cripple and obstruct it. The *polis* did not want to permit to culture any history or evolution; the education determined by the law of the land was intended to bind all generations and keep them at *one* level. Later, Plato too wanted it no different for his ideal state. So culture developed *in spite of the polis*; the *polis* helped indirectly, of course, and involuntarily, because in it an individual's ambition was stimulated greatly, so that once he had come to the path of intellectual development, he pursued that, too, as far as it would go. One should not evoke Pericles' panegyric as refutation: for it is only a great, optimistic delusion about the allegedly necessary connection between the *polis* and Athenian civilisation; just before the night falls on Athens (the plague and the break with tradition), Thucydides lets it shine resplendent once again like a transfiguring sunset, at whose sight we are to forget the bad day that went before it.

475

The European man and the destruction of nations. – Commerce and industry, traffic in books and letters, the commonality of all higher culture, quick changes of locality and landscape, the present-day nomadic life of all non-landowners – these conditions necessarily bring about a weakening and ultimately destruction of nations, or at least of European nations; so that a mixed race, that of the European man, has to originate from all of them, as the result of continual crossbreeding. The isolation of nations due to engendered *national* hostilities now works against this goal, consciously or unconsciously, but the mixing process goes on slowly, nevertheless, despite those intermittent counter-currents; this artificial nationalism, by the way, is as dangerous as artificial Catholicism was, for it is in essence a forcible state of emergency and martial law imposed by the few on the many, and requiring cunning, lies and force to remain respectable. It is not the self-interest of the many (the people), as one would have it, that urges this nationalism, but primarily the self-interest of certain royal dynasties, as well as that of certain commercial and social classes; once a man has understood this, he should be undaunted in presenting himself as a *good European* and should work actively on the merging of nations. The Germans, because of their age-old, proven trait of being the *nations' interpreter and mediator*, will be able to help in this process. – Incidentally, the whole problem of the *Jews* exists only within national states, inasmuch as their energy and higher intelligence, their capital of spirit and will, which accumulated from generation to generation in the long school of their suffering, must predominate to a degree that awakens envy and hatred; and so, in the literature of nearly all present-day nations – and, in fact, in proportion to their renewed nationalistic behaviour – there is an increase in the literary misconduct that leads the Jews to the slaughterhouse, as scapegoats for every possible public and private misfortune. As soon as it is no longer a matter of preserving nations, but rather of producing the strongest possible mixed European race, the Jew becomes as useful and desirable an ingredient as any other national quantity. Every nation, every man has disagreeable, even dangerous characteristics; it is cruel to demand that the Jew should be an exception. Those characteristics may even be especially dangerous and frightful in him, and perhaps the youthful Jew of the stock exchange is the most repugnant invention of the whole human race. Nevertheless, I would like to know how much one must excuse in the overall accounting of a people which, not without guilt on all our parts, has had the most sorrowful history of all peoples, and to whom we owe the noblest human being (Christ), the purest philosopher (Spinoza), the mightiest book and the most effective moral code in the world. Furthermore, in the darkest medieval times, when the Asiatic cloud had settled heavily over Europe, it was the Jewish freethinkers, scholars and doctors who, under the harshest personal pressure, held fast to the banner of enlightenment and intellectual independence, and defended Europe against Asia; we owe to their efforts not least that a more natural, rational and in any event unmythical explanation of the world could finally triumph again, and that the ring of culture which now links us to the enlightenment of Greco-Roman antiquity remained unbroken. If Christianity did everything possible to orientalise the Occident, then Judaism helped substantially to occidentalise it again and again, which, in a certain sense, is to say that it made Europe's history and task into a *continuation of the Greek*.

476

Apparent superiority of the Middle Ages. – The Middle Ages offers in the Church an institution with a quite universal goal, comprehending all men and aimed at their supposed highest interest; in contrast to it, the goals of states and nations, which modern history offers, make a disheartening impression; they appear petty, low, materialistic, geographically narrow. But we should not form our judgements because of these different impressions on our imagination; for the universal institution of the Church was reflecting artificial needs, based on fictions, which, if they were not yet present, it first had to produce (the need for redemption). The new institutions help in real states of need; and the time is coming when institutions will be formed in order to serve the common, true needs of all men, and to place that fantastic prototype, the Catholic Church, into the shadows of oblivion.

477

War essential. – It is vain rhapsodising and sentimentality to continue to expect much (even more, to expect a very great deal) from mankind once it has learned not to wage war. For the time being, we know of no other means to imbue exhausted peoples, as strongly and surely as every great war does, with that raw energy of the battleground, that deep impersonal hatred, that murderous coldbloodedness with a good conscience, that communal, organised ardour in destroying the enemy, that proud indifference to great losses, to one's own existence and to that of one's friends, that muted, earthquake-like convulsion of the soul. Afterwards, if conditions are favourable, the brooks and streams that have broken forth, tumbling stones and all kinds of debris along with them, and destroying the meadows of delicate cultures, will start to turn the wheels in the workshops of the spirit with new strength. Culture absolutely cannot do without passions, vices and acts of malice. – When the Imperial Romans had tired somewhat of wars, they tried to gain new strength by animal-baiting, gladiatorial contests and the persecution of Christians. The present-day English, who seem in general also to have renounced war, are using another means to produce anew those fading strengths: they have undertaken dangerous voyages of discovery, crossed oceans, climbed mountains, for scientific purposes, as is said, in truth to bring surplus energy home with them from every sort of adventure and danger. People will discover many other such surrogates for war, but perhaps that will make them understand ever more clearly that such a highly cultivated and therefore necessarily weary humanity as that of present-day Europe needs not only wars but the greatest and most terrible wars – that is, occasional relapses into barbarism – in order not to forfeit to the means of culture its culture and its very existence.

480

Envy and sloth in different directions. – The two opposing parties, the socialistic and the nationalistic – or however they are called in Europe's various countries – deserve one another: in both of them, envy and laziness are the moving powers. In the one camp, people want to work as little as possible with their hands; in the other, as little as possible with their heads; in nationalism, men hate and envy the outstanding individuals who develop on their own and are not willing to let themselves be placed among the rank and file for the purpose of collective action; in socialism, men hate and envy the better caste of society, outwardly in a more favourable position, whose actual duty, the production of the highest goods of culture, makes life inwardly all the more difficult and painful. Of course, if one can succeed in turning that spirit of collective action into the spirit of the higher social classes, then the socialistic throngs are quite right to try to bring themselves, externally too, to the level of the former, since inwardly, in heart and mind, they are already on the same level. – Live as higher men and persist in doing the deeds of higher culture – then everything alive will grant you your rights, and the social order, whose peak you represent, will be preserved from any evil eye or hand.

481

Great politics and its losses. – War and readiness for war do not cause a people to suffer its greatest losses because of the costs, the obstructions in trade and commerce, or the need to provide for the standing armies – however great these losses may be now, when eight European states spend the sum of two to three billion on them annually – rather, its greatest loss is that, year in and year out, the ablest, strongest, most industrious men are taken in extraordinary numbers from their own occupations and professions in order to be soldiers. Similarly, a people that prepares to engage in great politics and secure a decisive voice among the mightiest states does not suffer its greatest losses in the most obvious place. It is true that thenceforth it continually sacrifices a large number of its most outstanding talents on the 'altar of the

Fatherland', or to national ambition, while earlier, instead of being devoured by politics, they had other spheres of action open to them. But off to the side from these public hecatombs, and fundamentally much more frightful, a show goes on continually in one hundred thousand simultaneous acts: each able, industrious, intelligent, ambitious man of a people greedy for political glory is ruled by this greed and no longer belongs entirely to his own cause as he once did; every day, new questions and cares of the public good consume a daily tribute, taken from every citizen's mental and emotional capital: the sum of all these sacrifices and losses of individual energy and labour is so enormous that, almost necessarily, the political flowering of a people is followed by an intellectual impoverishment and exhaustion, a decreased ability to produce works that demand great concentration and singlemindedness. Finally, one may ask whether all this blossoming and splendour of the whole (which, after all, is only expressed as other states' fear of the new colossus, and the patronage, wrung from abroad, of national commerce and trade) is *worth it*, if all the nobler, more tender and spiritual plants once produced in such abundance on its soil have to be sacrificed to this gross and gaudy national flower.

531

The life of the enemy. – Whoever lives for the sake of combating an enemy has an interest in the enemy's staying alive.

633

Essentially, we are still the same people as those in the period of the Reformation: and how should it be otherwise? But we no longer allow ourselves certain means to gain victory for our opinion: this distinguishes us from that age and proves that we belong to a higher culture. These days, if a man still attacks and crushes opinions with suspicions and outbursts of rage, in the manner of men during the Reformation, he clearly betrays that he would have burnt his opponents had he lived in other times, and that he would have taken recourse to all the means of the Inquisition had he lived as an opponent of the Reformation. In its time, the Inquisition was reasonable, for it meant nothing other than the general martial law which had to be proclaimed over the whole domain of the Church, and which, like every state of martial law, justified the use of the most extreme means, namely under the assumption (which we no longer share with those people) that one *possessed* truth in the Church and *had* to preserve it at any cost, with any sacrifice, for the salvation of mankind. But now we will no longer concede so easily that anyone has the truth; the rigorous methods of inquiry have spread sufficient distrust and caution, so that we experience every man who represents opinions violently in word and deed as any enemy of our present culture, or at least as a backward person. And in fact, the fervour about *having* the truth counts very little today in relation to that other fervour, more gentle and silent to be sure, for seeking the truth, a search that does not tire of learning afresh and testing anew.

Translated by Marion Faber, with Stephen Lehmann

Miscellaneous Maxims and Opinions, 1879

179

Happiness of the age. – In two respects our age is to be accounted happy. With respect to the *past*, we enjoy all cultures and their productions, and nurture ourselves on the noblest blood of all periods. We stand sufficiently near to the magic of the forces from whose womb these periods are born to be able in passing to submit to their spell with pleasure and terror; whereas earlier cultures could only enjoy themselves and never looked beyond themselves, but were rather overarched by a bell of broader or narrower dome, through which indeed light streamed down to them, but which their gaze could not pierce. With respect to the *future*, there opens out to us for the first time a mighty, comprehensive vista of human and economic purposes engirdling the whole inhabited globe. At the same time, we feel conscious of a power ourselves to take this new task in hand without presumption, without requiring supernatural aids. Yes, whatever the result of our enterprise, however much we may have overestimated our strength, at any rate we need render account to no one but ourselves, and mankind can henceforth begin to do with itself what it will. – There are, it is true, peculiar human bees, who only know how to suck the bitterest and worst elements from the chalice of every flower. It is true that all flowers contain something that is not honey, but these bees may be allowed to feel in their own way about the happiness of our time and continue to build their hive of discomfort.

299

Pia fraus or something else. – I hope I am mistaken, but I think that in Germany of today a twofold sort of hypocrisy is set up as the duty of the moment for everyone. From imperial-political misgivings Germanism is demanded, and from social apprehensions Christianity, but both only in words and gestures, and particularly in ability to keep silent. It is the *veneer* that today costs so much and is paid for so highly; and for the benefit of the *spectators* the face of the nation assumes German and Christian wrinkles.

304

The revolution-spirit and the possession-spirit. – The only remedy against socialism that still lies in your power is to avoid provoking socialism: in other words, to live in moderation and contentment, to prevent as far as possible all lavish display and to aid the state as far as possible in its taxing of all superfluities and luxuries. You do not like this remedy? Then, you rich bourgeois who call yourselves 'Liberals', confess that it is your own inclination that you find so terrible and menacing in socialists, but allow to prevail in yourselves as unavoidable, as if with you it were something different. As you are constituted, if you had not your *property* and the cares of maintaining it, this bent of yours would make socialists of you. Possession alone differentiates you from them. If you wish to conquer the assailants of your prosperity, you must first conquer yourselves. – And if that prosperity only meant well-being, it would not be so external and provocative of envy; it would be more generous, more benevolent, more compensatory, more helpful. But the spurious, histrionic element in your pleasures, which lie more in the feeling of contrast (because others do not have them and feel envious) than in feelings of realised and heightened power – your houses, dresses, carriages, shops, the demands of your palates and your tables, your noisy operatic and musical enthusiasm; lastly your women, formed and fashioned but of base metal, gilded but without the ring of gold, chosen by you for show and considering themselves meant for show – these are the things that spread the poison of that national disease, which seizes the masses ever more and more as a socialistic heart-itch, but has its origin and breeding-place *in you*. Who shall now arrest this epidemic?

306

For the strengthening of parties. – Whoever wishes to strengthen a party internally should give it an opportunity of being forcibly treated with obvious injustice. The party thus acquires a capital of good conscience that it perhaps previously lacked.

310

Danger in wealth. – Only a man of *intellect* should hold *property*: otherwise property is *dangerous to the community*. For the owner, not knowing how to make use of the leisure which his possessions might secure to him, will *continue* to strive after more property. This strife will be his occupation, his strategy in the war with boredom. So in the end real wealth is produced from the moderate property that would be enough for an intellectual man. Such wealth, then, is the glittering outcrop of intellectual dependence and poverty, but it only *appears* quite different from what its humble origin might lead one to expect, because it can mask itself with culture and art – it can, in fact, *purchase* the mask. Hence it excites envy in the poor and uncultured – who at bottom always envy culture and see no mask in the mask – and gradually paves the way for a social revolution. For a gilded coarseness and a histrionic sounding of trumpets in the pretended enjoyment of culture inspires that class with the thought, 'It is only a matter of money' – whereas it is indeed to some extent a matter of money, but *far more of intellect*.

316

Welcome enemies. – The socialistic movements are today becoming more and more agreeable rather than terrifying to the dynastic governments, because by these movements they are provided with *a right and a weapon* for making exceptional rules, and can thus attack the figures that really fill them with terror, the democrats and anti-dynasts. – Towards all that such governments professedly detest they feel a secret cordiality and inclination. But they are compelled to veil their soul.

318

Of the mastery of them that know. – It is easy, ridiculously easy, to set up a model for the election of a legislative body. First of all the honest and reliable men of the nation, who at the same time are masters and experts in some one branch, have to become prominent by mutual scenting out and recognition. From these, by a narrower process of selection, the learned and expert of the first rank in each individual branch must again be chosen, also by mutual recognition and guarantee. If the legislative body be composed of these, it will finally be necessary, in each individual case, that only the voices and judgements of the most specialised experts should decide; the honesty of all the rest should have become so great that it is simply a matter of decency to leave the voting also in the hands of these men. The result would be that the law, in the strictest sense, would emanate from the intelligence of the most intelligent. – As things are now, voting is done by parties, and at every division there must be hundreds of uneasy consciences – among the ill-taught, the incapable of judgement, among those who merely repeat, imitate and go with the tide. Nothing lowers the dignity of a new law so much as this inherent shamefaced feeling of insincerity that necessarily results at every party division. But, as has been said, it is easy, ridiculously easy, to set up such a model: no power on earth is at present strong enough to realise such an ideal – unless the belief in the highest *utility of knowledge, and of those that know,* at last dawns even on the most hostile minds and is preferred to the prevalent belief in majorities. In the sense of such a future may our watchword be: 'More reverence for them that know, and down with all parties!'

320

Owls to Athens. – The governments of the great states have two instruments for keeping the people dependent in fear and obedience: a coarser, the army, and a more refined, the school. With the aid of the former they win over to their side the *ambition* of the higher strata and the *strength* of the lower, so far as both are characteristic of active and energetic men of moderate or inferior gifts. With the aid of the latter they win over *gifted* poverty, especially the intellectually pretentious semi-poverty of the middle classes. Above all, they make teachers of all grades into an intellectual court looking unconsciously 'towards the heights'. By putting obstacle after obstacle in the way of private schools and the wholly distasteful individual tuition they secure the disposal of a considerable number of educational posts, towards which numerous hungry and submissive eyes are turned to an extent five times as great as can ever be satisfied. These posts, however, must support the holder but meagrely, so that he maintains a feverish thirst for promotion and becomes still more closely attached to the views of the government. For it is always more advantageous to foster moderate discontent than contentment, the mother of courage, the grandmother of free thought and exuberance. By means of this physically and mentally bridled body of teachers, the youth of the country is as far as possible raised to a certain level of culture that is useful to the state and arranged on a suitable sliding-scale. Above all, the immature and ambitious minds of all classes are almost imperceptibly imbued with the idea that only a career which is recognised and hallmarked by the state can lead immediately to social distinction. The effect of this belief in government examinations and titles goes so far that even men who have remained independent and have risen by trade or handicraft still feel a pang of discontent in their hearts until their position too is marked and acknowledged by a gracious bestowal of rank and orders from above – until one becomes a 'somebody'. Finally, the state connects all these hundreds of offices and posts in its hands with the *obligation* of being trained and hallmarked in these state schools if one ever wishes to enter this charmed circle. Honour in society, daily bread, the possibility of a family, protection from above, the feeling of community in a common culture – all this forms a network of hopes into which every young man walks: how should he feel the slightest breath of mistrust? In the end, perhaps, the obligation of being a *soldier* for one year has become with everyone, after the lapse of a few generations, an unreflecting habit, an understood thing, with an eye to which we construct the plan of our lives quite early. Then the state can venture on the master-stroke of weaving *together* school *and* army, talent, ambition and strength by means of common advantages – that is, by attracting the *more highly gifted* and *cultivated* on favourable terms to the army and inspiring them with the military spirit of joyful obedience; so that finally, perhaps, they become attached permanently to the flag and endow it by their talents with an ever new and more brilliant lustre. Then nothing more is wanted but an opportunity for great wars. These are provided from professional reasons, and so in all *innocence*, by diplomats, aided by newspapers and stock exchanges. For 'the nation', as a nation of soldiers, need never be supplied with a good conscience in war – it has one already.

321

The press. – If we consider how even today all great political transactions glide upon the stage secretly and stealthily; how they are hidden by unimportant events, and seem small when close at hand; how they only show their far-reaching effect and leave the soil still quaking long after they have taken place – what significance can we attach to the press in its present position, with its daily expenditure of lung-power in order to bawl, to deafen, to excite, to terrify? – is it anything more than a *permanent false alarm*, which tries to lead our ears and our wits into a false direction?

324

Foreignisms. – A foreigner who travelled in Germany found favour or the reverse by certain assertions of his, according to the districts in which he stayed. All intelligent Swabians – he used to say – are coquettish. – The other Swabians still believed that Uhland was a poet and Goethe immoral. – The best about German novels now in vogue was that one need not read them, for one knew already what they contained. – The Berliner seemed more good-humoured than the South German, for he was all too fond of mocking and so could endure mockery himself, which the South German could not. – The intellect of the Germans was kept down by their beer and their newspapers: he recommended them tea and pamphlets, of course as a cure. – He advised us to contemplate the different nations of worn-out Europe and see how well each displayed some particular quality of old age, to the delight of those who sit before the great spectacle: how the French successfully represent the cleverness and amiability of old age, the English the experience and reserve, the Italians the innocence and candour. Can the other masks of old age be wanting? Where is the proud old man, the domineering old man, the covetous old man? – The most dangerous region in Germany was Saxony and Thuringia: nowhere else was there more mental agility, more knowledge of men, side by side with freedom of thought; and all this was so modestly veiled by the ugly dialect and the zealous officiousness of the inhabitants that one hardly noticed that one here had to deal with the intellectual drill sergeants of Germany, her teachers for good or evil. – The arrogance of the North Germans was kept in check by their tendency to obey, that of the South Germans by their tendency to make themselves comfortable. – It appeared to him that in their women German men possessed awkward but self-opinionated housewives, who lauded themselves so perseveringly that they had almost persuaded the world, and at any rate their husbands, of their peculiarly German housewifely virtue. – When the conversation turned on Germany's home and foreign policy, he used to say – he called it 'betray the secret' – that Germany's greatest statesman did not believe in great statesmen. – The future of Germans he found menaced and menacing, for Germans had forgotten how to *enjoy* themselves (an art that the Italians understood so well), but, by the great games of chance called wars and dynastic revolutions, had *accustomed themselves to emotionalism*, and consequently would one day have an uprising. For that is the strongest emotion that a nation can procure for itself. – The German socialist was all the more dangerous because impelled by no *definite* necessity: his trouble lay in not knowing what he wanted; so, even if he attained many of his objects, he would still pine away from desire in the midst of delights, just like Faust, but presumably like a very vulgar Faust. 'For the *Faust-Devil*', he finally exclaimed, 'by whom cultured Germans were so much plagued, was exorcised by Bismarck; but now the Devil has entered into the swine, and is worse than ever!'

The Wanderer and His Shadow, 1880

22

The principle of equilibrium. – The robber and the man of power who promises to protect a community from robbers are perhaps at bottom beings of the same mould, save that the latter attains his ends by other means than the former – that is to say, through regular imposts paid to him by the community, and no longer through forced contributions. (The same relation exists between merchant and pirate, who for a long period are one and the same person: where the one function appears to them inadvisable, they exercise the other. Even today mercantile morality is really nothing but a *refinement* on piratical morality – buying in the cheapest market, at prime cost if possible, and selling in the dearest.) The essential point is that the man of power promises to maintain the *equilibrium* against the robber, and herein the weak find a possibility of living. For either they must group themselves into an *equivalent* power, or they must subject themselves to someone of equivalent power (render service in return for his efforts). The latter course is generally preferred, because it really keeps two dangerous beings in check – the robber through the man of power, and the man of power through the standpoint of advantage; for the latter profits by treating his subjects with graciousness and tolerance, in order that they may support not only themselves but their ruler. As a matter of fact, conditions may still be hard and cruel enough, yet in comparison with the complete *annihilation* that was formerly always a possibility, men breathe freely. – The community is at first the organisation of the weak to counterbalance menacing forces. An organisation to outweigh those forces would be more advisable, if its members grew strong enough to destroy the adverse power: and when it is a question of one mighty oppressor, the *attempt* will certainly be made. But if the one man is the head of a clan, or if he has a large following, a rapid and decisive annihilation is improbable, and a long or permanent *feud* is only to be expected. This feud, however, involves the least desirable condition for the community, for it thereby loses the time to provide for its means of subsistence with the necessary regularity, and sees the product of all work hourly threatened. Hence the community prefers to raise its power of attack and defence to the exact plane on which the power of its dangerous neighbour stands, and to give him to understand that an equal weight now lies in its own side of the scales – so why not be good friends? – Thus *equilibrium* is a most important conception for the understanding of the ancient doctrines of law and morals. Equilibrium is, in fact, the basis of justice. When justice in ruder ages says, 'An eye for an eye, a tooth for a tooth', it presupposes the attainment of this equilibrium and tries to *maintain* it by means of this compensation; so that, when crime is committed, the injured party will not take the revenge of blind anger. By means of the *jus talionis* the equilibrium of the disturbed relations of power is *restored*, for in such primitive times an eye or an arm *more* means a bit more power, more weight. – In a community where all consider themselves equal, *disgrace* and *punishment* await crime – that is, violations of the principle of equilibrium. Disgrace is thrown into the scale as a counterweight against the encroaching individual, who has gained profit by his encroachment and now suffers losses, through disgrace, which annul and *outweigh* the previous profits. Punishment, in the same way, sets up a far greater counterweight against the preponderance which every criminal hopes to obtain – imprisonment as against a deed of violence, restitution and fines as against theft. Thus the sinner is *reminded* that his action has excluded him from the community and from its moral advantages, since the community treats him as an inferior, a weaker brother, an outsider. For this reason punishment is not merely retaliation, but has something *more*, something of the *cruelty of the state of nature*, and of *this* it would serve as a *reminder*.

26

Rule of law as a means. – Law, where it rests upon contracts between *equals*, holds good so long as the power of the parties to the contract remains equal or similar. Wisdom created law to end all feuds and *useless* expenditure among men on an equal footing. *Quite as definite* an end is put to this waste, however, when one party has *become* decidedly *weaker* than the other. Subjection enters and law *ceases*, but the result is the same as that attained by law. For now it is the *wisdom* of the superior which advises to *spare* the inferior and not uselessly to squander his strength. Thus the position of the inferior is often more favourable than that of the equal. – Thus rule of law is a temporary means counseled by wisdom, and not an end.

29

Envy and its nobler brother. – Where equality is really recognised and permanently established, we see the rise of that propensity that is generally considered immoral and would scarcely be conceivable in a state of nature: *envy*. The envious man is susceptible to every sign of individual superiority to the common herd and wishes to depress everyone once more to the level – or raise himself to the superior plane. Thus arise two different modes of action, which Hesiod designated good and bad Eris. In the same way, in a condition of equality there arises indignation that one man should fare badly *beneath* his dignity and equal rights, while another fares well *above* his equal rights. These latter, however, are emotions of *nobler* natures. They feel the want of justice and equity in things that are independent of the arbitrary choice of men: or, in other words, they desire the equality recognised by man to be recognised as well by Nature and chance. They are angry that men of equal merits should not have equal fortune.

31

Vanity as an anti-social offshoot. – As men, for the sake of security, have made themselves *equal* in order to found communities, but as also this conception is imposed by a sort of constraint and is entirely opposed to the instincts of the individual, so the more universal security is guaranteed, the more do new offshoots of the old instinct for predominance appear. Such offshoots appear in the setting-up of class distinctions, in the demand for professional dignities and privileges, and, generally speaking, in vanity (manners, dress, speech, and so forth). So as soon as danger to the community is apparent, the majority, who were unable to assert their preponderance in a time of universal peace, once more bring about the condition of equality, and for the time being the absurd privileges and vanities disappear. If the community, however, collapses utterly and anarchy reigns supreme, there arises the state of nature: an absolutely ruthless inequality as recounted by Thucydides in the case of Corcyra. Neither a natural justice nor a natural injustice exists.

39

Origin of rights. – Rights may be traced to *traditions*, traditions to momentary *agreements*. At some time or other men were mutually content with the consequences of making an agreement and, again, too indolent formally to renew it. Thus they went on living as if it had constantly been renewed, and gradually, when oblivion cast its veil over the origin, they thought they possessed a sacred, unalterable foundation on which every generation *had* to continue to build. Tradition was now a *compulsion*, even if it no longer involved the profit originally derived from making the agreement. – Here the *weak* have always found their strong fortress. They are inclined to regard the momentary agreement, the single act of grace as *valid eternally*.

87

Learning to write well. – The age of good speaking is over, because the age of city-state culture is over. The limit allowed by Aristotle to the great city – in which the herald must be able to make himself heard by the whole assembled community – troubles us as little as do any city-communities, us who even wish to be understood beyond the boundaries of nations. Therefore everyone who is a good European must learn *to write well, and to write better and better*. He cannot help himself, he must learn that: even if he was born in Germany, where bad writing is looked upon as a national privilege. Better writing means better thinking; always to discover matter more worthy of communication; to be able to communicate it properly; to be translatable into the tongues of neighbouring nations; to make oneself comprehensible to foreigners who learn our language; to work with the view of making all that is good common property and of giving free access everywhere to the free; finally, to *pave the way* for that still remote state of things, when the great task shall come for good Europeans – guidance and guardianship of the universal world culture. – Whoever preaches the opposite doctrine of not bothering about good writing and good reading – both virtues grow together and decline together – is really showing the peoples a way of becoming more and more *national*. He is intensifying the malady of this century, and is an enemy to good Europeans, an enemy to free spirits.

175

Mediocrity as a mask. – Mediocrity is the happiest mask which the superior mind can wear, because it does not lead the great majority – that is, the mediocre – to think that there is any disguise. Yet the superior mind assumes the mask just for their sake – so as not to irritate them, indeed, often from a feeling of pity and kindness.

181

Vanity as the greatest utility. – Originally the strong individual uses not only nature but even societies and weaker individuals as objects of rapine. He exploits them, so far as he can, and then passes on. As he lives from hand to mouth, alternating between hunger and superfluity, he kills more animals than he can eat, and robs and maltreats men more than is necessary. His manifestation of power is at the same time one of revenge against his cramped and worried existence. Furthermore, he wishes to be held more powerful than he is, and thus misuses opportunities; the accretion of fear that he begets being an accretion of power. He soon observes that he stands or falls not by what he *is* but by what he is *thought* to be. Here lies the origin of *vanity*. The man of power seeks by every means to increase others' *faith* in his power. – The thralls who tremble before him and serve him know, for their part, that they are worth just so much as they *appear* to him to be worth, and so they work with an eye to this valuation rather than to their own self-satisfaction. We know vanity only in its most weakened forms, in its idealisations and its small doses, because we live in a late and very emasculated state of society: originally vanity is of *the greatest utility*, the strongest means of preservation. And indeed vanity will be greater, the cleverer the individual, because an increase in the belief in power is easier than an increase in the power itself, but only for him who has intellect – or, as must be the case under primitive conditions, for him who is *cunning* and *crafty*.

220

Reaction against machine-culture. – The machine, itself a product of the highest mental powers, sets in motion hardly any but the lower, unthinking forces of the men who serve it. True, it unfetters a vast quantity of force which would otherwise lie dormant. But it does not communicate the impulse to climb higher, to improve, to become artistic. It creates *activity* and *monotony*, but this in the long run produces a counter-effect, a despairing boredom of the soul, which through machinery has learned to long for idleness in all its varieties.

221

The danger of enlightenment. – All the half-insane, theatrical, bestially cruel, licentious and especially sentimental and self-intoxicating elements which go to form the true *revolutionary substance*, and became flesh and spirit, before the Revolution, in Rousseau – all this composite being, with factitious enthusiasm, finally set even *the Enlightenment* upon its fanatical head, which thereby began itself to shine as in an illuminating halo. Yet the Enlightenment is essentially foreign to the Revolution, and, if left to itself, would have pierced silently through the clouds like a shaft of light, long content to transfigure individuals alone, and thus only slowly transfiguring national customs and institutions as well. But now, bound hand and foot to a violent and abrupt monster, the Enlightenment itself became violent and abrupt. Its danger has therefore become almost greater than its useful quality of liberation and illumination, which it introduced into the great revolutionary movement. Whoever grasps this will also know from what confusion it has to be extricated, from what impurities to be cleansed, so as then to *continue* the work of the Enlightenment *in himself*, and to strangle the Revolution at birth and nullify its effects.

226

Greek prudence. – As the desire for victory and pre-eminence is an ineradicable trait of human nature, older and more primitive than any respect of or joy in equality, the Greek state sanctioned gymnastic and artistic competitions among equals. In other words, it marked out an arena where this impulse to conquer would find a vent without jeopardising the political order. With the final decline of gymnastic and artistic contests the Greek state fell into a condition of profound unrest and dissolution.

275

The age of Cyclopean building. – The democratisation of Europe is irresistible: even he who would stem the tide uses those very means that democratic thought first put into man's hands, and he makes these means more handy and workable: and those who oppose democracy most on principle (I mean the spirits of revolution) seem only to exist in order, by the fear that they inspire, to drive forward the different parties faster and faster on the democratic course. Now we may well feel anxious for those who are working consciously and honourably for this future. There is something dreary and monotonous in their faces, and the grey dust seems to have been wafted into their very brains. Nevertheless, posterity may possibly some day laugh at our anxiety and see in the democratic work of several generations what we see in the building of stone dams and walls – an activity that necessarily covers clothes and face with a great deal of dust, and perhaps unavoidably makes the workers, too, a little dull-witted; but who would on that account desire such work undone? It seems that the democratisation of Europe is a link in the chain of those tremendous *prophylactic measures* which are the thought of the modern era, and whereby we separate ourselves from the Middle Ages. Now, and now only, is the age of cyclopean building! A final security in the foundations that the future may build on them without danger! Henceforth, an impossibility of the orchards of culture being once more destroyed overnight by wild, senseless mountain torrents! Dams and walls against barbarians, against plagues, against *physical and spiritual enslavement*! And all this understood at first roughly and literally, but gradually in an ever higher and more spiritual sense, so that all the measures here indicated may appear as the intellectual preparation of the highest artist in horticulture, who can only apply himself to his real task when the other is fully accomplished! – True, if we consider the long intervals of time that here lie between means and end, the great, supreme labour, straining the powers and minds of centuries, that is necessary in order to create or to provide each individual means, we must not bear too heavily upon the workers of the present when they loudly proclaim that the wall and the fence *are* already the end and the final goal; after all, no one yet sees the gardener and the fruit *for whose sake* the fence exists.

276

The right of universal suffrage. – The people did not give themselves universal suffrage but, wherever this is now in force, have received and accepted it as a temporary measure. But in any case the people have the right to return the gift if it does not satisfy their anticipations. This dissatisfaction seems universal today, for when, on any occasion where the vote is exercised, scarce two-thirds, indeed perhaps not even the majority of all voters, go to the polls, that very fact is a vote *against* the whole suffrage system. – On this point, in fact, we must pronounce a much sterner verdict. A law that enacts that the majority shall decide as to the welfare of all cannot be built up on the foundation that it alone has provided, for it is bound to require a far broader foundation, namely the *unanimity of all*. Universal suffrage must not only be the expression of the will of a majority, but of the whole country. Thus the dissent of a very small minority is already enough to set aside the system as impracticable; and the *abstention* from voting is in fact a dissent of this kind, which ruins the whole institution. The 'absolute veto' of the individual, or – not to be too minute – the veto of a few thousands, hangs over the system as the consequence of justice. On every occasion when it is employed, the system must, according to the nature of the participation, first prove that it is *still valid*.

280

More reverence for them that know. – In the competition of production and sale the *public* is made judge of the product. But the public has no special knowledge and judges by the *appearance* of the wares. In consequence, the art of appearance (and perhaps the taste for it) must increase under the dominance of competition, while on the other hand the quality of every product must deteriorate. The result will be, so far as reason does not fall in value, that one day an end will be put to that competition, and a new principle will win the day. Only the master of the craft should pronounce a verdict on the work, and the public should be dependent on the belief in the personality of the judge and his honesty. Accordingly, no anonymous work! At least an expert should be there as guarantor and pledge *his* name if the name of the creator is lacking or is unknown. The *cheapness* of an article is for the layman another kind of illusion and deceit, since only *durability* can decide that a thing is cheap and to what an extent. But it is difficult, and for a layman impossible, to judge of its durability. – Hence that which produces an effect on the eye and costs little at present gains the advantage – this being naturally machine-made work. Again, machinery – that is to say, the cause of the greatest rapidity and facility in production – favours the *most saleable* kind of article; otherwise it involves no tangible profit; it would be too little used and too often stand idle. But as to what is most saleable, the public, as above said, decides: it must be the most deceptive product – in other words, the thing that *appears* good and also *appears* cheap. Thus in the domain of labour our motto must also hold good: 'More respect for them that know!'

281

The danger of kings. – Democracy has it in its power, without any violent means, and only by a lawful pressure steadily exerted, to make the offices of king and emperor *hollow*, until only a zero remains, perhaps with the significance of every zero in that, while nothing in itself, it multiplies a number tenfold if placed in the right position. The office of king and emperor would remain a gorgeous ornament upon the simple and appropriate dress of democracy, a beautiful superfluity that democracy allows itself, a relic of all the historically venerable, primitive ornaments, indeed the symbol of history itself – and in this unique position a highly effective thing if, as above said, it does not stand alone, but is correctly *positioned*. – In order to avoid the danger of this nullification, kings hold by their teeth to their dignity as *warlords*. To this end they need wars, or in other words exceptional circumstances, in which that slow, lawful pressure of the democratic forces is relaxed.

284

The means towards genuine peace. – No government today will admit that it maintains an army in order to satisfy occasionally its passion for conquest.

The army is said to serve only defensive purposes. This morality, which justifies self-defence, is called in as the government's advocate. This means, however, reserving morality for ourselves and immorality for our neighbour, because he must be thought eager for attack and conquest if our state is forced to consider means of self-defence. – At the same time, by our explanation of our need of an army (because he denies the lust of attack just as our state does, and ostensibly also maintains his army for defensive reasons), we proclaim him a hypocrite and cunning criminal, who would only be too happy to *seize* by surprise, without any fighting, a harmless and unwary victim. In this attitude all states face each other today. They presuppose evil intentions on their neighbour's part and good intentions on their own. This hypothesis, however, is an *inhuman* notion, as bad as and worse than war. Indeed, at bottom it is a challenge and motive to war, foisting as it does upon the neighbouring state the charge of immorality, and thus provoking hostile intentions and acts. The doctrine of the army as a means of self-defence must be abjured as completely as the lust for conquest. Perhaps a memorable day will come when a nation renowned in wars and victories, distinguished by the highest development of military order and intelligence, and accustomed to make the heaviest sacrifice to these objects, will voluntarily exclaim, '*We will break our swords*' and will destroy its whole military system down to its last foundations. *Making ourselves defenceless, after having been the most strongly defended*, from a *loftiness* of sentiment – that is the means towards genuine peace, which must always rest upon a pacific disposition. The so-called armed peace that prevails at present in all countries is a sign of a bellicose disposition, of a disposition that trusts neither itself nor its neighbour and, partly from hate, partly from fear, refuses to lay down its weapons. Better to perish than to hate and fear, and *twice as far better to perish than to make oneself hated and feared* – this must some day become the supreme maxim of every political community! Our liberal representatives of the people, as is well known, have not the time for reflection on the nature of humanity, or else they would know that they are working in vain when they work for 'a gradual reduction of the military burden'. On the contrary, when the distress of this burden is greatest, the sort of God who alone can help here will be nearest. The tree of military glory can only be destroyed at one swoop, with one stroke of lightning. But, as you know, lightning comes from a cloud and from above.

285

Whether property can be reconciled with justice. – When the injustice of property is strongly felt – and the hand of the great clock is once more at this place – we formulate two methods of relieving this injustice: either equal distribution or abolition of private property and a return to state ownership. The latter method is especially dear to the hearts of our socialists, who are angry with that primitive Jew for saying, 'Thou shalt not steal'. In their view the seventh commandment should rather run, 'Thou shalt not possess'. – The former method was frequently tried in antiquity, always indeed on a small scale, and yet with poor success. From this failure we too may learn. 'Equal allotment of land' is easily enough said, but how much bitterness is aroused by the necessary division and separation, by the loss of time-honoured possessions, how much piety is wounded and sacrificed! We uproot the foundation of morality when we uproot boundary-stones. Again, how much acrimony among the new owners, how much envy and jealousy! For there have never been two really equal allotments of land, and if there were, man's envy of his neighbour would prevent him from believing in their equality. And how long would this equality, unhealthy and poisoned at the very roots, endure? In a few generations, by inheritance, here one allotment would come to five owners, there five allotments to one. Even supposing that men acquiesced in such abuses through the enactment of stern laws of inheritance, the same equal allotments would indeed exist, but there would also be needy malcontents, owning nothing but dislike of their relations and neighbours, and longing for a general upheaval. – If, however, by the *second* method we try to restore ownership to the *community* and make the individual but a temporary tenant, we interfere with agriculture. For man is opposed to all that is only a transitory possession, unblessed with his own care and sacrifice. With such property he merely exploits it like a robber or as worthless spendthrift. When Plato declares that egoism would be removed with the abolition of property, we may answer that, if egoism be taken away, man will no longer possess the four cardinal virtues either; as we must say that the most deadly plague could not injure mankind so terribly as if vanity were one day to disappear. Without vanity and egoism what are human virtues? By this I am far from meaning that these virtues are but varied names and masks for these two qualities. Plato's utopian refrain, which is still sung by socialists, rests upon a deficient knowledge of men. He lacked the historical science of moral emotions, the insight into the origin of the good and useful characteristics of the human soul. He believed, like all antiquity, in good and evil as in black and white – that is to say, in a radical difference between good and evil men and good and bad qualities. – In order that property may henceforth inspire more confidence and become more moral, we should keep open all the paths to the accumulation of *moderate* wealth through work, but should prevent the sudden and unearned acquisition of wealth. Accordingly, we should take all the branches of transport and trade which favour the accumulation of *great* wealth, especially, therefore, the money market, out of the hands of private persons or private companies, and look upon those who own too much, just as upon those who own nothing, as types fraught with danger to the community.

286

The value of labour. – If we try to determine the value of labour by the amount of time, industry, good or bad will, constraint, inventiveness or laziness, honesty or make-believe bestowed upon it, the valuation can never be a *just* one. For the whole personality would have to be thrown into the scale, and this is impossible. Here the motto is, 'judge not!' But after all the cry for justice is the cry we now hear from those who are dissatisfied with the present valuation of labour. If we reflect further we find every person non-responsible for his product, the labour; hence *merit* can never be derived from it, and every labour is as good or as bad as it must be through this or that necessary concatenation of forces and weaknesses, abilities and desires. The worker is not at liberty to say *whether* he shall work or not, or to decide *how* he shall work. Only the standpoints of *usefulness*, wider and narrower, have created the valuation of labour. What we at present call justice does very well in this sphere as a highly refined utility, which does not only consider the moment and exploit the immediate opportunity, but looks to the permanence of all conditions, and thus also keeps in view the well-being of the worker, his physical and spiritual contentment: *in order that* he and his posterity may work well for our posterity and become trustworthy for longer periods than the individual span of human life. The *exploitation* of the worker was, as we now understand, a piece of folly, a robbery at the expense of the future, a jeopardising of society. We almost have the war now, and in any case the expense of maintaining peace, of concluding treaties and winning confidence, will henceforth be very great, because the folly of the exploiters was very great and long-lasting.

289

Century-old quarantine. – Democratic institutions are centres of quarantine against the old plague of tyrannical desires. As such they are extremely useful and extremely tedious.

292

The victory of democracy. – All political powers today attempt to exploit the fear of socialism for their own strengthening. Yet in the long run democracy alone gains the advantage, for *all* parties are now compelled to flatter the 'people' and grant them facilities and liberties of all kinds, with the result that the people finally become omnipotent. The people are as far as possible removed from socialism as a doctrine of altering the acquisition of property. If once they get the steering-wheel into their hands, through great majorities in their parliaments, they will attack with progressive taxation the whole dominant system of capitalists, merchants, and financiers, and will in fact slowly create a middle class which may *forget* socialism like a disease that has been overcome. – The practical result of this increasing democratisation will next be a European league of nations, in which each individual nation, delimited by the proper geographical frontiers, has the position of a canton with its separate rights. Small account will be taken of the historic memories of previously existing nations, because the pious affection for these memories will be gradually uprooted under the democratic regime, with all its craze for novelty and experiment. The corrections of frontiers that will prove necessary will be so carried out as to serve the *interests* of the great cantons and at the same time that of the whole federation, but not that of any venerable memories. To find the standpoints for these corrections will be the task of future *diplomats*, who will have to be at the same time students of civilisation, agriculturists and commercial experts, with no armies but motives and utilities at their back. Then only will *foreign* and *domestic* politics be inseparably connected, whereas today the latter follows its proud dictator, and gathers in sorry baskets the stubble that is left over from the harvest of the former.

293

End and means of democracy. – Democracy tries to create and guarantee *independence* for as many as possible in their opinions, way of life and occupation. For this purpose democracy must withhold the political suffrage both from those who have nothing and from those who are really rich, as being the two intolerable classes of men. At the removal of these classes it must always work, because they are continually calling its task in question. In the same way democracy must prevent all measures that seem to aim at party organisation. For the three great enemies of independence, in that threefold sense, are the have-nots, the rich and the parties. I speak of democracy as of something yet to come. What at present goes by that name is distinguished from older forms of government only by the fact that it drives with *new horses*; the roads and the wheels are the same as of old. – Has the danger really become less with *these* conveyances of the commonwealth?

Translated by Paul V. Cohn with modifications

4
The Campaign against Morality, 1881–1885

Preface

In spite of the anti-Socialist Laws of 1878, the socialist movement was not fatally weakened and would continue to expand throughout the decade, its moderate forces content to work through parliamentary channels. In an effort to stem the growth of this movement, Bismarck offered an olive branch to German workers in the form of social welfare legislation, which was announced by Wilhelm I in the Royal Proclamation of November 17, 1881.

These events help to explain Nietzsche's continued preoccupation with socialism and the workers' movement. In *The Gay Science* (1882), Nietzsche provides a direct response to the Kaiser's famous speech announcing the new laws concerning accident and health insurance in the name of 'dignity' of work and the worker. He interprets the speech as indicative of the lack of distance between the workers and 'the most leisurely among us': 'The royal courtesy of the saying "we are all workers" would have been cynical and indecent as recently as the reign of Louis XIV'.[1] Nietzsche was opposed to the *Reich*'s socio-political concessions, believing that they would only contribute to a further radicalisation of the Social Democratic Party instead of quelling revolutionary sentiment. These events also explain why the theme of 'security' becomes so prominent in Nietzsche's work during this period. For example, he writes: 'the Socialists and state-idolaters of Europe could easily bring things to Chinese conditions and to a Chinese "happiness", with their measures for the amelioration and security of life'[2] and remarks elsewhere, that 'security is now worshipped as the supreme goddess'.[3]

The writings of 1881–85 testify to Nietzsche's concern with political life and display his antipathy towards the democratic vision of social equality and technological comfort offered by socialists and welfare-state liberals. The *Dawn* (1881) inaugurates Nietzsche's 'campaign against morality' (i.e. the 'morality that would un-self man' or 'selflessness')[4] and demonstrates how the Christian 'doctrine of the sympathetic affections' has insinuated itself into political life since 'the time of the French Revolution' and now constitutes the 'common ground' of 'all socialistic principles'.[5]

The 'socialist pied pipers',[6] with their collective goals, demand the sacrifice of the individual for the sake of becoming a 'useful member and instrument of the whole', while making workers 'wanton with wild hopes'[7] that one day they will be rescued from their miserable condition by a proletarian revolution. Nietzsche is still concerned that a violent revolution is possible and fears the prospect of sudden change.[8] The workers' desire for revolt in industrial society is explained in terms of the 'lack of a noble presence' in employers, whose vulgarity seems to challenge the very notion of an order of rank, thereby lending credibility to egalitarian ideals. This perception of vulgar 'captains of industry' leads the worker to believe that one's higher station in life is simply a matter of chance and fortune. If these magnates of commerce possessed a 'noble presence', there would be no socialism, Nietzsche argues, since the workers would be willing to 'submit to *slavery* of every kind, provided that the superior class above them constantly shows itself legitimately superior and *born* to command'.[9] Nietzsche considered all involuntarily accepted work (i.e. 'seeking work for the sake of pay') as a form of slavery, while acknowledging that society could not function without 'slaves'.[10]

In addition to this critique of the bourgeois class, Nietzsche offers a solution to the 'social question' and an equally direct contribution to the question of colonisation which focuses on social tensions. If workers, or 'factory slaves', as he calls them, cannot avoid 'becoming soured and malicious and conspiratorial' for being '*used up* as they are, like the parts of a machine', then he proposes that they leave Europe to become masters in some other region of the world and that the depleted workforce resulting from this mass exodus of labour could be solved by importing Chinese workers, 'industrious ants' who 'can be poor and happy'.[11] Nietzsche prefers this solution to the social question because he believes that socialists err in thinking that the workers' independence can be attained through the implementation of higher wages, which were, in fact, increased in 1882, or improved working conditions.

Nietzsche's critique of both the bourgeoisie and socialism and his proposed solutions to the social question still do not address the following challenge: how can aristocratic values emerge in increasingly middle-class and industrialised societies? He places little faith in Germany since the *Reich* has replaced culture with 'the political and national lunacy'.[12] Instead, he looks to the future, eagerly anticipating the coming of an age that will restore 'heroism' and then 'carry heroism into knowledge and wage war for the sake of ideas'. This transition to a 'higher age', he claims, will depend on 'brave preparatory human beings'.[13] Is Zarathustra an example of this 'brave preparatory human being'? His teachings seem to indicate that his task is to prepare the bridge to the Overman.

In the texts of this period Nietzsche often praises individualism, but an individualism that tends to fuse with autocracy, exemplified by autocrats such as Napoleon.[14] Nietzsche's concept of the individual must be qualified by what he means by 'noble' or 'aristocratic' (his reflections on aristocratic culture) and should not be confused with just any tyrant or demagogue. While his exemplary individuals reject universal norms and unconditional duties, they are, nevertheless, 'the seed-bearers of the future, the pioneers of spiritual colonisation and of a new construction of national and social unions'.[15] These individuals are creative artists of government, legislators of new values. But for now the development of the future ruling class Nietzsche foresees is being hindered by 'morality', the 'morality which is now striving with all its power to attain ... that green meadow happiness on earth, which consists in security, absence of danger, ease.... The two doctrines which it preaches most universally are "equality of rights" and "pity for all that suffers".'[16]

Nietzsche's writings of this period show an increased tendency towards class analysis and political psychology. With respect to the latter, he considers the psychology of political communications by way of both reflecting upon the dissimulative tactics of the higher type and the susceptibility of the masses to manipulation.[17] The first will apply to his recommendation for a gradual social transformation utilising existing institutions and the second, which appears to take for granted the irrationality of the lower classes,[18] to precisely what seduces them.

The political commentary that we encounter in *Thus Spoke Zarathustra* (1883–85) is consistent in many respects with Nietzsche's pre-Zarathustran writings. To begin with, Zarathustra regards the 'state', by which he means the modern democratic state, as the 'coldest of all cold monsters'.[19] In what appears to be a reference to Bismarck's 'democracy' (or at least his compromises), Zarathustra says that he has turned his back on today's rulers because they 'traffic and bargain for power – with the rabble'.[20] In opposition to the 'preachers of equality' with their underlying motive of revenge that masquerades as 'justice', Zarathustra offers his own conception of 'justice': 'Men are not equal'.[21] Zarathustra, as the 'adversary of all rabble and despot rule', declares that a *'new nobility'* is needed, but not 'a nobility which you could purchase like shopkeepers with shopkeepers' gold'. It is not the mob that should rule, but 'the best shall rule'.[22] When Zarathustra states that society seeks the ruler 'and *not* a "contract"',[23] he is not referring to the rule of kings (so there is no inkling in Nietzsche for monarchical reformism) for he proclaims: 'What does it now matter about kings!'[24]

Nietzsche's unpublished notes from the period 1883–85 contain some of his most important political insights, which either echo or supplement the views expressed in his published writings. Of particular importance is his declared opposition to socialism 'because it dreams ingenuously of "goodness, truth, beauty and equal rights"' and to 'parliamentary government and the power of the press, because they are the means whereby the herd become masters'.[25]

Although Nietzsche realises that Bismarck introduced universal suffrage as 'merely an expedient to steer clear of temporary difficulties' and that 'parliaments may be very useful to a strong and versatile statesman', he rejects 'universal suffrage', what he derisively refers to as 'the counting mania and the superstitious belief in majorities'.[26] An affirmative political voice seems to be emerging from this critique of popular representation, as Nietzsche declares: 'In this age of *suffrage universel*, in which everybody is allowed to sit in judgement upon everything and everybody, I feel compelled to re-establish *order of rank*'.[27] Universal suffrage represents the 'dominion of *inferior* men' and so 'it is necessary for *higher men* to declare war on the masses!'[28] The higher politics that he envisages is certainly not the Hohenzollern monarchy,[29] but rather a 'United Europe',[30] a concept which conceives of major transformations in international political relations, with England and America considered the danger, and the Slavs, the Jews and the Russians as indispensable allies.[31] This European Union will be forced into existence for economic reasons[32] and will amalgamate into one sovereign power complex 'in order to rule on earth'.[33] It is an idea inspired by Napoleon: 'the coming century will be found following in the footsteps of Napoleon…the man of greatest initiative and advanced views of modern times'.[34] Instrumental to this task will be the '*good Europeans*', described as 'atheists and immoralists',[35] who will prepare the ground for a reversal of values, which necessarily implies a material alteration of power relationships,[36] and negates 'the methods of "popular representation" and parliaments'),[37] but who know that 'for the present', it will be necessary to 'support the religions and the moralities of the herd instinct', since democratic Europe enhances weakness of will, it produces a trainable, intelligent, adaptive, herd animal, who will fall into the hands of the 'legislators of the future'.[38] What lies beyond Nietzsche's repudiation of socialism, the workers' movement, the parliamentary system of government and universal suffrage is an aristocratic radicalism that will provide the industrial age with the conditions necessary for producing a new elitist order.

Dawn: Thoughts on the Prejudices of Morality, 1881

71

The Christian vengeance against Rome. – Perhaps nothing is more fatiguing than the sight of a continual conqueror: for more than two hundred years the world had seen Rome overcoming one nation after another, the circle was closed, the whole future seemed to be fixed, everything was done with a view to its lasting for all time – when the Empire *built* anything it was erected with a view to being '*aere perennius*'. We, who know only the 'melancholy of ruins', can scarcely understand that totally different *melancholy of eternal construction*, from which men endeavoured to save themselves as best they could – with the light-hearted fancy of a Horace, for example. Others sought different consolations for the weariness which was closely akin to despair, against the deadening knowledge that from henceforth all progress of thought and heart would be hopeless, that the huge spider sat everywhere and mercilessly continued to drink all the blood within its reach, no matter where it might spring forth. This mute, century-old hatred of the wearied spectators against Rome, wherever Rome's domination extended, was at length vented in *Christianity*, which united Rome, 'the world' and 'sin' into a *single* conception. The Christians took their revenge on Rome by proclaiming the immediate and sudden destruction of the world; by once more introducing a future – for Rome had been able to transform everything into the history of its *own* past and present – a future in which Rome was no longer the most important factor; and by dreaming of the Last *Judgement* – while the crucified *Jew*, as the symbol of salvation, was the greatest derision on the superb provincial Roman governors, for now they seemed to be only the symbols of ruin and a 'world' ready to perish.

105

Pseudo-egoism. – The great majority of people, whatever they may think and say about their 'egoism', do nothing for their ego all their life long, but only for a phantom of this ego which has been formed in regard to them by their friends and communicated to them. As a consequence, they all live in a haze of impersonal and semi-personal opinions and of arbitrary and, as it were, poetic valuations: the one always in the head of another, and this head, again, in the head of somebody else – a queer world of phantasms which manages to give itself a rational appearance! This haze of opinions and habits grows in extent and lives almost independently of the people it surrounds; it is this haze which gives rise to the immense effect of general judgements on 'man' – all those men, who do not know themselves, believe in a bloodless abstraction which they call 'man', i.e. in a fiction; and every change caused in this abstraction by the judgements of powerful individualities (such as princes and philosophers) produces an extraordinary and irrational effect on the great majority – for the simple reason that not a single individual in this haze can oppose a real ego, an ego which is accessible to and fathomed by himself, to the universal pale fiction, which he could thereby destroy.

108

Some theses. – We should not give the individual, *insofar* as he desires his own happiness, any prescriptions or recommendations as to the road leading to happiness; for individual happiness arises from particular laws that are unknown to anybody, and it will only be hindered or obstructed by recommendations which come to him from outside sources. Those prescriptions which are called 'moral' are in reality directed against individuals and do not by any means want the happiness of such individuals. Th[e relation]ship of these prescriptions to the 'happiness and well-being of man[kind is] equally slight, it is even impossible to tie definite concepts to these words; still less can they be employed as guiding stars on the dark sea of moral aspirations. – It is a prejudice to think that morality is more favourable to the development of reason than immorality. – It is erroneous to suppose that the *unconscious aim* in the development of every conscious being (namely, animal, man, humanity, etc.) is its 'greatest happiness': on the contrary, there is a particular and incomparable happiness to be attained at every stage of our development, one that is neither high nor low, but a specific happiness. Evolution does not make happiness its goal; it aims merely at evolution and nothing else. – It is only if humanity had a universally recognised *goal* that we could propose 'thus and thus is the *right* course of action': for the time being there is no such goal. It follows that the pretensions of morality should not be brought into any relationship with mankind: this would be merely childish and irrational. – It is quite another thing to *recommend* a goal to mankind: this goal would then be something that would *depend on our own will* and pleasure. Provided that mankind in general agreed to adopt such a goal, it could then *impose* a moral law on itself, a law which would, at all events, be imposed at will. Up to now, however, the moral law has had to be placed *above* our own likes and dislikes: strictly speaking, men did not wish to *impose* this law on themselves; they wished to take it from somewhere, to *discover* it or to *let themselves be commanded by it* from somewhere.

112

On the natural history of rights and duties. – Our duties – are the rights of others over us. How have they acquired such rights? By taking us to be capable of contracting and of requiting, by positing us as similar and equal to them, and as a consequence entrusting us with something, educating, reproving, supporting us. We fulfil our duty – that is to say: we justify the idea of our power on the basis of which all these things were bestowed upon us, we give back in the measure in which we have been given to. It is thus our pride which bids us do our duty – when we do something for others in return for something they have done for us, what we are doing is restoring our self-regard – for in doing something for us, these others have impinged upon our sphere of power and would have continued to have a hand in it if we did not with the performance of our 'duty' practise a requital, that is to say impinge upon their power. The rights of others can relate only to that which lies within our power; it would be unreasonable if they wanted of us something we did not possess. Expressed more precisely: only to that which they believe lies within our power, provided it is the same thing we believe lies within our power. The same error could easily be made on either side: the feeling of duty depends upon our having the same *belief* in regard to the extent of our power as others have: that is to say, that we are able to promise certain things and bind ourselves to perform them ('freedom of will'). – My rights – consist of that part of my power which others have not only conceded to me, but which they wish me to preserve. How do these others arrive at that? First: through their prudence and fear and caution: whether in that they expect something similar from us in return (protection of their own rights); or in that they consider that a struggle with us would be perilous or to no purpose; or in that they see in any diminution of our force a disadvantage to themselves, since we would then be unsuited to forming an alliance with them in opposition to a hostile third power. *Then*: by donation and cession. In this case, others have enough and more than enough power to be able to dispose of some of it and to guarantee to him they have given it to the portion of it they have given: in doing so they presuppose a feeble sense of power in him who lets himself be thus donated to. That is how rights originate: recognised and guaranteed degrees of power. If power relationships undergo any material alteration, rights disappear and new ones are created – as is demonstrated in the continual disappearance and reformation of rights between nations. If our power is materially diminished, the feeling of those who have hitherto guaranteed our rights changes: they consider whether they can restore us to the full possession we formerly enjoyed – if they feel unable to do so, they henceforth deny our 'rights'. Likewise, if our power is materially increased, the feeling of those who have hitherto recognised it but whose recognition is no longer needed changes: they no doubt attempt to suppress it to its former level, they will try to intervene and in doing so will allude to their 'duty' – but this is only a futile playing with words. Where rights *prevail*, a certain condition and degree of power is being maintained, a diminution and increment warded off. The rights of others constitute a concession on the part of our sense of power to the sense of power of those others. If our power appears to be deeply shaken and broken, our rights cease to exist: conversely, if we have grown very much more powerful, the rights of others, as we have previously conceded them, cease to exist for us. – The 'man who wants to be fair' is in constant need of the subtle tact of a balance: he must be able to assess degrees of power and rights, which, given the transitory nature of human things, will never stay in equilibrium for very long but will usually be rising or sinking: – being fair is consequently difficult and demands much practise and good will, and very much very good *sense*. –

132

The echo of Christianity in morality. – 'On n'est bon que par la pitié: il faut donc qu'il y ait quelque pitié dans tous nos sentiments' – so says morality nowadays! And how does this come about? The fact that the man who performs social, sympathetic, disinterested and benevolent actions is now considered as the *moral* man: this is perhaps the most general effect, the most complete transformation that Christianity has produced in Europe; perhaps in spite of itself and not by any means because this was part of its essential doctrine.

But this was the residuum of those Christian feelings that prevailed at the time when the contrary and thoroughly selfish faith in the 'one thing needful', the absolute importance of eternal and *personal* salvation, together with the dogmas upon which this belief had rested, were gradually receding, and when the auxiliary beliefs in 'love' and 'love of one's neighbour', harmonising with the extraordinary practice of charity by the Church, were thereby coming to the front. The more people gradually became separated from the dogmas, the more did they seek some sort of *justification* for this separation in a cult of the love of humanity: not to fall short in this respect of the Christian ideal, but to excel it if possible, was the secret stimulus of all the French free-thinkers from Voltaire to Auguste Comte; and this latter with his famous moral formula *vivre pour autrui* has indeed out-Christianised even Christianity! It was Schopenhauer in Germany and John Stuart Mill in England who were the means of bringing into the greatest prominence this doctrine of sympathetic affections and of pity or utility to others as a principle of action; but these men themselves were only echoes. From about the time of the French Revolution these doctrines have manifested themselves in various places with enormous force. Since then they have shown themselves in their coarsest as well as their most subtle form, and all socialistic principles have almost involuntarily taken their stand on the common ground of this doctrine. At the present time there is perhaps no more widely spread prejudice than that of thinking that we *know* what really and truly constitutes morality. Everyone now seems to learn with *satisfaction* that society is beginning to *adapt* the individual to the general needs, and that it is *at the same time the happiness and sacrifice of each one* to consider himself as a useful member and instrument of the whole. They have still, however, doubts as to the form in which this whole is to be looked for, whether in a state already existing, or in one which has yet to be established, or in a nation, or in an international brotherhood, or in new and small economic communities. On this point there is still much reflection, doubt, struggling, excitement and passion; but it is pleasant and wonderful to observe the unanimity with which the ego is called upon to practise self-denial, until, in the form of adaptation to the whole, it once again secures its own fixed sphere of rights and duties – until, indeed, it has become something quite new and different. Nothing else is being attempted, whether admitted or not, than the complete transformation, even the weakening and suppression of the *individual*: the supporters of the majority never tire of enumerating and anathematising all that is bad, hostile, lavish, expensive and luxurious in the form of individual existence that has hitherto prevailed; they hope that society may be administered in a cheaper, less dangerous, more uniform and more harmonious way when nothing is left but *large bodies and their members*. All that is considered as *good* which in any way corresponds to this desire for grouping men into one particular society and to the minor cravings which necessarily accompany this desire – this is the chief *moral current* of our time; sympathy and social feelings are working hand in glove. (Kant is still outside of this movement: he expressly teaches that we should be insensible to the sufferings of others if our benevolence is to have any moral value – a doctrine which Schopenhauer, very angrily, as may easily be imagined, described as *Kantian absurdity*.)

146

Looking beyond our neighbour. – What? Ought the nature of true morality to consist for us in fixing our eyes on the most direct and immediate consequences of our action for other people and in our coming to a decision accordingly? This is only a narrow and bourgeois morality even though it may be a morality: but it seems to me that it would be a higher and freer viewpoint to *look beyond* these immediate consequences for our neighbour in order to encourage more distant purposes, *even at the risk of making others suffer* – as, for example, by encouraging the spirit of knowledge in spite of the certainty that our free thought will have the instant effect of plunging others into doubt, grief and even worse afflictions. Have we not at least the right to treat our neighbour as we treat ourselves? And if, where we are concerned, we do not think in such a narrow and bourgeois fashion of immediate consequences and sufferings, why *should* we be compelled to act thus in regard to our neighbour? Supposing that we felt ready to sacrifice ourselves, what is there to prevent us from sacrificing our neighbour together with ourselves – just as states and princes have hitherto sacrificed one citizen to the others, 'for the sake of the general interest' as they say? We too, however, have general interests, perhaps even more general than theirs: so why may we not sacrifice a few individuals of this generation for the benefit of generations to come? So that their affliction, anxiety, despair, blunders and misery may be deemed essential because a new plough is to break up the ground and render it fertile for all. Finally, we communicate the disposition to our neighbour by which he is enabled to *feel himself a victim*: we persuade him to carry out the task for which we employ him. Are we then devoid of all pity? If, however, we wish to achieve a victory over ourselves *beyond our pity*, is this not a higher and freer viewpoint and disposition than that in which we only feel safe after having ascertained whether an action *benefits or harms* our neighbour? On the contrary, it is by means of such sacrifice – including the sacrifice of ourselves *and our neighbour* – that we should strengthen and elevate the general sense of human *power*, even supposing that we attain nothing more than this. But even this itself would be a positive increase of *happiness*. Then, if even this – but not a word more! A glance is enough; you have understood me.

164

Perhaps premature. – It would seem at the present time that, under many different and misleading names, and often with a great want of clarity, those who do not feel themselves attached to morals and to established laws are taking the first initial steps to organise themselves and thus to create a *right* for themselves; while hitherto, as criminals, free-thinkers, immoral men and miscreants, they have lived beyond the pale of the law, under the ban of outlawry and bad conscience, corrupted and corrupting. On the whole, we should consider this as *right and proper*, although it may result in insecurity for the coming century and compel everyone to bear arms. – There is thereby a counterforce which continually reminds us that there is no morality that alone makes moral, and every ethic that affirms itself exclusively destroys too much good strength and costs humanity too dearly. The deviants, who are so often the inventive and fruitful ones, must no longer be sacrificed: it must never again be considered infamous to deviate from morality either in thought or actions; many new experiments of life and society must be made, and the world must be relieved from a tremendous burden of bad conscience. These general aims must be recognised and promoted by all who are honest and seek truth!

173

Those who commend work. – Behind the glorification of 'work' and the tireless talk of the 'blessings of work', I see the same covert ideas as in the praise of useful impersonal actions: the fear of everything individual. Fundamentally, one now feels when confronted with work – and what is meant is relentless industry from early till late – that such work is the best policeman, that it keeps everyone in bounds and can powerfully hinder the development of reason, of covetousness, of the desire for independence. For it uses up an extraordinary amount of nervous energy, which is thus denied to reflection, brooding, dreaming, worrying, loving, hating; it always sets a small goal in sight and guarantees easy and regular satisfactions. Thus a society in which there is continual hard work will have more security: and security is now worshipped as the supreme goddess. – And now! Horror! It is precisely the 'worker' who has become *dangerous*! The place is swarming with 'dangerous individuals'! And behind them, the danger of dangers – *the* individual!

174

Moral fashion of a commercial society. – Behind the principle of the present moral fashion: 'moral actions are actions performed out of sympathy for others', I see the social instinct of fear, which thus assumes an intellectual disguise: this instinct sets forth as its supreme, most important and most immediate principle that life shall be relieved of *all the dangerous characteristics* which it possessed in former times and that *everyone* must help with all his might towards the attainment of this end. It is for that reason that only those actions which keep in view the general security are called 'good'! – How little pleasure men must nowadays take in themselves when such a tyranny of fear prescribes their supreme moral law, if they make no objection when commanded to turn their eyes from themselves and to look away from themselves! And yet at the same time they have lynx-eyes for all the distress and suffering that exists elsewhere! Are we not, with this tremendous intention of ours of smoothing down every sharp edge of life, well on the way to turning mankind into *sand*? Sand! Small, soft, round, infinite sand! Is that your ideal, you heralds of the sympathetic affections? – In the meantime, the question itself remains unanswered whether we are of *more use* to our neighbour by immediately rushing to his side and *helping* him – which for the most part can only be done in a very superficial way, as otherwise it would become a tyrannical meddling and transforming – or by *creating* something out of ourselves which our neighbour can look upon with pleasure – something, for example, which may be compared to a beautiful, quiet and secluded garden, protected by high walls against storms and the dust of the roads, but likewise with a hospitable gate.

175

Fundamental idea of a commercial culture. – We have now an opportunity of watching the manifold growth of the culture of a society of which commerce is the soul, just as personal competition was the soul of culture among the ancient Greeks, and war, conquest and law among the ancient Romans. The tradesman is able to value everything without producing it, and to value it according to the requirements of the consumer rather than his own personal needs. 'How many and what class of people will consume this?' is his question of questions. Hence, he instinctively and incessantly employs this mode of valuation and applies it to everything, including the productions of art and science, and of thinkers, scholars, artists, statesmen, nations, political parties and even entire ages: with respect to everything produced or created he inquires into the supply and demand in order to estimate for himself the value of a thing. This, when once it has been made the principle of an entire culture, worked out to its most minute and subtle details, and imposed on every kind of will and knowledge, this is what you men of the coming century will be proud of – if the prophets of the commercial classes are right in putting that century into your possession! But I have little belief in these prophets. *Credat Judaeus Apella* – to speak with Horace.

179

As little state as possible! – All political and economic arrangements are not worth it, that precisely the most gifted spirits should not be permitted, or even obliged, to manage them: such a waste of spirit is at bottom worse than having none at all. These are and remain fields of work for lesser heads, and others than lesser heads ought not to be in the service of these workshops: better for the machinery to fall to pieces again! But as things now stand, with everybody believing he is obliged to *know* what is taking place here every day and neglecting his own work in order to be continually participating in it, the whole arrangement has become a great and ludicrous piece of insanity. The price being paid for 'general security' is much too high: and the most insane thing is that what is being produced is the very opposite of general security, a fact our dear century is undertaking to demonstrate: as if demonstration were needed! To make society secure against thieves and fireproof and infinitely amenable to every kind of trade and traffic, and to transform the state into a kind of providence in the good and bad sense – these are lower, mediocre and in no way indispensable goals which ought not to be pursued by means of the highest instruments *which in any way exist* – instruments which ought to be *reserved* for the highest and rarest objectives! Our age may talk about economy but it is in fact a squanderer: it squanders what is most precious, the spirit.

183

The old and the young. – 'There is something immoral about parliaments' – so many people still think – 'for in them views even *against* the government may be expressed'. – 'We should always adopt that view of a subject which our gracious lord commands' – this is the eleventh commandment in many an honest old head, especially in northern Germany. We laugh at it as an out-of-date fashion, but in former times it was morality itself! Perhaps we shall again some day laugh at that which is now considered as moral by a generation brought up under a parliamentary regime, namely, the policy of placing one's party before one's own wisdom and of answering every question concerning the public welfare in such a way as to fill the sails of the party with a favourable gust of wind. 'We must take that view of a subject which the position of our party calls for' – such would be the canon. In the service of such morals we may now behold every kind of sacrifice, even martyrdom and conquest over one's self.

184

The state as a product of the anarchists. – In countries inhabited by tractable men there are always a few backsliders and intractable people. For the present the latter have joined the socialists more than any other party. If it should happen that these people should one day lay down *laws*, then they may be relied upon to put themselves in iron chains and to practise a dreadful discipline: – *they know themselves*! And they will endure these harsh laws with the knowledge that they themselves have imposed them – the feeling of power, and of *this* particular power will be too recent among them and too attractive for them not to suffer anything for its sake.

188

Stimulants and food. – Nations are deceived so often because they are always *searching* for a deceiver, i.e. a stimulating wine for their senses. When they can only have *that*, they are glad to put up even with bad bread. Intoxication is to them more than nourishment – this is the bait with which they always let themselves be caught! What, to them, are men chosen from among themselves – although they may be the most expert specialists – as compared with the brilliant conquerors, or ancient and magnificent princely houses! In order that he may inspire them with faith, the demagogue must at least exhibit to them a prospect of conquest and splendour. People will always obey, and even do more than obey, provided that they can become intoxicated in doing so. We may not even offer them repose and pleasure without this laurel wreath and its maddening influence. This vulgar taste which ascribes *greater importance to intoxication than food* did not by any means originate in the lower ranks of the population: it was, on the contrary, transplanted there, and on this backward soil it grows in great abundance, while its real origin must be sought amongst the highest intellects, where it flourished for millennia. The people are the last *virgin soil* on which this brilliant weed can grow. Well, then, is it really to the people that we should entrust politics in order that they may thereby have their daily intoxication?

189

On grand politics. – Whatever may be the influence in grand politics of utilitarianism and the vanity of individuals and nations, the sharpest spur which urges them onwards is their *need for the feeling of power* – a need which rises not only in the souls of princes and rulers, but also gushes forth from time to time from inexhaustible sources in the people. The time comes again and again when the masses are *ready* to stake their lives and their fortunes, their consciences and their virtue, in order that they may secure that highest of all enjoyments and rule as a victorious, tyrannical and arbitrary nation over other nations (or at all events think that they rule). On occasions such as these, feelings of prodigality, sacrifice, hope, confidence, extraordinary audacity and enthusiasm will erupt so abundantly that a prince who is ambitious or far-sighted will be able to seize the opportunity for waging war, counting on the good conscience of his people to hide his injustice. Great conquerors have always given utterance to the pathetic language of virtue; they have always been surrounded by masses who felt themselves, as it were, in a state of exaltation and would listen to none but the most elevated oratory. The strange madness of moral judgements! When man experiences the feeling of power he feels and calls himself *good*; and at exactly the same time the others who have to *endure* his power call him *evil*! – Hesiod, in his fable of the epochs of mankind, has twice in succession depicted the same epoch, that of the heroes of Homer, and has thus made *two epochs out of one*: to those who lived under the terrible iron heel of those adventurous brutes [*Gewaltmenschen*], or had heard their ancestors speak of them, the epoch appeared to be *evil*; but the descendants of those chivalric races worshipped it as the *good* old times and as an almost ideally blissful age. The poet could thus not help doing what he did – his audience probably included the descendants of both races!

190

Former German culture. – When the Germans began to interest other European nations, which is not so very long ago, it was owing to a culture which they no longer possess today, and which they have indeed shaken off with a blind ardour, as if it had been some disease; and yet they have not been able to replace it by anything better than the political and national lunacy. They have in this way succeeded in becoming even more interesting to other nations than they were formerly through their culture: and may that satisfy them! It is nevertheless undeniable that this German culture has fooled Europeans and that it did not deserve the interest shown in it, and much less the imitation and emulation displayed by other nations in trying to rival it.

Let us look back for a moment to Schiller, Wilhelm von Humboldt, Schleiermacher, Hegel and Schelling; let us read their correspondence and mingle for a time with the large circle of their followers: what have they in common, what characteristics have they, that fill us, as we are now, partly with a feeling of nausea and partly with pitiful and touching emotions? First and foremost, the passion for appearing at all costs to be morally *exalted*, and then the desire for giving utterance to brilliant, feeble and inconsequential remarks, together with their intention of seeing everything (characters, passions, ages, customs) as beautiful – 'beautiful', unfortunately, in accordance with a bad and vague taste, which nevertheless pretended to be of Hellenic origin. We behold in these people a weak, good-natured and glistening idealism, which, above all, wished to exhibit noble attitudes and noble voices, something at once presumptuous and inoffensive, and animated by a cordial aversion to 'cold' or 'dry' reality – as also to anatomy, complete passions and every kind of philosophical temperance and scepticism, but especially towards natural science insofar as it was impossible to use it as religious symbolism. Goethe, in his own characteristic fashion, observed from afar these movements of German culture: placing himself beyond their influence, gently remonstrating, silent, more and more confirmed in his own better course. A little later, Schopenhauer also was an observer of these movements – a great deal of the world and devilry of the world had again been revealed to him and he spoke of it both roughly and enthusiastically, for there is a certain *beauty* in this devilry! And what was it, then, that really seduced the foreigners and prevented them from viewing this movement as did Goethe and Schopenhauer, or better, from ignoring it altogether? It was that dull lustre, that inexplicable starlight which formed a mysterious halo around this culture. The foreigners said to themselves: 'This is all very, very remote from us; our sight, hearing, understanding, enjoyment and powers of valuations are lost here, but in spite of that there may be some stars! There may be something in it! Is it possible that the Germans have quietly discovered some corner of heaven and settled there? We must try to come nearer to these Germans.' So they did begin to come nearer to the Germans, while not so very long afterwards the Germans put themselves to some trouble to get rid of this starlight halo: they knew only too well that they had not been in heaven – but only in a cloud!

200

Endurance of poverty. – There is one great advantage in noble extraction: it makes us endure poverty better.

201

The future of the nobility. – The demeanour of the nobility shows that in all the members of their body the consciousness of power is continually playing its fascinating game. Thus people of aristocratic habits, men or women, never sink worn out into a chair; when everyone else makes himself comfortable, as in a train, for example, they avoid reclining at their ease; they do not appear to get tired after standing at court for hours at a stretch; they do not furnish their houses in a comfortable manner, but in such a way as to produce the impression of something grand and imposing, as if they had to serve as a residence for greater (and taller) beings; they reply to a provocative speech with dignity and clarity of mind, and not as if scandalised, crushed, shamed or breathless in the plebeian fashion. As the aristocrat is able to preserve the appearance of being possessed of a superior physical force which never leaves him, he likewise wishes by his aspect of constant serenity and civility of disposition, even in the most trying circumstances, to convey the impression that his soul and spirit are equal to all dangers and surprises. A noble culture may resemble, so far as passions are concerned, either a horseman who takes pleasure in making his proud and fiery animal trot in the Spanish fashion – we have only to recollect the age of Louis XIV – or the rider who feels his horse dart away with him like a force of nature, to such a degree that both horse and rider come near losing their heads, but, owing to the enjoyment of the delight, do keep very clear heads: in both these cases this aristocratic culture breathes power, and if very often in its customs only the appearance of the feeling of power is required, nevertheless the real sense of superiority continues constantly to increase as the result of the impression which this display makes upon those who are not aristocrats. This indisputable happiness of aristocratic culture, based as it is on the feeling of superiority, is now beginning to rise to ever higher levels; for now, thanks to the free spirits, it is henceforth permissible and not dishonourable for people who have been born and reared in aristocratic circles to enter the domain of knowledge, where they may secure more intellectual consecrations and learn knightly duties even higher than those of former times, and where they may look up to that ideal of *victorious wisdom* which as yet no age has been able to set before itself with so good a conscience as the period which is about to dawn. Lastly, what is to be the occupation of the nobility in the future if it becomes more evident from day to day that it is *indecent* to take any part in politics?

204

Danäe and god in gold. – Whence arises this excessive impatience in our day which turns men into criminals even in circumstances which would be more likely to bring about the contrary tendency? What induces one man to use false weights, another to set his house on fire after having insured it for more than its value, a third to take part in counterfeiting, while three-fourths of our upper classes indulge in legalised fraud and suffer from the pangs of conscience that follow speculation and dealings on the stock exchange: what gives rise to all this? It is not real want – for their existence is by no means precarious; perhaps they have even enough to eat and drink without worrying – but they are urged on day and night by a terrible impatience at seeing their wealth pile up so slowly, and by an equally terrible longing and love for these heaps of gold. In this impatience and love, however, we see reappear once more that fanaticism of the *lust for power* which was stimulated in former times by the belief that we were in the possession of truth, a fanaticism which bore such beautiful names that we could dare to be inhuman *with a good conscience* (burning Jews, heretics and good books, and exterminating entire cultures superior to ours, such as those of Peru and Mexico). The means of this desire for power are changed in our day, but the same volcano is still smouldering, impatience and intemperate love call for their victims, and what was once done 'for the love of God' is now done for the love of money, i.e. for the love of that which *at present* affords us the highest feeling of power and good conscience.

205

The people of Israel. – One of the spectacles which the next century will invite us to witness is the decision regarding the fate of the European Jews. It is quite obvious now that they have cast their die and crossed their Rubicon: the only thing that remains for them is either to become masters of Europe or to lose Europe, as they once centuries ago lost Egypt, where they were confronted with similar alternatives. In Europe, however, they have gone through a schooling of eighteen centuries such as no other nation has ever undergone, and the experiences of this dreadful probationary period have benefited not only the Jewish community but, even to a greater extent, the individual. As a consequence of this, the resourcefulness of the modern Jews, in both mind and soul, is extraordinary. Amongst all the inhabitants of Europe it is the Jews least of all who try to escape from any deep distress by recourse to drink or to suicide, as other less gifted people are so prone to do. Every Jew can find in the history of his own family and of his ancestors a long record of instances of the greatest coolness and perseverance amid difficulties and dreadful situations, an artful cunning in fighting with misfortune and chance. And above all it is their bravery under the cloak of wretched submission, their heroic *spernere se sperni* that surpasses the virtues of all the saints. People wished to make them contemptible by treating them contemptibly for nearly twenty centuries and refusing them access to all honourable positions and dignities, and by pushing them further down into the meaner trades – and under this process indeed they have not become any cleaner. But contemptible? They have never ceased for a moment from believing themselves qualified for the very highest functions, nor have the virtues of the suffering ever ceased to adorn them. Their manner of honouring their parents and children, the rationality of their marriages and marriage customs, distinguishes them amongst all Europeans. Besides this, they have been able to create for themselves a sense of power and eternal vengeance from the very trades that were left to them (or to which they were abandoned). Even in extenuation of their usury we cannot help saying that, without this occasional pleasant and useful torture inflicted on their scorners, they would have experienced difficulty in preserving their self-respect for so long. For our self-respect depends on our ability to make reprisals in both good and bad things. Nevertheless, their revenge never urges them on too far, for they all have that liberty of mind, and even of soul, produced in men by frequent changes of place, climate and customs of neighbours and oppressors, they possess by far the greatest experience in all human intercourse, and even in their passions they exercise the caution which this experience has developed in them. They are so certain of their intellectual versatility and shrewdness that they never, even when reduced to the direst straits, have to earn their bread by manual labour as common workmen, porters, or farm hands. In their manners we can still see that they have never been inspired by chivalric and noble feelings, or that their bodies have ever been girt with fine weapons: a certain obtrusiveness alternates with a submissiveness which is often tender and almost always painful. Now, however, that they unavoidably intermarry more and more year after year with the finest nobility of Europe, they will soon have a considerable heritage of good intellectual and physical manners, so that in another hundred years they will appear sufficiently noble not to make those they dominate *ashamed* to have them as masters. And this is what is important! And therefore a settlement of the question is still premature! They themselves know very well that the conquest of Europe or any act of violence is not to be thought of; but they also know that some day or other Europe may, like a ripe fruit, drop into their hands, if they do not clutch at it too eagerly. In the meantime, it is necessary for them to distinguish themselves in all departments of European distinction and to stand in the front rank: until they shall have advanced so far as to determine themselves what distinction shall mean. Then they will be called the pioneers and guides of the Europeans whose modesty they will no longer offend. And then where shall an outlet be found for this abundant wealth of great impressions accumulated during such an extended period and representing Jewish history for every Jewish family, this wealth of passions, virtues, resolutions, resignations, struggles and conquests of all kinds – where can it find an outlet but in great intellectual men and works! On the day when the Jews will be able to exhibit to us as their own work such jewels and golden vessels as no European nation, with its shorter and less profound experience, can or could produce, when Israel shall have changed its eternal vengeance into an eternal benediction for Europe: then that seventh day will once more appear when the ancient Jewish God may *rejoice* in himself, in his creation, in his chosen people – and all, all of us, will rejoice with him!

206

The impossible class. – Poor, happy and independent! – that is possible together: Poor, happy and a slave! – that is possible too. And I can think of no better news I could give to our factory slaves: provided they do not consider it altogether *shameful* to be *used up* as they are, like the parts of a machine, and in a sense as stopgaps of human inventiveness! To the devil with the belief that higher pay could abolish the *essence* of their miserable condition – I mean their impersonal serfdom! To the devil with the idea of being persuaded into thinking that an increase in this impersonality, within the mechanical operation of a new society, could transform the shame of slavery into a virtue! To the devil with setting a price for which one remains a person no longer but becomes a part of a machine! Are you accomplices in the current folly of nations – the folly of wanting above all to produce as much as possible and to become as rich as possible? What you ought to do, rather, is to hold up to them the counter-calculation: how great a sum of *inner* value is thrown away in pursuit of this external goal! But where is your inner value if you no longer know what it is to breathe freely? If you no longer possess the slightest control over yourselves? If you all too often grow weary of yourselves, as of a stale drink? If you pay heed to the newspapers and leer at your wealthy neighbour, made covetous by the rapid rise and fall of power, money and opinions? If you no longer believe in philosophy that wears rags, in the candour of those without needs? If voluntary poverty and freedom from profession and marriage, such as would well suit the more spiritual among you, has become to you a laughingstock? Do your ears ring from the pipes of the socialist pied pipers, who want to make you wanton with wild hopes? Who bid you *to be prepared* and nothing further, prepared day upon day, so that you wait and wait for something to happen from outside, and in all other respects go on living as you have always lived – until this waiting turns to hunger and thirst and fever and madness, and at last the day of the *bestia triumphans* dawns in all its glory? – In contrast to all this, everyone ought to say to himself: 'better to go abroad, to seek to become *master* in new and savage regions of the world and above all master over myself; to keep moving from place to place for just as long as any sign of slavery seems to threaten me; to shun neither adventure nor war and, if the worst should come to the worst, to be prepared for death: all this rather than further to endure this indecent serfdom, rather than to go on becoming soured and malicious and conspiratorial!' This would be the right attitude of mind: the workers in Europe should declare that henceforth *as a class* they are a human impossibility, and not only, as is customary, a harsh and purposeless social arrangement. They should introduce an era of a vast swarming out from the European beehive, the like of which has never been seen before, and with this act of emigration in the grand manner protest against the machine, against capital and against the choice with which they are now threatened of becoming of *necessity* either slaves of the state or slaves of a revolutionary party. Let Europe be relieved of a fourth part of its inhabitants! They and it will be all the better for it! Only in distant lands and in the undertakings of swarming trains of colonists will it really become clear how much reason and fairness, how much healthy mistrust, mother Europe has embodied in her sons – sons who could no longer endure it with the dull old woman and were in danger of becoming as querulous, irritable and pleasure-seeking as she herself was. Outside of Europe the virtues of Europe will go on their wanderings with these workers; and that which was at home beginning to degenerate into dangerous discontent and criminal tendencies will, once outside, acquire a wild beautiful naturalness and be called heroism. – Thus a cleaner air would at last waft over old, over-populated and self-absorbed Europe! No matter if its 'workforce' should be a little depleted! Perhaps it may then be recalled that we grew accustomed to needing many things only when these needs became so *easy* to satisfy – we shall again relinquish some of them! Perhaps we shall also bring in numerous *Chinese*: and they will bring with them the modes of life and thought suitable to industrious ants. Indeed, they might as a whole contribute to the blood of restless and fretful Europe something of Asiatic calm and contemplativeness and – what is probably needed most – Asiatic *perseverance*.

245

The subtlety of the feeling of power. – Napoleon was greatly mortified at the fact that he could not speak well and he did not deceive himself in this respect: but his thirst for power, which never despised the slightest opportunity of showing itself, and which was still subtler than his subtle intellect, led him to speak even worse *than he could*. It was in this way that he revenged himself upon his own mortification (he was jealous of all his emotions because they possessed *power*) in order to enjoy his autocratic *pleasure*. He enjoyed this pleasure a second time in respect to the ears and judgement of his audience, as if it were good enough for them to be addressed in this way. He even secretly enjoyed the thought of bewildering their judgement and good taste by the thunder and lightning of his highest authority – that authority which lies in the union of power and genius – while both his judgement and his good taste held fast proudly and indifferently to the truth that he did not speak well. – Napoleon, as the complete and fully developed type of a single instinct, belongs to the mankind of antiquity whose characteristic – the simple construction and ingenious development and realisation of a single motif or of a few motifs – may be easily enough recognised in him.

262

The demon of power. – Neither necessity nor desire but the love of power is the demon of mankind. You may give men everything possible – health, food, shelter, entertainment – but they are and remain unhappy and capricious, for the demon lies in wait, and must be satisfied. Let everything else be taken away from them, and let this demon be satisfied, and then they will nearly be happy – as happy men and demons can be; but why do I repeat this? Luther has already said it, and better than I have done, in the verses: 'Let them take from us our body, goods, honour, children, wife: let it all go – the kingdom must yet remain to us!' Yes! Yes! The *'Reich'*!

272

The purification of the race. – It is probable that there are no pure races, but only races which have become purified, and even these are extremely rare. We more often meet with mixed races, among whom, together with the defects in the harmony of the bodily forms (for example, when the eyes do not accord with the mouth) we necessarily always find defects of harmony in habits and appreciations. (Livingstone heard someone say, 'God created white and black men, but the devil created the half-breeds.') Mixed races are always at the same time cross-cultures and cross-moralities: they are, as a rule, more evil, cruel and restless. Purity is the final result of innumerable adjustments, absorptions and eliminations; and progress towards purity in a race is shown by the fact that the latent strength in the race is more and more *restricted* to a few special functions, while it formerly had to carry out too many and often contradictory things. Such a restriction will always have the appearance of an *impoverishment*, and must be judged with prudence and moderation. In the long run, however, when the process of purification has come to a successful termination, all those forces which were formerly wasted in the struggle between the disharmonious qualities are at the disposal of the organism as a whole, and this is why purified races have always become *stronger* and *more beautiful*. – The Greeks may serve us as a model of a purified race and culture! – and it is to be hoped that some day a pure European race and culture may arise.

298

Hero worship and its fanatics. – The fanatic of an ideal that possesses flesh and blood is usually in the right so long as he *denies*, and in this he is usually right: he knows what he denies as well as he knows himself, for the simple reason that he comes from there, feels at home there, and has always the secret fear of being forced to return there some day. He therefore wishes to make his return impossible by the manner in which he denies. As soon as he begins to affirm, however, he half-closes his eyes and begins to idealise (frequently merely for the sake of annoying those who have stayed at home). We might say that there was something artistic about this – agreed, but there is also something dishonest about it. The idealist of a person imagines this person to be so far from him that he can no longer see him distinctly, and then he reinterprets what he still sees into something 'beautiful' – that is to say, symmetrical, vaguely outlined, indefinite. Since he wishes to worship from afar that ideal which floats on high in the distance, he finds it essential to build a temple for the object of his worship as a protection from the *profanum vulgus*. He brings into this temple for the object of his worship all the venerable and sanctified objects which he still possesses, so that his ideal may benefit by their charm, and that, *nourished* in this way, it may grow more and more divine. In the end he really succeeds in forming his god, but alas! there is someone who knows how all this has been done, viz. his intellectual conscience; and there is also someone who, quite unconsciously, begins to protest against these things, namely the deified one himself, who, in consequence of all this worship, praise and incense, now becomes completely unbearable and shows himself in the most obvious and dreadful manner to be non-divine and only too human. In a case like this there is only one means of escape left for such a fanatic; he patiently suffers himself and his fellows to be maltreated, and interprets all this misery *ad majorem dei gloriam* by a new kind of self-deceit and noble falsehood. He takes a stand against himself, and in doing so experiences, as an interpreter and ill-treated person, something like martyrdom – and in this way he climbs to the height of his conceit. Men of this kind lived about Napoleon, for example: indeed, perhaps it may have been he who inspired the soul of our century with that romantic prostration in the presence of 'genius' and the 'hero', which was so foreign to the spirit of rationalism of the nineteenth century – a man about whom even Byron was not ashamed to say that he was a 'worm compared with such a being'. (The formula of this prostration has been discovered by Thomas Carlyle, that arrogant old muddle-head and grumbler, who spent his long life in trying to romanticise the common sense of his Englishmen: but in vain!)

453

A moral interregnum. – Who is now in a position to describe that which will one day *supplant* moral feelings and judgements! – however certain we may be that these are founded on error, and that the building erected upon such foundations cannot be repaired: their obligation must gradually diminish from day to day, insofar as the obligation of reason does not diminish! To carry out the task of re-establishing the laws of life and action is still beyond the power of our sciences of physiology and medicine, society and solitude: though it is only from them that we can borrow the foundation-stones of new ideals (if not the new ideals themselves). Thus we live a *prelude* or *postlude*, according to our tastes and talents, and the best we can do in this *interregnum* is to be as much as possible our own *reges* and to establish small *experimental states*. We are experiments: if we want to be so!

526

Unwilling to be a symbol. – I sympathise with princes: they are not at liberty to discard their high rank even for a short time, and thus they come to know people only from the very uncomfortable position of constant dissimulation – their continual compulsion to represent something actually ends by making solemn ciphers of them. – Such is the fate of all those who deem it their duty to be symbols.

534

Small doses. – If we wish a change to be as deep and radical as possible, we must apply the remedy in minute doses, but unremittingly for long periods. What great action can be performed all *at once*? Let us therefore be careful not to exchange the moral conditions to which we are accustomed for a new valuation of things precipitately and violently – no, we may even wish to continue living in the old way for a long time to come, until probably at some very remote period we become aware of the fact that *the new valuation* has made itself the predominating power within us, and that its minute doses *to which we must henceforth become accustomed* have set up a new nature within us. – We now also begin to understand that the last attempt at a great change of valuations – that which concerned itself with political affairs – the 'Great Revolution' – was nothing *more* than a pathetic and bloody *piece of quackery* which, by means of sudden crises, was able to inspire a credulous Europe with the hope of a *sudden* recovery, and which has therefore made all political invalids *impatient and dangerous* up to this very moment.

Translated by J. M. Kennedy and R. J. Hollingdale with modifications

The Gay Science, 1882

5

Unconditional duties. – All those who feel that they need the strongest words and intonations, the most eloquent gestures and attitudes, in order to operate *at all* – revolutionary politicians, socialists, preachers of repentance with or without Christianity, with all of whom there must be no mere half-success – all these speak of 'duties', and indeed, always of duties, which have the character of being unconditional – without such they would have no right to their excessive pathos: they know that right well! They grasp, therefore, at philosophies of morality which preach some kind of categorical imperative, or they assimilate a good lump of religion, as, for example, Mazzini did. Because they want to be trusted unconditionally, it is first of all necessary for them to trust themselves unconditionally, on the basis of some ultimate, undebatable command, sublime in itself, as the ministers and instruments of which they would fain feel and announce themselves. Here we have the most natural and, for the most part, very influential opponents of moral enlightenment and scepticism: but they are rare. On the other hand, there is always a very numerous class of those opponents wherever interest teaches subjection, while repute and honour seem to forbid it. He who feels himself dishonoured at the thought of being the *instrument* of a prince, or of a party and sect, or even of financial power, for example, as the descendant of a proud, ancient family, but wishes just to be this instrument, or must be so before himself and before the public – such a person has need of pathetic principles which can at all times be appealed to:– principles of an unconditional *ought*, to which a person can subject himself without shame, and can show himself subjected. All more refined servility holds fast to the categorical imperative and is the mortal enemy of those who want to take away the unconditional character of duty; propriety demands this from them, and not only propriety.

10

A species of atavism. – I prefer to think of the rare men of an age as suddenly emerging after-shoots of past cultures, and of their persistent strength: like the atavism of a people and its civilisation: – there is thus still something in them to *think of*! They now seem strange, rare and extraordinary: and he who feels these forces in himself has to foster them in face of a different, opposing world; he has to defend them, honour them, and rear them to maturity: and he either becomes a great man thereby, or a deranged and eccentric person, if he does not altogether break down early. Formerly these rare qualities were usual and were consequently regarded as common: they did not distinguish people. Perhaps they were demanded and presupposed; it was impossible to become great with them, for indeed there was also no danger of becoming insane and solitary with them. – It is principally in the *old-established* families and castes of a people that such after-effects of old impulses present themselves, while there is no probability of such atavism where races, habits and valuations change too rapidly. For the tempo of the evolutional forces in peoples implies just as much as in music; for our case an andante of evolution is absolutely necessary, as the tempo of a passionate and slow spirit: – and the spirit of conserving families is certainly of that sort.

13

On the doctrine of the feeling of power. – We exercise our power over others by doing them good or by doing them ill – that is all we care for! *Doing ill* to those on whom we have to make our power felt; for pain is a far more sensitive means for that purpose than pleasure; pain always raises the question concerning its origin, while pleasure is inclined to stop with itself and not look backward. *Doing good* and being kind to those who are in any way already dependent on us (that is, who are accustomed to think of us as their causes); we want to increase their power because we thus increase our own, or we want to show them the advantage there is in being in our power; they thus become more contented with their position and more hostile to the enemies of *our* power and readier to contend with them.

If we make sacrifices in doing good or in doing ill, it does not alter the ultimate value of our actions. Even if we stake our life in the cause, as martyrs for the sake of our Church, it is a sacrifice to *our* desire for power, or for the purpose of conserving our feeling of power. He who under these circumstances feels that he 'is in possession of Truth', how many possessions does he not let go in order to preserve this feeling! What does he not throw overboard, in order to keep himself 'on top' – that is to say, *above* the others who lack 'the Truth'!

Certainly the condition we are in when we hurt others is rarely as pleasant, as purely pleasant, as that in which we benefit others; it is a sign that we still lack power, or it betrays ill-humour at this defect in us; it brings with it new dangers and uncertainties as to the power we already possess and clouds our horizon by the prospect of revenge, scorn, punishment and failure. Perhaps only those most susceptible to the feeling of power, and eager for it, will prefer to impress the seal of power on the resisting individual – those to whom the sight of the already subjugated person (the object of benevolence) is a burden and a tedium. What is decisive is how a person is accustomed to *season* his life; it is a matter of taste whether a person would rather have the slow or the sudden, the safe or the dangerous and daring increase of power; he seeks this or that seasoning always according to his temperament.

An easy prey is something contemptible to proud natures. They have an agreeable sensation only at the sight of men of unbroken spirit who could be enemies to them and at the sight of all possessions that are hard to come by. They are often hard towards the sufferer, for he is not worthy of their effort or their pride; but they show themselves so much the more courteous towards their *equals*, with whom strife and struggle would in any case be full of honour if the occasion for it should ever present itself. It is under the agreeable feelings of *this* perspective that the members of the knightly caste became accustomed to treating each other with exquisite courtesy.

Pity is the most pleasant feeling in those who have not much pride and have no prospect of great conquests; for them the easy prey – and that is what all who suffer are – is enchanting. Pity is praised as the virtue of prostitutes.

23

The characteristics of corruption. – Let us observe the following characteristics in that condition of society from time to time necessary, which is designated by the word 'corruption'.

Immediately upon the appearance of corruption anywhere, a motley *superstition* gets the upper hand and the previous universal belief of a people becomes colourless and impotent in comparison with it; for superstition is freethinking of the second rank – he who gives himself over to it selects certain forms and formulae which appeal to him and permits himself a right of choice. The superstitious man is always much more of a 'person' in comparison with the religious man, and a superstitious society will be one in which there are many individuals and a delight in individuality. Seen from this standpoint superstition always appears as a *progress* in comparison with belief and as a sign that the intellect becomes more independent and claims to have its rights. Those who reverence the old religion and the religious disposition then complain of corruption – they have hitherto also determined the usage of language and have given a bad repute to superstition, even among the freest spirits. Let us learn that it is a symptom of *enlightenment*. – Secondly, a society in which corruption takes a hold is blamed for exhaustion: for the appreciation of war, and the delight in war, perceptibly diminish in such a society, and the conveniences of life are now just as eagerly sought after as were military and gymnastic honours formerly. But one is accustomed to overlook the fact that the old national energy and national passion, which acquired a magnificent splendour in war and warlike games, has now transferred itself into innumerable private passions, and has merely become less visible; indeed in periods of 'corruption' the quantity and quality of the expended energy of a people is probably greater than ever, and the individual spends it lavishly, to such an extent as could not be done formerly – he was not then rich enough to do so! And thus it is precisely in times of 'exhaustion' that tragedy runs at large in and out of doors, it is then that ardent love and ardent hatred are born, and the flame of knowledge flashes heavenward in full blaze. – Thirdly, as if in amends for the reproach of superstition and exhaustion, it is customary to say of such periods of corruption that they are milder and that cruelty has then greatly diminished in comparison with the older, more credulous and stronger period. But to this praise I am just as little able to assent as to that reproach: I only grant so much – namely, that cruelty now becomes more refined, and its older forms are henceforth counter to the taste; but the wounding and torturing by word and look reaches its highest development in times of corruption – it is now only that *wickedness* is created, and the delight in wickedness. The men of the period of corruption are witty and calumnious; they know that there are yet other ways of murdering than by the dagger and ambush – they know also that all that is *well said* is believed in. – Fourthly, it is when 'morals decay' that those beings whom one calls tyrants first make their appearance; they are the forerunners of the *individual,* and as it were early matured *firstlings.* Yet a little while, and this fruit of fruits hangs ripe and yellow on the tree of a people – and only for the sake of such fruit did this tree exist! When the decay has reached its worst, and likewise the conflict of all sorts of tyrants, there always arises the Caesar, the final tyrant, who puts an end to the exhausted struggle for sovereignty by making the exhaustion work for him. In his time the individual is usually most mature, and consequently the 'culture' is highest and most fruitful, but not on his account nor through him: although the men of the highest culture love to flatter their Caesar by pretending that they are *his* creation. The truth, however, is that they need quietness externally, because they have disquietude and labour internally. In these times bribery and treason are at their height: for the love of the ego, then first discovered, is much more powerful than the love of the old, used-up, hackneyed 'fatherland'; and the need to be secure in one way or other against the frightful fluctuations of fortune, opens even the nobler hands, as soon as a richer and more powerful person shows himself ready to put gold into them. There is then so little certainty with regard to the future; people live only for the day: a psychical condition which enables every deceiver to play an easy game – people, of course, only let themselves be misled and bribed 'for the present' and reserve for themselves futurity and virtue. The individuals, as is well known, who only live for themselves, provide for the moment more than do their opposites, the herd men, because they consider themselves just as incalculable as the future; and similarly they attach themselves willingly to despots, because they believe themselves capable of activities and expedients, which can neither reckon on being understood by the multitude, nor on finding favour with them – but the tyrant or the Caesar understands the rights of the individual even in his excesses, and has an interest in speaking on behalf of a bolder private morality, and even in giving his hand to it. For he thinks of himself, and wishes people to think of him what Napoleon once uttered in his classical style: 'I have the right to answer by an eternal "thus I am" to everything about which complaint is brought against me. I am set apart from the world, I accept conditions from nobody. I wish people also to submit to my whims, and to take it quite as a straightforward matter if I should indulge in this or that diversion.' Thus spoke Napoleon once to his wife when she had reasons for calling in question the fidelity of her husband. – The times of corruption are the seasons when the apples fall from the tree: I mean the individuals, the seed-bearers of the future, the pioneers of spiritual colonisation, and of a new construction of national and social unions. Corruption is only an abusive term for the harvest time of a people.

24

Different dissatisfactions. – The feeble and as it were feminine dissatisfied people have ingenuity for beautifying and deepening life; the strong dissatisfied people – the masculine persons among them, to continue the metaphor – have ingenuity for improving and safeguarding life. The former show their weakness and feminine character by willingly letting themselves be temporarily deceived, and perhaps even by putting up with a little ecstasy and enthusiasm for a time, but on the whole they are never to be satisfied and suffer from the incurability of their dissatisfaction; moreover they are the patrons of all those who manage to concoct opiate and narcotic comforts, and on that account are averse to those who value the physician above the priest – they thereby encourage the *continuance* of actual distress! If there had not been a surplus of dissatisfied persons of this kind in Europe since the time of the Middle Ages the remarkable capacity of Europeans for constant *change* would perhaps not have originated at all; for the claims of the strong dissatisfied persons are too gross, and really too modest to resist being finally quieted down. China is an instance of a country in which dissatisfaction on a grand scale and the capacity for transformation died out many centuries ago; and the Socialists and state-idolaters of Europe could easily bring things to Chinese conditions and to a Chinese 'happiness', with their measures for the amelioration and security of life, provided that they could first of all root out the sicklier, more tender, more feminine dissatisfaction and romanticism which are still very abundant among us. Europe is an invalid who owes her best thanks to her incurability and the eternal transformations of her sufferings; these constant new situations, these equally constant new dangers, pains and media of information, have at last generated an intellectual sensitiveness which is almost equal to genius, and is in any case the mother of all genius.

31

Commerce and nobility. – Buying and selling is now regarded as something ordinary, like the art of reading and writing; everyone is now trained to it, even when he is not a tradesman and exercises himself daily in the art; precisely as formerly in the period of uncivilised humanity, everyone was a hunter and exercised himself day by day in the art of hunting. Hunting was then commonplace: but eventually it became a privilege of the powerful and noble and thereby lost the character of the commonplace and the ordinary – by ceasing to be necessary and by becoming an affair of fancy and luxury: – so it might become the same some day with buying and selling. Conditions of society are imaginable in which there will be no selling and buying, and in which the necessity for this art will become quite lost; perhaps it may then happen that individuals who are less subjected to the law of the prevailing condition of things will indulge in buying and selling as a *luxury of sentiment*. It is then only that commerce would acquire nobility, and the noble would then perhaps occupy themselves just as readily with commerce as they have done hitherto with war and politics: while on the other hand the valuation of politics might then have entirely altered. Already even politics ceases to be the art of the nobleman; and it is possible that one day it may be found to be so vulgar as to be brought, like all party literature and journalism, under the rubric 'Prostitution of the spirit'.

38

Explosive people. – When one considers how ready are the forces of young men for discharge, one does not wonder at seeing them decide so uncritically and with so little selection for this or that cause: that which attracts them is the sight of eagerness for a cause, as it were the sight of the burning fuse – not the cause itself. The more ingenious seducers on that account operate by holding out the prospect of an explosion to such persons and do not urge their cause by means of reasons; these powder kegs are not won over by means of reasons!

40

The lack of a noble presence. – Soldiers and their leaders have always a much higher mode of comportment towards one another than workers and their employers. At present at least, all militarily established civilisation still stands high above all so-called industrial culture; the latter, in its present form, is in general the meanest mode of existence that has ever been. It is simply the law of necessity that operates here: people want to live and have to sell themselves; but they despise him who exploits their necessity and *purchases* the worker. It is curious that the subjection to powerful, fear-inspiring and even dreadful individuals, to tyrants and military leaders, is not at all felt so painfully as the subjection to such undistinguished and uninteresting persons as the captains of industry; in the employer the worker usually sees merely a crafty, blood-sucking dog of a man, speculating on every necessity, whose name, form, character and reputation are altogether indifferent to him. It is probable that the manufacturers and great magnates of commerce have hitherto lacked too much all those forms and attributes of a *superior race*, which alone make persons interesting; if they had had the nobility of the nobly born in their looks and bearing, there would perhaps have been no socialism in the masses of the people. For these are really ready to submit to *slavery* of every kind, provided that the superior class above them constantly shows itself legitimately superior and *born* to command – by its noble presence! The commonest man feels that nobility is not to be improvised and that it is his part to honour it as the fruit of long periods of time – but the absence of superior presence, and the notorious vulgarity of manufacturers with red, fat hands, introduces the thought to him that it is only chance and fortune that has here elevated the one above the other; well then – so he reasons with himself – let *us* in our turn tempt chance and fortune! Let us in our turn throw the dice! – and socialism commences.

42

Work and boredom. – In respect to seeking work for the sake of pay, almost all men are alike at present in civilised countries; to all of them work is a means and not itself the end; on which account they are not very discriminating in the choice of work, provided it yields an abundant profit. But still there are rarer men who would rather perish than work without *delight* in their labour: the fastidious people, difficult to satisfy, whose object is not served by an abundant profit unless the work itself be the reward of all rewards. Artists and contemplative men of all kinds belong to this rare species of human beings; and also the idlers who spend their life in hunting and travelling, or in love affairs and adventures. They all seek toil and trouble in so far as these are associated with pleasure, and they want the severest and hardest labour, if it be necessary. In other respects, however, they have a resolute indolence, even should impoverishment, dishonour and danger to health and life be associated therewith. They are not so much afraid of boredom as of labour without pleasure; indeed they require much boredom if *their* work is to succeed. For the thinker and for all inventive spirits boredom is the unpleasant 'calm' of the soul which precedes the happy voyage and the dancing breezes; he must endure it, he must wait for the effect it has on him: – it is precisely this which lesser natures cannot at all experience! It is common to scare away boredom in every way, just as it is common to labour without pleasure. It perhaps distinguishes the Asians above the Europeans, that they are capable of a longer and profounder repose; even their narcotics operate slowly and require patience, in contrast to the obnoxious suddenness of the European poison, alcohol.

83

Translations. – One can estimate the amount of the historical sense which an age possesses by the way in which it makes *translations* and seeks to embody in itself past periods and literatures. The French of Corneille, and even the French of the Revolution, appropriated Roman antiquity in a manner for which we would no longer have the courage – owing to our superior historical sense. And Roman antiquity itself: how violently, and at the same time how naively, did it lay its hands on everything excellent and elevated belonging to the older Greek antiquity! How they translated these writings into the Roman present! How they wiped away intentionally and unconcernedly the wing-dust of the butterfly moment! It is thus that Horace now and then translated Alcaeus or Archilochus, it is thus that Propertius translated Callimachus and Philetas (poets of equal rank with Theocritus, if we *may* judge): of what consequence was it to them that the actual creator experienced this and that, and had inscribed the indication into his poem! As poets they were averse to the antiquarian, inquisitive spirit which precedes the historical sense; as poets they did not respect those essentially personal traits and names, nor anything peculiar to city, coast or century, such as its costume and mask, but at once put the present and the Roman in its place. They seem to us to ask: 'Should we not make the old new for ourselves and adjust ourselves to it? Should we not be allowed to inspire this dead body with our soul? For it is dead indeed: how loathsome is everything dead!' – They did not know the pleasure of the historical sense; the past and the alien was painful to them, and as Romans it was an incitement to a Roman conquest. In fact, they conquered when they translated – not only in that they omitted the historical: they also added allusions to the present; above all, they struck out the name of the poet and put their own in its place – not with the feeling of theft, but with the very best conscience of the *imperium Romanum*.

103

German music. – German music, more than any other, has now become European music; because the changes which Europe experienced through the Revolution have therein alone found expression; it is only German music that knows how to express the agitation of popular masses, the tremendous artificial uproar, which does not even need to be very noisy – while Italian opera, for example, knows only the choruses of domestics or soldiers, but not 'the people'. There is the additional fact that in all German music a profound *bourgeois* jealousy of the *noblesse* can be traced, especially a jealousy of *esprit* and *élégance*, as the expressions of a courtly, chivalrous, ancient and self-confident society. It is not music like that of Goethe's musician at the gate, which was pleasing also 'in the hall' and to the king as well; the idea is not: 'The knights looked on with martial air; with bashful eyes the ladies'. Even the Graces are not allowed in German music without a touch of remorse; it is only with Pleasantness, the country cousin of the Graces, that the German begins to feel morally at ease – and from this point up, more and more so, to his enthusiastic, learned and often gruff 'sublimity', the Beethoven-like sublimity. If we want to imagine the man of *this* music, merely imagine Beethoven as he appeared beside Goethe, say, at their meeting at Teplitz: as semi-barbarism beside culture, as the masses beside the nobility, as the good-natured man beside the good and more than 'good' man, as the visionary beside the artist, as the man needing comfort beside the comforted, as the man given to exaggeration and distrust beside the man of reason, as the crank and self-tormenter, as the foolishly enraptured, blessedly unfortunate, sincerely immoderate man, as the pretentious and awkward man – and altogether as the 'untamed man': it was thus that Goethe conceived and characterised him, Goethe, the exceptional German, for whom a music of equal rank has not yet been found! – Finally, let us consider whether the present continually extending contempt of melody and the stunting of the sense for melody among Germans should not be understood as a democratic impropriety and an after-effect of the Revolution? For melody has such an obvious delight in conformity to law, and such an aversion to everything evolving, unformed and arbitrary, that it sounds like a note out of the *ancient* European regime, and as a seduction and guidance back to it.

118

Benevolence. – Is it virtuous when a cell transforms itself into the function of a stronger cell? It must do so. And is it evil when the stronger one assimilates the other? It must do so likewise: it is necessary, for it has to have abundant substitutes and seeks to regenerate itself. One has therefore to distinguish the instinct of appropriation and the instinct of submission in benevolence, according as the stronger or the weaker feels benevolent. Gladness and covetousness are united in the stronger person, who wants to transform something to his function: gladness and desire to be coveted in the weaker person, who would like to become a function. The former case is essentially pity, a pleasant excitation of the instinct of appropriation at the sight of the weak: it is to be remembered, however, that 'strong' and 'weak' are relative conceptions.

136

The chosen people. – The Jews, who regard themselves as the chosen people among the nations, and that too because they are the moral genius among the nations (in virtue of their capacity for *despising* the human in themselves *more* than any other people) – the Jews have a pleasure in their divine monarch and saint similar to that which the French nobility had in Louis XIV. This nobility had allowed its power and autocracy to be taken from it, and had become contemptible: in order not to feel this, in order to be able to forget it, an *unequalled* royal magnificence, royal authority and plenitude of power was needed, to which there was access only for the nobility. As in accordance with this privilege they raised themselves to the elevation of the court, and from that elevation saw everything under them – saw everything contemptible – they got beyond all uneasiness of conscience. They thus elevated intentionally the tower of the royal power more and more into the clouds and set the final coping-stone of their own power upon it.

144

Religious wars. – The greatest advance of the masses hitherto has been religious wars, for it proves that the masses have begun to deal reverently with conceptions of things. Religious wars result only when human reason generally has been refined by the subtle disputes of sects; so that even the populace becomes punctilious and regards trifles as important, actually thinking it possible that the 'eternal salvation of the soul' may depend upon minute distinctions of concepts.

149

The failure of reformations. – It testifies to the higher culture of the Greeks, even in rather early ages, that attempts to establish new Greek religions frequently failed; it testifies that quite early on there must have been a multitude of dissimilar individuals in Greece, whose dissimilar troubles were not cured by a single recipe of faith and hope.

Pythagoras and Plato, perhaps also Empedocles, and much earlier the Orphic enthusiasts, aimed at founding new religions; and the two first-named were so endowed with the qualifications for founding religions that one cannot be sufficiently astonished at their failure: they just reached the point of founding sects. Every time that the Reformation of an entire people fails and only sects raise their leaders, one may conclude that the people already contains many types has begun to free itself from the rude herd instincts and the morality of mores: a momentous state of suspense, which one is accustomed to disparage as a mere decay of morals and corruption, although in fact it proclaims that the egg is approaching maturity and that the eggshell is about to be broken.

That Luther's Reformation succeeded in the North suggests that the North of Europe had remained backward in comparison with the South and still had requirements tolerably uniform in colour and kind; and there would have been no Christianising of Europe at all if the culture of the ancient world in the South had not been gradually barbarised through an excessive admixture of the blood of Teutonic barbarians, thus losing its cultural superiority.

The more universally and unconditionally an individual, or the thought of an individual, can operate, so much more homogeneous and so much lower must be the mass that is there operated upon, while counter-strivings betray internal counter-requirements that also want to be gratified and recognised. Conversely, we may always infer that a civilisation is really high when powerful and ambitious natures only produce a limited and sectarian effect. This is true also for the various arts and the field of knowledge. Where there is ruling there are masses; and where there are masses there is need of slavery. Where there is slavery the individuals are but few, and have the instincts and conscience of the herd opposed to them.

174

Apart. – Parliamentarianism, that is, public permission to choose between five main political opinions, insinuates itself into the favour of the numerous class who would like to *appear* independent and individual and like to fight for their opinions. After all, however, it is a matter of indifference whether one opinion is imposed upon the herd or five opinions are permitted to it. – He who deviates from the five public opinions and stands apart has always the whole herd against him.

176

Compassion. – The poor, ruling princes! All their rights now change unexpectedly into claims, and all these claims immediately sound like pretensions! And if they but say 'we' or 'my people', wicked old Europe begins to laugh. Verily, a chief master of ceremonies of the modern world would make little ceremony with them; perhaps he would decree that *'les souverains rangent aux parvenus'*.

188

Work. – How close work and the worker are now even to the most leisurely among us! The royal courtesy of the saying 'We are all workers' would have been cynical and indecent as recently as the reign of Louis XIV.

206

During the rain. – It rains and I think of the poor people who now crowd together with their many cares, which they are unaccustomed to conceal; all of them, therefore, ready and anxious to give pain to one another and thus provide themselves with a pitiable kind of comfort, even in bad weather. This, this only, is the poverty of the poor!

236

To move the crowd. Is it not necessary for him who wants to move the crowd to give a stage representation of himself? Has he not first to translate himself into the grotesquely obvious, and then set forth his whole personality and cause in that vulgarised and simplified fashion?

282

The gait. – There are mannerisms of the intellect by which even great minds betray that they originate from the mob, or from the semi-mob – it is principally the gait and step of their thoughts which betray them; they cannot walk. It was thus that even Napoleon, to his profound chagrin, could not walk 'legitimately' and in princely fashion on occasions when it was necessary to do so properly, as in great coronation processions and on similar occasions: even there he was always just the leader of a column-proud and brusque at the same time, and very self-conscious of it all. It is something laughable to see those writers who make the folding robes of their periods rustle around them: they want to cover their feet.

283

Preparatory human beings. – I greet all signs indicating that a more manly and warlike age is commencing, which will, above all, bring heroism again into honour! For it has to prepare the way for a yet higher age and gather the force which the latter will one day require – the age which will carry heroism into knowledge and wage war for the sake of ideas and their consequences. For that end many brave preparatory human beings are now needed, who, however, cannot originate out of nothing – and just as little out of the sand and slime of present-day civilisation and the culture of great cities: human beings silent, solitary and resolute, who know how to be content and persistent in invisible activity: human beings who with innate disposition seek in all things that which is to be overcome in them: human beings to whom cheerfulness, patience, simplicity and contempt of the great vanities belong just as much as do magnanimity in victory and indulgence to the trivial vanities of all the vanquished: human beings with an acute and independent judgement regarding all victors, and concerning the part which chance has played in the winning of victory and fame: human beings with their own festivals, their own workdays and their own periods of mourning; accustomed to command with perfect assurance and equally ready, if need be, to obey, proud in the one case as in the other, equally serving their own interests: men more imperilled, more productive, more happy! For believe me – the secret of realising the largest productivity and the greatest enjoyment of existence is to live in danger! Build your cities on the slope of Vesuvius! Send your ships into unexplored seas! Live in war with your equals and with yourselves! Be robbers and spoilers, you knowing ones, as long as you cannot be rulers and possessors! The time will soon pass when you can be satisfied to live like timorous deer concealed in the forests. Knowledge will finally stretch out her hand for that which belongs to her – she means to rule and possess, and you with her!

291

Genoa. – I have looked upon this city, its villas and pleasure grounds, and the wide circuit of its inhabited heights and slopes, for a considerable time: in the end I must say that I see faces out of past generations – this district is strewn with the images of bold and autocratic human beings. They have lived and have wanted to live on – they say so with their houses, built and decorated to last centuries, and not for the passing hour: they were well disposed to life, however ill-disposed they may often have been towards themselves. I always see the builder, how he casts his eye on all that is built around him far and near, and likewise on the city, the sea and the chain of mountains; how he expresses power and conquest with his gaze: all this he wishes to fit into his plan, and in the end make it his property by its becoming a portion of the same. The whole district is overgrown with this superb, insatiable egoism of the desire to possess and exploit; and as these human beings when abroad recognised no frontiers, and in their thirst for the new placed a new world beside the old, so also at home everyone rose up against everyone else, and devised some mode of expressing his superiority, and of placing between himself and his neighbour his personal illimitableness. Everyone won for himself his home once more by overpowering it with his architectural thoughts, and by transforming it into a delightful sight for his race. When we consider the mode of building cities in the north, the law, and the general delight in legality and obedience, impose upon us: we thereby divine the propensity to equality and submission which must have ruled in those builders.

Here, however, on turning every corner you find a human being by himself, who knows the sea, knows adventure, and knows the Orient, a human being who is averse to law and to neighbour, as if it bored him to have to do with them, a human being who scans all that is already old and established with envious glances: with a wonderful craftiness of fantasy, he would like, at least in thought, to establish all this anew, to lay his hands on it and introduce his meaning into it – if only for the passing hour of a sunny afternoon, when for once his insatiable and melancholy soul feels satiety, and when only what is his own, and nothing strange, may show itself to his eye.

329

Leisure and idleness. – There is an Indian savagery, a savagery peculiar to the Indian blood, in the manner in which the Americans strive after gold: and the breathless hurry of their work – the characteristic vice of the New World – already begins to infect old Europe and makes it savage also, spreading over it a strange lack of spirituality. One is now ashamed of repose: even long reflection almost causes remorse of conscience. Thinking is done with a stopwatch, as dining is done with the eyes fixed on the financial newspaper; we live like men who are continually 'afraid of letting opportunities slip'. 'Better do anything whatever, than nothing' – this principle also is a noose with which all culture and all higher taste may be strangled. And just as all form obviously disappears in the haste of workers, so the sense for form itself, the ear and the eye for the melody of movement, also disappear. The proof of this is the clumsy perspicuity which is now everywhere demanded in all positions where a person would like to be sincere with his fellows, in intercourse with friends, women, relatives, children, teachers, pupils, leaders and princes – one has no longer either time or energy for ceremonies, for roundabout courtesies, for any *esprit* in conversation, or for any *otium* whatever. For life in the pursuit of gain continually compels a person to consume his intellect, even to exhaustion, in constant dissimulation, overreaching or forestalling: the real virtue nowadays is to do something in a shorter time than another person. And so there are only rare hours of sincere intercourse *permitted*: in them, however, people are tired and would not only like 'to let themselves go', but to stretch their legs out wide in awkward style. The way people write their *letters* nowadays is quite in keeping with the age; their style and spirit will always be the true 'sign of the times'. If there be still enjoyment in society and in art, it is enjoyment such as overworked slaves provide for themselves. Oh, this moderation in 'joy' of our cultured and uncultured classes! Oh, this increasing suspiciousness of all enjoyment! Work is winning over more and more the good conscience to its side: the desire for enjoyment already calls itself 'need of recreation' and even begins to be ashamed of itself. 'One owes it to one's health', people say, when they are caught at a picnic. Indeed, it might soon go so far that one could not yield to the desire for the *vita contemplativa* (that is to say, excursions with thoughts and friends), without self-contempt and a bad conscience. Well! Formerly it was the very reverse: it was 'action' that suffered from a bad conscience. A person of good family concealed his work when need compelled him to labour. The slave laboured under the weight of the feeling that he did something contemptible – the 'doing' itself was something contemptible. 'Only in *otium* and *bellum* is there nobility and honour:' so rang the voice of ancient prejudice!

Translated by Thomas Common with modifications

Thus Spoke Zarathustra: A Book for Everyone and No One, 1883–1885

On the new idol

Somewhere there are still peoples and herds, but not with us, my brothers: here there are states.

What is that? Well! open now your ears unto me, for now will I say unto you my word concerning the death of peoples.

The state, is called the coldest of all cold monsters. Coldly it lies also; and this lie creeps from its mouth: 'I, the state, am the people.'

It is a lie! Creators were they who created peoples and hung a faith and a love over them: thus they served life.

Destroyers, are they who lay snares for many and call it the state: they hang a sword and a hundred cravings over them.

Where there is still a people, there the state is not understood, but hated as the evil eye and as sin against customs and rights.

This sign I give unto you: every people speaks its language of good and evil: this its neighbour understands not. Its language it has devised for itself in laws and customs.

But the state lies in all languages of good and evil; and whatever it says it lies – and whatever it has it has stolen.

False is everything in it; with stolen teeth it bites, the biting one. False are even its bowels. Confusion of language of good and evil; this sign I give unto you as the sign of the state. Verily, the will to death, indicates this sign! Verily, it beckons unto the preachers of death!

Many too many are born: for the superfluous ones was the state devised!

See just how it entices them to it, the many-too-many! How it swallows and chews and re-chews them!

'On earth there is nothing greater than I: it is I who am the regulating finger of God' – thus roars the monster. And not only the long-eared and short-sighted fall upon their knees!

Ah! even in your ears, you great souls, it whispers its gloomy lies! Ah! it finds out the rich hearts which willingly lavish themselves!

Yea, it finds you out too, you conquerors of the old god! Weary you became of the conflict, and now your weariness serves the new idol!

Heroes and honourable ones, it would set up around it, the new idol! Gladly it basks in the sunshine of good consciences – the cold monster!

Everything will it give you, if you worship it, the new idol: thus it purchases the lustre of your virtue and the glance of your proud eyes.

It seeks to allure by means of you, the many-too-many! Yea, a hellish artifice has here been devised, a death-horse jingling with the trappings of divine honours!

Yea, a dying for many has here been devised, which glorifies itself as life: verily, a hearty service unto all preachers of death!

State, I call it, where all are poison-drinkers, the good and the wicked: the state, where all lose themselves, the good and the wicked: the state, where the slow suicide of all – is called 'life'.

Just see these superfluous ones! They steal the works of the inventors and the treasures of the wise. Culture they call their theft – and everything becomes sickness and trouble unto them!

Just see these superfluous ones! Sick are they always; they vomit their bile and call it a newspaper. They devour one another and cannot even digest themselves.

Just see these superfluous ones! Wealth they acquire and become poorer thereby. Power they seek for and, above all, the lever of power, much money – these impotent ones!

See them clamber, these nimble apes! They clamber over one another, and thus scuffle into the mud and the abyss.

Towards the throne they all strive: it is their madness – as if happiness sat on the throne! Often sits filth on the throne – and often also the throne on filth.

Madmen they all seem to me, and clambering apes, and too eager. Badly smells their idol to me, the cold monster: badly they all smell to me, these idolaters.

My brothers, will you suffocate in the fumes of their maws and appetites! Better break the windows and jump into the fresh air!

Do escape the bad odour! Withdraw from the idolatry of the superfluous!

Do escape the bad odour! Withdraw from the steam of these human sacrifices!

Open still remains the earth for great souls. Empty are still many sites for lonesome and twosome, around which floats the odour of tranquil seas.

Open still remains a free life for great souls. Verily, he who possesses little is so much the less possessed: blessed be moderate poverty!

There, where the state ends, there only commences the man who is not superfluous: there commences the song of the necessary ones, the single and irreplaceable melody.

Where the state *ends* – look there, my brothers! Do you not see it, the rainbow and the bridges of the Overman?

Thus spoke Zarathustra.

On the rabble

Life is a well of delight; but where the rabble also drink, there all fountains are poisoned.

To everything clean am I well disposed; but I hate to see the grinning mouths and the thirst of the unclean.

They cast their eye down into the fountain: and now glance up to me their odious smile out of the fountain.

The holy water have they poisoned with their lustfulness; and when they called their filthy dreams 'delight', then poisoned they also the words.

Indignant becomes the flame when they put their damp hearts to the fire; the spirit itself bubbles and smokes when the rabble approach the fire.

Mawkish and over-mellow becomes the fruit in their hands: unsteady and withered at the top does their look make the fruit tree.

And many a one who has turned away from life has only turned away from the rabble: he hated to share with them fountain, flame and fruit.

And many a one who has gone into the wilderness and suffered thirst with beasts of prey, disliked only to sit at the cistern with filthy camel drivers.

And many a one who has come along as a destroyer, and as a hailstorm to all cornfields, wanted merely to put his foot into the jaws of the rabble and thus stop their throat.

And it is not the mouthful which has most choked me, to know that life itself requires enmity and death and torture-crosses – but I asked once, and suffocated almost with my question: What? Is the rabble also necessary for life? Are poisoned fountains necessary, and stinking fires, and filthy dreams and maggots in the bread of life?

Not my hatred, but my loathing, gnawed hungrily at my life! Ah, often became I weary of spirit, when I found even the rabble spiritual!

And on the rulers turned I my back, when I saw what they now call ruling: to traffic and bargain for power – with the rabble!

Amongst peoples of a strange language did I dwell with stopped ears: so that the language of their trafficking might remain strange unto me, and their bargaining for power. And holding my nose, I went morosely through all yesterdays and todays: verily, badly smell all yesterdays and todays of the scribbling rabble!

Like a cripple become deaf and blind and dumb: thus have I lived long; that I might not live with the power-rabble, the scribe-rabble and the pleasure-rabble.

Toilsomely did my spirit mount stairs, and cautiously; alms of delight were its refreshment; on the staff did life creep along with the blind one.

What has happened unto me? How have I freed myself from loathing? Who has rejuvenated my sight? How have I flown to the height where no rabble any longer sit at the wells?

Did my loathing itself create for me wings and fountain-divining powers? Verily, to the loftiest height had I to fly, to find again the well of delight!

Oh, I have found it, my brothers! Here on the loftiest height bubbles up for me the well of delight! And there is a life at whose waters none of the rabble drink with me!

Almost too violently do you flow for me, you fountain of delight! And often you empty the goblet again, in wanting to fill it!

And yet must I learn to approach you more modestly: far too violently does my heart still flow towards you.

My heart on which my summer burns, my short, hot, melancholy, over-happy summer: how my summer heart longs for your coolness!

Past, the lingering distress of my spring! Past, the wickedness of my snow-flakes in June! Summer have I become entirely, and summer-noontide!

A summer on the loftiest height, with cold fountains and blissful stillness: oh, come my friends, that the stillness may become more blissful!

For this is *our* height and our home: too high and steep do we here dwell for all uncleanly ones and their thirst.

Cast but your pure eyes into the well of my delight, my friends! How could it become turbid thereby! It shall laugh back to you with its purity.

On the tree, Future, build we our nest; eagles shall bring us lone ones food in their beaks!

Verily, no food of which the impure could be fellow-partakers! Fire, would they think they devoured, and burn their mouths!

Verily, no abodes do we here keep ready for the impure! An ice-cave to their bodies would our happiness be, and to their spirits!

And as strong winds will we live above them, neighbours to the eagles, neighbours to the snow, neighbours to the sun: thus live the strong winds. And like a wind will I one day blow among them, and with my spirit take the breath from their spirit: thus wills my future.

Verily, a strong wind is Zarathustra to all low places; and this counsel counsels he to his enemies, and to whatever spits and spews: 'Take care not to spit *against* the wind!'

Thus spoke Zarathustra.

On the tarantulas

Behold, this is the tarantula's den! Would you see the tarantula itself? Here hangs its web: touch this so that it may tremble.

There comes the tarantula willingly: Welcome, tarantula! Black on your back is your triangle and symbol; and I know also what is in your soul.

Revenge is in your soul: wherever you bite, there arises black scab; with revenge, your poison makes the soul giddy!

Thus do I speak unto you in parable, you who make the soul giddy, you preachers of *equality*! Tarantulas are you unto me, and secretly revengeful ones!

But I will soon bring your hiding places into the light: therefore, do I laugh in your face my laughter of the height. Therefore do I tear at your web, that your rage may lure you out of your den of lies, and that your revenge may leap forth from behind your word 'justice'.

Because, for *man to be redeemed from revenge*, that is for me the bridge to the highest hope, and a rainbow after long storms.

Otherwise, however, would the tarantulas have it. 'Let it be very justice for the world to become full of the storms of our vengeance' – thus do they talk to one another.

'Vengeance will we use, and insult, against all who are not like us' – thus do the tarantula hearts pledge themselves. 'And "will to equality" – that itself shall henceforth be the name of virtue; and against all that has power will we raise an outcry!'

You preachers of equality, the tyrant-frenzy of impotence cries thus in you for equality: your most secret tyrant-longings disguise themselves thus in virtue-words!

Fretted conceit and suppressed envy – perhaps your fathers' conceit and envy: in you they break forth as flame and frenzy of vengeance.

What the father has hidden comes out in the son; and often have I found in the son the father's revealed secret.

Inspired ones they resemble: but it is not the heart that inspires them – but vengeance. And when they become subtle and cold, it is not spirit, but envy, that makes them so.

Their jealousy leads them also into thinkers' paths; and this is the sign of their jealousy – they always go too far: so that their fatigue has at last to go to sleep on the snow.

In all their lamentations sounds vengeance, in all their eulogies is maleficence; and being judge seems to them bliss.

But thus do I counsel you, my friends: distrust all in whom the impulse to punish is powerful! They are people of bad race and lineage; out of their countenances peer the hangman and the sleuth-hound.

Distrust all those who talk much of their justice! Verily, in their souls not only honey is lacking. And when they call themselves 'the good and just', forget not that for them to be Pharisees, nothing is lacking but – power!

My friends, I will not be mixed up and confounded with others. There are those who preach my doctrine of life, and are at the same time preachers of equality, and tarantulas.

That they speak in favour of life, though they sit in their den, these poison-spiders, and withdrawn from life, is because they would thereby do injury.

To those would they thereby do injury who have power at present: for with those the preaching of death is still most at home.

Were it otherwise, then would the tarantulas teach otherwise: and they themselves were formerly the best world-maligners and heretic-burners.

With these preachers of equality will I not be mixed up and confounded. For thus speaks justice unto *me*: 'Men are not equal.'

And neither shall they become so! What would be my love to the Overman, if I spoke otherwise?

On a thousand bridges and piers shall they throng to the future, and always shall there be more war and inequality among them: thus does my great love make me speak!

Inventors of figures and phantoms shall they be in their hostilities; and with those figures and phantoms shall they yet fight with each other the supreme fight!

Good and evil, and rich and poor, and high and low, and all names of values: weapons shall they be, and sounding signs, that life must again and again surpass itself!

Aloft will it build itself with columns and stairs; life itself into remote distances would it gaze and out towards blissful beauties – therefore does it require elevation! And because it requires elevation, therefore does it require steps, and variance of steps and climbers! To rise strives life, and in rising to surpass itself.

And just behold, my friends! Here where the tarantula's den is, rises aloft an ancient temple's ruins – just behold it with enlightened eyes!

Verily, he who here towered aloft his thoughts in stone, knew as well as the wisest ones about the secret of life!

That there is struggle and inequality even in beauty, and war for power and supremacy: that does he here teach us in the plainest parable.

How divinely do vault and arch here contrast in the struggle: how with light and shade they strive against each other, the divinely striving ones.

Thus, steadfast and beautiful, let us also be enemies, my friends! Divinely will we strive against one another!

Alas! There has the tarantula bit me myself, my old enemy! Divinely steadfast and beautiful, it has bit me on the finger!

'Punishment must there be, and justice' – so thinks it: 'not gratuitously shall he here sing songs in honour of enmity!'

Yea, it has revenged itself! And alas! now will it make my soul also dizzy with revenge!

That I may not turn dizzy, however, bind me fast, my friends, to this pillar! Rather will I be a pillar-saint than a whirl of vengeance!

Verily, no cyclone or whirlwind is Zarathustra: and if he be a dancer, he is not at all a tarantula-dancer!

Thus spoke Zarathustra.

On old and new tablets

11

It is my pity with all the past that I see it is abandoned – abandoned to the favour, the spirit and the madness of every generation that comes, and reinterprets all that has been as its bridge!

A great despot might arise, an artful prodigy, who with approval and disapproval could strain and constrain all the past, until it became for him a bridge, a harbinger, a herald, and a cock crowing.

This, however, is the other danger and my other pity: he who is of the rabble, his thoughts go back to his grandfather; with his grandfather, however, does time cease.

Thus is all the past abandoned: for it might some day happen for the rabble to become master and drown all time in shallow waters.

Therefore, O my brothers, a *new nobility* is needed, which shall be the adversary of all rabble and despot rule, and shall inscribe anew the word 'noble' on new tables.

For many noble ones are needed, and many kinds of noble ones, for a new nobility! Or, as I once said in parable: 'Precisely this is godliness, that there are gods, but no God!'

12

O my brothers, I dedicate and direct you to a new nobility: you shall become procreators and cultivators and sowers of the future – verily, not to a nobility which you could purchase like shopkeepers with shopkeepers' gold; for little worth is all that has its price.

Let it not be your honour henceforth whence you come, but whither you go! Your will and your feet which seek to surpass you – let these be your new honour!

Verily, not that you have served a prince – of what account are princes now! – nor that you have become a bulwark to that which stands, that it may stand more firmly.

Not that your family has become courtly at courts, and that you have learned to stand, colourfully, like the flamingo for long hours in shallow pools: for ability to stand is a merit in courtiers; and all courtiers believe that unto blessedness after death comprises – permission to sit.

Nor even that a Spirit called Holy led your forefathers into promised lands, which I do not praise: for where the worst of all trees grew, the cross, in that land – there is nothing to praise! – and verily, wherever this 'Holy Spirit' led its knights, always in such campaigns did goats and geese, and wry-heads and guy-heads run foremost.

O my brothers, not backward shall your nobility gaze, but outward! Exiles shall you be from all fatherlands and forefatherlands!

Your *children's land* shall you love: let this love be your new nobility – the undiscovered in the remotest seas! For it do I bid your sails search and search!

Unto your children shall you make amends for being the children of your fathers: all the past shall you thus redeem! This new table do I place over you!

21

I love the brave: but it is not enough to be a swordsman, one must also know whereon to use swordsmanship!

And often is it greater bravery to keep quiet and pass by, that thereby one may reserve oneself for a worthier enemy!

You shall only have enemies to be hated; but not enemies to be despised: you must be proud of your enemies. Thus have I already taught.

For the worthier enemy, O my brothers, shall you reserve yourselves: therefore must you pass by many a one, especially many of the rabble, who din your ears with noise about people and peoples.

Keep your eye clear of their For and Against! There is there much right, much wrong: he who looks on becomes angry.

Therein viewing, therein hewing, they are the same thing: therefore depart into the forests and lay your sword to sleep!

Go your *own* ways! And let the people and peoples go theirs! – gloomy ways, verily, on which not a single hope glints any more!

Let there the shopkeeper rule, where all that still glitters is – shopkeepers' gold! It is the time of kings no longer: that which now calls itself the people is unworthy of kings.

See how these peoples themselves now do just like the shopkeepers: they pick up the smallest advantage out of all kinds of rubbish!

They set lures for one another, they lure things out of one another – that they call 'good neighbourliness'. O blessed remote period when a people said to itself: 'I will be *master* – over peoples!' For, my brothers, the best shall rule, the best also wills to rule! And where the teaching is different, there – the best is *lacking*.

25

He who has grown wise concerning old origins, behold, he will at last seek after the fountains of the future and new origins.

O my brothers, not long will it be until *new peoples* shall arise and new fountains shall rush down into new depths.

For the earthquake – it chokes up many wells, it causes much languishing: but it brings also to light inner powers and secrets. The earthquake discloses new fountains. In the earthquake of old peoples new fountains burst forth.

And whoever calls out: 'Behold, here is a well for many thirsty ones, one heart for many longing ones, one will for many instruments' – around him collects *a people*, that is to say, many attempting ones.

Who can command, who must obey – *that is there attempted*! Ah, with what long seeking and solving and failing and learning and re-attempting!

Human society: it is an attempt, so I teach – a long seeking: it seeks however the ruler! an attempt, my brothers! And *not* a 'contract'! Destroy, destroy that word of the soft-hearted and half-and-half!

Conversation with the kings
1

Zarathustra had not yet been an hour on his way in the mountains and forests, when he saw all at once a strange procession. Right on the path which he was about to descend came two kings walking, bedecked with crowns and purple girdles, and variegated like flamingos: they drove before them a laden ass. 'What do these kings want in my domain?' said Zarathustra in astonishment to his heart, and hid himself hastily behind a thicket. When, however, the kings approached him he said half-aloud, like one speaking only to himself: 'Strange! Strange! How does this harmonise? Two kings do I see – and only one ass!'

Thereupon the two kings halted; they smiled and looked towards the spot whence the voice proceeded and then looked into each other's faces. 'Such things do we also think among ourselves,' said the king on the right, 'but we do not utter them'.

The king on the left, however, shrugged his shoulders and answered: 'That may perhaps be a goatherd. Or a hermit who has lived too long among rocks and trees. For no society at all spoils also good manners.'

'Good manners?' replied angrily and bitterly the other king: 'what then do we run out of the way of? Is it not "good manners"? Our "good society"?'

'Better, verily, to live among hermits and goatherds than with our gilded, false, painted, over-rouged mob – even though it call itself "good society", 'even though it call itself "nobility." But there all is false and foul, above all the blood, thanks to old bad diseases and worse curers.

'The best and dearest to me at present is still a sound peasant, coarse, artful, obstinate and enduring: that is at present the noblest type.

'The peasant is at present the best; and the peasant type should be master! But it is the kingdom of the mob – I no longer let myself be deceived. The mob, however, means hodgepodge.

'Mob-hodgepodge: therein is everything mixed with everything, saint and swindler, *Junker* and Jew, and every beast out of Noah's Ark.

'Good manners! Everything is false and foul with us. No one knows any longer how to reverence: it is that precisely that we run away from. They are cloying, obtrusive dogs; they gild palm leaves.

'This loathing chokes me, that we kings ourselves have become false, draped and disguised with the old faded pomp of our ancestors, showpieces for the stupidest, the craftiest and whosoever at present traffics for power!

'We are not the first men and have nevertheless to stand for them: of this imposture have we at last become weary and disgusted.

'From the rabble have we gone out of the way, from all those bawlers and scribe-blowflies, from the shopkeepers' stench, the ambition fidgeting, the bad breath: phew to live among the rabble! 'Phew, to stand for the first men among the rabble! Ah, loathing! Loathing! Loathing! What does it now matter about us kings?'

'Your old sickness seizes you,' said here the king on the left, 'your loathing seizes you, my poor brother. You know, however, that someone hears us.'

Immediately thereupon, Zarathustra, who had opened ears and eyes to this talk, rose from his hiding place, advanced towards the kings and thus began:

'He who hearkens unto you, he who gladly hearkens unto you, is called Zarathustra.

'I am Zarathustra who once said: "What does it now matter about kings!" Forgive me, I rejoiced when you said to each other: "What does it matter about us kings!"

'Here, however, is *my* domain and dominion: what may you be seeking in my domain? Perhaps, however, you have found on your way what I seek: namely, the higher man.'

When the kings heard this, they beat their breasts and said with one voice: 'We are recognised!

'With the sword of your utterance sever you the thickest darkness of our hearts. You have discovered our distress; for behold, we are on our way to find the higher man – the man that is higher than we, although we are kings. To him do we convey this ass. For the highest man shall also be the highest lord on earth.

'There is no sorer misfortune in all human destiny than when the mighty of the earth are not also the first men. Then everything becomes false and distorted and monstrous.

'And when they are even the last men, and more beast than man, then rises and rises the mob in honour, and at last says even the mob-virtue: "Behold, I alone am virtue!"'

'What have I just heard?' answered Zarathustra. 'What wisdom in kings! I am enchanted, and verily, I have already promptings to make a rhyme upon it: even if it should happen to be a rhyme not suited for everyone's ears. I unlearned long ago to have consideration for long ears. Well then! Come now!'

(Here, however, it happened that the ass also found utterance: it said distinctly and with malevolence, Yea-Ah.)

'Once – methinks year One of our blessed Lord –

Drunk without wine, the Sybil thus deplored: "How ill things go! Oh, woe!

Decline! Decline! Never sank the world so low!

Rome became a whore and a fine whorehouse too,

Rome's Caesars became beasts, and God himself – a Jew!"'

Translated by Thomas Common with modifications

Nachlass Fragments, 1883–1885

KSA 10 7[26–27] 1883 WP 1026

It is not a fact that 'happiness follows virtue' – but it is the more powerful man who first declares his happy state to be virtue.

Evil actions belong to the powerful and virtuous: bad and base actions belong to the subjected.

The most powerful man, the creator, would have to be the most evil, in as much as he makes his ideal prevail over all men in opposition to their ideals and remoulds them according to his own image. Evil, in this respect, means hard, painful, enforced.

Such men as Napoleon must always return and always confirm our belief in the autocracy of the individual: he himself, however, was corrupted by the means he had to stoop to and lost *noblesse* of character. If he had *had to* prevail among another kind of man, he could have availed himself of other means; and thus it would not seem necessary that a *Caesar* must become bad.

KSA 11 25[105] 1884 WP 982

From war we must learn: (1) to associate death with those interests for which we are fighting – that makes *us* venerable; (2) we must learn to sacrifice *many* and to take our cause sufficiently seriously not to spare men; (3) we must practise inexorable discipline and allow ourselves violence and cunning in war.

KSA 11 25[174] 1884 WP 861

It is necessary for *higher men* to declare war on the masses! From all directions mediocre people are combining in order to make themselves master! Everything that pampers, that softens and that brings the 'people' or 'feminine' to the front operates in favour of *suffrage universel* – that is to say, the dominion of *inferior* men. But we must make reprisals and draw the whole state of affairs (which commenced in Europe with Christianity) to light and to judgement.

KSA 11 25[268] 1884

The peasant is the commonest type of *noblesse*: for he is dependent on himself most of all. Peasant blood is still the *best blood* in Germany, e.g. Luther, Niebuhr, Bismarck.

Where is an aristocratic family to be found in whose blood there is no venereal infection and corruption?

Bismarck a Slav. Let any one look on the faces of the Germans (one understands the astonishment of Napoleon when he saw the poet of Werther and got to see a *man!*): everything that possessed manly, overflowing blood went abroad: over the miserable populace which remained, the servant-souled people, there came an improvement from abroad, especially by means of *Slavonic blood*.

The nobility of the March Brandenburg and the Prussian nobility in general (and the peasant of certain North German districts) comprise at present the most *masculine* natures in Germany.

That the most *masculine men* rule is in order.

KSA 11 25[270] 1884 WP 998

Away from rulers and free of all bonds, live the highest men: and in the rulers they have their instruments.

KSA 11 25[343] 1884 WP 872

The rights which a man arrogates to himself are relative to the duties which he sets himself and to the tasks which he feels *capable of performing*. The great majority of men have no right to life and are only a misfortune to their higher fellows.

KSA 11 25[344] 1884 WP 874

The degeneration of the rulers and of the ruling classes has been the cause of all the great disorders in history! Without the Roman Caesars and Roman society, Christianity would never have prevailed.

When it occurs to inferior men to doubt whether higher men exist, then the danger is great! It is then that men finally discover that there are virtues even among inferior, suppressed and poor-spirited men, and that everybody is equal before God: which is the *non plus ultra* of all confounded nonsense that has ever appeared on earth! For ultimately higher men begin to measure themselves according to the standard of virtues upheld by the slaves – and discover that they are 'proud', etc., and that all their *higher* qualities should be condemned.

When Nero and Caracalla stood at the helm, it was then that the paradox arose: 'The lowest man is of more value than the one on the throne!' And thus the path was prepared for an *image of God* which was as remote as possible from the image of the most powerful – God on the cross!

KSA 11 26[9] 1884 WP 854

In this age of *suffrage universel*, in which everybody is allowed to sit in judgement upon everything and everybody, I feel compelled to re-establish *order of rank*.

KSA 11 26[282] 1884 WP 752

According to whether a people feels: 'the rights, the keenness of vision and the gift of leadership, etc., belong to the few' or 'to the many' – it constitutes an oligarchic or a democratic community.

Monarchy *represents* the belief in a man who is completely superior, a leader, a saviour, a demigod. Aristocracy represents the belief in an elite humanity and higher caste. Democracy represents the disbelief in all great human beings and in all elite societies: 'everybody is everybody else's equal'. 'At bottom we are one and all self-seeking cattle and mob.'

KSA 11 26[335] 1884

Can anyone be interested in this German *Reich*? Where is the new *thought*? Is it only a new combination of power? All the worse, if it does not know what it wants. Peace and *laissez-faire* are not types of politics for which I have any respect. Ruling and helping the highest thoughts to victory – the only thing that could make me interested in Germany. What do I care whether the Hohenzollern are there or not? – England's small-mindedness is presently the great danger on earth. I see more inclination towards greatness in the feelings of the Russian nihilists than in those of the English utilitarians. The German and the Slavonic races ought to grow into one another – and we require, too, the cleverest financiers, the Jews, in order to rule on earth.

KSA 11 26[336] 1884

1. The sense for reality
2. Break with the English principle of representation of the people, we require the representation of the great interests
3. We require an unconditional association with Russia and a new mutual platform which shall not permit any English spin-off to obtain mastery in Russia. No American future!
4. European politics are untenable and the constriction due to Christian views is a *very great mishap*. In Europe, all sensible people are sceptics, whether they admit it or not.

I think that we want to confine ourselves neither to Christian nor to American views.

KSA 11 26[360] 1884 WP 755

Socialists are particularly ridiculous in my eyes, because of their absurd optimism concerning the 'good man' who is supposed to be waiting in their cupboard and who will come into being when the present order of society has been overturned and has made way for natural instincts.

But the opposing party is quite as ludicrous, because it will not see the act of violence which lies beneath every law, the severity and egoism inherent in every kind of authority. 'I and my kind' will rule and prevail: whoever degenerates will be either expelled or annihilated – this was the fundamental feeling of all ancient legislation.

The idea of a higher order of man is hated much more profoundly than monarchs themselves. Anti-aristocracy: always uses hatred of monarchy as a mask –

KSA 11 26[417] 1884 WP 127

I am *delighted* at the military development of Europe, also at the inner anarchical conditions: the period of quietude and 'Chinadom' which Galiani prophesied for this century is now over. Personal and *manly* capacity, bodily capacity, recovers its value, valuations are becoming more physical, nutrition consists ever more and more of flesh. Beautiful men have once more become possible. Bloodless sneaks (with mandarins at their head, as Comte imagined them) are now a matter of the past. The barbarian in everyone of us is *affirmed*, even the wild animal. *Precisely on that account*, philosophers will have a better chance. – Kant is a scarecrow, some day!

KSA 11 26[449] 1884 WP 128

I have not yet seen *any* reasons to feel discouraged. He who acquires and preserves a strong will, together with a broad mind, has a more favourable chance now than ever. For the trainability of men has become exceedingly great in democratic Europe; men who learn easily, who readily adapt themselves, are the rule: the herd animal of a high order of intelligence is prepared. He who would command finds those who *must* obey: I have Napoleon and Bismarck in mind, for instance. The struggle against strong and unintelligent wills, which forms the greatest obstacle, is really insignificant. Who would not be able to knock down these 'objective' gentlemen with weak wills, like Ranke and Renan!

KSA 11 27[60] 1884 WP 983

The *education* which rears those ruling virtues that allow a man to become master of his benevolence and his pity, the great disciplinary virtues ('Forgive thine enemies' is mere child's play beside them), and the *passions of the creator*, must be elevated to the heights – we must cease from carving marble! The exceptional and powerful position of those creatures (compared with any princes hitherto): The Roman Caesar with Christ's soul.

KSA 11 34[109] 1885

N.B. Parliaments may be very useful to a strong and versatile statesman: he has something there to rely upon – every such thing must, however, be able to resist! – upon which he can throw a great deal of responsibility. On the whole, however, I could wish that the counting mania and the superstitious belief in majorities were not established in Germany, as with the Latin races, and that one could finally invent something new even in politics! It is senseless and dangerous to let the custom of universal suffrage – which is still but a short time under cultivation and could easily be uprooted – take a deeper root: while, of course, its introduction was merely an expedient to steer clear of temporary difficulties.

KSA 34[177] 1885 WP 753

I am opposed to 1. socialism because it dreams ingenuously of 'goodness, truth, beauty and equal rights': anarchy pursues the same ideal, but in a more brutal fashion. 2. I am opposed to parliamentary government and the power of the press, because they are the means whereby the herd become masters.

KSA 11 34[203] 1885

The condition of Europe in the next century will once again lead to the breeding of manly virtues, because men will live in continual danger. 'Universal military service' is already the curious antidote which we possess for the effeminacy of democratic ideas: and it has grown up out of the struggle of the nations. (Nations – men who speak one language and read the same newspapers, these men now call themselves 'nations' and would far too readily trace their descent from the same source and through the same history: which, however, even with the assistance of the most malignant lying in the past, they have not succeeded in doing.)

KSA 11 35[9] 1885 WP 132

How are *Good Europeans* such as ourselves distinguished from patriots?

In the first place, we are atheists and immoralists, but for the present we support the religions and the moralities of the herd instinct: for by means of them, a type of man is being prepared, which must one day fall into our hands, which must actually desire our hands.

Beyond good and evil, but we insist upon the unconditional and strict preservation of herd-morality.

We reserve ourselves the right to several kinds of philosophy which it is necessary to learn: under certain circumstances the pessimistic kind as a hammer; a European Buddhism might perhaps be indispensable.

We should probably support the development and the maturing of democratic tendencies: for they enhance weakness of will: in socialism we recognise a thorn which protects against being comfortable.

Attitude towards the people. Our prejudices; we pay attention to the results of interbreeding.

Detached, well-to-do, strong: irony concerning the 'press' and its culture. Our care: that scientific men should not become journalists. We despise any form of culture that tolerates newspaper reading or writing.

We make our accidental positions (like Goethe and Stendhal), our experiences, as foreground, and we lay stress on them, so that we may deceive concerning our backgrounds. We ourselves wait and avoid putting our heart into them. They serve us as refuges, such as a wanderer might require and use – but we avoid feeling at home in them.

We are ahead of our fellow men in possessing a *disciplina voluntatis*. All strength applied to development of *strength of the will*, an art that permits us to wear masks, an art of understanding beyond the affects (also to think in a 'supra-European' way, at times).

Preparation for becoming the legislators of the future, the masters of the earth, at least our children. Basic concern with marriages.

KSA 11 36[48] 1885 WP 129

Spiritual enlightenment is an unfailing means of making men uncertain, weak of will and needful of succour and support – in short, of developing the herd animal in them. That is why all great artists of government so far (Confucius in China, the *imperium Romanum*, Napoleon, the papacy at a time when they had the courage of their worldliness and frankly pursued power) in whom the ruling instincts that had prevailed until their time culminated, also made use of spiritual enlightenment; or at least allowed it to be supreme (after the style of the Popes of the Renaissance). The self-deception of the masses on this point, in every democracy for instance, is of the greatest possible value: all that makes men smaller and more amenable is pursued under the title 'progress'!

KSA 11 37[8] 1885 WP 957

The question, and at the same time the task, is approaching with hesitation, terrible as fate, but nevertheless inevitable: how shall the earth as a whole be ruled? And to what end shall man as a whole – no longer as a people or as a race – be reared and trained?

Legislative moralities are the principal means by which one can form mankind, according to the fancy of a creative and profound will: provided that such an artistic will of the first order gets the power into its own hands, and can make its creative will prevail over long periods in the form of legislation, religions and customs. At present, and probably for some time to come, one will seek such colossally creative men, such really great men, as I understand them, in vain: they will be lacking, until, after many disappointments, we are forced to begin to understand why it is they are lacking, and that nothing bars with greater hostility their rise and development, at present and for some time to come, than that which is now called simply 'morality' in Europe. Just as if there were no other kind of morality, and could be no other kind, than the one we have already characterised as herd morality. It is this morality which is now striving with all its power to attain to that green-meadow happiness on earth, which consists in security, absence of danger, ease, facilities for livelihood and, last but not least, 'if all goes well', even hopes to dispense with all kinds of shepherds or bellwethers. The two doctrines which it preaches most universally are 'equality of rights' and 'pity for all that suffers' – and it even regards suffering itself as something which must be abolished absolutely. That such ideas may be modern leads one to think very poorly of modernity.

He, however, who has reflected deeply concerning the question, how and where the plant man has hitherto grown most vigorously, is forced to believe that this has always taken place under the *reverse* conditions; that to this end the danger of the situation has to increase enormously, his inventive faculty and dissembling powers have to fight their way up under long oppression and compulsion, and his will to life has to be increased to the unconditioned will to power and to overpower: he believes that danger, severity, violence, peril in the street and in the heart, inequality of rights, secrecy, stoicism, seductive art and devilry of every kind – in short, the opposite of all herd desiderata – are necessary for the elevation of man. Such a morality with opposite designs, which would rear man upwards instead of to comfort and mediocrity; such a morality, with the intention of producing a ruling caste – the future *masters of the earth* – must, in order to be taught at all, introduce itself as if it were in some way correlated to the prevailing moral law, and must come forward under the cover of the latter's words and forms. But seeing that, to this end, a host of transitional and deceptive measures must be discovered, and that the life of a single individual stands for almost nothing in view of the accomplishment of such lengthy tasks and aims, the first thing that must be done is to rear *a new type* of man in whom the duration of the necessary will and the necessary instincts is guaranteed for many generations. This must be a new kind of ruling species and caste – this ought to be quite as clear as the somewhat lengthy and not easily expressed consequences of this thought. The aim should be to prepare a *reversal of values* for a particularly strong kind of man, most highly gifted in intellect and will and, to this end, slowly and cautiously to liberate in him a whole host of slandered instincts hitherto held in check: whoever reflects on this problem belongs to us, the free spirits – certainly not to that kind of 'free spirit' which has existed hitherto: for these desired practically the reverse. To this order, it seems to me, belong above all the pessimists of Europe, the poets and thinkers of a revolted idealism, in so far as their discontent with existence in general must consistently at least have led them to be dissatisfied with the man of the present; the same applies to certain insatiably ambitious artists who courageously and unconditionally fight against the herd animal for the special rights of higher men subdue all herd instincts and precautions of more exceptional minds by their seductive art. Thirdly and lastly, we should include in this group all those critics and historians by whom the discovery of the Old World, which has begun so happily – this was the work of the *new* Columbus, of German intellect – will be courageously continued (for we still stand in the very first stages of this conquest). For in the Old World, as a matter of fact, a different and more lordly morality ruled than that of today; and the man of antiquity, under the educational ban of his morality, was a stronger and deeper man than the man of today – up to the present he has been the only 'well-constituted man'. But the seductive power that antiquity exercises on such well turned out, i.e. on strong and enterprising, souls is the most subtle and effective of all anti-democratic and anti-Christian influences even today, just as it was in the time of the Renaissance.

KSA 11 37[9] 1885

I see over and beyond all these national wars, new 'empires', and whatever else lies in the foreground. What I am concerned with – for I see it preparing itself slowly and hesitatingly – is a United Europe. It was the only real work, the one impulse in the souls, of all the broad-minded and deep-thinking men of this century – this preparation of a new synthesis and the tentative effort to anticipate the future of 'the European'. Only in their weaker moments, or when they grew old, did they fall back again into the national narrowness of the 'Fatherlanders' – then they were once more 'patriots'. I am thinking of men like Napoleon, Goethe, Beethoven, Stendhal, Heinrich Heine, Schopenhauer; perhaps Richard Wagner likewise belongs to their number, concerning whom, as a successful type of German obscurity, nothing can be said without some such 'perhaps'.

But to the help of such minds as feel the need of a new unity there comes a great explanatory economic fact: the small states of Europe, I refer to all our present kingdoms and 'empires', will in a short time become economically untenable, owing to the mad, uncontrolled struggle for the possession of local and international trade. (Money is even now compelling European nations to amalgamate into one power.) In order, however, that Europe may engage in the battle for the mastery of the world with good prospects of victory – it is easy to perceive against whom this battle will be waged – she must probably 'come to an understanding' with England. The English colonies are needed for this struggle, just as much as modern Germany, to play her new role of broker and middleman, requires the colonial possessions of Holland. For no one any longer believes that England alone is strong enough to continue to act her old part for another fifty years; the impossibility of shutting out *homines novi* from the government will ruin her, and her continual change of political parties is a fatal obstacle to the carrying out of any tasks which need to be spread out over a long period of time – a man must today be a soldier first and foremost that he may not afterwards lose his credit as a merchant. Enough: here, as in other matters, the coming century will be found following in the footsteps of Napoleon, the first man and the man of greatest initiative and advanced views of modern times.

For the tasks of the next century, the methods of 'popular representation' and parliaments are the most inappropriate imaginable.

KSA 11 37[11] 1885 WP 125

Socialism – or the *tyranny* of the meanest and the most brainless, i.e. the superficial, the envious and the mummers, brought to its zenith – is, as a matter of fact, the logical conclusion of 'modern ideas' and their latent anarchy: but in the genial atmosphere of democratic well-being the capacity for forming resolutions or to finish, weakens. One follows – but no longer their reason. That is why socialism is on the whole a hopelessly bitter affair: and there is nothing more amusing than to observe the discord between the poisonous and desperate faces of today's socialists – and what wretched and nonsensical feelings does not their style reveal to us! – and the childish, lamblike happiness of their hopes and desires. Nevertheless, in many places in Europe, there may be violent hand-to-hand struggles and irruptions on their account: the coming century is likely to be convulsed in more than one spot, and the Paris Commune, which finds defenders and advocates even in Germany, will seem to have been but a slight indigestion compared with what is to come. Be this as it may, there will always be too many people of property for socialism ever to signify anything more than a sickness: and these people of property are like one man with one faith: 'one must possess something in order to *be* something'. This, however, is the oldest and most wholesome of all instincts; I should add: one must desire more than one has in order to *become* more. For this is the doctrine which life itself preaches to all living things: the morality of development. To have and to wish to have more – in a word, growth – that is life itself. In the doctrine of socialism 'a will to the negation of life' is but poorly concealed: the human beings and races who have devised a doctrine of this sort must be bungled. In fact, I even wish that a few experiments might be made to show that in a socialist society, life negates itself and cuts away its own roots. The earth is big enough and man is still unexhausted enough for a practical lesson of this sort and *demonstratio ad absurdum* – even if it were accomplished only by a vast expenditure of lives – to seem worthwhile to me. Still, socialism, like a restless mole under the soil of a society wallowing in stupidity, will be able to achieve something useful and salutary: it delays 'Peace on Earth' and the whole process of character-softening of the democratic herd animal; it forces the European to retain an extra supply of intellect, namely cunning and caution, and prevents his entirely abandoning the manly and warlike virtues, and to retain some remnant of spirit, of clarity, sobriety and coldness of the spirit – it also saves Europe awhile from the *marasmus femininus* which is threatening it.

KSA 11 40[26] 1885 WP 783

The two traits which characterise the modern European are apparently antagonistic – *individualism and the demand for equal rights*: this I am at last beginning to understand. The individual is an extremely vulnerable piece of vanity: this vanity, when it is conscious of its high degree of susceptibility to pain, demands that everyone should be made equal; that the individual should only stand *inter pares*. But in this way a social race is depicted in which, as a matter of fact, gifts and powers are on the whole equally distributed. The pride which would have loneliness and but few appreciators is quite beyond comprehension: really 'great' successes are only attained through the masses – indeed, we scarcely understand yet that a mob success is in reality only a small success; because *pulchrum est paucorum hominum*.

No morality will countenance order of rank among men, and the jurists know nothing of a communal conscience. The principle of individualism rejects *really great* men, and demands the most delicate vision for, and the speediest discovery of, a talent among people who are almost equal; and in as much as everyone has some modicum of talent in such late and civilised cultures – and can, therefore, expect to receive his share of honour – there is a more general flattering of modest merits today than there has ever been: it gives the age the appearance of *unlimited justice*. Its want of justice is to be found not in its unbounded hatred of tyrants and demagogues, even in the arts, but in its detestation of *noble* natures who scorn the fortune of the many. The demand for equal rights (i.e. the privilege of sitting in judgement on everything and everybody) is *anti-aristocratic*.

This age knows just as little concerning the vanished individual, the absorption in a great type, the desire not to be a personality. It was this that formerly constituted the distinction and ambition of many lofty natures (the greatest poets among them); or of the desire 'to be a city' as in Greece; or of Jesuitism, or of the Prussian officer corps and bureaucracy; or of apprenticeship and a continuation of the tradition of great masters: to all of which things, nonsocial conditions and the absence of *petty vanity* are necessary.

KSA 11 41[3] 1885 WP 942

The only nobility is that of birth and blood. (I do not refer here to the prefix 'von' and the *Almanach de Gotha*: this is a parenthesis for asses.) Wherever people speak of the 'aristocrats of the spirit', reasons are generally not lacking for concealing something; it is known to be a password among ambitious Jews. Spirit alone does not ennoble; on the contrary, something is always needed to ennoble the spirit. – What then is needed? – Blood.

Translated by J. M. Kennedy, A. Ludovici with modifications

5
Aristocratic Radical, 1886–1887

Preface

Nietzsche's 'campaign against morality' in its political dimension extends to the writings of 1886–87. In *Beyond Good and Evil*, the *'critique of modernity'* that Nietzsche describes as his task includes 'modern politics',[1] and the 'herd animal morality' he analyses finds expression in 'political and social arrangements'.[2] It is now more evident that he is increasingly critical of the *Reich* and its democratic concessions. In fact, his view in 1886 is that since its founding in 1871 the *Reich* has been making a progressive 'transition … to a levelling mediocrity, democracy'.[3] Democracy is declared to be a 'degenerating form of political organisation',[4] which makes men mediocre and reduces their value.

In the 1880s, democracy, socialism and anarchism, as species of egalitarianism, the 'herd instinct' or neo-Christianity,[5] are deployed virtually interchangeably, distinguished only by their respective tendency to violence or non-violence. While socialists in Nietzsche's Germany were ideologically divided with respect to whether or not they should participate in the *Reichstag*, anarchists were unanimous in their rejection of parliamentary processes and thus Nietzsche rightly identifies them as more 'furious' than the democrats.[6] This has significance for his cynical preference for democracy.

In *The Gay Science*, Nietzsche declares that he is 'homeless' in contemporary political society and encapsulates his oppositional programme as follows, invoking a real or imagined community:

> We 'conserve' nothing, nor would we return to any past age; we are not by any means 'liberal', we do not work for 'progress', we do not need first to stop our ears to the song of the marketplace and the sirens of the future – their song of 'equal rights', 'free society', 'no longer either masters or slaves', does not seduce us! We do not by any means consider it desirable that the realm of justice and peace should be established on earth.[7]

In offering a solution to the inevitable democratisation of Europe, Nietzsche assumes the role of a political prophet, declaring a new goal: 'the breeding of a new ruling caste for Europe'.[8]

As the prophet of this new ruling caste or new aristocracy, Nietzsche announces 'the necessity for new orders, even of a new slavery'.[9] He advises the active forces to strategically 'avail themselves of democratic Europe as the most suitable and supple instrument they can have for taking the fate of the earth into their own hands'.[10]

Nietzsche could not have made this assertion regarding new forms of slavery and others like it in these texts[11] without being aware of the anti-slavery movement in Germany, which commenced in 1887, or of the many efforts globally to eradicate slavery during the latter part of the nineteenth century, or of the signing of an international ban on the slave trade at the Berlin Conference of 1884. Nietzsche injects himself into a debate of his time when he disagrees with the 'Abolition of Slavery' because the imperialistic *'humanisation'* behind it involves 'the *annihilation of* a fundamentally different species' and claims a monopoly on the meaning of what is *human*.[12] Nietzsche's support of slavery here is made in favour of cultural variety; or because he thinks the 'elevation of culture'[13] depends on it: *'Every* elevation of the type "man" has so far been the work of an aristocratic society...a society believing in...an order of rank and differences of worth among human beings, and requiring slavery in some form or other.'[14] Aristocratic society believes in order of rank and class differences, the *pathos of distance* between classes.[15]

The new European ruling caste Nietzsche proposes entails the appearance of 'a new type of philosopher and commander'[16] whose task will be to revalue all values and laws on the basis of their own will to power. As Nietzsche is preparing the ground for this revaluation, he is constructing the basic political philosophy of these future active forces: thus his opposition to the natural law tradition and the principle of equality before the law,[17] his revaluation of law, or the 'conditions of law', as always *'exceptional conditions'* because they are based on power and 'the struggle of power complexes'.[18] The new type of philosopher is motivated towards a different level of 'psychical power', which accommodates itself to immoral (anti-Christian) actions,[19] which accompany 'every advance in culture', inspired by 'the Renaissance concept of *virtù*'.[20] Nietzsche's glorification of 'Renaissance *virtù*' (capacity, proficiency) was probably influenced by Jacob Burckhardt and situates him within an international movement, which included Stendhal and Gobineau in France, 'referred to in Germany as *Renaissancismus*'.[21]

Nietzsche believes that 'the democratisation of Europe will tend to the production of a type prepared for *slavery*' and will constitute 'an involuntary arrangement for the breeding of *tyrants*'[22] – 'a higher type of ruling and Caesarean spirits' – and thus he encourages its 'acceleration'.[23] Nietzsche models the new philosopher-legislator on Napoleon, the 'synthesis of the *inhuman* and *superhuman*'.[24]

After Europe's last political nobility of seventeenth- and eighteenth-century France was destroyed by 'the instincts of popular *ressentiment*', which '*privileged the rights of the majority*', Napoleon appeared with the 'delightful counter-slogan ... *privileged rights of the few*!'[25] He adulates Napoleon for being an enemy of modern ideas and sees him as 'one of the greatest continuators of the Renaissance',[26] an individual who possessed *virtù*.

Nietzsche interprets history as consisting of a struggle between 'two *opposing* values' summarised in the formula 'Rome against Judea, Judea against Rome'.[27] This history begins with the struggle between Roman aristocratic values and Jewish *ressentiment* values, a conflict that is subsequently resumed in the struggle between the Renaissance and the Lutheran Reformation, between the nobility of seventeenth- and eighteenth-century France and the populism of the French Revolution, between the values of the French Revolution and the personality of Napoleon. The Renaissance, for example, marked the return to the aristocratic classical tradition, while the French Revolution represented 'the last great slave insurrection',[28] the first being the Jewish revolt in ancient Rome.[29] In recounting this history, Nietzsche is applying his well-known distinction between master (noble) and slave moralities (a division which even structures the human body)[30] to certain developments in European history. Restoring the concept of master and slave and the antagonism it implies respectively corresponds with Nietzsche's affirmation of privilege and autocracy and his negation of the socialist formula, '*Ni dieu, ni maître*',[31] of the 'preference for the "*commune*" ... which all European socialists now share',[32] of the slave morality conveyed by democracy and anarchism.

Nietzsche's evocation of Napoleon as an exemplar was intended to capture his politics of the future, particularly his Napoleonic ideal for a politically and economically unified Europe.[33] Nietzsche adopted the expression, 'grand politics' (*grosse Politik*) to designate international politics, 'a higher form of politics specifically addressing European and world power conflicts',[34] and the formation of a European Union against 'the long spun-out comedy of ... petty statism, and its dynastic as well as democratic splinter wills.... the next century will bring the struggle for the dominion of the world – the *compulsion* to grand politics'.[35] In the political parlance of the time, the expression 'grand politics' was used to celebrate the accomplishments of Bismarck, the 'great statesman'. Critical of German nationalistic politics, Nietzsche dissociates the label 'grand politics' from the power politics of the *Reich* – Bismarck's policy of 'blood and iron'.[36] Bismarck (the 'statesman' Nietzsche refers to in *Beyond Good and Evil*) has not practised 'grand politics', but has merely constructed for the masses 'a new tower of Babel, some monstrosity of empire and power, they call "great" '.[37] Nietzsche questions whether Bismarck's ability to inspire nationalistic fervour in the people is a criterion of greatness when it comes at such a high price: the desolation of the German spirit.

There are a number of selections in this chapter expressing Nietzsche's repudiation of German anti-Semitism, which he considers to be a *ressentiment* movement.[38] Nietzsche is not only an opponent of anti-Semitism, which began to intensify in Germany in the 1880s, but is also critical of the misguided motivations of politicians claiming to reject anti-Semitism with policies that are only aimed at 'its dangerous excess' instead of being 'directed against the nature of the sentiment itself'.[39] Nietzsche recommends that all anti-Semites be sent into exile, which may be read as a diametric reaction to Bismarck's 'anti-Polish folly'.[40] To curry political favour, Bismarck pandered to public pressure demanding policies in support of German nationalism, and in 1885 ordered the expulsion from Prussia of 30,000 Poles and Jews of non-German nationality. Not 'nearly German enough to advocate nationalism [and] race-hatred',[41] Nietzsche opposed the government's action.

Though harshly critical of ancient Judaism,[42] Nietzsche, not inconsistently, supports Jewish assimilation.[43] But beyond this, the Jews play a highly significant role in his political thought, included as they are in his conception of a new ruling caste. Anyone concerned with the future of Europe will look to the Jews and the Russians as the 'surest and likeliest factors in the great play and battle of forces', for the 'Jews...are without doubt the strongest, toughest and purest race at present living in Europe'.[44] While in Russia, the 'power to will has been long stored up and accumulated' and 'waits threateningly to be discharged'.[45] Nietzsche viewed this Russian threat as cause for unifying Europe, whereas Bismarck dealt with the threat of war with the Tsarist empire with a peace proposal, the 'Reinsurance Treaty' (1887), which was an attempt to maintain an alliance with Russia following the breakdown of the Three Emperors' League.

After 1878, the Conservatives became a political force whose main innovation was to introduce the notion of a Christian state into the social, political and cultural fabric of the German nation. The Christian state 'derived its authority and justification from the Lutheran doctrine of the state',[46] thus Nietzsche's criticism of the Lutheran Reformation during this period is entirely appropriate.[47] In the early 1880s, Bismarck introduced 'practical Christianity' to justify his progressive social policy and offer 'a little more Christian concern for the welfare of the workers'.[48] The idea of the Christian state would also encompass, with the definitive end of the *Kulturkampf* in 1887, newly integrated Catholic interests, which would serve German colonial ambitions. Bismarck was drifting towards Rome just as Wagner had done.[49] It would also attract ultra-conservative circles around the *Kreuzzeitung* and Adolf Stöcker's Christian Social Movement. Yet these events were not enough to prevent Nietzsche from proclaiming that 'we see the religious community of Christianity shaken to its deepest foundations. The faith in God is overthrown, the faith in the Christian ascetic ideal is now fighting its last fight'.[50] Nietzsche's 'good Europeans' are described as having 'outgrown Christianity',[51] perhaps with a certain ambiguity regarding its preservation.[52] But it is the new philosopher whose conception haunts these pages, the vision of the 'man of the future...who restores to the earth its purpose and to human beings their hope, this Antichrist and anti-nihilist, this conqueror of God and of nothingness – *at some point he must come....*'[53]

Beyond Good and Evil: Prelude to a Philosophy of the Future, 1886

22

Let me be pardoned, as an old philologist who cannot desist from the mischief of putting his finger on bad modes of interpretation, but 'Nature's conformity to law', of which you physicists talk so proudly, as though – why, it exists only owing to your interpretation and bad 'philology'. It is no matter of fact, no 'text', but rather just a naively humanitarian adjustment and perversion of meaning, with which you make abundant concessions to the democratic instincts of the modern soul! 'Everywhere equality before the law – Nature is not different in that respect, nor better than we': a fine instance of secret motive, in which the vulgar antagonism to everything privileged and autocratic – likewise a second and more refined atheism – is once more disguised. '*Ni dieu, ni maître*' – that also is what you want; and therefore 'Hurrah for natural law!' – is it not so? But, as has been said, that is interpretation, not text; and somebody might come along, who, with opposite intentions and modes of interpretation, could read out of the same 'Nature', and with regard to the same phenomena, just the tyrannically inconsiderate and relentless enforcement of the claims of power – an interpreter who should so place the unexceptional and unconditional aspects of all 'Will to Power' before your eyes, that almost every word, and the word 'tyranny' itself, would eventually seem unsuitable, or like a weakening and softening metaphor – as being too human; and who should, nevertheless, end by asserting the same about this world as you do, namely, that it has a 'necessary' and 'calculable' course, *not*, however, because laws obtain in it, but because they are absolutely *lacking* and every power effects its ultimate consequences every moment. Granted that this also is only interpretation – and you will be eager enough to make this objection? – well, so much the better.

30

Our deepest insights must – and should – appear as follies, and under certain circumstances as crimes, when they come without permission to the ears of those who are not disposed and predestined for them. The exoteric and the esoteric, as they were formerly distinguished by philosophers – among the Indians, as among the Greeks, Persians and Muslims, in short, wherever people believed in order of rank and *not* in equality and equal rights – are not so much in contradistinction to one another in respect to the exoteric class, standing without, and viewing, estimating, measuring, and judging from the outside, and not from the inside; the more essential distinction is that the class in question views things from below upwards – while the esoteric class views things *from above downwards*. There are heights of the soul from which tragedy itself no longer appears to operate tragically; and if all the woe in the world were taken together, who would dare to decide whether the sight of it would *necessarily* seduce and constrain to sympathy, and thus to a doubling of that woe?... That which serves the higher class of men for nourishment or refreshment must almost be poison to an entirely different and lower order of human beings. The virtues of the common man would perhaps mean vice and weakness in a philosopher; it might be possible for a highly developed man, supposing him to degenerate and go to ruin, to acquire qualities thereby alone, for the sake of which he would have to be honoured as a saint in the lower world into which he had sunk. There are books which have an inverse value for the soul and the health according as the inferior soul and the lower vitality, or the higher and more powerful, make use of them. In the former case they are dangerous, disturbing, unsettling books, in the latter case they are heralds' calls which summon the bravest to *their* bravery. Books for the general reader are always vile-smelling books, the odour of paltry people clings to them. Where the populace eat and drink, and even where they reverence, it is accustomed to stink. One should not go into churches if one wishes to breathe *pure* air.

44

Need I say expressly after all this that they will be free, *very* free spirits, these philosophers of the future – as certainly also they will not be merely free spirits, but something more, higher, greater and fundamentally different, which does not wish to be misunderstood and mistaken? But while I say this, I feel under *obligation* almost as much to them as to ourselves (we free spirits who are their heralds and forerunners) to sweep away from ourselves altogether a stupid old prejudice and misunderstanding, which, like a fog, has too long made the conception of 'free spirit' obscure. In every country of Europe, and the same in America, there is at present something which makes an abuse of this name a very narrow, prepossessed, enchained class of spirits, who desire almost the opposite of what our intentions and instincts prompt – not to mention that in respect to the *new* philosophers who are appearing, they must still more be closed windows and bolted doors. Briefly and regrettably, they belong to the *levellers*, these wrongly named 'free spirits' – as glib-tongued and scribe-fingered slaves of the democratic taste and its 'modern ideas' all of them men without solitude, without personal solitude, blunt, honest fellows to whom neither courage nor honourable conduct ought to be denied, only they are not free and are ludicrously superficial, especially in their innate partiality for seeing the cause of almost *all* human misery and failure in the old forms in which society has so far existed – a notion which happily inverts the truth entirely! What they would fain attain with all their strength, is the universal, green-meadow happiness of the herd, together with security, safety, comfort and ease of life for everyone, their two most frequently chanted songs and doctrines are called 'equality of rights' and 'sympathy with all that suffers' – and suffering itself is looked upon by them as something which must be *abolished*. We opposite ones, however, who have opened our eye and conscience to the question how and where the plant 'man' has so far grown most vigorously, believe that this has always taken place under the opposite conditions, that for this end the dangerousness of his situation had to be increased enormously, his inventive faculty and dissembling power (his 'spirit') had to develop into subtlety and daring under long oppression and compulsion, and his will to life had to be increased to the unconditioned will to power – we believe that severity, violence, slavery, danger in the street and in the heart, secrecy, stoicism, tempter's art and devilry of every kind – that everything wicked, terrible, tyrannical, predatory and serpentine in man, serves as well for the elevation of the human species as its opposite – we do not even say enough when we only say *this much*, and in any case we find ourselves here, both with our speech and our silence, at the *other* extreme of all modern ideology and gregarious desirability, as their antipodes perhaps? What wonder that we 'free spirits' are not exactly the most communicative spirits? That we do not wish to betray in every respect *what* a spirit can free itself from, and *where* perhaps it will then be driven? And as to the import of the dangerous formula 'beyond good and evil', with which we at least avoid confusion, we *are* something other than *'libres-penseurs'*, *'liberi pensatori'*, *'Freidenker'* and whatever these honest advocates of 'modern ideas' like to call themselves. Having been at home, or at least guests, in many realms of the spirit, having escaped again and again from the gloomy, agreeable nooks in which preferences and prejudices, youth, origin, the accident of men and books, or even the weariness of travel seemed to confine us, full of malice against the seductions of dependency which he concealed in honours, money, positions or exaltation of the senses, grateful even for distress and the vicissitudes of illness, because they always free us from some rule and its 'prejudice', grateful to the god, devil, sheep and worm in us, inquisitive to a fault, investigators to the point of cruelty, with unhesitating fingers for the intangible, with teeth and stomachs for the most indigestible, ready for any business that requires sagacity and acute senses, ready for every adventure, owing to an excess of 'free will', with anterior and posterior souls, into the ultimate intentions of which it is difficult to pry, with foregrounds and backgrounds to the end of which no foot may run, hidden ones under the mantles of light, appropriators, although we resemble heirs and spendthrifts, arrangers and collectors from morning till night, misers of our wealth and our fully crammed drawers, economical in learning and forgetting, inventive in scheming, sometimes proud of tables of categories, sometimes pedants, sometimes night owls of work even in full day, if necessary, even scarecrows – and it is necessary nowadays, that is to say, inasmuch as we are the born, sworn, jealous friends of *solitude*, of our own profoundest midnight and midday solitude – such kind of men are we, we free spirits! And perhaps you are also something of the same kind, you coming ones, you *new* philosophers?

46

Faith such as early Christianity desired, and not infrequently achieved in the midst of a sceptical and southerly free-spirited world, which had centuries of struggle between philosophical schools behind it and in it, counting besides the education in tolerance which the *imperium Romanum* gave – this faith is not that sincere, austere slave faith by which perhaps a Luther or a Cromwell or some other northern barbarian of the spirit remained attached to his God and Christianity, it is much rather the faith of Pascal, which resembles in a terrible manner a continuous suicide of reason – a tough, long-lived, wormlike reason, which is not to be slain at once and with a single blow. The Christian faith from the beginning is sacrifice: the sacrifice of all freedom, all pride, all self-confidence of spirit, it is at the same time subjection, self-derision and self-mutilation. There is cruelty and religious Phoenicianism in this faith, which is adapted to a tender, many-sided and very fastidious conscience, it takes for granted that the subjection of the spirit is indescribably *painful*, that all the past and all the habits of such a spirit resist the *absurdissimum*, in the form of which 'faith' comes to it. Modern men, with their obtuseness as regards all Christian nomenclature, no longer have the sense for the terribly superlative conception which was implied to an antique taste by the paradox of the formula 'God on the cross'. There had never and nowhere been such boldness in inversion, nor anything at once so dreadful, questioning and questionable as this formula: it promised a revaluation of all ancient values – It was the Orient, the *profound* Orient, it was the Oriental slave who thus took revenge on Rome and its noble, light-minded toleration, on the Roman 'Catholicism' of faith, and it was always not the faith but the freedom from the faith, the half-stoical and smiling indifference to the seriousness of the faith, which made the slaves indignant at their masters and revolt against them. 'Enlightenment' causes revolt, for the slave desires the unconditioned, he understands nothing but the tyrannical, even in morals, he loves as he hates, without *nuance*, to the very depths, to the point of pain, to the point of sickness – his many *hidden* sufferings make him revolt against the noble taste which seems to *deny* suffering. The scepticism with regard to suffering, fundamentally only an attitude of aristocratic morality, was not the least of the causes, also, of the last great slave insurrection which began with the French Revolution.

61

The philosopher, as *we* free spirits understand him – as the man of the greatest responsibility, who has the conscience for the general development of mankind – will use religion for his disciplining and educating work, just as he will use the contemporary political and economic conditions. The selecting and disciplining influence – destructive, as well as creative and fashioning – which can be exercised by means of religion is manifold and varied, according to the sort of people placed under its spell and protection. For those who are strong and independent, destined and trained to command, in whom the judgement and skill of a ruling race is incorporated, religion is an additional means for overcoming resistance in the exercise of authority – as a bond which binds rulers and subjects in common, betraying and surrendering to the former the conscience of the latter, their inmost heart, which would like to escape obedience. And in the case of the unique natures of noble origin, if by virtue of superior spirituality they should incline to a more retired and contemplative life, reserving to themselves only the more refined forms of government (over chosen disciples or members of an order), religion itself may be used as a means for obtaining peace from the noise and trouble of managing *cruder* affairs, and for securing immunity from the *unavoidable* filth of all political agitation. The Brahmins, for instance, understood this fact. With the help of a religious organisation, they secured to themselves the power of nominating kings for the people, while their sentiments prompted them to keep apart and outside, as men with a higher and supra-royal mission. At the same time religion gives inducement and opportunity to some of the subjects to qualify themselves for future ruling and commanding the slowly ascending ranks and classes, which, through fortunate marriage customs, volitional power and delight in self-control, are on the increase. To them religion offers sufficient incentives and temptations to aspire to higher intellectuality and to experience the sentiments of authoritative self-control, of silence and of solitude. Asceticism and Puritanism are almost indispensable means of educating and ennobling a race which seeks to rise above its hereditary baseness and work itself upwards to future supremacy. And finally, to ordinary men, to the majority of the people who exist for service and general utility, and are only so far entitled to exist, religion gives invaluable contentedness with their lot and condition, peace of heart, ennoblement of obedience, additional social happiness and sympathy, with something of transfiguration and embellishment, something of justification of all the commonplaceness, all the meanness, all the semi-animal poverty of their souls. Religion, together with the religious significance of life, casts sunlight over such perpetually harassed men and makes even their own aspect endurable to them, it operates on them as the Epicurean philosophy usually operates on sufferers of a higher order, in a refreshing and refining manner, almost *turning* suffering *to account*, and in the end even hallowing and vindicating it. There is perhaps nothing so admirable in Christianity and Buddhism as their art of teaching even the lowest to elevate themselves by piety to a seemingly higher order of things, and thereby to retain their satisfaction with the actual world in which they find it difficult enough to live – this very difficulty being necessary.

199

Inasmuch as in all ages, as long as mankind has existed, there have also been human herds (family alliances, communities, tribes, peoples, states, churches) and always a great number who obey in proportion to the small number who command – in view, therefore, of the fact that obedience has been most practised and fostered among mankind so far, one may reasonably suppose that, generally speaking, the need for it is now innate in everyone, as a kind of *formal conscience* which gives the command 'Thou shalt unconditionally do something, unconditionally refrain from something', in short, 'Thou shalt'. This need tries to satisfy itself and to fill its form with a content, according to its strength, impatience and eagerness, it at once seizes as an omnivorous appetite with little selection and accepts whatever is shouted in its ear by all sorts of commanders – parents, teachers, laws, class prejudices or public opinion. The extraordinary limitation of human development, the hesitation, protractedness, frequent retrogression and going round in circles, is due to the fact that the herd instinct of obedience is transmitted best, and at the cost of the art of command. If we imagine this instinct increasing to its greatest extent, commanders and independent individuals will finally be lacking altogether, or they will suffer inwardly from a bad conscience and will have to impose a deception on themselves in the first place in order to be able to command just as if they also were only obeying. This condition of things actually exists in Europe at present – I call it the moral hypocrisy of the commanding class. They know no other way of protecting themselves from their bad conscience than by playing the role of executors of older and higher orders (of predecessors, of the constitution, of justice, of the law or of God himself), or they even justify themselves by maxims from the current opinions of the herd, as 'first servants of their people' or 'instruments of the public weal'. On the other hand, the herd man in Europe today assumes an air as if he were the only kind of man that is permissible, he glorifies his qualities, such as public spirit, kindness, deference, industry, temperance, modesty, indulgence, sympathy, by virtue of which he is gentle, endurable and useful to the herd, as the peculiarly human virtues. In cases, however, where it is believed that the leader and bellwether cannot be dispensed with, attempt after attempt is made today to replace commanders by the summing together of clever herd men: all representative constitutions, for example, are of this origin. In spite of all, what a blessing, what a deliverance from a weight becoming unendurable, is the appearance of an absolute ruler for these herd Europeans – of this fact the effect of the appearance of Napoleon was the last great proof: the history of the influence of Napoleon is almost the history of the higher happiness to which the entire century has attained in its worthiest individuals and periods.

200

The man of an age of dissolution which mixes the races with one another, who has the inheritance of a diversified descent in his body – that is to say, contrary, and often not only contrary, instincts and standards of value, which struggle with one another and are seldom at peace – such a man of late culture and broken lights will, on average, be a weak man. His fundamental desire is that the war which is *in him* should come to an end; happiness appears to him in the character of a soothing medicine and mode of thought (for instance, Epicurean or Christian); it is above all things the happiness of repose, of undisturbedness, of repletion, of final unity – it is the 'Sabbath of Sabbaths', to use the expression of the holy rhetorician St Augustine, who was himself such a man. – Should, however, the contrariety and conflict in such natures operate as an *additional* incentive and stimulus to life – and if, on the other hand, in addition to their powerful and irreconcilable instincts, they have also inherited and indoctrinated into them a proper mastery and subtlety for carrying on the conflict with themselves (that is to say, the faculty of self-control and self-deception), there then arise those marvellously incomprehensible and inexplicable beings, those enigmatic men, predestined for conquering and circumventing others, the finest examples of which are Alcibiades and Caesar (with whom I should like to associate the *first* of Europeans according to my taste, the Hohenstaufen Friedrich II), and among artists, perhaps, Leonardo da Vinci. They appear precisely in the same periods when that weaker type, with its longing for repose, comes to the fore; the two types are complementary to each other and spring from the same causes.

201

As long as the utility which determines moral estimates is only herd utility, as long as the preservation of the community is only kept in view, and the immoral is sought precisely and exclusively in what seems dangerous to the maintenance of the community, there can be no 'morality of love of one's neighbour'. Granted even that there is already a little constant exercise of consideration, sympathy, fairness, gentleness and mutual assistance, granted that even in this condition of society all those instincts are already active which are later distinguished by honourable names as 'virtues' and eventually almost coincide with the conception 'morality': in that period they do not as yet belong to the domain of moral valuations – they are still *extra-moral*. A sympathetic action, for instance, was called neither good nor bad, moral nor immoral, in the best period of the Romans; and even when it was praised, a sort of resentful disdain was compatible with this praise as soon as it was compared to a sympathetic action which contributed to the welfare of the whole, to the *res publica*. After all, 'love of the neighbour' is always a secondary matter, partly conventional and arbitrarily manifested in relation to our *fear of our neighbour*. After the fabric of society seems on the whole established and secured against external dangers, it is this fear of our neighbour which again creates new perspectives of moral valuation. Certain strong and dangerous instincts, such as love of enterprise, foolhardiness, revengefulness, astuteness, rapacity and love of power, which up till then had not only to be honoured from the point of view of general utility – under other names, of course, than those given here – but had to be fostered and cultivated (because they were perpetually required in the common danger against the common enemies), are now felt in their dangerousness to be doubly strong – when the outlets for them are lacking – and are gradually branded as immoral and given over to calumny. The contrary instincts and inclinations now attain to moral honour, the herd instinct gradually draws its conclusions. How much or how little danger to the community or to equality is contained in an opinion, a condition, an emotion, a disposition or an endowment – that is now the moral perspective, here again fear is the mother of morals. It is by the loftiest and strongest instincts, when they break out passionately and carry the individual far above and beyond the average, and the low level of the herd conscience, that the self-reliance of the community is destroyed, its belief in itself, its backbone, as it were, breaks, consequently these very instincts will be most branded and defamed. The lofty independent spirituality, the will to stand alone and even the cogent reason are felt to be dangers, everything that elevates the individual above the herd and is a source of fear to the neighbour is henceforth called *evil*, the tolerant, unassuming, self-adapting, self-equalising disposition, the *mediocrity* of desires, attains to moral distinction and honour. Finally, under very peaceful circumstances, there is always less opportunity and necessity for training the feelings to severity and rigour, and now every form of severity, even in justice, begins to trouble the conscience, a lofty and rigorous nobleness and self-responsibility almost offends and awakens distrust, 'the lamb' and still more 'the sheep' win respect. There is a point of diseased mellowness and effeminacy in the history of society, at which society itself takes the part of him who injures it, the part of the *criminal*, and does so, in fact, seriously and honestly. To punish appears to it to be somehow unfair – it is certain that the idea of 'punishment' and 'the obligation to punish' are then painful and alarming to people. 'Is it not sufficient if the criminal be rendered *harmless*? Why should we still punish? Punishment itself is terrible.' – With these questions herd morality, the morality of fear, draws its ultimate conclusion. If one could at all do away with danger, the cause of fear, one would have done away with this morality at the same time, it would no longer be necessary, it *would not consider itself* any longer necessary! – Whoever examines the conscience of present-day Europeans will always elicit the same imperative from its thousand moral folds and hidden recesses, the imperative of the timidity of the herd 'we wish that some time or other there may be *nothing more to fear!*' Some day – the will and the way to this day are now called 'progress' across Europe.

202

Let us say once again what we have already said a hundred times, for people's ears today are unwilling to hear such truths – *our* truths. We know well enough how offensive it sounds when anyone plainly and without metaphor counts man among the animals, but it will be accounted to us almost a *crime* that it is precisely in respect to men of 'modern ideas' that we have constantly applied the terms 'herd', 'herd instincts' and such like expressions. What use is it? We cannot do otherwise, for it is precisely here that our new insight is. We have found that in all the principal moral judgements, Europe has become unanimous, including likewise the countries where European influence prevails in Europe: people evidently *know* what Socrates thought he did not know and what the famous serpent of old once promised to teach – they 'know' today what is good and evil. It must then sound hard and be offensive to the ear when we always insist that that which here thinks it knows, that which here glorifies itself with praise and blame, and calls itself good, is the instinct of the herd human animal, the instinct which has come and is ever coming more and more to the fore, to preponderance and supremacy over other instincts, according to the increasing physiological approximation and resemblance of which it is the symptom. *Morality in Europe at present is herd animal morality*, and therefore, as we understand the matter, only one kind of human morality, beside which, before which and after which many other moralities, and above all *higher* moralities, are or should be possible. Against such a 'possibility', against such a 'should be', however, this morality defends itself with all its strength, it says obstinately and inexorably, 'I am morality itself and nothing else is morality!' Indeed, with the help of a religion which has humoured and flattered the most sublime desires of the herd animal, things have reached such a point that we always find a more visible expression of this morality even in political and social arrangements: the *democratic* movement is the heir of the Christian movement. That its *tempo*, however, is much too slow and somnolent for the more impatient ones, for those who are sick and distracted by the herd instinct, is indicated by the increasingly furious howling, and always less disguised teeth-gnashing of the anarchist dogs, who are now roaming the highways of European culture. Apparently in opposition to the peacefully industrious democrats and Revolution ideologues, and still more so to the awkward philosophasters and fraternity visionaries who call themselves socialists and want a 'free society', those are really at one with them all in their thorough and instinctive hostility to every form of society other than that of the *autonomous* herd (to the extent even of repudiating the notions 'master' and 'servant' – *ni dieu ni maître*, according to a socialist formula); at one in their tenacious opposition to every special claim, every special right and privilege (this means ultimately opposition to *every* right, for when all are equal, no one needs 'rights' any longer); at one in their distrust of punitive justice (as though it were a violation of the weak, unfair to the *necessary* consequences of all former society); but equally at one in their religion of pity, in their compassion for all that feels, lives and suffers (down to the very animals, up even to 'God' – the extravagance of 'sympathy for God' belongs to a democratic age); altogether at one in the cry and impatience of their sympathy, in their deadly hatred of suffering generally, in their almost feminine incapacity for witnessing it or *allowing* it; at one in their involuntary plunge into gloom and heart-softening, under the spell of which Europe seems to be threatened with a new Buddhism; at one in their belief in the morality of *mutual* sympathy, as though it were morality in itself, the climax, the *attained* climax of mankind, the sole hope of the future, the consolation of the present, the great discharge from all the obligations of the past; altogether at one in their belief in the community as the *deliverer*, in the herd, and therefore in 'themselves'.

203

We who hold a different belief – we who regard the democratic movement not only as a degenerating form of political organisation, but as equivalent to a degenerating, waning type of man, making him mediocre and lowering his value: where have we to pin our hopes? In *new philosophers* – there is no other alternative: in minds strong and original enough to initiate opposite estimates of value, to revalue and invert 'eternal valuations'; in forerunners, in men of the future, who in the present shall fix the constraints and tie the knots which will compel millennia to take *new* paths. To teach man the future of humanity as his *will*, as depending on a human will, and to make preparation for vast, hazardous enterprises and collective attempts in breeding and educating, in order to put an end to the frightful rule of folly and chance which has so far gone by the name of 'history' (the folly of the 'greatest number' is only its latest form) – for that purpose a new type of philosopher and commander will some time or other be needed, at the very idea of which everything that has existed in the way of occult, terrible and benevolent beings might appear pale and dwarfed. The image of such leaders hovers before *our* eyes: – is it lawful for me to say it aloud, you free spirits? The conditions which one would partly have to create and partly utilise for their genesis; the presumptive methods and tests by virtue of which a soul should grow up to such an elevation and power as to feel a *constraint* to these tasks; a revaluation of values, under the new pressure and hammer of which a conscience should be steeled and a heart transformed into brass so as to bear the weight of such responsibility; and on the other hand the necessity for such leaders, the dreadful danger that they might be lacking, or miscarry and degenerate: – these are *our* real anxieties and glooms, you know it well, you free spirits! These are the heavy, distant thoughts and storms which sweep across the skies of our life. There are few pains so grievous as to have seen, divined or experienced how an exceptional man has lost his way and deteriorated; but he who has the rare eye for the universal danger of 'man' himself *deteriorating*, he who like us has recognised the extraordinary fortuitousness which has so far played its game in respect to the future of mankind – a game in which neither the hand, nor even a 'finger of God' has participated! – he who divines the fate that is hidden under the idiotic unwariness and blind confidence of 'modern ideas', and still more under the whole of Christo-European morality – suffers from an anguish with which no other is to be compared. He sees at a glance all that could still *be made out of man* through a favourable accumulation and augmentation of human powers and arrangements; he knows with all the knowledge of his conviction how unexhausted man still is for the greatest possibilities and how often in the past the type man has stood in presence of mysterious decisions and new paths: – he knows still better from his most painful recollections on what wretched obstacles promising developments of the highest rank have so far usually gone to pieces, broken down, sunk and become contemptible. The *universal degeneracy of mankind* to the level of the 'man of the future' – as idealised by the socialistic fools and flatheads – this degeneracy and dwarfing of man into the perfect herd animal (or as they call it, to a man of 'free society'), this brutalising of man into a dwarf animal with equal rights and claims, is undoubtedly *possible*! He who has thought through this possibility to its ultimate conclusion knows *another* loathing unknown to the rest of mankind – and perhaps also a new *mission*!

208

When a philosopher today makes known that he is not a sceptic – I hope that has been gathered from the foregoing description of the objective spirit? – people all hear it impatiently; they regard him on that account with some apprehension, they would like to ask so many, many questions … indeed among timid hearers, of whom there are now so many, he is henceforth considered dangerous. With his repudiation of scepticism it seems to them as if they heard some evil, threatening sound in the distance, as if a new kind of explosive were being tried somewhere, a dynamite of the spirit, perhaps a newly discovered Russian *nihiline*, a pessimism *bonae voluntatis*, that not only denies, means denial, but – dreadful thought! – *practises* denial. Against this kind of 'good will'– a will to the veritable, actual negation of life – there is, as is generally acknowledged today, no better soporific and sedative than scepticism, the mild, pleasing, lulling poppy of scepticism; and Hamlet himself is now prescribed by the doctors of the day as an antidote to the 'spirit' and its underground noises. 'Are not our ears already full of bad sounds?' say the sceptics, as lovers of repose, and almost as a kind of safety police; 'this subterranean No is terrible! Be still, you pessimistic moles!' The sceptic, in effect, that delicate creature, is far too easily frightened; his conscience is schooled so as to start at every No, and even at that sharp, decided Yes, and feels something like a bite thereby. Yes! and No! – they seem to him opposed to morality; he loves, on the contrary, to make a festival to his virtue by a noble aloofness, while perhaps he says with Montaigne: 'What do I know?' Or with Socrates: 'I know that I know nothing.' Or: 'Here I do not trust myself, no door is open to me.' Or: 'Even if the door were open, why should I enter immediately?' Or: 'What is the use of any hasty hypotheses? It might quite well be in good taste to make no hypotheses at all. Are you absolutely obliged to straighten at once what is crooked? To stuff every hole with some kind of oakum? Is there not time enough for that? Has not the time leisure? Oh, you demons, can you not at all *wait*? The uncertain also has its charms, the Sphinx, too, is a Circe, and Circe, too, was a philosopher.' – Thus does a sceptic console himself; and in truth he needs some consolation. For scepticism is the most spiritual expression of a certain many-sided physiological temperament, which in ordinary language is called nervous debility and sickliness; it arises whenever races or classes which have been long separated, decisively and suddenly mix with one another. In the new generation, which has inherited as it were different standards and valuations in its blood, everything is disquiet, derangement, doubt and tentativeness; the best powers operate restrictively, the very virtues prevent each other from growing and becoming strong, equilibrium, ballast and perpendicular stability are lacking in body and soul. That, however, which is most diseased and degenerated in such nondescripts is the *will*; they are no longer familiar with independence of decision or the courageous feeling of pleasure in willing – they are doubtful of the 'freedom of the will' even in their dreams. Our present-day Europe, the scene of a senseless, precipitate attempt at a radical blending of classes, and *consequently* of races, is therefore sceptical in all its heights and depths, sometimes exhibiting the mobile scepticism which springs impatiently and wantonly from branch to branch, sometimes with gloomy aspect, like a cloud overcharged with interrogative signs – and often sick unto death of its will! Paralysis of will, where do we not find this cripple sitting today! And yet how often bedecked! How seductively ornamented! There are the finest gala dresses and disguises for this disease, and that, for instance, most of what places itself today in the showcases as 'objectivity', 'the scientific spirit', *'l'art pour l'art'* and 'pure voluntary knowledge' is only decked-out scepticism and paralysis of the will – I am ready to answer for this diagnosis of the European disease – The disease of the will is diffused unequally over Europe, it is worst and most varied where culture has longest prevailed, it decreases according as 'the barbarian' still – or again – asserts his claims under the loose drapery of Western culture. It is therefore in the France of today, as can be readily disclosed and comprehended, that the will is most infirm, and France, which has always had a masterly aptitude for converting even the portentous crises of its spirit into something charming and seductive, now manifests emphatically its intellectual ascendancy over

Europe by being the school and exhibition of all the charms of scepticism. The power to will and to persist, moreover, in a resolution is already somewhat stronger in Germany, and again in the north of Germany it is stronger than in central Germany, it is considerably stronger in England, Spain and Corsica, associated with phlegm in the former and with hard skulls in the latter – not to mention Italy, which is too young yet to know what it wants and must first show whether it can exercise will, but it is strongest and most surprising of all in that immense middle empire where Europe, as it were, flows back to Asia – namely, in Russia. There the power to will has been long stored up and accumulated, there the will – uncertain whether to be negative or affirmative – waits threateningly to be discharged (to borrow a pet phrase from our physicists). Perhaps not only Indian wars and complications in Asia would be necessary to free Europe from its greatest danger, but also internal subversion, the shattering of the empire into small states, and above all the introduction of parliamentary imbecility, together with the obligation of everyone to read his newspaper at breakfast. I do not say this as one who desires it, in my heart I should rather prefer the contrary – I mean such an increase in the threatening attitude of Russia that Europe would have to make up its mind to become equally threatening – namely, to *acquire one will* by means of a new caste that would rule Europe, a persistent, dreadful will of its own, that can set its aims thousands of years ahead; so that the long spun-out comedy of its petty statism and its dynastic as well as democratic splinter wills might finally be brought to a close. The time for petty politics is past; the next century will bring the struggle for the dominion of the world – the *compulsion* to grand politics.

209

As to how far the new warlike age on which we Europeans have evidently entered may perhaps favour the growth of another and stronger kind of scepticism, I should like to express myself initially merely by a parable, which the lovers of German history will already understand. That unscrupulous enthusiast for big, handsome grenadiers (who, as King of Prussia, brought into being a military and sceptical genius – and thus, in reality, the new and now triumphantly emerged type of German), the problematic, mad father of Friedrich the Great, had on one point the very knack and lucky grasp of the genius: he knew what was then lacking in Germany, the want of which was a hundred times more alarming and serious than any lack of culture and social form – his ill-will towards the young Friedrich resulted from the anxiety of a profound instinct. *Men were lacking*; and he suspected to his most bitter regret that his own son was not man enough. There, however, he deceived himself; but who would not have deceived himself in his position? He saw his son lapse into atheism, to the *esprit*, to the pleasant frivolity of clever Frenchmen – he saw in the background the great bloodsucker, the spider of scepticism; he suspected the incurable wretchedness of a heart no longer hard enough for either evil or good, and of a broken will that no longer commands, is no longer *able* to command. Meanwhile, however, there grew up in his son that new kind of harder and more dangerous scepticism – who knows *to what extent* it was encouraged by his father's hatred and the icy melancholy of a will condemned to solitude? – the scepticism of daring manliness, which is closely related to the genius for war and conquest, and made its first entrance into Germany in the person of the great Friedrich. This scepticism despises and nevertheless grasps; it undermines and takes possession; it does not believe, but it does not lose itself in the process; it gives the spirit a dangerous liberty, but it keeps strict guard over the heart. It is the *German* form of scepticism, which, as a continued Friedrichianism, risen to the highest spirituality, has kept Europe for a considerable time under the dominion of the German spirit and its critical and historical distrust. Owing to the insuperably strong and tough masculine character of the great German philologists and historical critics (who, rightly estimated, were also all of them artists of destruction and dissolution), a *new* conception of the German spirit gradually established itself – in spite of all Romanticism in music and philosophy – in which the leaning towards masculine scepticism was decidedly prominent whether, for instance, as fearlessness of gaze, as courage and sternness of the dissecting hand, or as resolute will to hazardous voyages of discovery, to spiritualised North Pole expeditions under bleak and threatening skies. There may be good grounds for it when warm-blooded and superficial humanitarians cross themselves before this spirit, *Cet esprit fataliste, ironique, Mephistophelique,* as Michelet calls it, not without a shudder. But if one would realise how characteristic is this fear of the 'man' in the German spirit which awakened Europe out of its 'dogmatic slumber', let us call to mind the former conception which had to be overcome by this new one – and that it is not so very long ago that a masculinised woman could dare, with unbridled presumption, to recommend the Germans to the interest of Europe as gentle, good-hearted, weak-willed and poetic fools. Finally, let us only understand profoundly enough Napoleon's astonishment when he saw Goethe: it reveals what had been regarded for centuries as the 'German spirit' *'Voilà un homme!'* – that meant: 'But this is a *man*! And I only expected to see a German!'

210

Supposing, then, that in the picture of the philosophers of the future some trait suggests the question of whether they must not perhaps be sceptics in the last-mentioned sense, something in them would only be designated thereby – and *not* they themselves. With equal right they might call themselves critics, and assuredly they will be men of experiments. By the name with which I ventured to baptise them, I have already expressly emphasised their attempting and their love of attempting: is this because, as critics in body and soul, they will love to make use of experiments in a new and perhaps wider and more dangerous sense? In their passion for knowledge, will they have to go further in daring and painful attempts than the sensitive and pampered taste of a democratic century can approve of? – There is no doubt these coming ones will be least able to dispense with the serious and not unscrupulous qualities which distinguish the critic from the sceptic; I mean the certainty as to standards of worth, the conscious employment of a unity of method, the wary courage, the standing alone and the capacity for self-responsibility, indeed, they will avow among themselves a *delight* in denial and dissection, and a certain considerate cruelty, which knows how to handle the knife surely and deftly, even when the heart bleeds. They will be *harder* (and perhaps not always towards themselves only) than humane people may desire, they will not deal with the 'truth' in order that it may 'please' them or 'elevate' and 'inspire' them – they will rather have little faith in '*truth*' bringing with it such revels for the feelings. They will smile, those rigorous spirits, when anyone says in their presence: 'That thought lifts me up, why should it not be true?' Or: 'That work enchants me, why should it not be beautiful?' Or: 'That artist enlarges me, why should he not be great?' Perhaps they will not only have a smile, but a genuine disgust for all that is thus rapturous, idealistic, feminine and hermaphroditic, and if anyone could look into their innermost hearts, he would not easily find there the intention to reconcile 'Christian sentiments' with 'antique taste' or even with 'modern parliamentarianism' (the kind of reconciliation necessarily found even among philosophers in our very uncertain and consequently very conciliatory century). Critical discipline, and every habit that conduces to purity and rigour in intellectual matters, will not only be demanded from them by these philosophers of the future, they may even make a display of them as their special adornment – nevertheless they will not want to be called critics on that account. It will seem to them no small indignity to philosophy to have it decreed, as is so welcome today, that 'philosophy itself is criticism and critical science – and nothing else whatever!' Though this estimate of philosophy may enjoy the approval of all the positivists of France and Germany (and possibly it even flattered the heart and taste of *Kant*: let us call to mind the titles of his principal works), our new philosophers will say, nevertheless, that critics are instruments of the philosopher, and just on that account, as instruments, they are far from being philosophers themselves! Even the great Chinaman of Konigsberg was only a great critic.

211

I insist that people finally cease confounding philosophical workers, and in general scientific men, with philosophers – that precisely here one should strictly give 'each his own' and not give those far too much, these far too little. It may be necessary for the education of the real philosopher that he himself should have once stood upon all those steps upon which his servants, the scientific workers of philosophy, remain standing, and *must* remain standing, he himself must perhaps have been critic, and dogmatist, and historian, and besides, poet, and collector, and traveller, and riddle-reader, and moralist, and seer, and 'free spirit', and almost everything, in order to traverse the whole range of human values and estimations, and that he may *be able* with a variety of eyes and consciences to look from a height to any distance, from a depth up to any height, from a nook into any expanse. But all these are only preliminary conditions for his task; this task itself demands something else – it requires him *to create values*. The philosophical workers, following the excellent pattern of Kant and Hegel, have to fix and formalise some great existing body of valuations – that is to say, former *determinations of value*, creations of value, which have become prevalent, and are for a time called 'truths'– whether in the domain of the *logical*, the *political* (moral) or the *artistic*. It is for these investigators to make whatever has happened and been esteemed so far conspicuous, conceivable, intelligible and manageable, to shorten everything long, even 'time' itself, and to *subjugate* the entire past: an immense and wonderful task, in the carrying out of which all refined pride, all tenacious will, can surely find satisfaction. *The real philosophers, however, are commanders and lawgivers*; they say: 'Thus *shall* it be!' They determine first the Whither and the Why of mankind, and in so doing set aside the previous labour of all philosophical workers and all subjugators of the past – they grasp at the future with a creative hand, and whatever is and was becomes for them a means, an instrument, a hammer. Their 'knowing' is *creating*, their creating is lawgiving, their will to truth is – *will to power*. – Are there such philosophers at present? Have there ever been such philosophers? *Must* there not be such philosophers some day? ...

212

It is always more obvious to me that the philosopher, as a man *indispensable* for tomorrow and the day after tomorrow, has ever found himself, and has been *obliged* to find himself, in opposition to the day in which he lives; his enemy has always been the ideal of his day. So far all those extraordinary advancers of humanity whom one calls philosophers – who rarely regarded themselves as lovers of wisdom, but rather as disagreeable fools and dangerous interrogators – have found their mission, their hard, involuntary, imperative mission (in the end, however, the greatness of their mission), in being the bad conscience of their age. In putting the vivisector's scalpel to the breast of the very *virtues of their age*, they have betrayed their own secret; it has been for the sake of a *new* greatness of man, a new, untrodden path to his aggrandisement. They have always disclosed how much hypocrisy, indolence, self-indulgence and self-neglect, how much falsehood was concealed under the most venerated types of contemporary morality, how much virtue was *outlived*, they have always said, 'We must remove there to where *you* are least at home'. In the face of a world of 'modern ideas', which would like to confine everyone in a corner, in a 'specialty', a philosopher, if there could be philosophers today, would be compelled to place the greatness of man, the conception of 'greatness', precisely in his comprehensiveness and multifariousness, in his all-roundness, he would even determine worth and rank according to the amount and variety of that which a man could bear and take upon himself, according to the *extent* to which a man could stretch his responsibility. Today the taste and virtue of the age weaken and attenuate the will, nothing is so adapted to the spirit of the age as weakness of will, consequently, in the ideal of the philosopher, strength of will, hardness and capacity for prolonged resolution, must specially be included in the conception of 'greatness', with as good a right as the opposite doctrine, with its ideal of a silly, renouncing, humble, selfless humanity, was suited to an opposite age – such as the sixteenth century, which suffered from its accumulated energy of will and from the wildest torrents and floods of selfishness. In the time of Socrates, among men only of worn-out instincts, old conservative Athenians who let themselves go – 'for the sake of happiness' as they said, for the sake of pleasure, as their conduct indicated – and who had continually on their lips the old pompous words to which they had long forfeited the right by the life they led, *irony* was perhaps necessary for greatness of soul, the wicked Socratic assurance of the old physician and plebeian, who cut ruthlessly into his own flesh as into the flesh and heart of the 'noble', with a look that said plainly enough: 'Do not dissemble before me! Here – we are equal!' At present, on the contrary, when throughout Europe the herd animal alone attains to honours, and dispenses honours, when 'equality of rights' can too readily be transformed into equality in wrongs – I mean to say into a general war against everything rare, strange and privileged, against the higher man, the higher soul, the higher duty, the higher responsibility, the creative power and masterfulness – at present it belongs to the conception of 'greatness' to be noble, to wish to be apart, to be capable of being different, to stand alone, to have to live by personal initiative, and the philosopher will betray something of his own ideal when he asserts: 'He shall be the greatest who can be the most solitary, the most concealed, the most divergent, the man beyond good and evil, the master of his virtues, and of super-abundance of will; precisely this shall be called *greatness*: as diversified as can be entire, as ample as can be full.' And to ask once more the question: Is greatness *possible* – today?

225

Whether it be hedonism, pessimism, utilitarianism or eudaemonism, all those modes of thinking which measure the worth of things according to *pleasure* and *pain*, that is, according to prevailing circumstances and secondary considerations, are plausible modes of thought and naiveties, which everyone conscious of *creative* powers and an artist's conscience will look down upon with scorn, though not without pity. Pity for you! – to be sure, that is not pity as you understand it; it is not pity for social 'distress', for 'society' with its sick and misfortunate, for the hereditarily vicious and defective who lie on the ground around us; still less is it pity for the grumbling, vexed, revolutionary slave classes who strive after power – they call it 'freedom'. *Our* pity is a higher and farsighted sympathy: – we see how *man* dwarfs himself, how *you* dwarf him! And there are moments when we view *your* pity with an indescribable anguish, when we resist it – when we regard your seriousness as more dangerous than any kind of levity. You want, if possible – and there is not a more foolish 'if possible' – *to abolish suffering*; and we? – It really seems that we would rather have it increased and made worse than it has ever been! Well-being, as you understand it – is certainly not a goal; it seems to us an *end*; a condition which at once renders man ludicrous and contemptible – and makes his destruction *desirable*! The discipline of suffering, of *great* suffering – do you not know that it is only *this* discipline that has produced all the elevations of humanity so far? The tension of soul in misfortune which communicates to it its energy, its shuddering in view of rack and ruin, its inventiveness and bravery in undergoing, enduring, interpreting and exploiting misfortune, and whatever depth, mystery, disguise, spirit, artifice or greatness has been bestowed upon the soul – has it not been bestowed through suffering, through the discipline of great suffering? In man *creature* and *creator* are united: in man there is not only matter, shred, excess, clay, mire, folly, chaos; there is also the creator, the sculptor, the hardness of the hammer, the divinity of the spectator and the seventh day – do you understand this contrast? And that *your* sympathy for the 'creature in man' applies to that which has to be fashioned, bruised, forged, stretched, roasted and refined – to that which must necessarily *suffer* and *is meant* to suffer? And our pity – do you not understand what our *reverse* pity applies to when it resists your pity as the worst of all pampering and enervation? – So it is pity *against* pity! – But to repeat it once more, there are higher problems than the problems of pleasure and pain and pity; and all systems of philosophy which deal only with these are naiveties.

228

I hope to be forgiven for discovering that all moral philosophy so far has been tedious and has belonged to the soporific appliances – and that 'virtue', in my opinion, has been *more* injured by the *tediousness* of its advocates than by anything else; at the same time, however, I would not wish to overlook their general usefulness. It is desirable that as few people as possible should reflect upon morals, and consequently it is very desirable that morals should not some day become interesting! But let us not be afraid! Things still remain today as they have always been: I see no one in Europe who has (or *discloses*) an idea of the fact that philosophising concerning morals might be conducted in a dangerous, captious and ensnaring manner – that *calamity* might be involved there. Observe, for example, the indefatigable, inevitable English Utilitarians: how ponderously and respectably they stalk on, stalk along (a Homeric metaphor expresses it better) in the footsteps of Bentham, just as he had already stalked in the footsteps of the respectable Helvetius! (No, he was not a dangerous man, Helvetius, *ce senateur Pococurante*, to use an expression of Galiani.) No new thought, nothing of the nature of a finer turning or better expression of an old thought, not even a proper history of what has been previously thought on the subject: an *impossible* literature, taking it all in all, unless one knows how to flavour it with some mischief. In effect, the old English vice called *cant*, which is *moral Tartuffery*, has insinuated itself also into these moralists (whom one must certainly read with an eye to their motives if one *must* read them), concealed this time under the new form of the scientific spirit; moreover, they are not without a secret struggle with the pangs of conscience, from which a race of former Puritans must naturally suffer in all their scientific tinkering with morals. (Is not a moralist the opposite of a Puritan? That is to say, as a thinker who regards morality as questionable, as worthy of interrogation, in short, as a problem? Is moralising not – immoral?) In the end, they all want English morality to be recognised as authoritative, inasmuch as mankind, or the 'general utility' or 'the happiness of the greatest number' – no! the happiness of *England* will be best served thereby. They would like, by all means, to convince themselves that the striving after English happiness, by which I mean after *comfort* and *fashion* (and in the highest instance, a seat in Parliament), is at the same time the true path of virtue; in fact, that in so far as there has been virtue in the world so far, it has consisted in such striving. Not one of those ponderous, conscience-stricken herd animals (who undertake to advocate the cause of egoism as conducive to the general welfare) wants to have any knowledge or inkling of the facts that the 'general welfare' is no ideal, no goal, no notion that can ever be grasped, but is only a nostrum – that what is fair to one *may not* be fair at all to another, that the requirement of one morality for all is really detrimental to higher men, in short, that there is an *order of rank* between man and man, and consequently between morality and morality. They are an unassuming and fundamentally mediocre species of men, these utilitarian Englishmen, and, as already remarked, in so far as they are tedious, one cannot think highly enough of their utility. ...

238

To be mistaken in the fundamental problem of 'man and woman', to deny here the profoundest antagonism and the necessity for an eternally hostile tension, to dream here perhaps of equal rights, equal training, equal claims and obligations: that is a *typical* trait of shallow-mindedness; and a thinker who has proved himself shallow at this dangerous spot – shallow in instinct! – may generally be regarded as suspect, no more, as betrayed, as discovered; he will probably prove too 'short' for all fundamental questions of life, future as well as present, and will be unable to descend into *any* of the depths. On the other hand, a man who has depth of spirit as well as of desires, and has also the depth of benevolence which is capable of severity and harshness, and easily confounded with them, can only think of woman as *Orientals* do: he must conceive of her as a possession, as confinable property, as a being predestined for service and accomplishing her mission in that – he must take his stand in this matter on the immense rationality of Asia, on the superiority of the instinct of Asia, as the Greeks did formerly; those best heirs and scholars of Asia – who, as is well known, with their *increasing* culture and range of power, from Homer to the time of Pericles, became gradually *stricter* towards woman, in short, more Oriental. *How* necessary, *how* logical, even *how* humanely desirable this was let us consider for ourselves!

239

The weaker sex has in no previous age been treated with so much respect by men as at present – this belongs to the tendency and fundamental taste of democracy, in the same way as disrespectfulness to old age – what wonder is it that abuse should be immediately made of this respect? They want more, they learn to make claims, the tribute of respect is at last felt to be insulting; rivalry for rights, indeed actual strife itself, would be preferable: in a word, woman is losing modesty. And let us immediately add that she is also losing taste. She is unlearning to *fear* man: but the woman who 'unlearns to fear' sacrifices her most womanly instincts. That woman should venture forward when the fear-inspiring quality in man – or more definitely, the *man* in man – is no longer either desired or fully developed is reasonable enough and also intelligible enough; what is more difficult to understand is that precisely thereby – woman deteriorates. This is what is happening today: let us not deceive ourselves about it! Wherever the industrial spirit has triumphed over the military and aristocratic spirit, woman strives for the economic and legal independence of a clerk: 'woman as clerk' is inscribed on the portal of the modern society which is in the process of formation. While she thus appropriates new rights, aspires to be 'master' and inscribes 'progress' of woman on her flags and banners, the very opposite realises itself with terrible obviousness: *woman retrogresses*. Since the French Revolution the influence of woman in Europe has *declined* in proportion as she has increased her rights and claims; and the 'emancipation of woman', insofar as it is desired and demanded by women themselves (and not only by shallow males), thus proves to be a remarkable symptom of the increased weakening and deadening of the most womanly instincts. There is *stupidity* in this movement, an almost masculine stupidity, of which a well-reared woman – who is always a sensible woman – might be heartily ashamed. To lose the intuition as to the ground on which she can most surely achieve victory; to neglect exercise in the use of her proper weapons; to let herself go before man, perhaps even 'to the book', where formerly she kept herself in control and in refined, artful humility; to neutralise with her virtuous audacity man's faith in a *veiled*, fundamentally different ideal in woman, something eternally, necessarily feminine; to emphatically and loquaciously dissuade man from the idea that woman must be cherished, cared for, protected and indulged, like some delicate, strangely wild and often pleasing domestic animal; the clumsy and indignant collection of everything of the nature of servitude and bondage which the position of woman in the hitherto existing order of society has entailed and still entails (as though slavery were a counterargument and not a condition of every higher culture, of every elevation of culture): – what does all this mean, if not a disintegration of womanly instincts, a defeminising? Certainly, there are enough idiotic friends and corrupters of woman among the learned asses of the masculine sex, who advise woman to defeminise herself in this manner and to imitate all the stupidities from which 'man' in Europe, European 'manliness', suffers – who would like to lower woman to 'general culture', indeed even to newspaper reading and meddling in politics. in some places they wish even to turn women into free spirits and literary workers: as though a woman lacking piety would not be perfectly obnoxious or ludicrous to a profound and godless man; – almost everywhere her nerves are being ruined by the most morbid and dangerous kind of music (our latest German music), and she is daily being made more hysterical and more incapable of fulfilling her first and last function, that of bearing robust children. They wish to 'cultivate' her in general still more and intend, as they say, to make the 'weaker sex' *strong* by culture: as if history did not teach most emphatically that the 'cultivating' of mankind and his weakening – that is to say, the weakening, dissipating and languishing of his *force of will* – have always kept pace with one another, and that the most powerful and influential women in the world (and lastly, the mother of Napoleon) had just to thank their force of will – and not their schoolmasters – for their power and ascendancy over men. That which inspires respect in woman, and often enough fear also, is her *nature*, which is more 'natural' than that of man, her genuine, carnivore-like, cunning flexibility, her tiger claws within the glove, her *naiveté* in egoism, her untrainability and innate wildness, the incomprehensibleness, extent and deviation of her desires and virtues. That which, in spite of fear, excites one's pity for the dangerous and beautiful cat that is 'woman' is that she seems more afflicted, more vulnerable, more in need of love and more destined to disillusionment than any other creature. Fear and pity – it is with these feelings that man has so far stood in the presence of woman, always with one foot already steeped in tragedy, which rends while it delights – What? And all that is now to come to an end? And the *disenchantment* of woman is in progress? The tediousness of woman is slowly evolving? Oh Europe! Europe! We know the horned animal which was always most attractive to you, from which danger is ever again threatening you! Your old fable might once more become 'history' – an immense stupidity might once again overwhelm you and carry you away! And no God concealed beneath it – No! only an 'idea', a 'modern idea'!

241

We 'good Europeans' we also have hours when we allow ourselves a warm-hearted patriotism, a plunge and relapse into old loves and narrow views – I have just given an example of it – hours of national excitement, of patriotic anguish and all sorts of old-fashioned floods of sentiment. Duller spirits may perhaps only get done with what confines its operations in us to hours and plays itself out in hours – in a considerable time: some in half a year, others in half a lifetime, according to the speed and strength with which they digest and 'change their material'. Indeed, I could think of sluggish, hesitating races, which even in our rapidly moving Europe would require half a century before they could surmount such atavistic attacks of patriotism and attachment to the land and return once more to reason, that is to say, to 'good Europeanism'. And while digressing on this possibility, I happened to overhear a conversation between two old patriots – they were evidently both hard of hearing and consequently spoke all the louder. '*He* has as much, and knows as much, philosophy as a peasant or a corps student,' said the one – 'he is still innocent. But what does that matter today! It is the age of the masses: they lie on their belly before everything that is massive. And so also in politics. A statesman who erects for them a new tower of Babel, some monstrosity of empire and power, they call "great" – what does it matter that we more prudent and conservative ones do not meanwhile give up the old belief that it is only the great thought that gives greatness to an action or affair. Supposing a statesman were to bring his people into the position of being obliged henceforth to practise "grand politics", for which they were by nature ill-endowed and prepared, so that they would have to sacrifice their old and reliable virtues out of love to a new and doubtful mediocrity; – supposing a statesman were to condemn his people generally to "practise politics" when they have so far had something better to do and think about, and when in the depths of their souls they have been unable to free themselves from a prudent loathing of the restlessness, emptiness and noisy wrangling of the essentially politics-practising nations; – supposing such a statesman were to awaken the slumbering passions and avidities of his people, were to make a stigma out of their former diffidence and delight in aloofness, an offence out of their exoticism and hidden permanency, were to depreciate their most radical proclivities, subvert their consciences, make their minds narrow and their tastes "national" – What! a statesman who should do all this, which his people would have to do penance for throughout their whole future, if they had a future, such a statesman would be *great*, would he?' – 'Undoubtedly!' replied the other old patriot vehemently, 'Otherwise he *could not* have done it! It was mad perhaps to wish such a thing! But perhaps everything great has been just as mad at its commencement!' – 'Misuse of words!' cried his interlocutor, contradictorily – 'Strong! Strong! Strong and mad! *Not* great!' – The old men had obviously become heated as they thus shouted their 'truths' in each other's faces, but I, in my happiness and separateness, considered how soon a stronger one may become master of the strong, and also that there is a compensation for the intellectual trivialising of a nation – namely, in the deepening of another.

242

Whether we call it 'civilisation', 'humanising' or 'progress', which now distinguishes the European, whether we call it simply, without praise or blame, by the political formula the *democratic* movement in Europe – behind all the moral and political foregrounds pointed to by such formulas, an immense *physiological process* goes on, which is ever extending the process of the assimilation of Europeans, their increasing detachment from the conditions under which, climatically and hereditarily, united races originate, their increasing independence of every definite milieu, that for centuries would like to inscribe itself with equal demands on soul and body – that is to say, the slow emergence of an essentially *supranational* and nomadic species of man, who possesses, physiologically speaking, a maximum of the art and power of adaptation as his typical distinction. This process of the *evolving European*, which can be retarded in its *tempo* by great relapses, but will perhaps just gain and grow thereby in vehemence and depth – the still raging storm and stress of 'national sentiment' pertains to it, and also the anarchism which is appearing at present – this process will probably arrive at results on which its naive propagators and panegyrists, the apostles of 'modern ideas', would least care to reckon. The same new conditions under which on an average a levelling and mediocritisation of man will take place – a useful, industrious, variously serviceable and clever herd man – are in the highest degree suitable to give rise to exceptional men of the most dangerous and attractive qualities. For, while the capacity for adaptation, which is every day trying changing conditions and begins a new work with every generation, almost with every decade, makes the *powerfulness* of the type impossible; while the collective impression of such future Europeans will probably be that of numerous, loquacious, weak-willed and very handy workmen who *require* a master, a commander, as they require their daily bread; while, therefore, the democratising of Europe will tend to the production of a type prepared for *slavery* in the most subtle sense of the term: the *strong* man will necessarily, in individual and exceptional cases, become stronger and richer than he has perhaps ever been before – owing to the lack of prejudice of his schooling, owing to the immense variety of practice, art and disguise. I mean to say that the democratising of Europe is at the same time an involuntary arrangement for the breeding of *tyrants* – taking the word in all its meanings, even in its most spiritual sense.

244

There was a time when it was customary to call Germans 'deep' by way of distinction; but now that the most successful type of new Germanism is covetous of other honours, and perhaps misses 'smartness' in all that has depth, it is almost opportune and patriotic to doubt whether we did not formerly deceive ourselves with that commendation: in short, whether German depth is not at bottom something different and worse – and something from which, thank God, we are on the point of successfully ridding ourselves. Let us try, then, to learn anew with regard to German depth; the only thing necessary for the purpose is a little vivisection of the German soul. – The German soul is above all manifold, varied in its source, aggregated and superimposed, rather than actually built: this is owing to its origin. A German who would embolden himself to assert 'Two souls, alas, dwell in my breast' would make a bad guess at the truth or, more correctly, would fall far short of the truth about the number of souls. As a people made up of the most extraordinary mix and mingling of races, perhaps even with a preponderance of the pre-Aryan element as the 'people of the centre' in every sense of the term, the Germans are more intangible, more ample, more contradictory, more unknown, more incalculable, more surprising and even more terrifying than other peoples are to themselves: – they elude *definition* and are thus uniquely the despair of the French. It *is* characteristic of the Germans that the question: 'What is German?' never dies out among them. Kotzebue certainly knew his Germans well enough: 'We are known,' they cried jubilantly to him – but Sand also thought he knew them. Jean Paul knew what he was doing when he declared himself incensed at Fichte's lying but patriotic flatteries and exaggerations – but it is probable that Goethe thought differently about Germans from Jean Paul, even though he acknowledged him to be right with regard to Fichte. It is a question what Goethe really thought about the Germans. – But about the many things around him he never spoke of explicitly, and all his life he knew how to keep a canny silence – probably he had good reason for it. It is certain that it was not the 'Wars of Liberation' that made him look up more joyfully, any more than it was the French Revolution – the event on account of which he *reconstructed* his *Faust*, and indeed the whole problem of 'man', was the appearance of Napoleon. There are words of Goethe in which he condemns with impatient severity, as from a foreign land, that which Germans take a pride in: he once defined the famous German turn of mind as 'Indulgence towards its own and others' weaknesses'. Was he wrong? It is characteristic of Germans that one is seldom entirely wrong about them. The German soul has passages and galleries in it, there are caves, hiding places and dungeons in it; its disorder has much of the charm of the mysterious, the German is well acquainted with the byways to chaos. And as everything loves its symbol, so the German loves the clouds and all that is obscure, evolving, crepuscular, damp and shrouded, it seems to him that everything uncertain, undeveloped, self-displacing and growing is 'deep'. The German himself does not *exist,* he is *becoming,* he is 'developing himself'. 'Development' is therefore the essentially German discovery and hit in the great domain of philosophical formulas – a ruling idea, which, together with German beer and German music, is labouring to Germanise all Europe. Foreigners are astonished and attracted by the riddles which the conflicting nature at the basis of the German soul propounds to them (riddles which Hegel systematised and Richard Wagner has set to music). 'Good-natured and spiteful' – such a juxtaposition, preposterous in the case of every other people, is unfortunately only too often justified in Germany; one has only to live for a while among Swabians to know this! The clumsiness of the German scholar and his social distastefulness agree alarmingly well with his physical rope-dancing and nimble boldness, of which all the gods have learned to be afraid. If anyone wishes to see the 'German soul' demonstrated *ad oculos*, let him only look at German taste, at German arts and manners: what boorish indifference to 'taste'! How the noblest and the commonest stand there in juxtaposition! How disorderly and how rich is the whole constitution of this soul! The German *drags* at his soul, he drags at everything he experiences. He digests his events badly; he never gets 'done' with them; and German depth is often only a difficult, hesitating 'digestion'. And just as all chronic invalids, all dyspeptics, like what is convenient, so the German loves 'frankness' and 'honesty'; it is so *convenient* to be frank and honest! – This confiding, this complaisance, this revealing the hand of German *honesty*, is probably the most dangerous and most successful disguise which the German is up to today: it is his true Mephistophelean art; with this he can 'still achieve much'! The German lets himself go, and while gazing with faithful, blue, empty German eyes – and other countries immediately confound him with his dressing gown! – I meant to say that, let 'German depth' be what it will – among ourselves alone we perhaps take the liberty to laugh at it – we shall do well to continue henceforth to honour its appearance and good name and not barter away too cheaply our old reputation as a people of depth for Prussian 'smartness' and Berlin wit and sand. It is wise for a people to pose and *let* itself be regarded as profound, clumsy, good-natured, honest and foolish: it might even be – profound to do so! Finally, we should do honour to our name – we are not called the *'tiusche' Volk* (deceptive people) for nothing...

251

It must be taken into the bargain if various clouds and disturbances – in short, slight attacks of stupidity – pass over the spirit of a people that suffers and *wants* to suffer from national nervous fever and political ambition: for instance, among present-day Germans there is successively the anti-French folly, the anti-Semitic folly, the anti-Polish folly, the Christian-romantic folly, the Wagnerian folly, the Teutonic folly, the Prussian folly (just look at those poor historians, the Sybels and Treitschkes, and their closely bandaged heads), and whatever else these little obscurations of the German spirit and conscience may be called. May it be forgiven me that I too, when on a short daring sojourn on very infected ground, did not remain wholly immune from the disease, but like everyone else began to entertain thoughts about matters which did not concern me – the first symptom of political infection. About the Jews, for instance, listen to the following: – I have never yet met a German who was favourably inclined to the Jews; and however decided the repudiation of actual anti-Semitism may be on the part of all prudent and political men, this prudence and policy are not perhaps directed against the nature of the sentiment itself, but only against its dangerous excess, and especially against the distasteful and infamous expression of this excess of sentiment; – on this point we must not deceive ourselves. That Germany has amply *sufficient* Jews, that the German stomach, the German blood, has difficulty (and will long have difficulty) in disposing only of this quantity of 'Jew' – as the Italian, the Frenchman and the Englishman have done by means of a stronger digestion: – that is the unmistakable declaration and language of a general instinct, to which one must listen and according to which one must act. 'Let no more Jews come in! And shut the doors, especially towards the East (also towards Austria)!' – thus commands the instinct of a people whose nature is still feeble and uncertain so that it could be easily wiped out, easily extinguished, by a stronger race. The Jews, however, are without doubt the strongest, toughest and purest race at present living in Europe, they know how to succeed even under the worst conditions (in fact, better than under favourable ones), by means of virtues of some sort, which one would like today to label as vices – owing above all to a resolute faith which does not need to be ashamed before 'modern ideas', they alter only, *when* they do alter, in the same way that the Russian Empire makes its conquest – as an empire that has plenty of time and is not of yesterday – namely, according to the principle 'as slowly as possible'! A thinker who has the future of Europe at heart will, in all his perspectives concerning the future, calculate upon the Jews, as he will calculate upon the Russians, as above all the surest and likeliest factors in the great play and battle of forces. That which is at present called a 'nation' in Europe, and is really rather a *res facta* than *nata* (indeed, sometimes confusingly similar to a *res ficta et picta*), is in every case something evolving, young, easily ousted and not yet a race, much less such a race *aere perennius*, as the Jews are: such 'nations' should most carefully avoid all hot-headed rivalry and hostility! It is certain that the Jews, if they desired it – or were driven to it, as the anti-Semites seem to wish – *could* now have the ascendancy, no, literally the supremacy, over Europe, that they are *not* working and planning for that end is equally certain. Meanwhile, they rather wish and desire, even somewhat importunely, to be assimilated and absorbed by Europe, they long to be finally settled, authorised and respected somewhere, and wish to put an end to the nomadic life, to the 'wandering Jew' – and one should certainly take account of this impulse and tendency, and *make advances* to it (it possibly means a mitigation of the Jewish instincts), for which purpose it would perhaps be useful and fair to banish the anti-Semitic screamers from the country. One should make advances with all prudence, and with selection, pretty much as the English nobility does. It stands to reason that the more powerful and strongly marked types of new Germanism could enter into relation with the Jews with the least hesitation, for instance, the noble officer from the Prussian border: it would be interesting in many ways to see whether the genius for money and patience (and especially some intellect and intellectuality – sadly lacking in the place referred to) could not in addition be annexed and trained to the hereditary art of commanding and obeying – for both of which the country in question now has a classic reputation. But here it is expedient to break off my festal discourse and my sprightly Germanomania for I have already reached my *serious topic*, the 'European problem' as I understand it, the breeding of a new ruling caste for Europe.

254

Even at present France is still the seat of the most intellectual and refined culture of Europe, it is still the foremost school of taste; but one must know how to find this 'France of taste'. He who belongs to it keeps himself well hidden: – they may be a small number in whom it lives and is embodied, besides perhaps being men who do not stand upon the strongest legs, in part fatalists, hypochondriacs, invalids, in part persons over-indulged, over-refined, such as have the *ambition* to conceal themselves. They have all something in common: they keep their ears closed in the presence of the delirious folly and noisy spouting of the democratic *bourgeois*. In fact, a besotted and brutalised France at present sprawls in the foreground – it recently celebrated a veritable orgy of bad taste, and at the same time of self-admiration, at the funeral of Victor Hugo. There is also something else common to them: a predilection to resist intellectual Germanising – and a still greater inability to do so! In this France of the intellect, which is also a France of pessimism, Schopenhauer has perhaps become more at home and more indigenous than he has ever been in Germany; not to speak of Heinrich Heine, who has long ago been reincarnated in the more refined and fastidious lyric poets of Paris; or of Hegel, who at present, in the form of Taine – the *first* among living historians – exercises an almost tyrannical influence. As regards Richard Wagner, however, the more French music learns to adapt itself to the actual needs of the *ame moderne*, the more will it 'Wagnerise'; one can safely predict that in advance – it is already taking place sufficiently! There are, however, three things which the French can still boast of with pride as their heritage and possession, and as indelible tokens of their ancient intellectual superiority in Europe, in spite of all voluntary or involuntary Germanising and vulgarising of taste. *First*, the capacity for artistic emotion, for devotion to 'form', for which the expression *l'art pour l'art*, along with numerous others, has been coined: – such capacity has not been lacking in France for three centuries; and owing to its reverence for the 'small number', it has again and again made a sort of chamber music of literature possible, which is sought for in vain elsewhere in Europe. – The *second* thing whereby the French can lay claim to a superiority over Europe is their ancient, many-sided, *moralistic* culture, owing to which one finds on average, even in the petty *romanciers* of the newspapers and chance *boulevardiers de Paris*, a psychological sensitivity and curiosity, of which, for example, one has no conception (to say nothing of the thing itself!) in Germany. The Germans lack a couple of centuries of the moralistic work which, as mentioned, France has not spared herself: those who call the Germans 'naive' on that account commend them for a defect. (As the opposite of the German inexperience and innocence *in voluptate psychologica*, which is not too remotely associated with the tediousness of German intercourse – and as the most successful expression of genuine French curiosity and inventive talent in this domain of delicate thrills, Henri Beyle [Stendhal] may be noted; that remarkable anticipatory and precursor human being, who, with a Napoleonic *tempo*, traversed *his* Europe, in fact, several centuries of the European soul, as a surveyor and discoverer of this soul: – it has required two generations to *overtake* him one way or other, to work out much later some of the riddles that perplexed and enraptured him – this strange Epicurean and man of interrogation, the last great psychologist of France). – There is yet a *third* claim to superiority: in the French character there is a successful half-way synthesis of the North and South, which makes them comprehend many things, and enjoins upon them other things an Englishman can never comprehend. Their temperament, turned alternately to and from the South, in which from time to time the Provençal and Ligurian blood foams over, shields them from the dreadful, northern grey-on-grey, from sunless conceptual-spectrism and from poverty of blood – our *German* infirmity of taste, for the excessive prevalence of which at the present, blood and iron, that is to say 'grand politics', has with great resolution been prescribed (according to a dangerous healing art, which teaches me to wait and wait, but not yet hope). – There is also still in France a pre-understanding and ready welcome for those rarer and rarely gratified men who are too comprehensive to find satisfaction in any kind of fatherlandishness and know how to love the South when in the North and the North when in the South – the born Midlanders, the 'good Europeans'. For them *Bizet* has made music, this latest genius who has seen a new beauty and seduction – who has discovered a piece of the *South in music*.

256

Owing to the morbid estrangement which the insanity of nationality has induced and still induces among the nations of Europe, owing also to the short-sighted and quick-handed politicians, who with the help of this insanity are currently in power and do not suspect to what extent the disintegrating policy they pursue must necessarily be only an interim policy – owing to all this and much else that is altogether unmentionable at present, the most unmistakable signs that *Europe wishes to be one* are now overlooked, or arbitrarily and falsely misinterpreted. With all the more profound and comprehensive men of this century, the real general tendency of the mysterious labour of their souls was to prepare the way for that new *synthesis* and tentatively to anticipate the European of the future; only in their simulations or in their weaker moments, in old age perhaps, did they belong to the 'fatherlands' – they only rested from themselves when they became 'patriots'. I think of such men as Napoleon, Goethe, Beethoven, Stendhal, Heinrich Heine, Schopenhauer: it must not be held against me if I also count Richard Wagner among them, about whom one must not let oneself be deceived by his own misunderstandings (geniuses like him have seldom the right to understand themselves), still less, of course, by the unseemly noise with which he is now resisted and opposed in France: the fact remains, nevertheless, that Richard Wagner and the *later French Romanticism* of the 1840s are most closely and intimately related to one another. They are akin, fundamentally akin, in all the heights and depths of their requirements; it is Europe, the *one* Europe, whose soul presses urgently and longingly, outwards and upwards, in their multifarious and boisterous art – Whither? Into a new light? Towards a new sun? But who would attempt to express accurately what all these masters of new modes of speech could not express distinctly? It is certain that the same storm and stress tormented them, that they *went in search* in the same way, these last great seekers! All of them steeped in literature up to their eyes and ears – the first artists of universal literary culture – for the most part themselves writers, poets, intermediaries and blenders of the arts and the senses (Wagner, as musician is reckoned among painters, as poet among musicians, as artist generally among actors); all of them fanatics for expression 'at any cost' – I specially mention Delacroix, the nearest to Wagner; all of them great discoverers in the realm of the sublime, also of the loathsome and dreadful, still greater discoverers in effect, in display, in the art of display windows; all of them talented far beyond their genius, out and out *virtuosi*, with mysterious accesses to all that seduces, allures, constrains and upsets; born enemies of logic and of the straight line, hankering after the strange, the exotic, the monstrous, the crooked and the self-contradictory; as men, Tantaluses of the will, plebeian parvenus, who knew themselves to be incapable of a noble *tempo* or of a *lento* in life and action – think of Balzac, for instance – unfettered workers almost destroying themselves by work; antinomians and rebels in manners, ambitious and insatiable, without equilibrium and enjoyment; all of them finally shattering and sinking before the Christian cross (and with right and reason, for who of them would have been sufficiently profound and sufficiently original for an *anti-Christian* philosophy?); – on the whole, a boldly daring, splendidly overbearing class of higher human beings who soared, and tore others along, to the heights – who had first to teach their century – and it is the century of the *masses* – the concept 'higher man' .... Let the German friends of Richard Wagner unite to advise as to whether there is anything purely German in Wagnerian art, or whether its distinction does not consist precisely in coming from *supra-German* sources and impulses: in which connection it may not be underrated how indispensable Paris was to the development of his type, which the strength of his instincts made him long to visit at the most decisive time – and how the whole style of his proceedings, of his self-apostolate, could only perfect itself in sight of the French socialistic original. On a more subtle comparison it will perhaps be found, to the honour of Richard Wagner's German nature, that he has acted in everything with more strength, daring, severity and elevation than a nineteenth-century Frenchman could have done – owing to the circumstance that we Germans are as yet closer to barbarism than the French; – perhaps even the most remarkable creation of Richard Wagner is not only at present, but for ever inaccessible, incomprehensible and inimitable to the whole latter-day Latin race: the figure of Siegfried, that *very free* man, who is probably far too free, too hard, too cheerful, too healthy, too *anti-Catholic* for the taste of old and mellow cultured nations. He may even have been a sin against Romanticism, this anti-Latin Siegfried: well, Wagner atoned fully for this sin in his sad old days, when – anticipating a taste which has meanwhile migrated into politics – he began, with the religious vehemence peculiar to him, to preach, at least, *the way to Rome.*...

257

Every elevation of the type 'man' has so far been the work of an aristocratic society and so it will always be – a society believing in a long scale of an order of rank and differences of worth among human beings, and requiring slavery in some form or other. Without the *pathos of distance*, such as grows out of the incarnated difference of classes, out of the constant out-looking and down-looking of the ruling caste on subordinates and instruments, and out of their equally constant practice of obeying and commanding, of keeping down and keeping at a distance – that other more mysterious pathos could never have arisen, the longing for an ever new widening of distance within the soul itself, the formation of ever higher, rarer, further, more extended, more comprehensive states, in short, just the elevation of the type 'man', the continued 'self-surmounting of man' to use a moral formula in a supra-moral sense. To be sure, one must not resign oneself to any humanitarian illusions about the history of the origin of an aristocratic society (that is to say, of the preliminary condition for the elevation of the type 'man'): the truth is hard. Let us acknowledge without prejudice how every higher culture so far has *originated*! Men with a still natural nature, barbarians in every terrible sense of the word, predatory men, still in possession of unbroken strength of will and desire for power, threw themselves upon weaker, more moral, more peaceful races (perhaps trading or cattle-rearing communities), or upon old mellow civilisations in which the vital force was finally flickering out in brilliant fireworks of wit and depravity. At the commencement, the noble caste was always the barbarian caste: their superiority did not consist first of all in their physical, but in their psychical power – they were more *complete* men (which at every point also implies the same as 'more complete beasts').

258

Corruption – as the indication that anarchy threatens to break out among the instincts, and that the foundation of the emotions, called 'life' is convulsed – is something radically different according to the organisation in which it manifests itself. When, for instance, an aristocracy like that of France at the beginning of the Revolution jettisoned its privileges with sublime disgust and sacrificed itself to an excess of its moral sentiments it was corruption: – it was really only the closing act of the corruption which had existed for centuries, by virtue of which that aristocracy had abdicated step by step its privileges and lowered itself to a *function* of royalty (in the end even to its decoration and parade dress). The essential thing, however, in a good and healthy aristocracy is that it should not regard itself as a function either of the kingship or the commonwealth, but as their *significance* and highest justification – that it should therefore accept with a good conscience the sacrifice of a legion of individuals, who, *for its sake*, must be kept down and reduced to imperfect men, to slaves and instruments. Its fundamental belief must be precisely that society is *not* allowed to exist for its own sake, but only as a foundation and scaffolding, by means of which a select class of beings may be able to elevate themselves to their higher duties and in general to a higher *existence*: like those sun-seeking climbing plants in Java – they are called *Sipo Matador* – which encircle an oak so long and so often with their arms, until at last, high above it, but supported by it, they can unfold their tops in the open light and exhibit their happiness.

259

To refrain mutually from injury, from violence, from exploitation, and put one's will on a par with that of others: this may result in a certain rough sense in good conduct among individuals when the necessary conditions pertain (namely, the actual similarity of the individuals in amount of force and degree of worth, and their correlation within one organisation). As soon, however, as one wished to take this principle more generally, and if possible even as the *fundamental principle of society*, it would immediately disclose what it really is – namely, a will to the *denial* of life, a principle of dissolution and decay. Here one must think profoundly to the very basis and resist all sentimental weakness: life itself is *essentially* appropriation, injury, conquest of the strange and weak, suppression, severity, obtrusion of peculiar forms, incorporation, and at the least, putting it at its mildest, exploitation; – but why should one forever use precisely these words on which for ages a disparaging purpose has been stamped? Even the organisation within which, as was previously supposed, the individuals treat each other as equal – it takes place in every healthy aristocracy – must itself, if it be a living and not a dying organisation, do all that towards other bodies, which the individuals within it refrain from doing to each other: it will have to be the incarnate will to power, it will endeavour to grow, to gain ground, attract to itself and acquire ascendancy – not owing to any morality or immorality, but because it *lives* and because life *is* precisely will to power. On no point, however, is the ordinary consciousness of Europeans more unwilling to be corrected than on this matter, people now rave everywhere, even under the guise of science, about imminent conditions of society in which 'the exploiting character' is to be absent – that sounds to my ears as if they promised to invent a mode of life which should refrain from all organic functions. 'Exploitation' does not belong to a depraved or imperfect and primitive society, it belongs to the nature of the living being as a primary organic function, it is a consequence of the intrinsic will to power, which is precisely the will of life. – Granting that as a theory this is a novelty – as a reality it is the *fundamental fact* of all history: let us be so far honest towards ourselves!

260

In a tour through the many finer and coarser moralities which have so far prevailed or still prevail on the earth, I found certain traits recurring regularly together and connected with one another, until finally two primary types revealed themselves to me and a radical distinction was brought to light. There is *master morality* and *slave morality* – I would at once add, however, that in all higher and mixed cultures, there are also attempts at the reconciliation of the two moralities, but one finds still more often a confusion and mutual misunderstanding of them, indeed sometimes their close juxtaposition – even in the same man, within one soul. The distinctions of moral values have either originated in a ruling caste, pleasantly conscious of being different from the ruled – or among the ruled class, the slaves and dependants of all sorts. In the first case, when it is the rulers who determine the conception 'good' it is the exalted, proud disposition which is regarded as the distinguishing feature, and that which determines the order of rank. The noble type of man separates from himself the beings in whom the opposite of this exalted, proud disposition displays itself: he despises them. Let it at once be noted that in this first kind of morality the antithesis 'good' and 'bad' means practically the same as 'noble' and 'despicable' – the antithesis 'good' and *'evil'* has a different origin. The cowardly, the timid, the insignificant and those thinking merely of narrow utility are despised; moreover, also, the distrustful, with their constrained glances, the self-abasing, the dog-like kind of men who let themselves be abused, the mendicant flatterers and above all the liars: – it is a fundamental belief of all aristocrats that the common people are untruthful. 'We truthful ones' – the nobility in ancient Greece called themselves. It is obvious that everywhere the designations of moral value were at first applied to *men*; and were only derivatively and at a later period applied to *actions*; it is a gross mistake, therefore, when historians of morals start with questions like 'Why have sympathetic actions been praised?' The noble type of man regards *himself* as determining values; he does not need others' approval; he passes judgement: 'What is injurious to me is injurious in itself'; he knows that it is he himself only who confers honour on things; he is a *creator of values*. He honours whatever he recognises in himself: such morality equals self-glorification. In the foreground there is the sense of plenitude, of power, which seeks to overflow, the happiness of high tension, the consciousness of a wealth which we would like to give and bestow: – the noble human being also helps the unfortunate, but not – or rarely – out of pity, but rather from an impulse generated by the superabundance of power. The noble human being honours himself as the powerful one, also as one who has power over himself, who knows how to speak and how to be silent, who takes pleasure in subjecting himself to severity and harshness, and has reverence for all that is severe and harsh. 'Wotan placed a hard heart in my breast,' says an old Scandinavian saga: it is thus rightly expressed from the soul of a proud Viking. Such a type of human being is even proud of not being made for pity; the hero of the saga therefore adds warningly: 'He who has not a hard heart when young will never have one.' The noble and brave who think thus are the furthest removed from the morality which sees precisely in pity, or in acting for the good of others, or in *désintéressement*, the characteristic of the moral; faith in oneself, pride in oneself, a radical enmity and irony towards 'selflessness' belong as definitely to noble morality as do careless scorn and precaution in the presence of sympathy and a 'warm heart'. – It is the powerful who *know* how to honour, it is their art, their domain for invention. The profound reverence for age and for tradition – all law rests on this double reverence – the belief and prejudice in favour of ancestors and unfavourable to newcomers is typical in the morality of the powerful; and if, conversely, men of 'modern ideas' believe almost instinctively in 'progress' and the 'future' and are more and more lacking in respect for old age, the ignoble origin of these 'ideas' has complacently betrayed itself thereby. A morality of the ruling class, however, is more especially foreign and irritating to present-day taste in the sternness of its principle that one has duties only to one's equals; that one may act towards beings of a lower rank, towards all that is foreign, just as seems good to one, or 'as the heart desires', and in any case 'beyond good and evil': it is here that pity and similar sentiments can find a place. The ability and obligation to exercise prolonged gratitude and prolonged revenge – both only within a circle of equals – artfulness in retaliation, *raffinement* of the idea in friendship, a certain need to have enemies (as outlets for the emotions of envy, quarrelsomeness, arrogance – in fact, in order to be a good *friend*): all these are typical characteristics of the noble morality, which, as has been pointed out, is not the morality of 'modern ideas' and is therefore at present difficult to realise, and also to unearth and disclose. – It is otherwise with the second type of morality, *slave morality*. Supposing that the abused, the oppressed, the suffering, the unemancipated, the weary and those uncertain of themselves should moralise, what will be the common element in their moral estimates? Probably a pessimistic suspicion with regard to the entire situation of man will find expression, perhaps a condemnation of man, together with his situation. The slave has an unfavourable eye for the virtues of the powerful; he has a scepticism and distrust, a *refinement* of distrust of everything 'good' that is there honoured – he would like to persuade himself that the happiness found there is not genuine. On the other hand, *those* qualities which serve to alleviate the existence of sufferers are brought into prominence and flooded with light; it is here that pity, the kind, helping hand, the warm heart, patience, diligence, humility and friendliness attain honour; for here these are the most useful qualities and almost the only means of supporting the burden of existence. Slave morality is essentially the morality of utility. Here is the seat of the origin of the famous antithesis 'good' and 'evil': – power and dangerousness are assumed to reside in the evil, a certain dreadfulness, subtlety and strength, which do not admit of being despised. According to slave morality, therefore, the 'evil' man invokes fear; according to master morality, it is precisely the 'good' man who invokes fear and seeks to do so, while the bad man is regarded as despicable. The contrast attains its maximum when, in accordance with the logical consequences of slave morality, a shade of depreciation – it may be slight and well-intentioned – at last attaches itself to the 'good' man of this morality; because, according to the servile mode of thought, the good man must in any case be the *safe* man: he is good-natured, easily deceived, perhaps a little stupid, *un bonhomme*. Everywhere that slave morality gains ascendancy, language shows a tendency to approximate the significations of the words 'good' and 'stupid'. – A last fundamental difference: the desire for *freedom*, the instinct for happiness and the refinements of the feeling of liberty belong as necessarily to slave morals and morality as artifice and enthusiasm in reverence and devotion are the usual symptoms of an aristocratic mode of thinking and estimating. – Thus we can understand without further detail why love *as a passion* – it is our European specialty – must absolutely be of noble origin; as is well known, its invention is due to the Provençal knight-poets, those brilliant, ingenious men of the *'gai saber'* to whom Europe owes so much, and almost owes itself.

261

Vanity is one of the things which are perhaps most difficult for a noble human being to understand: he will be tempted to deny it, where another kind of man thinks he sees it self-evidently. The problem for him is to represent to his mind beings who seek to create a good opinion of themselves which they themselves do not possess – and consequently also do not 'deserve' – and who yet *believe* in this good opinion afterwards. This seems to him on the one hand such bad taste and so self-disrespectful, and on the other hand so grotesquely unreasonable, that he would like to consider vanity an exception and is doubtful about it in most cases when it is spoken of. He will say, for instance: 'I may be mistaken about my value, and on the other hand may nevertheless demand that my value should be acknowledged by others precisely as I rate it: – that, however, is not vanity (but self-conceit or, in most cases, that which is called "humility," and also "modesty").' Or he will even say: 'For many reasons I can delight in the good opinion of others, perhaps because I love and honour them, and rejoice in all their joys, perhaps also because their good opinion endorses and strengthens my belief in my own good opinion, perhaps because the good opinion of others, even in cases where I do not share it is useful to me, or gives promise of usefulness: – all this, however, is not vanity.' The human being of noble character must first bring it home forcibly to his mind, especially with the aid of history, that, from time immemorial, in all social strata in any way dependent, the ordinary man *was* only that which he *passed for*: – not being at all accustomed to fix values, he did not assign even to himself any other value than that which his master assigned to him (it is the peculiar *right of masters* to create values). It may be looked upon as the result of an extraordinary atavism that the ordinary man, even today, is still always *waiting* for an opinion about himself and then instinctively submitting himself to it; yet by no means only to a 'good' opinion, but also to a bad and unjust one (think, for instance, of the greater part of the self-appreciations and self-depreciations which believing women learn from their confessors and which in general the believing Christian learns from his Church). In fact, conformably to the slow rise of the democratic social order (and its cause, the blending of the blood of masters and slaves), the originally noble and rare impulse of the masters to assign a value to themselves and to 'think well' of themselves, will now be more and more encouraged and extended; but it has at all times an older, ampler and more radically ingrained propensity opposed to it – and in the phenomenon of 'vanity' this older propensity overmasters the younger. The vain person rejoices at *every* good opinion which he hears about himself (quite apart from the point of view of its usefulness and equally regardless of its truth or falsehood), just as he suffers from every bad opinion: for he subjects himself to both, he feels himself subjected to both, by that oldest instinct of subjection which breaks forth in him. – It is 'the slave' in the vain person's blood, the remnants of the slave's cunning – and how much of the 'slave' is still left in woman, for instance! – which seeks to *seduce* to good opinions of itself; it is the slave, too, who immediately afterwards prostrates himself before these opinions, as though he had not called them forth. – And to repeat it again: vanity is an atavism.

262

A *species* originates and a type becomes established and strong in the long struggle with essentially constant *unfavourable* conditions. On the other hand, it is known by the experience of breeders that species which receive superabundant nourishment, and in general a surplus of protection and care, immediately tend in the most marked way to develop variations and are fertile in prodigies and monstrosities (as well as in monstrous vices). Now look at an aristocratic commonwealth, say an ancient Greek *polis*, or Venice, as a voluntary or involuntary contrivance for the purpose of *breeding* human beings; there are there human beings beside one another, thrown on their own resources, who want to make their species prevail, chiefly because they *must* prevail or else run the terrible risk of being exterminated. The favour, the superabundance, the protection are there lacking under which variations are fostered; the species needs itself as species, as something which, precisely by virtue of its hardness, its uniformity and simplicity of structure, can in general prevail and make itself permanent in constant struggle with its neighbours, or with rebellious or rebellion-threatening vassals. The most varied experience teaches it what are the qualities to which it principally owes the fact that it still exists, in spite of all gods and men, and has so far been victorious: these qualities it calls virtues, and these virtues alone it develops to maturity. It does so with severity, indeed it desires severity; every aristocratic morality is intolerant in the education of youth, in the control of women, in marriage customs, in the relations of old and young, in the penal laws (which have an eye only for the degenerating): it counts intolerance itself among the virtues in the name of 'justice'. A type with few, but very marked features, a species of severe, warlike, wisely silent, reserved and reticent men (and as such, with the most delicate sensibility for the charm and nuances of society) is thus established, unaffected by the vicissitudes of generations; the constant struggle with uniform *unfavourable* conditions is, as already remarked, the cause of a type becoming stable and hard. Finally, however, a happy state of affairs results, the enormous tension is relaxed; there are perhaps no more enemies among the neighbouring peoples, and the means of life, even of the enjoyment of life, are present in superabundance. At a stroke the bond and constraint of the old discipline are severed: it is no longer regarded as necessary, as a condition of existence – if it would continue, it can only do so as a form of *luxury*, as an archaising *taste*. Variations, whether they be deviations (into the higher, finer and rarer) or deteriorations and monstrosities appear suddenly on the scene in the greatest exuberance and splendour; the individual dares to be individual and detach himself. At this turning point of history there manifest themselves, side by side, and often mixed and enmeshed, a magnificent, manifold, jungle-like growth and upward striving, a kind of *tropical tempo* in the rivalry of growth, and an extraordinary decay and self-destruction, owing to the savagely opposing and seemingly exploding egoisms, which strive with one another 'for sun and light' and can no longer assign any limit, restraint or consideration for themselves by means of the previously existing morality. It was this morality itself which piled up strength massively, which bent the bow in so threatening a manner: – it is now 'out of date', it is getting 'out of date'. The dangerous and disquieting point has been reached when the greater, more manifold, more comprehensive life *is lived beyond* the old morality; the 'individual' stands out and is obliged to have recourse to his own lawgiving, his own arts and artifices for self-preservation, self-elevation and self-deliverance. Nothing but new 'Whys', nothing but new 'Hows', no longer any common formulas, misunderstanding and disregard in league with each other, decay, deterioration and the highest desires frightfully entangled, the genius of the race overflowing from all the cornucopias of good and bad, a portentous simultaneity of spring and autumn, full of new charms and mysteries peculiar to the fresh, still unexhausted, still unwearied corruption. Danger is again present, the mother of morality, great danger; this time shifted into the individual, into the neighbour and friend, into the street, into their own child, into their own heart, into all the most personal and secret recesses of their desires and volitions. What will the moral philosophers who appear at this time have to preach? They discover, these acute onlookers and loafers, that the end is soon approaching, that everything around them decays and produces decay, that nothing will endure until the day after tomorrow, except one species of man, the incurably *mediocre*. The mediocre alone have a prospect of continuing and propagating themselves – they will be the men of the future, the sole survivors; 'Be like them! Become mediocre!' is now the only morality which has still a significance, which still obtains a hearing. – But it is difficult to preach this morality of mediocrity! It can never avow what it is and what it desires! It has to talk of moderation and dignity and duty and brotherly love – it will have difficulty *in concealing its irony*!

265

At the risk of displeasing innocent ears, I submit that egoism belongs to the essence of a noble soul, I mean the unalterable belief that to a being such as 'we' other beings must naturally be subordinate and have to sacrifice themselves. The noble soul accepts the fact of its egoism without question and also without consciousness of harshness, constraint or arbitrariness, but rather as something that may have its basis in the primary law of things: – if it sought a designation for it, it would say: 'It is justice itself.' It acknowledges under certain circumstances, which made it hesitate at first, that there are other equally privileged ones; as soon as it has settled this question of rank it moves among those equals and equally privileged ones with the same assurance, as regards modesty and delicate respect, which it enjoys in intercourse with itself – in accordance with an innate heavenly mechanism which all the stars understand. It is an *additional* instance of its egoism, this artfulness and self-limitation in intercourse with its equals – every star is a similar egoist; it honours *itself* in them and in the rights which it concedes to them, it has no doubt that the exchange of honours and rights, as the *essence* of all intercourse, belongs also to the natural condition of things. The noble soul gives as it takes, prompted by the passionate and sensitive instinct of requital, which is at the root of its nature. The notion of 'favour' has, *inter pares*, neither significance nor good repute; there may be a sublime way of letting gifts, as it were, light upon one from above, and of drinking them thirstily like dewdrops; but for those arts and displays the noble soul has no aptitude. Its egoism hinders it here: in general, it looks 'up' unwillingly – it looks either *forward*, horizontally and deliberately, or downwards – *it knows that it is on a height.*

Translated by Helen Zimmern with modifications

The Gay Science, Book V, 1887

356

How things will become more 'artistic' in Europe. – In the present day, in our transition period when so much ceases to compel men, providing a living still compels almost all male Europeans to adopt a definite *role*, their so-called calling; some have the freedom, an apparent freedom, to choose this role themselves, but most have it chosen for them. The result is strange enough. Almost all Europeans confound themselves with their role when they advance in age; they themselves are the victims of their 'good acting', they have forgotten how much chance, mood and caprice swayed them when their 'calling' was decided – and how many other roles they perhaps *could* have played: for it is now too late! Looked at more closely, we see that their characters have actually *evolved* out of their role, nature out of art. There were ages in which people believed with unshaken confidence, even with piety, in their predestination for this very occupation, for that very mode of livelihood, and would not at all acknowledge chance, or the fortuitous role, or arbitrariness. Ranks, guilds and hereditary trade privileges succeeded, with the help of this faith, in rearing those monsters of social pyramids which distinguished the Middle Ages, and of which at all events one thing remains to their credit: durability (and duration is a value of the first rank on earth!). But there are opposite ages, really democratic, in which people tend to abandon this faith, and a sort of cocky faith and opposite point of view comes more and more to the fore, the Athenian faith which is first observed in the Periclean age, the American faith of the present day, which wants also more and more to become a European faith: whereby the individual is convinced that he can do almost anything, that he *can play almost any role,* whereby everyone experiments with himself, improvises, tries anew, tries with delight, whereby all nature ceases and becomes art…. The Greeks, having adopted this *role faith* – an artist's faith, if you will – underwent step by step, as is well known, a curious transformation, not in every respect worthy of imitation: *they became actual actors*; and as such they enchanted, they overcame the entire world, and at last even 'the power that had overcome the world' (for the *Graeculus histrio* conquered Rome, and *not* Greek culture, as the naive are accustomed to say …). What I fear, however, and what is at present obvious, if we desire to perceive it, is that we modern men are already on the same road; and whenever a man begins to discover in what respect he plays a role, and to what extent he *can* be an actor, he *becomes* an actor…. With this a new flora and fauna of men springs up, which cannot grow in more stable, more restricted eras – or is left 'at the bottom' under the ban and suspicion of infamy. It is thus that the most interesting and insane periods of history always make their appearance, in which 'actors', *all* kinds of actors, are the real masters. As this happens, another species of man is always more and more injured, and in the end made impossible: above all, the great 'architects'; the building power is now being paralysed; the courage that makes plans for the distant future is disheartened; there begins to be a lack of organising geniuses. Who is there who would now venture to undertake projects that would require thousands of years for their completion? The fundamental faith is dying out, on the basis of which one could calculate, promise and anticipate the future in one's plan, and to sacrifice the future to them – namely, the faith that man has value and significance only insofar as he is *a stone in a great building*; for which purpose he has first of all to be *solid*, a 'stone'…Above all, not an actor! In short, this fact will be hushed up for some considerable time to come! – that which henceforth will no longer be built, and *can* no longer be built, is – a society in the old sense of the term; to build that, everything is lacking, above all the material. *None of us are any longer material for a society*: that is a truth for which the time has come! It seems to me a matter of indifference that meanwhile the most short-sighted, perhaps the most honest, and at any rate the noisiest species of men of the present day, our good socialists, believe, hope, dream and above all scream and scribble almost the opposite; in fact, one already reads their slogan of the future, 'free society', on every table and wall. Free society? Indeed! Indeed! But you know, gentlemen, what is required for building that? Wooden iron! The famous wooden iron! And it must not even be wooden …

358

The peasant rebellion of the spirit. – We Europeans find ourselves in sight of a vast world of ruins, where some things still tower, while other objects stand mouldering and dismal, where most things however already lie on the ground, picturesque enough – where were there ever finer ruins? – overgrown with weeds, large and small. It is the Church which is this city of decay: we see the religious community of Christianity shaken to its deepest foundations. Faith in God is overthrown, faith in the Christian ascetic ideal is now fighting its last fight. Such a long and solidly built work as Christianity – it was the last construction of the Romans! – could not of course be demolished all at once; every sort of earthquake had to shake it, every sort of spirit which bores, digs, gnaws and moulders had to assist in the work of destruction. But what is strangest is that those who have exerted themselves most to retain and preserve Christianity have been precisely those who did most to destroy it – the Germans. It seems that the Germans do not understand the nature of a Church. Are they not spiritual enough or not distrustful enough to do so? In any case the structure of the Church rests on a *southern* freedom and enlightenment of the spirit, and similarly on a southern suspicion of nature, man and spirit; it rests on knowledge of man and experience of man, entirely different from what the North has had. The Lutheran Reformation in all its breadth was the indignation of simplicity against 'multiplicity'. To speak cautiously, it was a coarse, honest misunderstanding, in which much is to be forgiven – people did not understand the mode of expression of a *victorious* Church and only saw corruption; they misunderstood the noble scepticism, the *luxury* of scepticism and tolerance which every victorious, self-confident power permits itself... One overlooks the fact readily enough at present that as regards all cardinal questions concerning power Luther's disposition was calamitously short-sighted, superficial and imprudent – and above all, as a man of the common people, he lacked all the hereditary qualities of a ruling caste and all the instincts for power; so that his work, his intention to restore the work of the Romans, merely became involuntarily and unconsciously the beginning of a work of destruction. He unravelled, he tore up with honest rage, where the old spider had spun longest and most carefully. He surrendered the sacred books into the hands of everyone – they thereby got at last into the hands of the philologists, that is to say, the annihilators of every faith based on books. He demolished the concept of 'the Church' in that he repudiated the faith in the inspiration of the church councils: for only under the supposition that the inspiring spirit which had founded the Church still lives in it, still builds it, still goes on building its house, does the concept of the 'Church' retain its power. He gave back to the priest sexual intercourse: but three-quarters of the reverence of which the common people, especially all the women among the common people, are capable, rests on the faith that an exceptional man in this respect will also be an exceptional man in other respects. It is precisely here that the popular belief in something superhuman in man, in a miracle, in the saving God in man, has its most subtle and insidious advocate. After Luther had given a wife to the priest, he had *to take from him* auricular confession;

that was psychologically right: but thereby he practically did away with the Christian priest himself, whose profoundest utility has always consisted in his being a sacred ear, a silent well and a grave for secrets. 'Every man his own priest' – behind such a formula and their peasant cunning there was concealed in Luther the profoundest hatred of 'higher men' and of the rule of 'higher men' as the Church had conceived them. Luther disowned an ideal which he did not know how to attain, while he seemed to combat and detest the degeneration of this ideal. As a matter of fact, he, the impossible monk, repudiated the *rule* of the *homines religiosi*; he consequently brought about precisely the same thing within the ecclesiastical social order that he fought so impatiently in the civic order – namely a 'peasant rebellion'. – As to all that grew out of his Reformation afterwards, good and bad, which can at present be almost counted up – who would be naïve enough to praise or blame Luther simply on account of these results? He is innocent of all; he had no idea what he did. The art of making the European spirit shallower especially in the North, or *more good-natured*, if people would rather hear it designated by a moral expression, undoubtedly took a clever step in advance in the Lutheran Reformation; and similarly there grew out of it the mobility and disquietude of the spirit, its thirst for independence, its faith in the right to freedom and its 'naturalness'. If people wish to ascribe to the Reformation in the last instance the merit of having prepared and favoured that which we at present honour as 'modern science' they must of course add that it is also accessory to bringing about the degeneration of the modern scholar, with his lack of reverence, of shame and of profundity; and that it is also responsible for all naive candour and plain dealing in matters of knowledge, in short for the *plebeianism of the spirit* which is peculiar to the last two centuries and from which even pessimism has not yet liberated us. 'Modern ideas' also belong to this peasant rebellion of the North against the colder, more ambiguous, more suspicious spirit of the South, which has built itself its greatest monument in the Christian Church. Let us not forget in the end what a Church is, and especially in contrast to every 'state': a Church is above all a structure for ruling which secures to the *most spiritual* men the highest rank, and *believes* in the power of spirituality so far as to forbid itself the use of all the cruder instruments of force. Through this alone the Church is under all circumstances a *nobler* institution than the state. –

362

Our faith that Europe will become more virile. – We owe it to Napoleon (and not to the French Revolution, which aimed at the 'brotherhood' of nations and a blossoming universal exchange of hearts) that several warlike centuries, which have not had their like in past history, may now follow one another – in short, that we have entered *the classical age of war*, war at the same time scientific and popular, on the grandest scale (as regards weapons, talents and discipline), to which all future millennia will look back with envy and awe for its perfection: – for the national movement out of which this war glory springs is only the counter-shock against Napoleon and would not have existed without him. He should receive credit some day for the fact that in Europe *man* has again become master over the businessman and the philistine; perhaps even over 'woman' also, who has become pampered owing to Christianity and the enthusiastic spirit of the eighteenth century, and still more owing to 'modern ideas'. Napoleon, who saw in modern ideas, and in civilisation itself, something like a personal enemy, has by this hostility proved himself one of the greatest continuators of the Renaissance: he has brought to the surface a whole slab of antiquity, perhaps the decisive piece, the piece of granite. And who knows whether this slab of antiquity will in the end become master over the national movement, and will have to make itself in a *positive* sense the heir and continuator of Napoleon: – who, as one knows, wanted one unified Europe, which was to be *mistress of the earth*. –

377

We who are homeless. – Among the Europeans of today there are not lacking those who may call themselves homeless ones in a way which is at once a distinction and an honour; it is by them that my secret wisdom and *gaya scienza* is especially to be laid to heart! For their fate is hard, their hope uncertain; it is a clever feat to devise consolation for them. But what good does it do! We children of the future, how *could* we be at home in the present? We are antipathetic to all ideals which could make us feel at home in this fragile, broken-down, transition period; and as for its 'realities', we do not believe in their *endurance*. The ice which still supports has become very thin: the thawing wind blows; we ourselves, the homeless ones, are a force that breaks the ice, and the other too thin 'realities' ... We 'conserve' nothing, nor would we return to any past age; we are not by any means 'liberal', we do not work for 'progress', we do not need first to stop our ears to the song of the marketplace and the sirens of the future – their song of 'equal rights', 'free society', 'no longer either masters or slaves', does not seduce us! We do not by any means consider it desirable that the realm of justice and peace should be established on earth (because under any circumstances it would be the realm of the profoundest mediocrity and *chinoiserie*); we rejoice in all men who like ourselves love danger, war and adventure, who do not make compromises, nor let themselves be captured, reconciled and castrated; we count ourselves among the conquerors; we think about the necessity for new orders, even of a new slavery – for every strengthening and elevation of the type 'man' also involves a new form of slavery. Is it not obvious that with all this we must feel ill at ease in an age which claims the honour of being the most humane, gentle and just that the sun has ever seen? What a pity that at the mere mention of these fine words the thoughts at the bottom of our hearts are all the more unpleasant, what we find in them is only the expression – or the masquerade – of profound weakening, exhaustion, age and declining power! What can it matter to us what kind of tinsel the sick may use to cover up his weakness? He may parade it as his *virtue*; there is no doubt whatever that weakness makes people gentle, oh so gentle, so just, so inoffensive, so 'humane'! – The 'religion of pity' to which people would like to convert us – yes, we know sufficiently well the hysterical little men and women who need this religion at present as a cloak and adornment! We are no humanitarians; we should not dare to speak of our 'love of mankind'; for that, a person of our stamp is not enough of an actor! Or not sufficiently Saint-Simonist, not sufficiently French. A person must have been afflicted with a *Gallic* excess of erotic susceptibility and amorous impatience even to approach mankind honourably with his lewdness…. Mankind! Was there ever a more hideous old woman among all old women (unless perhaps it were 'truth': a question for philosophers)? No, we do not love mankind! On the other hand, we are not nearly 'German' enough, in the sense in which the word 'German' is current at present, to advocate nationalism and race hatred, or take delight in the national scabies of the heart and blood-poisoning, on account of which the nations of Europe are at present bounded off and secluded from one another as if by quarantine. We are too unprejudiced for that, too perverse, too fastidious; also too well informed and too 'travelled'. We prefer much rather to live on mountains, apart, 'untimely', in past or future centuries, in order merely to spare ourselves the silent rage to which we know we should be condemned as eyewitnesses of politics that are desolating the German spirit by making it vain, and that is a *petty* politics besides: – will it not be necessary for this system to plant itself between two mortal hatreds lest its own creation should immediately collapse? Will it not *be obliged* to desire the perpetuation of the petty-state system of Europe?…We homeless ones are too diverse and mixed in race and descent for 'modern men' and are consequently little tempted to participate in the falsified racial self-admiration and lewdness which at present display themselves in Germany, as signs of German sentiment, and which strike one as doubly false and unbecoming among the people of the 'historical sense'. We are, in a word – and it shall be our word of honour! – *good Europeans*, the heirs of Europe, the rich, over-wealthy heirs, but also overly obligated heirs of thousands of years of European spirit. As such, we have also outgrown Christianity and are disinclined to it – and just because we have grown *out of* it, because our ancestors were Christians uncompromising in their Christian integrity, who willingly sacrificed possessions and positions, blood and fatherland, for the sake of their faith. We – do the same. For what, then? For our unbelief? For all sorts of unbelief? No, you know better than that, my friends! The hidden *Yes* in you is stronger than all the Nos and Maybes, of which you and your age are afflicted like a disease; and when you are obliged to put out to sea, you emigrants, you too are compelled to this by – a *faith*!…

Translated by Thomas Common with modifications

On the Genealogy of Morals: A Polemical Tract, 1887

First Essay, Good and Evil, Good and Bad

4

I was given a hint of the *right* direction by this question: What, from an etymological perspective, do the meanings of 'good' as manifested in different languages really mean? There I found that all of them lead back to the *same conceptual transformation*, that everywhere 'noble' or 'aristocratic' in a social sense is the fundamental concept out of which 'good' in the sense of 'spiritually noble', 'aristocratic', 'spiritually high-minded', 'spiritually privileged' necessarily develop – a development which always runs parallel with that other one which finally transforms 'common', 'plebeian' and 'low' into the concept 'bad'. The most eloquent example of the latter is the German word *schlecht* [bad] itself – which is identical with the word *schlicht* [plain] – compare *schlechtweg* [plainly] and *schlechterdings* [simply]. Originally these words designated the plain, common man, but without any suspicious sideglance, simply in contrast to the noble man. Around the time of the Thirty Years' War approximately – hence late enough – this sense changed into the one used today.

As far as the genealogy of morals is concerned, this point strikes me as a *fundamental* insight – that it was first discovered so late we can ascribe to the repressive influence which the democratic prejudice in the modern world exercises over all questions of origin. And this occurs even in the apparently objective realm of natural science and physiology, a point which I can only hint at here. But the sort of mischief this prejudice can cause, once it has become unleashed to the point of hatred, particularly where morality and history are concerned, is revealed in the notorious case of Buckle: the *plebeian nature* of the modern spirit, which originated in England, broke out once again on its home soil, as violently as a muddy volcano and with the same salty, overloud and common eloquence with which all previous volcanoes have spoken. –

5

With respect to *our* problem – which for good reasons we can call a *quiet* problem, so refined that it directs itself only to a few ears – there is no little interest in establishing the point that often in those words and roots which designate 'good' there still shines through the main nuance of what made the nobility feel they were men of higher rank. It is true that in most cases they perhaps named themselves simply after their superiority in power (as 'the powerful' 'the masters', 'those in command') or after the most visible sign of their superiority, for example, as 'the rich' or 'the owners' (that is the meaning of *arya*, and the corresponding words in Persian and Slavic). But they also named themselves after a *typical characteristic*, and that is the case which is our concern here. For instance, they called themselves 'the truthful' – above all the Greek nobility, whose mouthpiece is the Megarian poet Theognis. The word developed for this characteristic – *esthlos* [good, brave] – indicates, according to its root, a man who *is*, who possesses reality, who really exists, who is true. Then, with a subjective transformation, it indicates the true as the truthful. In this phase of conceptual transformation it became the slogan and catchphrase for the nobility, and its sense shifted entirely to 'aristocratic' to mark a distinction from the *lying* common man, as Theognis takes and presents him, until finally, after the decline of the nobility, the word remains as a designation of spiritual *noblesse* and becomes, as it were, ripe and sweet. In the word *kakos* [bad, ugly, ill-born, mean, craven] as in the word *deilos* [cowardly, worthless] (the plebeian in contrast to the *agathos* [good, well-born]) cowardice is emphasised. This perhaps provides a hint about the direction in which we have to seek the etymological origin for the multiple meanings of *agathos*. In the Latin word *malus* [bad] (which I place alongside *melas* [black]) the common man could be designated as the dark-coloured, above all as the dark-haired (*'hic niger est'* ['this man is black']), as the pre-Aryan inhabitant of Italian soil, who stood out from those who became dominant, the blond, that is, the conquering race of Aryans, most clearly through this colour. At any rate, the Gaelic race offers me an exactly corresponding case. The word *fin* (for example, in the name *Fin-Gal*), the term designating nobility and finally the good, noble and pure, originally referred to the blond-headed man in contrast to the dark, black-haired, original inhabitants.

Incidentally, the Celts were a thoroughly blond race. People are wrong when they link the traces of a basically dark-haired population, which are noticeable on the carefully prepared ethnographic maps of Germany, with any Celtic origin and mixing of blood, as Virchow does. It is much rather the case that in these places the *pre-Aryan* population of Germany emerged. (The same is true for almost all of Europe: essentially the conquered race finally attained the upper hand once again in colour, shortness of skull, perhaps even in the intellectual and social instincts. Who can confirm for us whether modern democracy, even more modern anarchism, and indeed that preference for the *'commune'*, for the most primitive form of society, which all European socialists now share, does not indicate a monstrous *counterattack*, and that the ruling and *master race*, the Aryans, is not being defeated, even physiologically?)

The Latin word *bonus* [good] I believe I can explicate as 'the warrior', provided that I am correct in tracing *bonus* back to an older word *duonus* (compare *bellum* [war] = *duellum* [war] = *duenlum*, which seems to me to contain that word *duonus*). Hence, *bonus* as a man of war, of division (*duo*), as a warrior. We can see what constituted a man's 'goodness' in ancient Rome. What about our German word *gut* [good] itself? Does it not indicate *'den Göttlichen'* [the godlike man], the man of *'göttlichen Geschlechts'* [the godlike race]? And is it not identical to the popular (originally noble) name for the Goths? The basis for this hypothesis does not have a place here. –

7

You will have already guessed how easily the priestly way of evaluating could split from the knightly-aristocratic and then continue to evolve into its opposite. Such a development receives a special stimulus every time the priest caste and the warrior caste confront each other jealously and are not willing to agree. The knightly-aristocratic value judgements have as their basic assumption a powerful physicality, a blooming, rich, even overflowing health, together with those things which are required to maintain these qualities – war, adventure, hunting, dancing, war games, in general everything which involves strong, free, happy action. The priestly-noble method of evaluating has, as we saw, other preconditions: these make it difficult enough for them when it comes to war! As is well known, priests are the most *evil of enemies* – but why? Because they are the most powerless. Out of powerlessness, their hate grows into something immense and uncanny, something most spiritual and most poisonous. Those who have been the greatest haters in world history and the most ingenious haters have always been priests – in comparison with the spirit of priestly revenge all the remaining spirits are hardly worth considering. Human history would be a really stupid affair without that spirit which entered it because of the powerless. Let us quickly consider the greatest example. Everything on earth which has been done against 'the nobles', 'the powerful', 'the masters', 'the ones in power' is not worth mentioning in comparison with what *the Jews* have done against them – the Jews, that priestly people, who could get back at their enemies and oppressors only through a radical revaluation of their enemies' values, that is, through an act of the *most spiritual revenge*. For only this was appropriate to a priestly people with the most deeply rooted priestly desire for revenge. In opposition to the aristocratic value equation (good = noble = powerful = beautiful = fortunate = loved by God), it was the Jews who, with a consistency inspiring fear, dared this reversal and hung on to it with the teeth of the most profound hatred (the hatred of the powerless), saying, 'Only those who suffer are good; the poor, the powerless, the low are the only good people; the suffering, those in need, the sick, the ugly are also the only pious people; only they are blessed by God; for them alone there is beatitude. By contrast, you privileged and powerful people, you are for all eternity the evil, the cruel, the lecherous, the insatiable, the godless – you will also be the unblessed, the cursed, and the damned for all eternity!' We know *who* inherited this Jewish revaluation of values. In connection with that huge and immeasurably disastrous initiative which the Jews launched with this most fundamental of all declarations of war, I recall the sentence I wrote on another occasion (in *Beyond Good and Evil*, section 195) – namely, that with the Jews *the slave revolt in morality* begins: that revolt which has a history of two thousand years behind it and which today we no longer notice because it has triumphed.

10

The slave revolt in morality begins when *ressentiment* itself becomes creative and gives birth to values: the *ressentiment* of those beings who are prevented from a genuinely active reaction and who compensate for that with a merely imaginary vengeance. While all noble morality grows out of a triumphant self-affirmation, slave morality from the start says No to what is 'outside', 'other', 'a non-self'. And *this* No is its creative act. This transformation of the glance which confers value – this *necessary* projection towards what is outer instead of back onto itself – that is inherent in *ressentiment*. In order to arise, slave morality always requires first an opposing world, a world outside itself. Physiologically speaking, it needs external stimuli in order to act at all. Its action is basically reaction.

The reverse is the case with the noble method of valuing: it acts and grows spontaneously. It seeks its opposite only to affirm itself even more gratefully, with even more rejoicing. Its negative concept of 'low', 'common', 'bad' is only a pale contrasting image after the fact in relation to its positive basic concept, thoroughly steeped in life and passion, 'We, the noble, good, beautiful, and happy!' When the noble way of evaluating makes a mistake and abuses reality, that happens with reference to the sphere which it does *not* know well enough, indeed, the sphere which it has strongly resisted getting to know: under certain circumstances it misjudges the sphere it despises – the sphere of the common man, the low people. On the other hand, we should consider that even assuming that the feeling of contempt, of looking down or of looking superior *falsifies* the image of the person despised, it will at any rate still be a much less serious falsification than that perpetrated on its opponent – naturally, *in effigie* – by the repressed hatred and vengeance of the powerless. In fact, in contempt there is too much negligence, too much dismissiveness, too much looking away and impatience, all mixed together, even too much joy, for it to be capable of converting its object into a truly distorted monster.

We should not fail to hear the almost benevolent nuances which for a Greek noble, for example, lay in all the words with which he set himself above the lower people – how a constant form of pity, consideration and forbearance is mixed in there, sweetening the words, to the point where almost all words which refer to the common man finally remain as expressions for 'unhappy', 'pitiable' (compare *deilos* [cowardly], *deilaios* [paltry], *poneros* [oppressed by toil, wretched], *mochtheros* [suffering, wretched] – the last two basically designating the common man as a slave worker and beast of burden). On the other hand, for the Greek ear the words 'bad', 'low', 'unhappy' have never stopped echoing a single note, one tone colour, in which 'unhappy' predominates. That is the inheritance of the old, noble, aristocratic way of evaluating, which does not betray its principles even in contempt. (Philologists might recall the sense in which *oizyros* [miserable], *anolbos* [unblessed], *tlemon* [wretched], *dystychein* [unfortunate], *xymphora* [misfortune] were used.) The 'well born' *felt* that they were the 'happy ones'; they did not have to construct their happiness artificially first by looking at their enemies, or in some circumstance talk themselves into it, to *lie to themselves* (the way all men of *ressentiment* do). Similarly they knew, as complete men, overloaded with power and thus *necessarily* active, that they must not separate action from happiness. They considered being active to be necessarily associated with happiness (that is where the phrase *eu prattein* [do well, succeed] derives its origin) – all this is very much the opposite of 'happiness' at the level of the powerless, the oppressed, those festering with poisonous and hostile feelings, among whom happiness is expressed essentially as a narcotic, an anaesthetic, peace and quiet, 'sabbath', relaxation of the soul, stretching one's limbs, in short, something *passive*.

While the noble man lives for himself with trust and candour (*gennaios*, meaning 'of noble birth' stresses the nuance 'upright' and also probably 'naïve'); the man of *ressentiment* is neither upright nor naïve, nor honest and direct with himself. His soul *squints*. His spirit loves hiding places, secret paths and backdoors. Everything furtive attracts him as *his* world, *his* security, *his* refreshment. He understands how to remain silent, not forgetting, waiting, temporarily diminishing himself, humiliating himself. A race of such men of *ressentiment* will necessarily end up *cleverer* than any noble race. It will value cleverness to a very different extent, that is, as a condition of existence of the utmost importance; whereas cleverness among noble men easily acquires a delicate aftertaste of luxury and sophistication. Here it is not nearly as important as the complete certainty of the ruling *unconscious* instincts or even a certain lack of cleverness, something like brave recklessness, whether in the face of danger or of an enemy, or wildly enthusiastic, sudden outbursts of anger, love, reverence, thankfulness and vengefulness, by which in all ages noble souls have recognised each other. The *ressentiment* of the noble man himself, if it comes over him, consumes and exhausts itself in an immediate reaction and therefore does not *poison*. On the other hand, in countless cases it simply does not appear at all; whereas, in the case of all weak and powerless people, it is unavoidable.

The noble man cannot take his enemies, his misfortunes, even his *bad deeds* seriously for very long – that is the mark of strong, complete natures, in whom there is a surplus of plastic, creative, healing power, as well as the power to forget (a good example from the modern world is Mirabeau, who had no memory of the insults and maliciousness people directed at him, and who therefore could not forgive, because he forgot). Such a man with a single shrug throws off all those worms which eat into other men. Only here is possible – provided that it is at all possible on earth – real *'love* for one's enemy'. How much reverence a noble man has for his enemies! And such a reverence is already a bridge to love. In fact, he demands his enemy for himself, as his badge of honour. Indeed, he has no enemy other than one in whom there is nothing to despise and a *great deal* to respect! By contrast, imagine 'the enemy' as a man of *ressentiment* conceives him – and right here we have his action, his creation: he has conceptualised 'the evil enemy', *'the evil one'*, as a fundamental idea – in opposition to which he now conceives of an opposite image and counterpart, a 'good man' – himself!...

16

Let us bring this to a conclusion. The two *opposing* values 'good and bad', 'good and evil' have fought a fearful battle on earth for thousands of years. If it is true that the latter pair of opposites has for a long time had the upper hand, there is still no lack of places where the battle still rages without a final conclusion. We could even say that in the intervening period the battle has been constantly drawn to greater heights and even greater depths and has become continuously more spiritual, so that today there is perhaps no more decisive mark of a *'higher nature'*, a more spiritual nature, than that it is split in this sense and is truly still a battleground for these opposites.

The symbol of this battle, written in a script which has remained legible throughout human history up to the present, is 'Rome against Judea, Judea against Rome'. To this point there has been no greater event than *this* war, *this* posing of a question, *this* contradiction between these deadly enemies. Rome felt that there was, in the Jew, something contrary to nature itself, something like its monstrous polar opposite. In Rome the Jew was considered *'guilty* of hatred against the entire human race'. And that view was correct, to the extent we are right to link the salvation and the future of the human race to the unconditional rule of aristocratic values, Roman values.

By contrast, how did the Jews feel about Rome? We can guess that from a thousand signs, but it is sufficient to treat oneself again to the Apocalypse of John, that wildest of all written outbursts which vengeance has on its conscience. (Incidentally, we must not underestimate the deep consistency of the Christian instinct, when it signed this very book of hate with the name of the disciple of love, the same disciple to whom it attributed that wildly enthusiastic amorous gospel – there is some truth to this, no matter how much literary counterfeiting may have been necessary for that book to make the point.) The Romans were indeed the strong and noble ones, stronger and nobler ones have hitherto never existed on earth, have never even been dreamed of. Everything they left as relics, every inscription, is delightful, provided that we can guess *what* was doing the writing there. By contrast, the Jews were *par excellence* that priestly people of *ressentiment*, who possessed an unparalleled genius for popular morality. Just compare people with related talents – say, the Chinese or the Germans – with the Jews in order to understand who is ranked first and who is ranked fifth.

Which of them has *proved victorious* for the time being, Rome or Judea? Surely there is not the slightest doubt. Just think of who it is people bow down to today in Rome as the personification of all the highest values – and not only in Rome, but over almost half the earth, all the places where people have become merely tame or want to become tame – in front of *three Jews*, as we know, and *one Jewess* (in front of Jesus of Nazareth, the fisherman Peter, the carpet worker Paul, and the mother of the first-mentioned Jesus, named Mary). Now this is very remarkable: without doubt Rome has been conquered. It is true that in the Renaissance there was a brilliant, incredible reawakening of the classical ideal, the noble way of evaluating everything. Rome itself behaved like someone who had woken up from a coma induced by the pressure of the new Jewish Rome built over it, which looked like an ecumenical synagogue and was called 'the Church'. But immediately Judea triumphed again, thanks to that basically vulgar (German and English) movement of *ressentiment*, which we call the Reformation, together with what had to follow as a consequence, the re-establishment of the Church, as well as the re-establishment of the old grave-like tranquillity of classical Rome.

In what is an even more decisive and deeper sense, Judea once again was victorious over the classical ideal at the time of the French Revolution. The last political nobility which we had in Europe, that of the seventeenth and eighteenth *French* centuries, broke apart under the instincts of popular *ressentiment* – never on earth has there been heard a greater rejoicing, a noisier enthusiasm! It is true that in the midst of all this the most dreadful and most unexpected events took place: the embodiment of Antiquity's ideal itself rose with unheard-of splendour before the eyes and the conscience of humanity – and once again, stronger, simpler and more urgently than ever, rang out, in opposition to the old lie, to the slogan of *ressentiment* about the *privileged rights of the majority*, in opposition to that will for a low condition, abasement, equality, for the decline and extinguishing of man – in opposition to all that, there rang out a fearsome and delightful counter-slogan about the *privileged rights of the few*! As a last signpost to a *different* road, Napoleon appeared, the most singular and late-born man there ever was, and in him the problem of the *inherently noble ideal* was made flesh. We might well think about *what* sort of a problem that is: Napoleon, this synthesis of the *inhuman* and the *superhuman* ...

Second Essay, Guilt, Bad Conscience and Related Matters
11

Now a critical word about recently published attempts to find the origin of justice in quite a different place – that is, in *ressentiment*. But first let me speak a word in the ear of the psychologists, provided that they have any desire to study *ressentiment* itself up close for once: this plant grows most beautifully today among anarchists and anti-Semites – in addition, it blooms, as it always has, in hidden places, like the violet, although it has a different fragrance. And since like always has to emerge from like, it is not surprising to see attempts coming forward again from just such circles, as they have already done many times before... to sanctify *revenge* in the name of *justice*, as if justice were basically simply a further development of a feeling of being injured, and to bring belated respect to *reactive* emotions generally, all of them, using the idea of revenge. With this last point I personally take the least offence. It even seems to me a *service* so far as the entire biological problem is concerned (in connection with which the worth of these emotions has been underestimated up to now). The only thing I am calling attention to is the fact that it is the very idea of *ressentiment* itself out of which this new emphasis on scientific fairness grows (which favours hate, envy, malevolence, suspicion, rancour and revenge). This 'scientific fairness' ceases immediately and gives way to tones of mortal enmity and prejudice as soon as it deals with another group of emotions which, it strikes me, have a much higher biological worth than those reactive ones and which therefore have earned the right to be *scientifically* assessed and given a high value – namely, the truly *active* emotions, like desire for mastery, greediness, and so on (E. Dühring, *The Value of Life*: *A Course in Philosophy*, the whole book really).

So much against this tendency in general: but in connection with Dühring's single principle that we must seek the homeland of justice in the land of the reactive feeling, we must, for love of the truth, rudely turn this around by setting out a different principle: the *last* territory to be conquered by the spirit of justice is the land of reactive feeling! If it is truly the case that the just man remains just even towards someone who has injured him (and not just cold, moderate, strange, indifferent: being just is always a *positive* attitude), if even under the sudden attack of personal injury, ridicule and suspicion the gaze of the lofty, clear, deep and benevolent objectivity of the just and *judging* eye does not grow dark, well, that is a piece of perfection and the highest mastery on earth, even something that it would be wise for people not to expect, or that in any event they should not *believe* in too easily. It is certainly true that, on average, even among the most just people even a small dose of hostility, malice and insinuation is enough to make them see red and drive fairness from their eyes. The active, aggressive, over-reaching human being is always placed a hundred steps closer to justice than the reactive person. For him it is not even necessary in the slightest to estimate an object falsely and with bias, the way the reactive man does and must do. Thus, as a matter of fact, at all times the aggressive human being – the stronger, braver, nobler – has always had on his side a *better* conscience as well as a *more independent* eye. And by contrast, we can already guess who generally has the invention of 'bad conscience' on his conscience – the man of *ressentiment*!

Finally, let us look in history: up to now in what area has the whole implementation of law in general as well as the essential need for law been at home? Could it be in the area of the reactive human being? That is entirely wrong. It is much more the case that it has been at home with active, strong, spontaneous and aggressive men. Historically considered, the law on earth – let me say this to the annoyance of the above-mentioned agitator (who himself once made the confession: 'The doctrine of revenge runs through all my work and efforts as the red thread of justice') – represents that very struggle *against* the reactive feelings, the war with them on the part of active and aggressive powers, which have partly expended their strength to bring a halt to, or restrain, reactive pathos and to force some settlement with it. Everywhere where justice is practised, where justice is upheld, we see a power stronger in relation to a weaker power standing beneath it (groups or individuals), seeking ways to bring an end among the latter to the mindless rage of *ressentiment*, partly by dragging the object of *ressentiment* out of the hands of revenge, partly by setting in the place of revenge a battle against the enemies of peace and order, partly by coming up with compensations, proposing them, under certain circumstances making them compulsory, sometimes establishing certain equivalents for injuries as a norm, which, from now on, *ressentiment* is channelled into once and for all. The most decisive factor, however, which the highest power carries out and sets in place against the superiority of the feelings of hostility and animosity – something that power always does as soon as it is somehow strong enough to do so – is to set up the *law*, the imperative explanation of those things which, in its own eyes, are considered permissible and legal and things which are considered forbidden and illegal. By treating, after the establishment of the law, attacks and arbitrary acts of individuals or entire groups as an outrage against the law, as rebellion against the highest power itself, the authorities steer the feeling of those beneath them away from the immediate harm caused by such outrages and thus, in the long run, achieve the reverse of what all revenge desires, which sees only the viewpoint of the injured party and considers only that to be valid. From now on, the eye becomes trained to evaluate actions *impersonally*, even the eye of the harmed party itself (although this would be the very last thing to occur, as I have remarked earlier).

Consequently, only with the institution of the law is there 'justice' and 'injustice' (and *not*, as Dühring will have it, from the time of the injurious action). To talk of justice and injustice *in themselves* makes no sense whatsoever – it is obvious that *in themselves* harming, oppressing, exploiting, destroying cannot be 'unjust', inasmuch as life *essentially* works that way, that is, in its basic functions it harms, oppresses, exploits and destroys – and cannot be conceived at all without these characteristics. We must acknowledge something even more alarming – the fact that from the highest biological standpoint, conditions of law must always be *exceptional*, partial restrictions on the basic will to live, which is set on power – they are subordinate to the overall purpose of this will as its individual means, that is, as means to create *larger* units of power. A legal system conceived of as sovereign and universal, not as a means in the struggle of power complexes, but as a means *against* all struggles in general, something along the lines of Dühring's communist cliché in which each will must be considered as equal to every other will, that would be a principle *hostile to life*, a destroyer and dissolver of the human being, an assassination attempt on the future of the human being, a sign of exhaustion, a secret path to nothingness.

17

Inherent in this hypothesis about the origin of bad conscience is, first, the assumption that this change was not gradual or voluntary and did not manifest an organic growth into new conditions, but was a break, a leap, something forced, an irrefutable disaster, against which there was no struggle or any *ressentiment*. Secondly, it assumes that the moulding of a populace which had hitherto been unchecked and shapeless into a fixed form, just as it was initiated by an act of violence, was carried to its conclusion by nothing but sheer acts of violence, that consequently the oldest 'state' emerged as a terrible tyranny, an oppressive and inconsiderate machine, and continued working until such a raw material of people and semi-animals finally were not only thoroughly kneaded and submissive but also given a *shape*.

I used the word 'state' – it is self-evident who is meant by that term – some pack of blond beasts of prey, a race of conquerors and masters, which, organised for war and with the power to organise, without forethought, sets its terrifying paws on a subordinate population which may perhaps be vast in numbers but is still without any form, is still wandering aimlessly. That is surely the way the 'state' began on earth. I believe that that fantasy has been done away with which sees the beginning of the state in some 'contract'. He who can command, who is naturally a 'master', who comes forward with violence in his actions and gestures – what has he to do with contracts! We cannot negotiate with such beings. They arrive like fate, without cause, reason, consideration or pretext. They are present as lightning is present, too terrible, too sudden, too convincing, too 'different' even to become hated. Their work is an instinctive creation of forms, the imposition of forms. They are the most involuntary and unconscious artists in existence. Where they appear something new is soon present, a *living* power structure, something in which the parts and functions are demarcated and coordinated, in which there is no place for anything which does not first derive its 'meaning' from its relationship to the totality. These men, these natural organisers, have no idea what guilt, responsibility and consideration are. In them that terrible egoism of the artist is in control, which stares out like bronze and sees himself, in his work, eternally justified, just like a mother is in her child. *They* are not the ones in whom 'bad conscience' developed – that point is obvious from the outset. But this ugly plant would not have grown *without them*. It would have failed if an immense amount of freedom had not been driven from the world under the pressure of their hammer blows, their artistic violence – or at least driven out of sight and, as it were, had become *latent*. This powerful *instinct for freedom*, once made latent – we already understand how – this instinct repulsed, repressed, imprisoned inside, and finally able to discharge and direct itself only against itself – that and that alone is what *bad conscience* is in its beginnings.

18

We need to be careful not to entertain a low opinion of this entire phenomenon simply because it is from the start ugly and painful. Basically, it is the same active force which is at work on a grander scale in those artists of power and organisers who build states. Here it is internally, on a smaller and more mean-spirited scale, directed backward into 'the labyrinth of the breast' to quote Goethe, and it creates for itself bad conscience and builds negative ideals, that very *instinct for freedom* (to use my own phrase, the will to power). But the material on which the shaping and violating nature of this force directs itself here is man himself, all his old animal self, and *not*, as in that greater and more striking phenomenon, *another* man or *other* men. This furtive violation of the self, this artistic cruelty, this pleasure in giving a shape to oneself as if to a tough, resistant, suffering material, to burn into it a will, a critique, a contradiction, a contempt, a denial – this uncanny and horribly pleasurable work of a soul willingly divided against itself, which makes itself suffer for the pleasure of creating suffering, all this *active* 'bad conscience', as the essential womb of ideal and imaginative events, finally brought to light – we have already guessed – also an abundance of strange new beauty and affirmation, perhaps for the first time the idea of the beautiful. For what would be 'beautiful' if its opposite had not yet come to an awareness of itself, if ugliness had not already said to itself, 'I am ugly'? ...

At least, after this hint one paradox will be less puzzling – how contradictory concepts, like *selflessness*, *self-denial* and *self-sacrifice*, can connote an ideal, something beautiful. And beyond that, one thing we do know – I have no doubt about it – namely, the nature of the *pleasure* which the selfless, self-denying, self-sacrificing person experiences from the beginning: this pleasure belongs to cruelty.

So much for the moment on the origin of the 'unegoistic' as something of *moral* worth and on the demarcation of the soil out of which this value has grown: only bad conscience, only the will to abuse the self, provides the condition for the *value* of the unegoistic.

24

I'll conclude with three question marks – that is clear enough. You may perhaps ask me, 'Is an ideal being built up here or shattered?'

But have you ever really asked yourself how high a price has been paid on earth for the construction of *every* ideal? How much reality had to be constantly vilified and misunderstood, how many lies had to be consecrated, how many consciences corrupted, how much 'God' had to be sacrificed each time? If a temple is to be erected, *a temple must be destroyed*: that is the law – show me an instance where it has not been fulfilled!...

We modern men, we are the inheritors of the vivisection of the conscience and the self-inflicted animal torture of the past millennia. That is what we have had the longest practice doing, that is perhaps our artistry – in any case it is something we have *refined*, the corruption of our taste. For too long man has looked at his natural inclinations with an 'evil eye' so that finally in him they have become twinned with 'bad conscience'. An attempt to reverse this might in itself be possible, but who is strong enough for that, that is, to link with bad conscience the *unnatural* inclinations, all those aspirations for what lies beyond us, those things which go against our senses, against our instincts, against nature, against animals – in short, the ideals that have hitherto existed, all the ideals which are hostile to life and which have vilified the world? To whom can we turn to today with *such* hopes and demands?...

We would have precisely the *good* men against us as well, of course, as the comfortable, the complacent, the vain, the quixotic, the tired.

What is more offensive, what cuts us off more fundamentally from these others than letting them take some note of the severity and loftiness with which we deal with ourselves? And by contrast how obliging, how friendly all the world is in relation to us, as soon as we act as all the world does and 'let ourselves go' just like everyone else!...

To attain the goal I am talking about demands a *different* sort of spirit from those that really exist at this time: spirits empowered by war and victory, for whom conquest, adventure, danger and even pain have become a necessity. That would require getting acclimatised to keen, high air, winter wanderings, to ice and mountains in every sense. That would require even a kind of sublime maliciousness, an ultimate self-conscious wilfulness of knowledge, which comes with robust health. Briefly put, that would unfortunately require such *great health*!...

Is this even possible today?... But at some time or other, in a more powerful time than this mouldy, self-doubting present, he must nonetheless come to us, the *redeeming* man of great love and contempt, the creative spirit, whose driving power will enable him to distance himself from any aloofness or beyond, whose isolation is misunderstood by people as if it were a flight *from* reality, whereas it is his immersion, burial and absorption *into* nothing but reality, so that once he comes out of it into the light again, he brings back the *redemption* of this reality, its redemption from the curse which the previous ideal had laid upon it. This man of the future, who will release us from that earlier ideal and, in so doing, from those things *which had to grow from it*, from the great loathing, from the will to nothingness, from nihilism – that stroke of noon and of the great decision which makes the will free once again, who restores to the earth its purpose and to human beings their hope, this Antichrist and anti-nihilist, this conqueror of God and of nothingness – *at some point he must come.*

Third Essay, What Do Ascetic Ideals Mean?

14

The more normal this pathology is among human beings – and we cannot deny its normality – the higher we should esteem the rare cases of spiritual and physical power, humanity's *strokes of luck*, and the more vigorously successful people should protect themselves from the worst air, the air of the sick. Do people do that?...

The sick are the greatest danger to the healthy. For strong people disaster does *not* come from the strongest, but from the weakest. Are we aware of that?...

If we consider the big picture, we should not want any diminution of the fear we have of human beings, for this fear compels the strong to be strong and, in some circumstances, terrible. That fear *sustains* the successful type of people. What we should fear, what has a disastrous effect unlike any other, would not be a great fear of man but a great *loathing* for man or, for the same reasons, a great *pity* for man. If these both were one day to mate, then something utterly uncanny would immediately appear in the world, the 'last will' of man, his will to nothingness, nihilism. As a matter of fact, much to that effect has been prepared. Whoever possesses not only a nose to smell with, but also eyes and ears, senses almost everywhere, no matter where he goes nowadays, an air like that found in an insane asylum or hospital. I am speaking, as usual, of people's cultural surroundings, of every kind of 'Europe' on this earth. The *sick* are the great danger to humanity – *not* the evil men, *not* the 'beasts of prey'. Those people who are from the outset failures, oppressed, broken – they are the ones, the *weakest*, who most undermine life among human beings, who in the most perilous way poison and question our trust in life, in humanity, in ourselves. Where can we escape that downcast glance with which people carry their deep sorrow, that reversed gaze of the born failure which betrays how such a man speaks to himself, that gaze which is a sigh. 'I wish I could be someone else!' – that is what this glance sighs. 'But there is no hope here. I am who I am. How could I detach myself from myself? And yet I *have had enough of myself!*'

On such a ground of contempt for oneself, a truly swampy ground, grows every weed, every poisonous plant – all of them so small, so hidden, so dishonest, so sweet. Here the worms of angry and resentful feelings swarm; here the air stinks of secrets and duplicity; here is constantly woven the net of the most malicious conspiracy – the conspiracy of those who are suffering at the hands of successful and victorious people; here the appearance of the victor is *hated.* And what dishonesty not to acknowledge this hatred as hatred! What an extravagance of grand words and attitudes, what an art of 'decent' slander! These failures – what noble eloquence flows from their lips! How much sugary, slimy, humble resignation swims in their eyes! What do they really want? At least to *make a show of* justice, love, wisdom, superiority – that is the ambition of these 'lowest' people, the sick! And how clever such an ambition makes people! For let us admire the skilful counterfeiting with which people here imitate the trade-marks of virtue, even its resounding tinkle, the golden sound of virtue. They have now taken a lease on virtue entirely for themselves, these weak and hopelessly sick people – there is no doubt about that. 'We alone are the good, the just' – that is what they imply: 'We alone are the *homines bonae voluntatis*' [men of good will]. They wander among us, personifications of reproach, like warnings to us, as if health, success, strength, pride and a feeling of power were inherently depraved, for which people *must* some day atone, and atone bitterly. How ready they are, at bottom, to make one pay, how they thirst to be *hangmen*! Among them there are plenty of people disguised as judges seeking revenge. They always have the word 'justice' in their mouths, like poisonous saliva, with their lips always pursed, ever ready to spit at anything which does not look discontented and goes on its way in good spirits. Among them there is no lack of that most disgusting species of vain people, the lying monsters who aim to present themselves as 'beautiful souls', and carry off to market their ruined sensuality, wrapped up in verse and other swaddling clothes, as 'purity of heart' – the species of self-gratifiers and moral masturbators. The will of the sick to present *some* form or other of superiority, their instinct for secret paths leading to a tyranny over the healthy – where can we not find it, this very will to power of the weakest people!

The sick woman, in particular: no one outdoes her in refined ways to control others, to exert pressure, to tyrannise. For that purpose, the sick woman spares nothing living or dead. She disinters the most deeply buried things (the Bogos say 'woman is a hyena').

Take a look into the background of every family, every corporation, every community – everywhere you see the struggle of the sick against the healthy, a quiet struggle for the most part, with a little poison, with pinpricks, with deceitful expressions of silent suffering, but now and then also with that sick man's Phariseeism of *loud* gestures, whose favourite role is 'noble indignation'. It likes to make itself heard all the way into the consecrated rooms of science, that hoarse, booming indignation of the pathologically sick hounds, the biting insincerity and rage of such 'noble' Pharisees (once again I remind readers who have ears of Eugen Dühring, that apostle of revenge from Berlin, who in today's Germany makes the most indecent and most revolting use of moralistic gibberish – Dühring, the pre-eminent moral braggart we have today, unexcelled even among those like him, the anti-Semites).

They are all men of *ressentiment*, these physiologically impaired and worm-eaten men, a whole quivering earthly kingdom of subterranean revenge, inexhaustible, insatiable in its outbursts against the fortunate, and equally in its masquerades of revenge, its pretexts for revenge. When would they attain their ultimate, most refined, most sublime triumph of revenge? Undoubtedly, if they could succeed in pushing their own wretchedness, all misery in general, into the consciences of the fortunate, so that the latter one day might begin to be ashamed of their good fortune and perhaps would say to themselves, 'It's shameful to be fortunate. *There is too much misery!*'

But there could be no greater and more fateful misunderstanding than if, through this process, the fortunate, the successful, the powerful in body and soul should start to doubt their *right to happiness*. Away with this 'inverted world'! Away with this disgraceful softening of feelings! That the sick should *not* make the healthy sick – and that would be such a softening – that should surely be the ruling point of view on earth. But that would require above all else that the healthy remain *separated* from the sick, protected even from the gaze of sick people, so that they do not confuse themselves with the ill. Or would it perhaps be their task to attend to the sick or be their doctors? ...

But they could not misjudge or negate *their* task more seriously – something higher *should* never demean itself by becoming the tool of something lower. The pathos of distance *should* keep the tasks of the two groups forever separate! Their right to exist, the privilege of a bell with a perfect ring in comparison to one that is cracked and off key, is a thousand times greater. They alone are *guarantors* of the future; they alone stand as a *pledge* for humanity's future. The sick can never have the ability or obligation to do what *they* can do, what *they* should do. But if they are to be able to do what *they* alone should do, how can they have the freedom to make themselves the doctor, the consoler, the 'saviour' of the sick? ...

And therefore let us have fresh air! fresh air! In any case, let us keep away from all cultural insane asylums and hospitals! And for that let us have good companionship, *our* companionship! Or loneliness, if that is necessary! But by all means let us stay away from the foul stench of inner corruption and the hidden, worm-eaten rottenness of disease! ... In that way, my friends, we can defend ourselves, at least for a little while, against the two nastiest scourges which may be lying in wait precisely for us – against a *great disgust with man* and against a *great pity for man!* ...

Translated by Ian Johnston and Nathalie Lachance

Nachlass Fragments, 1885–1887

KSA 12 1[56] 1885–86 WP 975

To remain objective, severe, firm and hard while making a thought prevail – perhaps the *forte* of artists; but if for this purpose one needs human beings (as teachers, statesmen, etc.), then the repose and coldness and hardness soon vanish. In natures like Caesar and Napoleon, we are able to divine something of the nature of 'disinterestedness' in their work on their marble, whatever the number of men that are sacrificed in the process may be. In this direction lies the future of higher men: to bear the greatest responsibility and *not to go to rack and ruin because of it*. – Hitherto the deceptions of inspiration have almost always been necessary for a man not to lose *faith in his own hand* and *in his right to his task*.

KSA 12 2[13] 1885–86 WP 954

... A question recurs, a seductive and unsettling question perhaps: it may be whispered into the ears of those who have a right to such doubtful questions, the strongest souls of today whose dominion over themselves is unswerving: would it not be high time, now that the type 'herd animal' is developing more and more in Europe, to make an attempt at a fundamental, artificial and conscious *breeding* of the opposite type and its virtues? And would not the democratic movement itself find for the first time a sort of goal, salvation and justification, if someone appeared *who availed himself of it* – by finally producing beside its new and sublime development of slavery (– that is what European democracy must become ultimately) a higher type of ruling and Caesarean spirits, who would at last find his way to its new and sublime form of slavery, who would also *need* this new slavery? For new, hitherto impossible, visions, for *his* visions? For *his* tasks?

KSA 12 2[57] 1885–86 WP 960

From now on there will be such favourable preconditions for greater ruling powers as have never yet been found on earth. And this is by no means the most important point. The establishment has been made possible of international race unions which will set themselves the task of breeding a ruling race, the future 'masters of the earth'; – a new, vast aristocracy based on the most severe self-discipline, in which the will of philosophical men of power and artist-tyrants will be stamped on thousands of years: a higher type of men which, thanks to their preponderance of will, knowledge, wealth and influence, will avail themselves of democratic Europe as the most suitable and supple instrument they can have for taking the fate of the earth into their own hands, and working as artists upon man himself.

Enough, the time is coming, in which one will unlearn politics.

KSA 12 2[76] 1885–86 WP 660

Regarding the order of rank:
I. *On the physiology of power*
The aristocracy in the body, the majority of the rulers (fight of tissues)?
   Slavery and the division of labour: the higher type alone possible through the *oppression* of the lower to a function
      Pleasure and pain not contraries. The feeling of power.

Nutrition only a result of the insatiable lust of appropriation, of the will to power.

Procreation, decay supervening when the ruling cells are too weak to organise that which was appropriated. It is the *shaping* force which always wants to have a continual supply of new 'new material' (more 'force'). The masterly construction of an organism out of an egg.

'The mechanical interpretation': wants nothing but quantities: but the real force is in the quality. Mechanics can therefore only describe processes; it cannot explain them.

'Purpose'. Start out from the 'sagacity' of plants.

The concept of 'meliorism': *not* only greater complexity, but greater *power* (it need not be only greater mass –).

Conclusion concerning the evolution of humankind: the road to perfection lies in bringing forth the most powerful individuals, for whose use the great masses would be converted into a mere tool (that is to say, into the most intelligent and flexible tool possible). ...

KSA 12 5[61] 1886–87 WP 953

A period when man has a surplus of power at his disposal: science aims at establishing this *slavery of nature*.

Then man acquires *leisure*: to *develop* himself into something new and higher. New aristocracy

Then a large number of virtues which are now *conditions of existence* are superseded. Qualities which are no longer needed are *consequently* lost.

We no longer need virtues: *consequently* we are losing them: likewise the morality of 'one thing is needful', of the salvation of the soul, and of immortality: these were means *to make man capable* of enormous *self-tyranny* (through the emotion of great *fear* :::

the different kinds of needs by means of whose discipline man is formed: need teaches work, thought, self-control

* * *

Physiological purification and strengthening

The *new aristocracy* is in need of an opposite which it may combat: it must be driven to extremes in order to maintain itself.

The two futures of mankind:

(1) the consequence of a levelling down to mediocrity
(2) conscious elevation and self-development

a doctrine which would cleave a *gulf*: it maintains the *highest and the lowest types* (it destroys the intermediate) the aristocracies, both spiritual and temporal, which have existed so far prove *nothing* against the necessity of a new aristocracy.

Theory of the formation of leadership instead of sociology

KSA 12 9[34] 1887 WP 763

Workers should learn to feel as *soldiers* do. Remuneration, a salary, but no payment! No relationship between payment and *effort*! Rather, the individual should, *according to his kind*, be so placed as to *achieve* the *highest* that is compatible with his powers.

KSA 12 9[145] 1887 WP 776

Concerning the 'Machiavellianism' of power.
(unconscious *Machiavellianism*)
The *will to power* appears

(a) among the oppressed and slaves of all kinds, in the form of will to '*freedom*': the mere fact of breaking loose from something seems to be an end in itself (in a religio-moral sense: 'one is only answerable to one's own conscience', 'evangelical freedom,' etc.).
(b) in the case of a stronger type, ascending to power, in the form of the will to overpower, if this fails, then it shrinks to the will to '*justice*' – that is to say, to the will *to the same measure of rights* as the ruling type possesses (the fight for rights ...)
(c) in the case of the strongest, richest, most independent, most courageous, in the form of '*love* of humanity', of the 'people', of the gospel, of truth, of God; in the form of pity, 'self-sacrifice,' etc. in the form of overpowering, of deeds of capture, of imposing service on someone; in the form of an instinctive reckoning of oneself as part of a great mass of power to which *one attempts to give a direction*: the hero, the prophet, the Caesar, the Saviour, the shepherd (– sexuality also belongs to this category; it *wants* to overpower something, possess it utterly, and it *appears* to abandon itself ...) at bottom it is only the love of one's 'instrument', of one's 'horse' – the conviction that things *belong* to one because one is in a position to *use* them.

'Freedom,' 'Justice' and 'Love'!!!

KSA 12 9[146] 1887 WP 98

Against Rousseau. – *Unfortunately*, man is no longer sufficiently evil; Rousseau's opponents, who say that 'man is a beast of prey', are unfortunately wrong. Not the corruption of man, but the softening and moralising of him is the curse; in the very sphere which Rousseau attacked most violently was the type of man who was still *relatively* strong and successful to be found (– the type which still possessed the great passions intact, will to power, will to pleasure, the will and ability to command). The man of the eighteenth century must be compared with the man of the Renaissance (also with the man of the seventeenth century in France) if the matter is to be understood at all: Rousseau is a symptom of self-contempt and of inflamed vanity – both signs that the dominating will is lacking: he, as a man holding a grudge, moralises and seeks the *cause* of his own misery in the *ruling* classes.

KSA 12 9[153] 1887 WP 898

The strong of the future

What necessity on the one hand and accident on the other have attained, the conditions from which a *stronger type* may be reared: this we are now able to understand and to *will* consciously: we can now create those conditions under which such an elevation is possible

Until now, education has always kept in mind the benefits of society: *not* the potential benefits for the future, but the benefits for the existing society. What people required were 'instruments' for this society. Provided the *wealth of forces were greater*, it would be possible to think of a draining of forces, the aim of which would not be to benefit society, but to benefit the future.

This task would have to be brought forward, if people would better grasp to what extent the present form of society is in a state of transition, that sooner or later *it will no longer be able to exist for its own sake*: but only as a means in the hands of a stronger race.

The increasing belittlement of man is precisely the impelling power which leads one to think of the cultivation of a *stronger race*: a race which would have a surplus precisely there where the dwarfed species was weak and growing weaker (will, responsibility, self-reliance, the ability to postulate aims for oneself).

The *means* would be those which history teaches: *isolation* by means of preservative interests which would be the reverse of the average ones today; exercise in revalued valuations; distance as pathos; a clean conscience in what today is most underrated and most prohibited.

The *levelling* of the European is the great process which cannot be arrested; it should even be accelerated.

The necessity of *cleaving gulfs, of distance*, of the *order of rank*, is therefore imperative; *not* the necessity of retarding the process above mentioned.

As soon as it is attained, this *levelled down* species requires *justification*: its justification is that it serves a higher and sovereign type, which stands upon it and can only thus rise to its task.

Not only a ruling race whose task would be consummated in ruling alone: but a race with *vital spheres* of its own, with an overflow of energy for beauty, bravery, culture, manners even in spiritual matters; an *affirmative* race which would be able to allow itself every kind of great luxury...strong enough to be able to dispense with the tyranny of the imperative of virtue, rich enough to be in no need of economy or pedantry; beyond good and evil; a hothouse for peculiar and selected plants.

KSA 12 9[154] 1887 WP 1027

Man is the *beast* and *super-beast*; higher man is the brute and the overman: these opposites belong to each other. With every growth of man towards greatness and loftiness, he also grows downwards into the depths and into the terrible: we should not desire the one without the other – or, better still: the more fundamentally we desire the one, the more completely we shall achieve the other.

KSA 12 9[173] 1887 WP 315

Morality in the valuation of races and classes

In view of the fact that *the passions* and *fundamental instincts* in every race and class say something about their conditions of existence (– at least about the conditions under which they have for the longest time been able to prevail:)

: means to claim that they are 'virtuous': that they change their character, shed their skins, and blot out their past

: means that they should cease from differentiating themselves from others

: means that they are getting to resemble each other in their needs and aspirations – more clearly: *that they are declining*...

The will to *one kind* of morality is merely the *tyranny* of the particular type, which is adapted to that kind of morality, over other types: it is the annihilation or general levelling in favour of the prevailing type (whether it aims at making a type harmless or at exploiting it)

'Abolition of Slavery' – a so-called tribute to 'human dignity'; in truth, the *annihilation of* a fundamentally different species (– the undermining *of* its values and its happiness –)

The qualities which constitute the strength *of* an *opposing race* or class are declared to be the *most evil* and pernicious things it has: for by means of them, it harms us (its 'virtues' are slandered and rechristened)

When a man or a people *harm us*, their action constitutes an *objection* against them: but from their point of view *we* are desirable, because we are such as can be useful to them.

The demand for 'humanisation' (which quite naively believes to be in possession of the formula 'What is human?') is Tartuffery, beneath the cover of which a very definite type of man strives to attain to power: or, more precisely, a very particular kind of instinct – the *herd instinct*.

'The equality of men': this is what lies *concealed* behind the tendency *of making* ever more and more men *alike* as men.

The 'interested nature' with regard to common morality (trick: to turn the great passions, power and property, into the protectors of virtue).

To what extent do all kinds of *businessmen* and money-grabbers, all those, who give and take credit, find it *necessary* to promote the levelling of all characters and notions of value: *international trade and exchange* of all kind compel and almost *buy* virtue.

The same applies to the *state* and to any sort of rule with regard to officials and soldiers; the same applies to science, in order that it may work with assurance and sparing its forces.

The same applies to the *priesthood*.

– Common morality is thus enforced here, because it is advantageous; and, in order to make it triumph, war and violence are waged against immorality – with what 'right'? Without any right whatsoever; but in accordance with the instinct of self-preservation. The same classes avail themselves of *immorality* when it serves their purpose to do so.

KSA 12 9[180] 1887 WP 884

Händel, Leibniz, Goethe and Bismarck – characteristic of the *strong German type*. Harmlessly living among opposites, full of that supple kind of strength which cautiously avoids convictions and doctrines, by using the one as a weapon against the other, and reserving absolute freedom for themselves.

KSA 12 10[5] 1887 WP 1017

In the place of Rousseau's 'man of Nature' the nineteenth century has discovered a much *more genuine* image of 'Man' – it had the courage to do this... On the whole, the Christian concept of 'man' has in a way been reinstalled. What we have not had the courage to do was to endorse precisely *this* 'man in itself', and to see the future of mankind guaranteed in him. In the same way, we did *not* dare to regard the *growth in the terrible side* of man's character as an accompanying feature of every advance in culture; in this sense we are still under the influence of the Christian ideal, and side *with it* against paganism, and likewise against the Renaissance concept of *virtù*. But the key of culture is not to be found in this way: and *in praxi* we still have the forgeries of history in favour of the 'good man' (as if he alone constituted the *progress* of humanity) and we have the *socialistic ideal* (i.e. the *residue* of Christianity and of Rousseau in the de-Christianised world).

The fight against the eighteenth century: its *highest overcoming* in Goethe and *Napoleon*. Schopenhauer, too, fights against the eighteenth century; but he returns involuntarily to the seventeenth – he is a modern Pascal, with Pascalian valuations *without* Christianity... Schopenhauer was not strong enough to invent a new *Yes*.

Napoleon: understood here is the necessary relationship between the higher and the terrible man. 'Man' reinstated; and her due of contempt and fear restored to woman. 'Totality' as health and highest activity; the straight line and grand style in action rediscovered; the mightiest of all instincts, that of life itself, the lust of dominion, affirmed.

KSA 12 10[117] 1887 WP 361

I have declared war against the anaemic Christian ideal (together with what is closely related to it), not because I want to annihilate it, but only to put an end to its *tyranny* and clear the way for other *ideals*, for *more robust* ideals... The *continuance* of the Christian ideal belongs to the most desirable of desiderata: if only for the sake of the ideals which wish to take their stand beside it and perhaps above it – they must have opponents, and *strong ones* too, in order to grow *strong* themselves. – That is why we immoralists require the *power of morality*: our instinct of self-preservation insists upon our *opponents* maintaining their strength – insists on our becoming *master of them*. –

Translated by A. Ludovici with modifications – Nathalie Lachance

6
The Antichrist, 1888

Preface

In a letter to Heinrich Köselitz, dated June 20, 1888, five days after the death of Emperor Friedrich III, Nietzsche writes: 'The death of Emperor Friedrich moved me; in the end he was a little shimmering light of free thought, the last hope for Germany. Now begins the rule of Stöcker; I am drawing the consequences and know already that my *Will to Power* will now be confiscated in Germany.'[1] For liberals of the era, the death of the Emperor after a brief reign of just three months ended all hope for a less repressive political climate in the *Reich*, for the Emperor had wished to strengthen the parliamentary system. Although anti-liberal, Nietzsche had similar concerns about increasing political repression, but his principal target was the 'Christian state' which had recently re-emerged in Germany after nearly half a century in abeyance. Thus Nietzsche's final year of intellectual activity is marked by his unprecedented 'Curse on Christianity',[2] including a continuing critique of the political ideologies that share its 'ancestry': democracy, socialism, anarchism.[3]

The Protestant Christian state ideal was resuscitated by the anti-Semitic court chaplain Adolf Stöcker, who received enthusiastic support from the newly proclaimed Emperor Wilhelm II. Nietzsche denounced the Emperor's association with Stöcker, claiming that 'the court preacher *canaille*' should not be 'close to the higher circles',[4] for 'what has hurt the court more than the court preacher'?[5] What had hurt the court more, Nietzsche is asking, than the anti-Semitic historiography that had now become *reichsdeutsche*?[6] Stöcker's Christian anti-Semitic views were representative of a pervasive political and cultural anti-Semitism in Germany, an expression of the *ressentiment* which Nietzsche also associated with Treitschke, Dühring and Wagner, although Stöcker's anti-Semitism was not racial. For reasons which were relevant to his conception of a new European ruling caste, Nietzsche energetically opposed this anti-Semitic trend in German society, which was gradually consolidating itself as an inextricable appendage of the Christian state, developing through Stöcker's Christian Social movement, Wilhelm von Hammerstein's *Kreuzzeitung*, and working to convert the German Conservative Party.

Under the conservative regime of Wilhelm II, Nietzsche feared that his 1888 writings would be banned as 'sacrilegious' or 'a danger to public morals' (in violation of Germany's anti-blasphemy laws) or construed as being *lèse-majesté*,[7] a fear that never arose under Friedrich III's brief but 'shimmering light of free thought'. In October 1888, Professor Geffcken, the former adviser to Crown Prince Friedrich Wilhelm (later Emperor Friedrich III) was prosecuted, at Bismarck's insistence, for high treason for publishing excerpts from the Crown Prince's diaries written during the Franco-Prussian war. For Nietzsche, the Geffcken case was a reminder of the perils of publishing under the reign of Wilhelm II.[8] Nietzsche was concerned that, if published, the *Antichrist* would be confiscated immediately, so his plan was to first publish *Ecce Homo* in order to 'test what risks' he could 'take with the German ideas of freedom of speech'.[9] The laws in effect were draconian and *The Antichrist* would not be published until 1895.

The re-emergence of the Christian state in the late 1880s was arguably the event which galvanised the writing of *The Antichrist*, where Nietzsche, confronting the danger, delivers the following warning: '*And* let us not underestimate the fatal influence which crept out of Christianity into politics!'[10] In 1888, Nietzsche declares war on the Christian state and Christianity: 'there must be no *compromise*…man must eliminate, annihilate, wage war – the Christian-nihilistic standard of value must still be withdrawn from all things and attacked beneath every disguise'.[11] In this note, Nietzsche does not appear to want to maintain the agonistic ideal he had described in 'Homer's Contest', given his stress on *annihilation*, but elsewhere argues for the strategic preservation of the Church, which he recognises as a strategy common to the 'political realm', to 'every party', to 'grand politics'. In fact, Nietzsche is embracing the negative integration strategies of the *Reich* when he writes: 'we immoralists and anti-Christians see our advantage in the survival of the Church…. A new creation, more particularly, like the new *Reich*, has more need of enemies than friends: only as a contrast does it begin to feel necessary, only as a contrast does it *become* necessary.'[12] This remark indicates Nietzsche's subjection to the perspective of *Realpolitik* which sees 'Machiavellian' practices at the basis of the Christian state[13] and the Bismarckian *Reich*.[14]

Although he was no ally of Stöcker's, Bismarck's policy of 'practical Christianity' went hand in hand with the Christian state ideal in acknowledging that 'only the Christian religion can redeem the social reality'.[15] Similarly, the large Conservative presence in the *Reichstag* following the 1887 *Kartell* elections upheld the dissemination of the Christian ideal to the spheres of legislation, public affairs and education, which Nietzsche condemned as intrusive and along lines approximating his early critique of the *Kulturstaat*.[16] For Nietzsche, the very notion of a *Kulturstaat* is flawed since 'culture and the state...are antagonists...all great periods of culture have been periods of political decline'.[17] This applies no less when the state becomes Christian. Thus when Nietzsche refers to himself as 'the last anti-political German',[18] he means that he is pro-cultural as well as anti-democratic, as he distinguishes himself from 'mere citizens of the *Reich*'[19] and considers the *Reich* to be a partial democracy.

Nietzsche's denunciation of the Christian state is only one aspect of his critique of the German *Reich*. In *Twilight of the Idols*, in defence of 'aristocratic' culture, Nietzsche renounces the *Reich's* devotion to 'power...grand politics...economics...parliamentarianism and military interests',[20] virtually everything that defines it as a state. As evidence of the way he construes its government, he finds inimical its *democratic* foundation in 'the most washed-out and despised of ideas, universal suffrage and equal rights for all'.[21] Nietzsche's objection to the 'theory of equal rights' (whose history he plots from early Christianity to the French Revolution)[22] is that it has undermined the 'aristocratic outlook'[23] and has destroyed 'the multiplicity of types', 'the *pathos of distance*...proper to all *strong* ages'.[24]

Nietzsche assesses the worth of nations, institutions and human beings according to what he considers to be the fundamental value antithesis: *Christian* values (i.e. *décadence* values) versus *noble* values.[25] Both 'modern democracy' ('a decaying form of the state')[26] and 'liberal institutions'[27] are expressions of the former, while 'the aristocratic commonwealths like those of Rome and Venice',[28] the Hindu caste system or the Russia of Nietzsche's own era ('the opposite of all wretched European petty-statism')[29] are expressions of the latter. This value antithesis also informs and animates the contrast between the Renaissance and German culture which is a recurring theme in the writings of 1888. For Nietzsche, the Renaissance was the 'last *great* age',[30] an attempt to restore noble values. German culture produced the Lutheran Reformation and consequently deprived Europe of the 'harvest' of the Renaissance. It also fought the Wars of Liberation (1813–15) which 'cheated Europe out of...the miracle of meaning, in the existence of Napoleon', a late representative of the Renaissance, who 'was strong enough to consolidate Europe and to convert it into a political and *economic* unity for the sake of a world government'.[31] When Nietzsche invokes his 'revaluation of all values', the Renaissance is cited as an *exemplum*.[32] And when he invokes the Renaissance notion of *virtù*,[33] it calls forth 'a type of supreme achievement', the *Übermensch* and his uncanny double, Cesare Borgia.[34] The noble is the anti-Christian. Accordingly, when Nietzsche praises the Hindu caste system and the Law-Book of Manu – the *order of rank* it affirms – and declares its superiority over the Bible,[35] it is a deliberate offence to the Christian state.

In Nietzsche's notebook entries and correspondence from his final year, anti-Semites, the German *Reich* and the Hohenzollern dynasty are the principal targets of his wrath. Nietzsche entitles some of his last notes 'War to the Death to the House of Hohenzollern' and labels Bismarck 'the idiot *par excellence* among all statesmen'.[36] In a letter to Helen Zimmern, written not long before his complete mental collapse, Nietzsche confides that he will devote the next few years to an '*"Attentat"* (a "bomb attack") against Christianity that will be so explosive that it will send Bismarck's *"Reich"*, the "Triple Alliance",[37] and other geopolitical "splendours" sky-high'.[38] By this time, Nietzsche had already penned letters to Wilhelm II and Bismarck. To Wilhelm II he announces an impending crisis, the 'deepest conscience-collision' in the history of mankind, and claims that he speaks in the name of *truth*, not as a fanatic: 'For when this volcano becomes active, we shall have convulsions on the earth as have never been seen.'[39]

Twilight of the Idols: Or How One Philosophises with a Hammer, 1888

Morality as Anti-Nature

3

The spiritualisation of sensuality is called *love*: it is a great triumph over Christianity. Another triumph is our spiritualisation of *hostility*. It consists in the fact that we are beginning to realise very profoundly the value of having enemies: in short, that with them we are forced to act and to think precisely the reverse of what we previously acted and thought. In all ages the Church wished to annihilate its enemies: we, we immoralists and anti-Christians, see our advantage in the survival of the Church. Even in the political realm, hostility has now become more spiritual – much more cautious, much more thoughtful and much more moderate. Almost every party sees that its self-preservation is best served if its opposition does not lose its strength; and the same applies to grand politics. A new creation more particularly, such as the new *Reich*, has greater need of enemies than friends: only as a contrast does it begin to feel necessary, only as a contrast does it *become* necessary. And we behave in precisely the same way to the 'inner enemy': in this quarter too we have spiritualised hostility, in this quarter too we have understood its value. A man is productive only insofar as he is rich in extremes; he can remain young only on condition that his soul does not begin to take things easy and to long for peace. Nothing has grown more alien to us than that old desire – 'peace of the soul' – which is the aim of Christianity. Nothing could make us less envious than the moral cow and the well-fed happiness of a clean conscience. The man who has renounced war has renounced a *great* life. In many cases, of course, 'peace of the soul' is merely a misunderstanding – it is something *very different* which has failed to find a more honest name. Without either circumlocution or prejudice I will suggest a few cases. 'Peace of the soul' may, for instance, be the sweet effulgence of rich animality in the realm of morality (or religion). Or the beginning of weariness, the first shadow which evening, of every kind of evening, casts. Or a sign that the air is humid and that the wind is blowing up from the South. Or unconscious gratitude for good digestion (sometimes called 'brotherly love'). Or the serenity of the convalescent, on whose lips all things taste new and who bides his time. Or the condition which follows upon a thorough gratification of our strongest passion, the well-being of unaccustomed satiety. Or the senility of our will, of our desires and of our vices. Or laziness, coaxed by vanity into decking itself out in a moral garb. Or the appearance of a state of long suspense and of agonising uncertainty, by a state of certainty, of even terrible certainty. Or the expression of ripeness and mastery in the midst of a task, of a creative work, of a production, of a thing willed, the calm breathing that denotes *attained* 'freedom of will'. Who knows? – maybe *The Twilight of the Idols* is only a sort of 'peace of the soul' ...

The 'Improvers' of Mankind

3

Now let us consider the other case which is called morality, the case of the *breeding* of a particular race and species. The most magnificent example of this is offered by Indian morality and is sanctioned religiously as the 'Law of Manu'. In this book the task is set of breeding no less than four races at the same time: a priestly race, a warrior race, a merchant and agricultural race, and finally a race of servants – the Sudras. It is quite obvious that we are no longer in a circus watching animal tamers. To have conceived even the plan for such a breeding programme presupposes the existence of a man who is a hundred times milder and more reasonable than the mere lion tamer. One breathes more freely after stepping out of the Christian atmosphere of disease and dungeons into this healthier, higher and more expansive world. What a wretched thing the New Testament is beside Manu, what an evil odour hangs around it! – But even this organisation found it necessary to be *terrible* – not this time in a struggle with the beast, but with his opposite, the unbred human being, the mish-mash human being, the Chandala. And once again it had no other means to render him harmless, to make him weak, than by making him *sick* – it was the struggle with the 'great number'. Nothing perhaps is more offensive to our feelings than these protective measures on the part of Indian morality. The third edict, for instance (*Avadana-Sastra* I), which treats 'of impure vegetables', ordains that the only nourishment that the Chandala should be allowed must consist of garlic and onions, as the holy scriptures forbid their being given grain or fruit with grains, water and fire. The same edict declares that the water which they need must be drawn neither from rivers or wells, nor from ponds, but only out of ditches leading to swamps and out of the holes left by the prints of animals. They are likewise forbidden to wash either their laundry or *themselves*, since the water which is graciously granted to them must only be used for quenching their thirst. Finally, Sudra women are forbidden to assist Chandala women in childbirth, while Chandala women are also forbidden to *assist each other* at such times. The success of sanitary regulations of this kind could not fail to make themselves felt; deadly epidemics, ghastly venereal diseases followed again by 'the law of the knife', that is to say circumcision, was prescribed for male children and the removal of the small labia from the females. Manu himself says: 'the Chandala are the fruit of adultery, incest and crime (– this is the *necessary* consequence of the concept of breeding). Their clothes shall consist only of the rags torn from corpses, their dishes shall be the fragments of broken pottery, their ornaments shall be made of old iron and their religion shall be the worship of evil spirits. They shall wander without rest from place to place. They are forbidden to write from left to right or to use their right hand in writing: the use of the right hand and writing from left to right are reserved for people of virtue, for people of *race*.' –

5

The morality of *breeding* and the morality of *taming*, in the means which they adopt in order to prevail, are quite worthy of each other: we may lay down as a leading principle that in order to create morality a man must have the absolute will to immorality. This is the great and strange problem with which I have so long been occupied: the psychology of the 'improvers' of mankind. A small and at bottom perfectly insignificant fact, known as the *pia fraus* first gave me access to this problem: the *pia fraus*, the heirloom of all philosophers and priests who 'improved' mankind. Neither Manu, nor Plato, nor Confucius, nor the Jewish and Christian teachers have ever doubted their right to lie. They never doubted that they had *very different rights*. To express oneself in a formula, one might say:– *all means* which have been used so far with the object of making mankind moral were through and through *immoral*.

What the Germans Lack

1

Among Germans today it does not suffice to have spirit; you also need the courage of your spiritual convictions ...

Perhaps I know the Germans, perhaps I may even tell them a few truths. The new Germany represents such an enormous store of inherited and acquired capacity that for some time it might spend this amassed treasure even with some prodigality. It is no high culture that has ultimately become prevalent with this modern tendency, nor is it by any means delicate taste or noble beauty of the instincts; but rather a number of more manly virtues than any that other European countries can show. An amount of good spirits and self-respect, plenty of firmness in social relations and in the reciprocity of duties; much industry and much perseverance – and a certain inherited moderation which is much more in need of a spur than of a brake. Let me add that in this country people still obey without feeling that obedience humiliates.... And no one despises his opponent.

You observe that it is my desire to be fair to the Germans: and in this respect I should not like to be untrue to myself, – I must therefore also state my objections to them. It costs a good deal to attain to a position of power; for power *makes one stupid*.... The Germans – they were once called a people of thinkers: do they really think at all today? Today the Germans are bored with spirit, they mistrust spirit; politics have swallowed up all seriousness for really spiritual matters – *Deutschland, Deutschland, über alles*. I fear this was the death-blow to German philosophy. 'Are there any German philosophers? Are there any German poets? Are there any *good* German books?' people ask me abroad. I blush; but with that courage which is peculiar to me, even in moments of desperation, I reply: 'Yes, Bismarck!' – Could I have dared to confess what books are read today? Cursed instinct of mediocrity! –

4

Even a cursory assessment shows that it is not only obvious that German culture is in decline, but that there are sufficient reasons why this is the case. After all, nobody can spend more than he has:– this is true of individuals, it is also true of nations. If you spend your strength to gain power, grand politics, economics, world commerce, parliamentarianism and military interests – if you take the quantum of understanding, seriousness, will and self-overcoming that you represent and expend it in one particular direction, then there will not be any left for the other direction. Culture and the state – let no one be deceived on this point – are antagonists: *'Kultur Staat'* is merely a modern idea. The one lives off the other, the one flourishes at the expense of the other. All great periods of culture have been periods of political decline; that which is great from the standpoint of culture was always unpolitical – even *anti-political*. Goethe's heart opened at the phenomenon of Napoleon – it closed at the thought of the 'Wars of Liberation'.... At the very moment when Germany emerged as a great power, France won new importance as a *cultural power*. Even today a large amount of new seriousness and new passion of the spirit has emigrated to Paris; the question of pessimism, for instance, and the question of Wagner; in France almost all psychological and artistic questions are considered with incomparably more subtlety and thoroughness than they are in Germany, – the Germans are even incapable of this kind of earnestness. In the history of European culture the rise of the *Reich* signifies, above all, a displacement of the centre of gravity. Everywhere people are already aware of this: in things that really matter – and these after all constitute culture – the Germans are no longer worth considering. I ask you, can you show me one single spirit who could be mentioned in the same breath with other European thinkers, like your Goethe, your Hegel, your Heinrich Heine and your Schopenhauer? – The fact that there is no longer a single German philosopher worth mentioning is an increasing wonder. –

5

Everything that matters has been lost sight of by the entire system of higher education in Germany: the end quite as much as the means to that end. People forget that education, that *Bildung*, is itself an end – and *not* 'the *Reich*' – they forget that the *educator* is required for this end – and not the secondary school teacher and university scholar. Educators are needed who are themselves educated, superior and noble spirits, who can prove that they are thus qualified, that they are ripe and mellow products of culture at every moment of their lives, in word and in gesture; – not the learned louts who, like 'superior wet-nurses', are now thrust upon the youth of the land by secondary schools and universities. With a few rare exceptions, what is lacking in Germany is the first prerequisite of education – that is to say, the educators; hence the decline of German culture. One of those rarest exceptions is my highly respected friend Jacob Burckhardt of Basel: to him above all is Basel indebted for its foremost position in the humanities. – What the 'higher schools' in Germany really do accomplish is this, they brutally train a vast number of young men, in the smallest amount of time possible, to become *useful and exploitable* servants of the state. 'Higher education' and vast *numbers* – these terms contradict each other from the start. All superior education can only concern the exception: a man must be privileged in order to have a right to such a great privilege. All great and beautiful things cannot be a common possession: *pulchrum est paucorum hominum*. – What is it that is *bringing about* the decline of German culture? The fact that 'higher education' is no longer a privilege – the democratisation of *Bildung* which has become *common* and commonplace.... Nor must it be forgotten that the privileges of the military profession by urging *far too many* to attend the higher schools, involve the downfall of the latter. In Germany today nobody is at liberty to give his children a noble education: in regard to their teachers, their curricula and their educational aims, our 'higher schools' are one and all established upon a fundamentally doubtful mediocre basis. Everywhere, too, a hastiness which is unbecoming reigns supreme; just as if something would be forfeited if the young man were not 'finished' at the age of twenty-three or did not know how to reply to the fundamental question, 'which calling should I choose?' – The higher kind of man, if you please, does not like 'callings' precisely because he knows himself to be called. He has time, he takes time, he cannot possibly think of becoming 'finished' – in the matter of higher culture, a man of thirty years is a beginner, a child. Our overcrowded secondary schools, our overworked, foolishly manufactured secondary school teachers, are a scandal: maybe there are very serious *motives* for defending this state of affairs, as was shown quite recently by the professors of Heidelberg; but there can be no *grounds* for doing so.

Skirmishes of an Untimely Man

34

Christian and anarchist. – When the anarchist, as the mouthpiece of the decaying strata of society, raises his voice in splendid indignation for 'rights', 'justice', 'equal rights' he is only groaning under the burden of his ignorance, which cannot understand *why* he actually suffers – what his poverty consists of – the poverty of life. An instinct of causality is active in him: someone must be responsible for his being in a bad way. His 'splendid indignation' alone relieves him somewhat, it is a pleasure for all poor devils to grumble – it gives them a little intoxicating sensation of power. The very act of complaining, the mere fact that one bewails one's lot, may lend such a charm to life that on that account alone one is ready to endure it. There is a modicum of revenge in every complaint. One casts one's afflictions and, under certain circumstances, even one's baseness, in the teeth of those who are different, as if their condition were an injustice, a *forbidden* privilege. 'Since I am *canaille* you ought to be one too.' It is upon such reasoning that revolutions are based. – To bewail one's lot is always despicable: it is always the outcome of weakness. Whether one ascribes one's afflictions to others or to one's self, it is all the same. The socialist does the former, the Christian, for instance, does the latter. That which is common to both attitudes, or rather that which is equally ignoble in them both, is the fact that somebody must be to *blame* if one is suffering – in short, that the sufferer treats himself with the honey of revenge to allay his anguish. The objects towards which this lust of vengeance, like a lust of pleasure, are directed, are purely accidental causes. In all directions the sufferer finds reasons for cooling his petty passion for revenge. If he is a Christian, I repeat, he finds these reasons in himself. The Christian and the anarchist – both are *décadents*. But even when the Christian condemns, slanders and sullies the world, he is actuated by precisely the same instinct as that which leads the socialist worker to curse, calumniate and besmirch society. The 'Last Judgement' itself is still the sweetest solace to revenge – revolution, as the socialist worker expects it, only thought of as a little more remote. The notion of a 'beyond' as well – why a beyond, if not to denigrate *this* world? ...

37

Whether we have become more moral? – As might have been expected, the whole *ferocity* of moral stupidity, which, as is well known, passes for morality itself in Germany, hurled itself against my concept 'beyond good and evil': I could tell you some nice tales about this. Above all, people tried to make me see the 'incontestable superiority' of our age in regard to moral sentiment and the *progress* we had made in these matters. Compared with *us* a Cesare Borgia was by no means to be represented as a 'higher man', a sort of overman, which I declared him to be. The editor of the Swiss newspaper the *Bund* went so far as not only to express his admiration for the courage displayed by my enterprise, but also to pretend to 'understand' that the intended purpose of my work was to abolish all decent feeling. Much obliged! In reply, I venture to raise the following question: *have we really become more moral?* The fact that everybody believes that we have is in itself an objection to the belief.... We modern men, so extremely delicate and susceptible, full of consideration one for the other, actually dare to suppose that the sensitive humanity which we all display, this unanimity which we have at last acquired in sparing and helping and trusting one another, marks a definite step forward and shows us to be far ahead of the man of the Renaissance. But every age thinks the same, it is *bound* to think the same. This at least is certain, that we should not dare to stand amid the conditions which prevailed during the Renaissance, we should not even dare to imagine ourselves in those conditions: our nerves could not endure that reality, not to speak of our muscles. The inability to do this, however, does not denote any progress; but simply the different and more senile quality of our particular nature, its greater weakness, delicacy and susceptibility, out of which a morality *more rich in consideration* was bound to arise. If we imagine our delicacy and senility, our physiological decrepitude as nonexistent, our morality of 'humanisation' would immediately lose all value – no morality has value *per se* – it would even fill us with scorn. On the other hand, do not let us doubt that we moderns, wrapped as we are in the thick cotton wool of our humanitarianism which would shrink even from grazing a stone, would present a comedy to Cesare Borgia's contemporaries which would literally make them die of laughter. We are indeed, without knowing it, utterly ridiculous with our modern 'virtues' .... The decline of the instincts of hostility and of those instincts that arouse suspicion – for this, if anything, is what constitutes our progress – is only one of the results manifested by the general decline in *vitality*: it requires a hundred times more trouble and caution to live such a dependent and senile existence. In such circumstances everybody gives everybody else a helping hand, and, to a certain extent, everybody is either sick or a nurse to the sick. This is then called 'virtue': among those men who knew a different life – that is to say, a fuller, more profligate, more super-abundant sort of life, it might have been called by another name – possibly 'cowardice' or 'vileness' or 'old woman's morality'.... Our softening of manners – this is my claim; this if you will is my *innovation* – is the outcome of our decline; conversely, hardness and terribleness in morals may be the result of an excess of life. When the latter state prevails, much is dared, much is challenged and much is also *squandered*. That which formerly was simply the spice of life would now be our *poison*. To be indifferent – even this is a form of strength – for that, likewise, we are too senile, too decrepit: our morality of sympathy, against which I was the first to raise a finger of warning, that which might be called *moral impressionism*, is one symptom more of the excessive physiological irritability which is peculiar to everything *décadent*. That movement which attempted to introduce itself in a scientific manner on the shoulders of Schopenhauer's morality of pity – a very sad attempt! – is in its essence the movement of *décadence* in morality, and as such it is intimately related to Christian morality. Strong ages and noble cultures see something contemptible in pity, in the 'love of one's neighbour' and in a lack of egoism and of self-esteem. – Ages should be measured according to their *positive forces*; – valued by this standard that prodigal and fateful age of the Renaissance, appears as the last *great* age, while we moderns with our anxious care of ourselves and love of our neighbours, with all our unassuming virtues of industry, equity and scientific method – with our lust of collection, of economy and of mechanism – represent a *weak age*.... Our virtues are necessarily determined, and are even stimulated, by our weakness. 'Equality', a certain definite process of making everybody uniform, which only finds its expression in the theory of equal rights, is essentially bound up with a declining culture: the chasm between man and man, class and class, the multiplicity of types, the will to be one's self and to distinguish one's self – that, in fact, which I call the *pathos of distance* is proper to all *strong* ages. The force of tension – no, the tension itself, between extremes grows slighter every day – the extremes themselves are tending to become obliterated to the point of becoming identical. All our political theories and state constitutions, not by any means excepting 'The German *Reich*', are the logical consequences, the necessary consequences of decline; the unconscious effect of *décadence* has begun to dominate even the ideals of the various sciences. My objection to the whole of English and French sociology still continues to be this, that it knows only the *décadent form* of society from experience, and with perfectly childlike innocence takes the instincts of decline as the *norm*, the standard of sociological valuations. *Descending* life, the decay of all organising power – that is to say, of all that power which separates, cleaves gulfs and establishes rank above and below, formulated itself in modern sociology as *the* ideal. Our socialists are *décadents*: but Herbert Spencer was also a *décadent*: *he* saw something to be desired in the triumph of altruism! ...

38

My conception of freedom. – Sometimes the value of a thing does not lie in that which it helps us to achieve, but in the amount we have to pay for it – what it *costs* us. For instance, liberal institutions straightaway cease to be liberal the moment they are soundly established: once this is attained no more grievous and more thorough enemies of freedom exist than liberal institutions! One knows, of course, what they bring about: they undermine the will to power, they are the levelling of mountain and valley exalted to a morality, they make people small, cowardly and pleasure-loving – by means of them the herd animal invariably triumphs. Liberalism, or, in other words, *herd-animalisation*.... The same institutions, so long as they are fought for, produce quite other results; then indeed they promote the cause of freedom quite powerfully. Regarded more closely, it is war that produces these results, war in favour of liberal institutions, which, as war, allows the illiberal instincts to subsist. For war trains men to be free. For what is freedom? Freedom is the will to be responsible for ourselves. It is to preserve the distance which separates us from other men. To grow more indifferent to hardship, to severity, to privation and even to life itself. To be ready to sacrifice men for one's cause, one's self included. Freedom denotes that the virile instincts which rejoice in war and in victory prevail over other instincts; for instance, over the instincts of 'happiness'. The man who has won his freedom, and how much more so the spirit that has won its freedom, tramples ruthlessly upon that contemptible kind of comfort which shopkeepers, Christians, cows, women, Englishmen and other democrats worship in their dreams. The free man is a *warrior*. – How is freedom measured in individuals as well as in nations? According to the resistance which has to be overcome, according to the pains which it costs to remain *aloft*. The highest type of free man would have to be sought where the greatest resistance has continually to be overcome: five paces away from tyranny, on the very threshold of the danger of servitude. This is psychologically true if by the word 'tyrants' we mean inexorable and terrible instincts which challenge the *maximum* amount of authority and discipline to oppose them – the finest example of this is Julius Caesar; it is also true politically: just examine the course of history. The nations which were worth anything, which *got to be* worth anything, never attained to that condition under liberal institutions: *great danger* made out of them something which deserves reverence, that danger which alone can make us aware of our resources, our virtues, our means of defence, our weapons, our genius – which compels us to be strong....First principle: a man must need strength, otherwise he will never attain it. – Those great forcing-houses for the strong, for the strongest kind of men that have ever existed on earth, the aristocratic commonwealths like those of Rome and Venice, understood freedom precisely as I understand the word: as something that one has and that one has *not*, as something that one *wants*, something one *conquers*.

39

Critique of modernity. – Our institutions are no longer any good; on this point we are all agreed. But the fault does not lie with them; but with *us*. Now that we have lost all the instincts out of which institutions grow, the latter on their part are beginning to disappear from our midst because we are no longer fit for them. Democracy has always been the death agony of the power of organisation: already in *Human All-too-Human*, I pointed out that modern democracy, together with its half-measures, of which the 'German *Reich*' is an example, was a decaying form of the state. For institutions to be possible there must exist a sort of will, instinct, imperative, which cannot be otherwise than anti-liberal to the point of malice: the will to tradition, to authority, to responsibility for centuries to come, to *solidarity* between succeeding generations forwards and backwards *in infinitum*. If this will is present, something is founded which resembles the *imperium Romanum*: or Russia, the *only* great nation today that has some lasting power and grit in her, that can bide her time, that can still promise something. – Russia the opposite of all wretched European petty-statism and neurasthenia, which the foundation of the German *Reich* has brought to a crisis. The whole of the West no longer possesses those instincts from which institutions spring, out of which a *future* grows: maybe nothing is more opposed to its 'modern spirit' than these things. People live for the present, they live at top speed – they certainly live without any sense of responsibility; and this is precisely what they call 'freedom.' Everything in institutions which *makes* them institutions, is scorned, loathed and repudiated: everybody is in mortal fear of a new slavery, wherever the word 'authority' is so much as whispered. The *décadence* of the valuing instinct, in our politicians and in our political parties, goes so far that they instinctively prefer that which acts as a solvent, that which precipitates the final catastrophe ...

40

The labour question. – The mere fact that there is such a thing as the labour question is due to stupidity, or at bottom to degenerate instincts which are the cause of *all* the stupidity of modern times. Concerning certain things no questions ought to be asked: the first imperative of instinct. For the life of me I cannot see what people want to do with the European worker now that they have made a question of him. He is far too comfortable to cease from questioning more and more, and with ever less modesty. After all, he has the majority on his side. There is now not the slightest hope that a modest and self-sufficient sort of human being, a Chinese type, will come into being in this quarter: and this would have been the reasonable course, it was even a dire necessity. What has been done? Everything has been done with the view to nipping the very prerequisite of this accomplishment in the bud – with the most frivolous thoughtlessness those selfsame instincts by means of which the worker becomes possible as a class, possible *for himself*, have been destroyed root and branch. The worker has qualified for military service; he has been granted the right to organise and to vote: is it any wonder that he already regards his own existence as one of distress (expressed morally, as an *injustice*)? But, again I ask, what do people want? If they desire a certain end, then they should also desire the means. If they want slaves, then it is foolish to educate them to be masters. –

41

'Freedom which I do *not* mean ...' In an age like the present, it simply adds to one's peril to be left to one's instincts. The instincts contradict, disturb and destroy each other; I have already defined the *modern* as physiological self-contradiction. A reasonable system of education would insist upon at least one of these instinct-systems *being paralysed* beneath an iron pressure in order to allow others to assert their power, to grow strong and to dominate. At present, the only conceivable way of making the individual possible would be to *prune* him:– of making him possible – that is to say, *whole*.... The very reverse occurs. Independence, free development and *laisser aller* are clamoured for most violently precisely by those for whom no restraint *could be too severe* – this is true *in politicis*, it is true in art. But this is a symptom of *décadence*: our modern notion of 'freedom' is one more proof of the degeneration of instinct.

43

Whispered to the conservatives. – That which we did not know formerly, and know now, or might know if we chose – is the fact that a *retrograde formation*, a reversion in any sense or degree, is absolutely impossible. We physiologists at least are aware of this. But all priests and moralists have believed in it – they *wished* to drag and force man back to a *former* standard of virtue. Morality has always been a Procrustean bed. Even the politicians have imitated the preachers of virtue in this matter. There are still parties today which dream of the crab-like *retrogression* of all things as their goal. But not everyone can be a crab. It cannot be helped: we *must* go forward – that is to say step by step further and further into *décadence* (– this is my definition of modern 'progress' ...). We can *hinder* this development, and thus dam up and accumulate degeneration itself and render it more convulsive, more *volcanic*: we cannot do more.

44

My conception of genius. – Great men, like great ages, are explosive material in which a stupendous amount of power is accumulated; their precondition is always historical and physiological; they are the outcome of the fact that for eons energy has been collected, stored, saved and conserved for their use, and that no explosion has taken place. When the tension in the mass has become sufficiently excessive, the most incidental stimulus suffices in order to summon 'genius', 'great deeds' and momentous fate into the world. What, then, is the good of all environment, historical periods, '*Zeitgeist*' and 'public opinion'? – Take the case of Napoleon. Revolutionary France, and even more pre-revolutionary France, would have brought forward a type which was the very opposite of Napoleon: it actually *did* produce such a type. And because Napoleon was something *different*, the heir of a stronger, older, more ancient civilisation than that which in France was dying off, he became master there, he was the only master there. Great men are necessary, the age in which they appear is accidental; the fact that they almost invariably master their age is accounted for simply by the fact that they are stronger, that they are older and that power has been stored longer for them. The relation of a genius to his age is like that which exists between strength and weakness and between maturity and youth: the age is relatively always very much younger, thinner, less mature, less resolute and more childish. The fact that general opinion in France today is *utterly different* on this very point (in Germany too, but that is of no consequence); the fact that in that country the milieu theory – a regular neuropathic notion – has become sacrosanct and almost scientific, and finds acceptance even among the physiologists, is a very bad and exceedingly depressing sign. In England too the same belief prevails: but nobody will be surprised at that. The Englishman knows only two ways of understanding the genius and the 'great man': either *democratically* in the style of Buckle, or *religiously* after the manner of Carlyle. – The *danger* which great men and great ages represent is simply extraordinary; every kind of exhaustion and sterility follows in their wake. The great man is an end; the great age – the Renaissance for instance – is an end. The genius – in work and in deed – is necessarily a squanderer: the fact that *he spends himself*...constitutes his greatness. The instinct of self-preservation is, as it were, suspended in him; the overpowering pressure of outflowing energy in him forbids any such protection and prudence. People call this 'self-sacrifice', they praise his 'heroism', his indifference to his own well-being, his utter devotion to an idea, a great cause, a fatherland: all misunderstandings....He flows out, he flows over, he consumes himself, he does not spare himself – and does all this with fateful necessity, irrevocably, involuntarily, just as a river involuntarily bursts its dams. But, owing to the fact that humanity has been highly indebted to such explosives, it has endowed them with many things, for instance, with a kind of *higher morality*....This is indeed the sort of gratitude that humanity is capable of: it *misunderstands* its benefactors. –

48

Progress in my sense – I also speak of a 'return to nature', although it is not a process of going back but of going up – up into lofty, free and even terrible nature and naturalness; such a nature as can play with great tasks and *may* play with them....To speak in *a parable*, Napoleon was an example of a return to nature, as I understand it (for instance, *in rebus tacticis*, and still more, as military experts know, in strategy). But Rousseau – where did he want to return? Rousseau, this first modern man, idealist and *canaille* in *one* person; who was in need of moral 'dignity' in order even to endure the sight of his own person – sick with unbridled vanity and wanton self-contempt; this abortion, who erected his tent on the threshold of modernity, also wanted a 'return to nature' – but, I ask once more, where did he wish to return? – I hate Rousseau, even *in* the Revolution itself: the latter was the historical expression of this hybrid of idealist and *canaille*. The bloody farce which this Revolution ultimately became, its 'immorality', concerns me but slightly; what I loathe however is its Rousseauesque *morality* – the so-called 'truths' of the Revolution, by means of which it still exercises power and draws all flat and mediocre things over to its side. The doctrine of equality!.... But there is no more deadly poison than this; for it *seems* to proceed from the very lips of justice, whereas in reality it draws the curtain down on all justice.... 'To equals equality, to unequals inequality' – *that* would be the real slogan of justice and that which follows from it. 'Never make unequal things equal.' – The fact that so much horror and blood are associated with this doctrine of equality has lent this 'modern idea' *par excellence* such a halo of fire and glory that the Revolution as a drama has misled even the most noble minds. – That after all is no reason for honouring it the more. – I can see only one who regarded it as it should be regarded – that is to say, with *loathing* – Goethe ...

49

Goethe. – no mere German, but a European event: a magnificent attempt to overcome the eighteenth century by means of a return to nature, by means of an *ascent* to the naturalness of the Renaissance, a kind of self-overcoming on the part of the century in question. – He bore the strongest instincts of this century in his breast: its sentimentality and idolatry of nature, its anti-historical, idealistic, unreal and revolutionary spirit (the latter is only a form of the unreal). He enlisted history, natural science, antiquity, as well as Spinoza and above all practical activity, in his service. He drew a host of very definite horizons around him; far from liberating himself from life, he plunged right into it; he did not give in; he took as much as he could on his own shoulders and into his heart. That to which he aspired was *totality*; he was opposed to the sundering of reason, sensuality, feeling and will (as preached with most repulsive scholasticism by Kant, the antipodes of Goethe); he disciplined himself into a harmonious whole, he *created* himself.... Goethe, in the midst of an age of unreal sentiment was a convinced realist: he said yes to everything that was like himself in this regard – there was no greater event in his life than that *ens realissimum*, called Napoleon. Goethe conceived a strong, highly cultured man, skilful in all bodily accomplishments, able to keep himself in check, having a feeling of reverence for himself, and so constituted as to be able to risk the full enjoyment of naturalness in all its rich profusion and be strong enough for this freedom; a man of tolerance, not out of weakness, but out of strength, because he knows how to turn to his own advantage that which would ruin the mediocre nature; a man to whom nothing is any longer forbidden, unless it be weakness either as a vice or as a virtue.... Such a spirit who has *become free* appears in the middle of the universe with a cheerful and trusting fatalism; he believes that only individual things are loathsome and that as a whole everything is redeemed and affirmed – *he no longer denies* .... But such a faith is the highest of all faiths: I gave it the name of *Dionysus*.

Translated by A. Ludovici with modifications

The Antichrist: A Curse on Christianity, 1888

2

What is good? Whatever heightens the feeling of power in man, the will to power, power itself.
  What is evil? – Whatever springs from weakness.
  What is happiness? – The feeling that power is *growing* – that resistance is overcome.
  Not contentment, but more power; *not* peace at any price, but war; *not* virtue, but efficiency (virtue in the Renaissance sense, *virtù*, virtue that is moraline-free).
  The weak and the ill-constituted shall perish: first principle of *our* love of mankind. And one should help them to it.
  What is more harmful than any vice? – Active pity for the ill-constituted and the weak – Christianity...

3

The problem that I set here is not what shall replace mankind in the order of living creatures (– man is an *end* –): but what type of man must be *bred*, must be *willed*, as being the most valuable, the most worthy of life, the most secure guarantee of the future.
  This more valuable type has appeared often enough in the past: but always as a stroke of luck, as an exception, never as deliberately *willed*. Very often he has been precisely the most feared; hitherto he has been almost *the* terror of terrors; – and out of that terror the opposite type has been willed, bred and *attained*: the domestic animal, the herd animal, the sick animal man – the Christian.

4

Mankind surely does *not* represent an evolution towards a better or stronger or higher level, as progress is now understood. This 'progress' is merely a modern idea, which is to say, a false idea. The European of today, in his essential worth, falls far below the European of the Renaissance; the process of evolution does *not* necessarily mean elevation, enhancement, strengthening.
  True enough, it succeeds in isolated and individual cases in various parts of the world and under the most widely different cultures, and in these cases a *higher type* certainly manifests itself; something which, compared to mankind as a whole, appears as a sort of overman. Successes like this, real strokes of luck have always been possible, and will remain possible, perhaps, for all time to come. Even whole races, tribes and nations may occasionally represent such a *lucky strike*.

37

– Our age is proud of its historical sense: how, then, could it delude itself into believing that the *crude fable of the miracle worker and Redeemer* constituted the beginnings of Christianity – and that everything spiritual and symbolic in it only came later? Quite to the contrary, the whole history of Christianity – from the death on the cross onwards – is the history of a progressively clumsier misunderstanding of an *original* symbolism. With every extension of Christianity among larger and cruder masses, even less capable of grasping the principles that gave birth to it, the need arose to make it more and more *vulgar* and *barbarous* – it absorbed the teachings and rites of all the *subterranean* cults of the *imperium Romanum*, and the absurdities engendered by all sorts of sickly reasoning. It was the fate of Christianity that its faith had to become as sickly, as low and as vulgar as the needs were sickly, low and vulgar to which it had to administer. A *sickly barbarism* finally lifts itself to power as the Church – the Church, that incarnation of deadly hostility against all integrity, against all loftiness of soul, against all discipline of the spirit, against all spontaneous and kindly humanity. – *Christian* values – *noble* values: it is only we, we spirits who have *become free*, who have re-established this greatest of all antitheses in values! ...

38

– I cannot, at this point, avoid a sigh. There are days when I am afflicted with a feeling blacker than the blackest melancholy – *contempt of man*. Let me leave no doubt as to *what* I despise, *whom* I despise: it is the man of today, the man with whom I am unhappily contemporaneous. The man of today – I am suffocated by his foul breath!... Towards the past, like all who understand, I am full of tolerance, which is to say, *magnanimous* self-control: with gloomy caution I pass through whole millennia of this madhouse of a world, call it 'Christianity', 'Christian faith' or the 'Christian Church', what you will – I take care not to hold mankind responsible for its lunacies. But my feeling changes and breaks out irresistibly the moment I enter modern times, *our* times. Our age *knows better*... What was formerly merely sickly now becomes indecent – it is indecent to be a Christian today. *And here my disgust begins.* – I look about me: not a word survives of what was once called 'truth'; we can no longer bear to hear a priest pronounce the word. Even a man who makes the most modest pretensions to integrity *must* know that a theologian, a priest, a pope today not only errs when he speaks, but actually *lies* – and that he no longer escapes blame for his lie through 'innocence' or 'ignorance'. The priest knows, as everyone knows, that there is no longer any 'God' or any 'sinner' or any 'Redeemer' – that 'free will' and the 'moral world order' are *lies* – serious reflection, the profound self-overcoming of the spirit, *allow* no man to pretend that he does *not* know it. *All* the ideas of the Church are now recognised for what they are – the worst counterfeits in existence, invented to debase nature and all natural values; the priest himself is seen as he actually is – as the most dangerous form of parasite, as the venomous spider of creation. We know, our *conscience* now knows – just *what* the real value of all those sinister inventions of priest and Church has been and *what ends they have served*, with their debasement of humanity to a state of self-pollution, the very sight of which excites loathing – the concepts 'beyond', 'the Last Judgement', 'the immortality of the soul' the 'soul' itself: they are all merely so many instruments of torture, systems of cruelty, whereby the priest becomes master and remains master. Everyone knows this, *but nevertheless things remain as they were*. What has become of the last trace of decent feeling, of self-respect, when our statesmen, otherwise an unconventional class of men and thoroughly anti-Christian in their acts, now call themselves Christians and take communion?...A young prince at the head of his armies, magnificent as the expression of the egoism and arrogance of his people – and yet shamelessly acknowledging, that he is a Christian!...*Whom*, then, does Christianity deny? *What* does it call 'the world'? To be a soldier, to be a judge, to be a patriot; to defend one's self; to protect one's honour; to desire one's own advantage; to be proud, every act of everyday, every instinct, every valuation that shows itself in a *deed* is now anti-Christian: what a *monster of falsehood* the modern man must be to call himself nevertheless, and *without* shame, a Christian! –

43

When the centre of gravity of life is placed *not* in life itself, but in the 'beyond' – *in nothingness* – then one has taken away its centre of gravity altogether. The great lie of personal immortality destroys all reason, all natural instinct – henceforth, everything in the instincts that is beneficial, that promotes life and that safeguards the future is a cause of suspicion. To live like this so that life no longer has any meaning: *this* now becomes the 'meaning' of life. Why be public-spirited? Why take any pride in descent and forefathers? Why labour together, trust one another or concern oneself about the common good and try to serve it?...Merely so many 'temptations', so many strayings from the 'straight path' – '*One* thing only is necessary'. That every man, because he has an 'immortal soul', is as good as every other man; that in an infinite universe of things the 'salvation' of *every* individual may lay claim to eternal importance; that insignificant bigots and the three-quarters madmen may assume that the laws of nature are constantly *suspended* on their behalf – it is impossible to lavish too much contempt upon such a magnification of every sort of selfishness to infinity, to *insolence*. And yet Christianity has to thank precisely *this* miserable flattery of personal vanity for its *triumph* – it was thus that it lured all the ill-constituted, the dissatisfied, the fallen upon evil days, the whole detritus and dross of humanity to its side. The 'salvation of the soul' – in plain English: 'the world revolves around *me*'. The poisonous doctrine '*equal* rights for all' has been propagated as a Christian principle: out of the secret nooks and crannies of bad instinct Christianity has waged a deadly war upon all feelings of respect and distance between man and man, which is to say, upon the first *prerequisite* to every step upward, to every development of culture – out of the *ressentiment* of the masses it has forged its chief weapons against *us*, against everything noble, joyous and high-spirited on earth, against our happiness on earth. To allow 'immortality' to every Peter and Paul was the greatest, the most vicious outrage upon *noble* humanity ever perpetrated – *And* let us not underestimate the fatal influence which crept out of Christianity into politics! Today no one has the courage to demand privileges, the right of dominion, respect for himself and his equals – for the *pathos of distance*. Our politics is sick with this lack of courage! – The aristocratic outlook has been undermined by the lie of the equality of souls; and if belief in the 'privileges of the majority' makes and *will continue to make* revolutions – it is Christianity, let us not doubt it, *Christian* value judgements, which convert every revolution into a carnival of blood and crime! Christianity is a revolt of all creatures that creep on the ground against everything that has *height*: the gospel of the 'lowly' *lowers*...

51

The fact that faith, under certain circumstances, may work for blessedness, but that this blessedness produced by an *idée fixe* by no means makes the idea itself true, and the fact that faith actually moves no mountains, but instead *raises them up* where there were none before: all this is made sufficiently clear by a walk through a *lunatic asylum. Not*, of course, to a priest: for his instincts prompt him to the lie that sickness is not sickness and lunatic asylums are not lunatic asylums. Christianity finds sickness *necessary*, just as Greek culture had need of a superabundance of health – the actual ulterior purpose of the whole system of salvation of the Church is to *make* people ill. And the Church itself – does it not set up a Catholic lunatic asylum as the ultimate ideal? – The whole earth as a madhouse? – The sort of religious man that the Church *wants* is a typical *décadent*; the moment at which a religious crisis dominates a people is always marked by epidemics of nervous disorder; the 'inner world' of the religious man is so like the 'inner world' of the overexcited and exhausted that it is difficult to distinguish between them; the 'highest' states, held up before mankind by Christianity as being of supreme value, are actually forms of epilepsy – the Church has granted the name of holy only to lunatics or to gigantic frauds *in majorem dei honorem*. Once I ventured to designate the whole Christian system of *training* in penance and redemption (now best studied in England) as a method of producing a *folie circulaire* upon a soil already prepared for it, which is to say, a soil that is thoroughly unhealthy. Not everyone may be a Christian: one is not 'converted' to Christianity – one must first be sick enough for it...We others, who have the *courage* for health *and* likewise for contempt – we may well despise a religion that teaches misunderstanding of the body! That refuses to rid itself of the superstition about the soul! That makes a 'virtue' of insufficient nourishment! That combats health as a sort of enemy, devil, temptation! that persuades itself that it is possible to carry a 'perfect soul' in a cadaver of a body, and that, to this end, had to devise for itself a new concept of 'perfection', a pale, sickly, idiotically ecstatic state of existence, so-called 'holiness' – a holiness that is itself merely a series of symptoms of an impoverished, enervated and incurably disordered body! ... The Christian movement, as a European movement, was from the start no more than a general uprising of all sorts of outcast and refuse elements (who now, under the cover of Christianity, aspire to power). It does *not* represent the decay of a race; it represents, on the contrary, a conglomeration of *décadence* products from all quarters, thronging together and seeking one another out. It was *not*, as has been thought, the corruption of antiquity, of *noble* antiquity, which made Christianity possible; one cannot too sharply challenge the scholarly imbecility which today maintains that theory. At the time when the sick and corrupt Chandala strata in the whole *imperium* were Christianised, the *contrary type*, the nobility, reached its finest and ripest development. The majority became master; democracy, with its Christian instincts, *triumphed*. Christianity was not 'national', it was not based on race – it appealed to all the varieties of men disinherited by life, it had its allies everywhere. Christianity has the rancour of the sick at its very core – the instinct against the *healthy*, against *health*. Everything that is well-constituted, proud, gallant and, above all, beautiful gives offence to its ears and eyes. Again I remind you of Paul's priceless words: 'And God hath chosen the *weak* things of the world, the *foolish* things of the world, the *base* things of the world, and things which are *despised*': *this* was the formula; *in hoc signo* the *décadence* triumphed. – God on the cross – is man always to miss the frightful inner significance of this symbol? – Everything that suffers, everything that hangs on the cross, is *divine*. We all hang on the cross, consequently *we* are divine. We alone are divine. Christianity was thus a victory: a *nobler* outlook was destroyed by it – Christianity remains to this day the greatest misfortune of humanity. –

54

Do not let yourself be deceived: great intellects are sceptical. Zarathustra is a sceptic. The strength, the *freedom* which proceed from intellectual power, from a superabundance of intellectual power, *manifest* themselves as scepticism. Men of fixed convictions do not count when it comes to determining what is fundamental in values and lack of values. Men of convictions are prisoners. They do not see far enough, they do not see what is *below* them: whereas a man who wishes to join in the discussion of value and disvalue must be able to see five hundred convictions *beneath* him – and *behind* him. A spirit who aspires to great things, and who wants the means to them, is necessarily sceptical. Freedom from any sort of conviction *belongs* to strength and to an independent point of view. That great passion which is at once the foundation and the power of a sceptic's existence, and is both more enlightened and more despotic than he is himself, drafts the whole of his intellect into its service; it makes him unscrupulous; it gives him courage to employ unholy means; under certain circumstances it does not *begrudge* him even convictions. Conviction as a means: one may achieve a good deal by means of a conviction. A great passion makes use of and uses up convictions; it does not yield to them – it knows itself to be sovereign. – On the contrary, the need of faith, of some thing unconditioned by Yes or No, of Carlylism, if I may be permitted the word, is a need of *weakness*. The man of faith, the 'believer' of any sort, is necessarily a dependent man – such a man cannot posit *himself* as a goal, nor can he find goals within himself. The 'believer' does not belong to himself; he can only be a means to an end; he must be *used up*; he needs someone to use him up. His instinct gives the highest honours to a morality of self-abnegation; he is prompted to embrace it by everything: his prudence, his experience, his vanity. Every sort of faith is in itself evidence of self-abnegation, of self-alienation. When one reflects how necessary it is to the great majority that there be regulations to restrain them from without and hold them fast, and to what extent control, or, in a higher sense, *slavery*, is the one and only condition which makes for the well-being of the weak-willed man, and especially woman, then one at once understands conviction and 'faith'. To the man with convictions they are his backbone. To *avoid* seeing many things, to be impartial about nothing, to be a party man through and through, to estimate all values strictly and infallibly – these are conditions necessary to the existence of such a man. But by the same token they are *antagonists* of the truthful man – of the truth. The believer is not free to answer the question 'true' or 'not true' according to the dictates of his own conscience: integrity on *this* point would bring about his instant downfall. The pathological limitations of his vision turn the man of convictions into a fanatic – Savonarola, Luther, Rousseau, Robespierre, Saint-Simon – these types stand in opposition to the strong spirit who has *become* free. But the grandiose attitudes of these *sick* intellects, these intellectual epileptics, influence the great masses – fanatics are picturesque, and mankind prefers observing poses to listening to *reasons*.

56

– In the last analysis it comes to this: what is the *end* of lying? The fact that, in Christianity, 'holy' ends are lacking is *my* objection to the means it employs. Only *bad* ends appear: the poisoning, the slandering, the denial of life, the despising of the body, the degradation and self-violation of man by the concept of sin – *therefore*, its means are also bad. – I have a contrary feeling when I read the Law-Book of Manu, an incomparably more intellectual and superior work, which it would be a sin against the *intelligence* to so much as *name* in the same breath with the Bible. It is easy to see why: there is a genuine philosophy behind it, *in* it, not merely an evil-smelling mess of Jewish rabbinism and superstition – it gives even the most fastidious psychologist something to sink his teeth into. And, *not* to forget what is most important, it differs fundamentally from every kind of Bible: by means of it the *noble* orders, the philosophers and the warriors keep the masses under control; it is full of noble valuations, it shows a feeling of perfection, an affirmation of life and triumphant feeling towards self and life – the *sun* shines upon the whole book. – All the things on which Christianity vents its fathomless vulgarity – for example, procreation, women and marriage – are here treated seriously, with respect and with love and confidence. How can anyone really put into the hands of children and ladies a book which contains such vile things as this: 'to avoid fornication, let every man have his own wife, and let every woman have her own husband; it is better to marry than to burn'? And is it *possible* to be a Christian so long as the origin of man is Christianised, which is to say, *befouled*, by the doctrine of the *immaculata conceptio*?... I know of no book in which so many delicate and kindly things are said of women as in the Law-Book of Manu; these old grey beards and saints have a way of being gallant to women that it would be impossible, perhaps, to surpass. 'The mouth of a woman,' it says in one place, 'the breasts of a maiden, the prayer of a child and the smoke of sacrifice are always pure.' In another place: 'there is nothing purer than the light of the sun, the shadow cast by a cow, air, water, fire and the breath of a maiden.' Finally, in still another place – perhaps this is also a holy lie – 'all the orifices of the body above the navel are pure, and all below are impure. Only in the maiden is the whole body pure.'

57

One catches the *unholiness* of Christian means *in flagranti* by the simple process of putting the ends sought by Christianity beside the ends sought by the Law-Book of Manu – by putting these enormously antithetical ends under a bright light. The critic of Christianity cannot evade the necessity of making Christianity *contemptible*. – A book of laws such as the Law-Book of Manu has the same origin as every other good law-book: it epitomises the experience, the sagacity and the ethical experimentation of long centuries; it brings things to a conclusion; it no longer creates. The prerequisite to a codification of this sort is recognition of the fact that the means which establish the authority of a slowly and painfully attained *truth* are fundamentally different from those which one would make use of to prove it. A law-book never recites the utility, the grounds, the casuistical antecedents of a law: for if it did so it would lose the imperative tone, the 'thou shalt' on which obedience is based. The problem lies exactly here. – At a certain point in the evolution of a people, the class within it of the greatest insight, which is to say, the greatest hindsight and foresight, declares that the series of experiences determining how all shall live – or *can* live – has come to an end. The object now is to reap as rich and as complete a harvest as possible from the days of experiment and *hard* experience. In consequence, the thing that is to be avoided above everything is further experimentation – the continuation of the state in which values are fluent, and are tested, chosen and criticised *ad infinitum*. Against this a double wall is set up: on the one hand, *revelation*, which is the assumption that the reasons lying behind the laws are *not* of human origin, that they were *not* sought out and found by a slow process and after many errors, but that they are of divine ancestry, and came into being complete, perfect, without a history, as a free gift, a miracle; and on the other hand, *tradition*, which is the assumption that the law has remained unchanged from time immemorial and that it is impious and a crime against one's forefathers to question it. The authority of the law is thus grounded on the thesis: God gave it and the fathers *lived* it. – The higher motive of such procedure lies in the design to distract consciousness, step by step, from its concern with notions of right living (that is to say, those that have been *proved* to be right by wide and carefully considered experience), so that instinct attains to a perfect automatism – a primary necessity to every sort of mastery, to every sort of perfection in the art of life. To draw up such a law-book as Manu's means to lay before a people the possibility of future mastery, of attainable perfection – it permits them to aspire to the highest reaches of the art of life. *To that end the law must be made unconscious*: that is the aim of every holy lie. – The *order of castes*, the highest, the dominating law, is merely the ratification of an *order of nature*, of a natural law of the first rank, over which no arbitrary fiat, no 'modern idea', can exert any influence. In every healthy society there are three physiological types, gravitating toward differentiation but mutually conditioning one another, and each of these has its own hygiene, its own sphere of work, its own special mastery and feeling of perfection. It is *not* Manu but nature that sets in one class those who are chiefly intellectual, in another those who are marked by muscular strength and temperament, and in a third those who are distinguished in neither one way or the other, but show only mediocrity – the last-named represents the great majority, and the first two the select. The superior caste – I call it the *fewest* – has, as the most perfect, the privileges of the few: it stands for happiness, for beauty, for everything good upon earth. Only the most intellectual of men have any right to beauty, to the beautiful; only in them can goodness escape being weakness. *Pulchrum est paucorum hominum*: goodness is a privilege. Nothing could be more unbecoming to them than uncouth manners or a pessimistic look, or an eye that sees *ugliness* – or indignation against the general aspect of things. Indignation is the privilege of the Chandala; so is pessimism. '*The world is perfect*' – so prompts the instinct of the intellectual, the instinct of the man who says yes to life. 'Imperfection, whatever is *inferior* to us, distance, the pathos of distance, even the Chandala themselves are parts of this perfection.' The most intelligent men, like the *strongest*, find their happiness where others see only disaster: in the labyrinth, in being hard with themselves and with others, in effort; their delight is in self-mastery; in them asceticism becomes second nature, a necessity, an instinct. They regard a difficult task as a privilege; to them it is *recreation* to play with burdens that would crush all others. Knowledge – a form of asceticism. – They are the most honourable kind of men: but that does not prevent them being the most cheerful and most amiable. They rule, not because they want to, but because they *are*; they are not at liberty to come second. – The *second caste*: to this belong the guardians of the law, the keepers of order and security, the more noble warriors, above all, the king as the highest form of warrior, judge and protector of the law. The second in rank constitute the executive arm of the intellectuals, the next to them in rank, taking from them all that is *rough* in the business of ruling – their followers, their right hand, their most apt disciples. – In all this, I repeat, there is nothing arbitrary, nothing 'made up'; whatever is to the *contrary* is made up – by it nature is brought to shame. The order of castes, the *order of rank*, simply formulates the supreme law of life itself; the separation of the three types is necessary to the maintenance of society and to the evolution of higher types, and the highest types – the *inequality* of rights is essential to the existence of any rights at all. – A right is a privilege. Everyone enjoys the privileges that accord with his state of existence. Let us not underestimate the privileges of the *mediocre*. Life is always harder as one mounts the *heights* – the cold increases, responsibility increases. A high culture is a pyramid: it can stand only on a broad base; its primary prerequisite is a strong and soundly consolidated mediocrity. The handicrafts, commerce, agriculture, *science*, the greater part of art, in brief, the whole range of *occupational* activities, are compatible only with mediocre ability and aspiration; such callings would be out of place for exceptional men; the instincts which belong to them stand as much opposed to aristocracy as to anarchism. The fact that a man is publicly useful, that he is a wheel, a function, is evidence of a natural predisposition; it is not *society*, but the only sort of happiness that the majority are capable of, that makes them intelligent machines. To the mediocre mediocrity is a form of happiness; they have a natural instinct for mastering one thing, for specialisation. It would be altogether unworthy of a profound intellect to see anything objectionable in mediocrity in itself. It is, in fact, the *first* prerequisite to the appearance of the exceptional: it is a necessary condition to a high degree of culture. When the exceptional man handles the mediocre man with more delicate fingers than he applies to himself or to his equals, this is not merely kindness of heart – it is simply his *duty*. Whom do I hate most heartily among the rabble of today? The rabble of Socialists, the apostles of the Chandala, who undermine the worker's instincts, his pleasure, his sense of contentment with his petty existence – who make him envious and teach him revenge. Wrong never lies in unequal rights; it lies in the assertion of 'equal' rights. What is *bad*? But I have already answered: all that proceeds from weakness, from envy, from *revenge*. – The anarchist and the Christian have a common ancestry.

58

In point of fact, the end for which one lies makes a great difference: whether one preserves thereby or *destroys*. There is a perfect likeness between *Christian* and *anarchist*: their object, their instinct, points only towards destruction. One need only turn to history for proof of this: there it appears with appalling clarity. We have just studied a code of religious legislation whose object it was to convert the conditions which cause life to *flourish* into an 'eternal' social organisation, – Christianity found its mission in putting an end to such an organisation, *because life flourished under it*. There the benefits that reason had produced during long ages of experiment and insecurity were applied to the most remote uses, and an effort was made to bring home a harvest that should be as large, as rich and as complete as possible; here, on the contrary, the harvest is *blighted* overnight. That which stood there *aere perennius*, the *imperium Romanum*, the most magnificent form of organisation under difficult conditions that has ever been achieved, and compared to which everything before it and after it appears as patchwork, bungling, *dilettantism* – those holy anarchists made it a matter of 'piety' to destroy 'the world', *which is to say*, the *imperium Romanum*, so that in the end not a stone stood upon another – and even Germans and other such louts were able to become its masters. The Christian and the anarchist: both are *décadents*; both are incapable of any act that is not disintegrating, poisonous, degenerating, *bloodsucking*; both have an instinct of *mortal hatred* of everything that stands up, and is great, and has durability, and promises life a future. Christianity was the vampire of the *imperium Romanum* – overnight it destroyed the vast achievement of the Romans: the conquest of the soil for a great culture *that could await its time*. Can it be that this fact is not yet understood? The *imperium Romanum* that we know, and that the history of the Roman provinces teaches us to know better and better – this most admirable of all works of art in the grand style was merely the beginning, and the structure to follow was designed to *prove* itself through thousands of years. To this day, nothing on a like scale *sub specie aeterni* has been brought into being or even dreamed of! – This organisation was strong enough to withstand bad emperors: the accident of personality has nothing to do with such things – the *first* principle of all genuinely great architecture. But it was not strong enough to stand up to the *most corrupt* of all forms of corruption – against *Christians*...These stealthy worms, which under the cover of night, mist and duplicity crept upon every individual, sucking him dry of all earnest interest in *real* things, of all instinct for *reality* – this cowardly, effeminate and sugar-coated gang gradually alienated all 'souls', bit by bit, from that colossal edifice, turning against it all the meritorious, manly and noble natures that had found in the cause of Rome their own cause, their own serious purpose, their own *pride*. The underhanded bigotry, the secrecy of the conventicle, concepts as black as hell, such as the sacrifice of the innocent, the *unio mystica* in the drinking of blood, above all, the slowly rekindled fire of revenge, of Chandala revenge – all *that* sort of thing became master of Rome: the same kind of religion which, in a pre-existent form, Epicurus had combated. One has but to read Lucretius to know *what* Epicurus made war upon – *not* paganism, but 'Christianity', which is to say, the corruption of souls by means of the concepts of guilt, punishment and immortality. – He combated the *subterranean* cults, the whole of latent Christianity – to deny immortality was already a form of genuine *salvation*. – Epicurus had triumphed, and every respectable intellect in Rome was Epicurean – *when Paul appeared*. Paul, the Chandala hatred against Rome, against 'the world', in the flesh and inspired by genius – the Jew, the *eternal* Jew *par excellence*. What he saw was how, with the aid of the small sectarian Christian movement that stood apart from Judaism, a 'world fire' might be kindled; how, with the symbol of 'God on the cross', all secret rebellions, all the fruits of anarchist agitation in the Empire, might be amalgamated into one immense power. 'Salvation is of the Jews.' – Christianity is the formula for exceeding *and* summing up the subterranean cults of all varieties, that of Osiris, that of the Great Mother, that of Mithras, for instance: in his discernment of this fact the genius of Paul showed itself. His instinct was here so sure that, with reckless violence to the truth, he put the ideas which lent fascination to every sort of Chandala religion into the mouth of the 'Saviour' as his own inventions, and not only into the mouth – he *made* out of him something that even a priest of Mithras could understand. This was his revelation at Damascus: he grasped the fact that he *needed* belief in immortality in order to rob 'the world' of its value, that the concept of 'hell' would master Rome – that the notion of a 'beyond' is the *death of life*. Nihilist and Christian: they rhyme in German, and they do more than rhyme.

59

The whole labour of the ancient world *in vain*: I have no word to describe the feelings that such an enormity arouses in me. – And, considering the fact that its labour was merely preparatory, that with granite self-confidence it laid only the foundations for a work to go on for thousands of years, the whole *meaning* of antiquity disappears!... To what end the Greeks? To what end the Romans? – All the prerequisites to a learned culture, all the *methods* of science, were already there; man had already perfected the great and incomparable art of reading profitably – that first necessity to the tradition of culture, the unity of the sciences; the natural sciences, in alliance with mathematics and mechanics, were on the right track – *the sense of fact*, the last and more valuable of all the senses, had its schools, and its traditions already centuries old! Is all this properly understood? Everything *essential* to the beginning of the work was ready; – and the *most* essential, it cannot be said too often, are methods, and also the most difficult to develop, and the longest opposed by habit and laziness. What we have today reconquered, with unspeakable self-discipline, for ourselves – for certain bad instincts, certain Christian instincts, still lurk in our bodies – that is to say, a keen eye for reality, a cautious hand, patience and seriousness in the least things, the whole *integrity* of knowledge – all these things were already there more than two thousand years ago! *More*, there was also a refined and excellent tact and taste! *Not* as mere brain-drilling! *Not* as 'German' culture, with its loutish manners! But as body, as bearing, as instinct – in short, as reality. *All in vain*! Overnight it became merely a memory! – The Greeks! The Romans! The nobility of instinct, taste, methodical inquiry, genius for organisation and administration, faith in and the *will* to secure the future of man, a great Yes to everything entering into the *imperium Romanum* and palpable to all the senses, a grand style that was beyond mere art, but had become reality, truth, *life* – All overwhelmed in a night, but not by a convulsion of nature! Not trampled to death by Teutons and others of heavy hoof! But brought to shame by crafty, sneaking, invisible, anaemic vampires! Not conquered – only sucked dry!...Hidden vengefulness, petty envy, became *master*! Everything wretched, intrinsically ailing and invaded by bad feelings, the whole *ghetto existence* of the soul, was at once *on top*! – One needs but read any of the Christian agitators, for example, St Augustine, in order to realise, in order to smell, what filthy fellows rose to the top. It would be an error, however, to assume that there was any lack of understanding in the leaders of the Christian movement: – oh, but they were clever, clever to the point of holiness, these fathers of the Church! What they lacked was something quite different. Nature neglected – perhaps forgot – to give them even the most modest endowment of respectable, of upright, of *cleanly* instincts. Between ourselves, they are not even men. If Islam despises Christianity, it has a thousand-fold right to do so: Islam at least assumes that it is dealing with *men*.

60

Christianity destroyed for us the whole harvest of ancient culture, and later it also destroyed for us the whole harvest of the culture of Islam. The wonderful culture of the Moors in Spain, which was fundamentally nearer to *us* and appealed more to our senses and tastes than that of Rome and Greece, was *trampled* (– I do not say by what sort of feet –) Why? Because it had to thank noble and manly instincts for its origin – because it said Yes to life, even to the rare and refined luxury of Moorish life!...The crusaders later made war on something before which it would have been more fitting for them to have grovelled in the dust – a culture beside which even that of our nineteenth century seems very poor and very 'senile'. – What they wanted, of course, was booty: the Orient was rich. Let us put to one side our prejudices! The crusades were a higher form of piracy, nothing more! The German nobility, which is fundamentally a Viking nobility, was in its element there: the Church knew only too well how the German nobility was to be *won*. The German noble, always the 'Swiss guard' of the Church, always in the service of every bad instinct of the Church – *but well paid*. Consider the fact that it is precisely the aid of German swords and German blood and valour that has enabled the Church to carry through its war to the death upon everything noble on earth! At this point a host of painful questions suggest themselves. The German nobility stands *outside* the history of the higher culture: the reason is obvious Christianity, alcohol – the two *great* means of corruption. Intrinsically there should be no more choice between Islam and Christianity than there is between an Arab and a Jew. The decision is already reached; nobody remains at liberty to choose here. Either a man is a Chandala or he is not. 'War to the knife with Rome! Peace and friendship with Islam!': this was the feeling, this was the *act*, of that great free spirit, that genius among German emperors, Friedrich II. What! Must a German first be a genius, a free spirit, before he can feel *decently*? I cannot make out how a German could ever feel *Christian* ...

61

Here it becomes necessary to call up a memory that must be a hundred times more painful to Germans. The Germans have destroyed for Europe the last great harvest of culture that Europe was ever to reap – the *Renaissance*. Is it understood at last, *will* it ever be understood, *what* the Renaissance was? *The revaluation of Christian values* – an attempt by all available means, all instincts and all the resources of genius to bring about the triumph of the *opposite* values, the more *noble* values. This has been the one great war of the past; there has never been a more critical question than that of the Renaissance – it is *my* question too; there has never been a form of *attack* more fundamental, more direct, or more violently delivered by a whole front upon the centre of the enemy! To attack at the critical place, at the very seat of Christianity, and there enthrone the more noble values – that is to say, to *insinuate* them into the instincts, into the most fundamental needs and appetites of those sitting there. I see before me the *possibility* of a perfectly heavenly enchantment and spectacle:– it seems to me to scintillate with all the vibrations of a fine and delicate beauty, and within it there is an art so divine, so infernally divine, that one might search in vain for thousands of years for another such possibility; I see a spectacle so rich in significance and at the same time so wonderfully full of paradox that it should arouse all the gods on Olympus to immortal laughter – *Cesare Borgia as pope*!...Am I understood?...Well then, *that* would have been the sort of triumph that *I* alone am longing for today –: by it Christianity would have been *swept away*! – What happened? A German monk, Luther, came to Rome. This monk, with all the vengeful instincts of an unsuccessful priest in him, raised a rebellion *against* the Renaissance in Rome. Instead of grasping, with profound gratitude, the miracle that had taken place: the conquest of Christianity at its *capital* – instead of this, his hatred was stimulated by the spectacle. A religious man thinks only of himself. – Luther saw only the *depravity* of the papacy at the very moment when the opposite was becoming apparent: the old corruption, the *peccatum originale*, Christianity itself, no longer occupied the papal throne! Instead, there was life! Instead, there was the triumph of life! Instead, there was a great Yes to all lofty, beautiful and daring things! ... And Luther *restored the Church*: he attacked it. The Renaissance – an event without meaning, a great futility! – Ah, these Germans, what they have not cost us! *Futility* – that has always been the work of the Germans. – The Reformation; Leibniz; Kant and so-called German philosophy; the 'Wars of Liberation'; the *Reich* – every time a futile substitute for something that once existed, for something *irrecoverable*. These Germans, I confess, are *my* enemies: I despise all their uncleanliness in concept and valuation, their cowardice before every honest Yes and No. For nearly a thousand years they have tangled and confused everything their fingers have touched; they have on their conscience all the half-way measures, all the three-eighths-way measures, that Europe is sick of – they also have on their conscience the uncleanest variety of Christianity that exists, and the most incurable and indestructible – Protestantism. If mankind never rids itself of Christianity the *Germans* will be to blame ...

62

With this I come to a conclusion and pronounce my judgement. I *condemn* Christianity; I bring against the Christian Church the most terrible of all the accusations that an accuser has ever had in his mouth. It is, to me, the greatest of all imaginable corruptions; it seeks to work the ultimate corruption, the worst possible corruption. The Christian Church has left nothing untouched by its depravity; it has turned every value into worthlessness, every truth into a lie and every integrity into baseness of soul. Let anyone dare to speak to me of its 'humanitarian' blessings! Its deepest necessities range it against any effort to *abolish* distress; it lives by distress; it *creates* distress to make *itself* immortal. For example, the worm of sin: it was the Church that first endowed mankind with this misery! – The 'equality of souls before God' – this fraud, this *pretext* for the *rancune* of all the base-minded – this explosive concept, ending in revolution, the modern idea, and the notion of overthrowing the whole social order – this is *Christian* dynamite. 'Humanitarian' blessings of Christianity! To breed out of *humanitas* a self-contradiction, an art of self-violation, a will to lie at any price, an aversion and contempt for all good and honest instincts! All this, to me, is the 'humanitarianism' of Christianity! – Parasitism as the *only* practice of the Church; with its anaemic and 'holy' ideals, sucking all the blood, all the love, all the hope out of life; the beyond as the will to deny all reality; the cross as the distinguishing mark of the most subterranean conspiracy ever heard of – against health, beauty, well-being, intellect, *kindness* of soul – *against life itself* ...

This eternal accusation against Christianity I shall inscribe on all walls, wherever walls are to be found – I have letters that even the blind will be able to see. I call Christianity the one great curse, the one great intrinsic depravity, the one great instinct of revenge, for which no means are venomous enough, or secret, subterranean and *small* enough – I call it the one immortal blemish upon the human race ...

And mankind reckons *time* from the *dies nefastus* when this fatality arose – from the *first* day of Christianity! – *Why not rather from its last?* – *From today?* – Revaluation of all values! ...

Translated by H. L. Mencken with modifications

Ecce Homo: How One Becomes What One Is, 1888

Why I am so wise

3

First version
This *dual* series of experiences, this means of access to two worlds that seem so separate, finds an exact reflection in my own nature – I am a *Doppelgänger*, I have a 'second' face, as well as a first. And perhaps also a third...The very nature of my origin allowed me an outlook transcending merely local, merely national and limited horizons, it cost me no effort to be a 'good European'. On the other hand, I am perhaps more German than modern Germans, mere citizens of the German *Reich* could possibly be – I, the last *anti-political* German. And yet my ancestors were Polish noblemen: it is owing to them that I have so much race instinct in my blood. Who knows? perhaps even the *liberum veto*. When I think of how often I have been accosted as a Pole when travelling, even by Poles themselves, and how seldom I have been taken for a German, it seems to me as if I belonged to those who have but a sprinkling of German in them. But my mother, Franziska Oehler, is at any rate very German; as is also my paternal grandmother, Erdmuthe Krause. The latter spent the whole of her youth in good old Weimar, not without coming into contact with Goethe's circle. Her brother, Krause, professor of theology in Königsberg, was called to the post of general superintendent at Weimar after Herder's death. It is not unlikely that her mother, my great-grandmother, appears in young Goethe's diary under the name of 'Muthgen'. The husband of her second marriage was superintendent Nietzsche of Eilenburg; on 10 October, 1813, the year of the great war, when Napoleon with his general staff entered Eilenburg, she gave birth to a son. As a Saxon, she was a great admirer of Napoleon; perhaps I still am, too. My father, born in 1813, died in 1849. Before taking over the pastorship of the parish of Röcken, not far from Lützen, he had lived for some years in the castle of Altenburg, where he had charge of the education of the four princesses. His pupils are now the Queen of Hanover, the Grand Duchess Constantine, the Grand Duchess of Altenburg and the Princess Therese of Saxe-Altenburg. He was full of pious respect for the Prussian king, Friedrich Wilhelm IV, from whom he obtained his

living at Röcken; the events of 1848 caused him great sorrow. As I was born on 15 October, the birthday of the above-named king, I naturally received the Hohenzollern name *Friedrich* Wilhelm. There was at all events one advantage in the choice of this day: my birthday throughout my entire childhood was a public holiday. – I regard it as a great privilege to have had such a father: it even seems to me that this exhausts all that I can claim in the matter of privileges – *not* including life, the great Yes to life. What I owe to him above all is this, that I do not need any special intention, but merely patience, in order to enter involuntarily into a world of higher and finer things: there I am at home, there alone does my profoundest passion have free play. The fact that I almost paid for this privilege with my life, certainly does not make it a poor bargain. – In order to understand even a little of my *Zarathustra*, perhaps a man must be similarly conditioned as I am – with one foot *beyond* life.

Revised version
I consider the fact that I had such a father as a great privilege: the peasants he preached to – for, after he had spent several years at the court of Altenburg, he was a preacher in his final years – said that the angels must look like he did. And with this I touch on the question of race. I am a pure-blooded Polish nobleman, in whom there is no drop of bad blood, least of all German blood. When I look for my profoundest opposite, the incalculable pettiness of the instincts, I always find my mother and my sister – to be related to such *canaille* would be a blasphemy against my divinity. The treatment I have received from my mother and my sister up to the present fills me with inexpressible horror: there is an absolutely hellish machine at work here, operating with infallible certainty at the precise moment when I am most vulnerable – at my highest moments... for then one needs all one's strength to counter such a poisonous viper... physiological contiguity renders such a *disharmonia praestabilita* possible... But I confess that the deepest objection to the 'eternal recurrence', my real idea from the abyss, is always my mother and my sister. – However, even as a Pole I am an incredible atavism. One would have to go back centuries in order to find this noblest of races ever to exist on earth exhibiting its instincts as pristinely as I exhibit them. Over and against everything today that calls itself *noblesse* I possess a sovereign feeling of distinction, – I would not do the young German Kaiser the honour of being my coachman. There is one single case in which I acknowledge my equal – I confess it with profound gratitude. Frau Cosima Wagner is the noblest nature by far and, in order not to leave a single word unsaid, I say that Richard Wagner was by far the man most akin to me... The rest is silence... All prevailing concepts about degrees of consanguinity are utter physiological nonsense. Even today the Pope insists on trafficking in such absurdity. One is *least* akin to one's parents: it would be the utmost mark of vulgarity to be related to one's parents. Higher natures have their origins infinitely farther back, from them a great deal had to be accumulated, saved

and hoarded over long periods of time. The great individuals are the oldest: I do not understand it, but Julius Caesar could be my father – or Alexander, this Dionysus incarnate... At the very moment I am writing this, the mail brings me a Dionysus-head ...

Why I write such good books

1

I am one thing, my writings are another. Here, before I speak of the books themselves, I shall touch on the question of their intelligibility or *un*intelligibility. I shall do this in as casual a manner as the occasion demands; for the time has by no means come for this question. My time has not yet come either; some are born posthumously. One day institutions will be needed in which men will live and teach, as I understand living and teaching; maybe, also, by that time, chairs will be founded and endowed for the interpretation of *Zarathustra*. But I should regard it as a complete contradiction of myself if I expected to find ears *and hands* for my truths today: the fact that no one hears me, that no one accepts my ideas today, is not only understandable, it even seems right to me. I do not wish to be mistaken for another – and to this end I must not mistake myself. To repeat what I have already said, I can point to but few instances of ill-will in my life: and as for literary ill-will, I could mention scarcely a single example. On the other hand, I have met with far too much *pure foolishness*! It seems to me that to take one of my books into his hands is one of the rarest honours that a man can pay himself – even supposing that he first takes off his shoes, not to mention his boots... When on one occasion Dr Heinrich von Stein honestly complained that he could not understand a word of my *Zarathustra*, I said to him that this was just as it should be: to have understood six sentences in that book – that is to say, to have *experienced* them – raises a man to a higher level among mortals than 'modern' men can attain. With this feeling of distance how could I even wish to be read by the 'moderns' whom I know! My triumph is just the opposite of what Schopenhauer's was – I say *'non legor, non legar'*. – Not that I should like to underestimate the pleasure I have derived from the *innocence* with which my works have frequently been contradicted. As late as last summer, at a time when I was attempting, perhaps by means of my weighty, all-too-weighty literature, to throw the rest of literature off balance, a professor from the University of Berlin kindly suggested that I ought to make use of a different form: no one could read such stuff as I wrote. – Finally, it was not Germany, but Switzerland that presented me with the two most extreme cases. An article by Dr V. Widmann in the *Bund* about *Beyond Good and Evil*, with the title 'Nietzsche's Dangerous Book', and an overview of all my works by Herr Karl Spitteler, also in the *Bund*, constitute a maximum in my life – I shall not say of what... The latter treated my *Zarathustra*, for instance, as 'advanced exercises in style' and expressed the wish that I concern myself with content too at some later point; Dr Widmann assured me of his respect for the courage I showed in endeavouring to abolish all decent feelings. Thanks to some small accident of faith, every sentence in these criticisms seemed, with a consistency that I could not but admire, to be an inverted truth. In fact, it was most remarkable that all one had to do was to 'revalue all values' in order to hit the nail on the head with regard to me, instead of striking my head with the nail... I am more particularly anxious therefore to come up with an explanation. After all, no one can draw more out of things, books included, than he already knows. A man has no ears for that to which experience has given him no access. To take an extreme case, suppose a book contains simply incidents which lie quite outside the range of general or even rare experience – suppose it to be the *first* language to express a whole series of experiences. In this case nothing it contains will really be heard at all and, thanks to an auditory illusion, people will believe that where nothing is heard there is nothing to hear... This, at least, has been my usual experience and proves, if you will, the originality of my experience. He who thought he had understood something in my work had as a rule adjusted something in it to his own image – not infrequently the very opposite of myself, an 'idealist', for instance. He who understood nothing in my work would deny that I was worth considering at all. – The word 'overman', which designates a type of supreme achievement, as opposed to 'modern' men, to 'good' men, to Christians and other nihilists – a word which in the mouth of Zarathustra, the annihilator of morality, acquires a very profound meaning – is understood almost everywhere, and with perfect innocence, in the light of those very values whose opposite Zarathustra was meant to represent – that is to say, as an 'ideal' type, a higher kind of man, half-'saint' and half-'genius'... Other scholarly oxen have suspected me of Darwinism on account of this word: even the 'hero cult' of that great unconscious and involuntary swindler Carlyle, – a cult which I repudiated with such roguish malice – was recognised in my doctrine. Once, when I whispered to a man that he would do better to seek for the Overman in a Cesare Borgia than in a Parsifal, he could not believe his ears. The fact that I am quite free from curiosity in regard to criticisms of my books, more particularly when they appear in newspapers, will have to be forgiven me. My friends and my publishers know this and never mention such things to me. In one particular case, I once saw all the sins that had been committed against a single book – it was *Beyond Good and Evil*; I could tell you a nice story about it. Would you believe it? Is it possible that the *Nationalzeitung* – a Prussian newspaper, to keep my foreign readers informed: for my own part, if I may say so, I read only the *Journal des Débats* – actually managed to understand the book as a 'sign of the times', as the real and genuine *Junker philosophy*, for which the *Kreuzzeitung* had not sufficient courage?

The case of Wagner: A musician's problem

2

But here nothing shall stop me from being blunt and from telling the Germans a few hard truths: *who else would do it?* I refer to their laxity *in historicis*. Not only have German historians entirely lost the *breadth of vision* which enables one to grasp the course of culture and the values of culture; not only are they all political (or Church) buffoons; but they have also actually *banned* this very breadth of vision. A man must first and foremost be 'German', he must belong to the 'race'; only then can he pass judgement on all values and lack of values *in historicis* – only then can he establish them... To be German is in itself an argument, *Deutschland, Deutschland über alles* is a principle; the Teutons represent the 'moral world order' in history; compared with the *imperium Romanum*, they are the upholders of freedom; compared with the eighteenth century, they are the restorers of morality, of the 'categorical imperative'. There is such a thing as historiography that is *reichsdeutsche*; there is even, I fear, an anti-Semitic one – there is also a *court* historiography, and Herr von Treitschke is not ashamed... An idiotic opinion *in historicis*, an observation made by Vischer – an aesthetic Swabian, fortunately a deceased one – recently made the rounds of the German newspapers as a 'truth' to which every German *must assent*. The observation was this: 'The Renaissance *and* the Reformation only together constitute a whole – the aesthetic rebirth *and* the moral rebirth.' When I hear such things, I lose all patience and I feel inclined, I even feel it my duty, to tell the Germans *just what* they have on their conscience. *Every great crime against culture for the last four centuries lies on their conscience*... And always for the same reason, always owing to their innermost *cowardice* in the face of reality, which is also cowardice in the face of truth; always owing to their untruthfulness which has become almost instinctive in them – in short, their 'idealism'. It was the Germans who caused Europe to lose the fruits, the whole meaning of her last period of greatness – the period of the Renaissance. At a moment when a higher order of values, the noble values, that said Yes to life, and that guaranteed a future, had succeeded in triumphing over the opposite values, the *values of degeneration*, in the very seat of Christianity itself – and *even in the instincts of those sitting there* – Luther, that cursed monk, not only restored the Church, but, what was a thousand times worse, restored Christianity, and at a time too when it lay defeated. Christianity, the denial of the will to life, exalted to a religion! Luther was an impossible monk who, thanks to his own 'impossibility', attacked the Church and in so doing restored it! Catholics would be perfectly justified in celebrating feasts in honour of Luther and in producing festival plays in his honour. Luther and the 'moral rebirth'! May all psychology go to the devil! Without a shadow of a doubt the Germans are idealists. On two occasions when, at the cost of enormous courage and self-control, an upright, unequivocal and perfectly scientific attitude of mind had been attained, the Germans were able to discover backstairs leading down to the old 'ideal' again, compromises between truth and the 'ideal', and, in short, formulas for the right to reject science and to perpetrate lies. Leibniz and Kant – these two great breaks upon the intellectual honesty of Europe! Finally, at a moment when there appeared on the bridge that spanned two centuries of *décadence* a superior force of genius and will became visible which was strong enough to consolidate Europe and to convert it into a political and *economic* unity for the sake of a world government – the Germans, with their Wars of Liberation, cheated Europe out of the meaning, the miracle of meaning, in the existence of Napoleon. As a result, they laid on their conscience everything that followed, everything that exists today, the most *anti-cultural* sickness and unreason there is, nationalism – this *névrose nationale* from which Europe is suffering acutely; this immortalising of European particularism, of *petty* politics. They have robbed Europe itself of its significance, of its reason – and have steered it into a *dead end*. Is there anyone except me who knows a way out of this *dead end*? – A task which would be great enough to *unite* nations again?

Why I am a destiny

1

I know my fate. There will come a day when my name will recall the memory of something formidable – a crisis the like of which has never been known on earth, the memory of the most profound clash of consciences and the passing of a sentence upon all which had been believed, demanded and hallowed so far. I am not a man, I am dynamite. – And with all that, there is nothing in me of a founder of a religion. – Religions are affairs for the mob; after coming in contact with a religious man, I always feel that I must wash my hands…I require no 'believers', it is my opinion that I am too full of malice to believe even in myself; I never address myself to the masses…I am horribly frightened that one day I shall be pronounced 'holy'. You will understand why I publish this book *beforehand* – it is to prevent people from wronging me. I refuse to be a saint; I would rather be a buffoon. Maybe I am a buffoon. And I am in spite of that, or rather *not* in spite of it, the mouthpiece of truth; for nobody has ever existed more mendacious than a saint. But my truth is *terrible*: because *lies* have been called truth so far. *Revaluation of all Values*, this is my formula for mankind's supreme self-examination – a step which in me became flesh and genius. My fate ordained that I should be the first, *decent* human being, and that I should feel myself opposed to the lies of millennia. I was the first to *discover* truth, and for the simple reason that I was the first who became conscious of lies as lies – that is to say, I smelled it as such. My genius resides in my nostrils. I contradict as no one has contradicted before, and am nevertheless the opposite of a No-saying spirit. I am the *bearer of glad tidings*, the like of which has never existed before; I have discovered tasks of such lofty greatness that, until my time, no one had any idea of such things. Mankind can begin to have fresh hopes, only now that I have lived. Thus, I am necessarily a man of fate. For when truth enters into a fight against the lies of ages, upheavals are bound to ensue, and a convulsion of earthquakes, followed by a moving of mountains and valleys, such as the world has never yet imagined even in its dreams. The concept of politics will have then merged entirely into a war of spirits. All power structures from the old order of society will have exploded – for they are all based on lies: there will be wars, the like of which have never been seen on earth before. It is only beginning with me that the earth knows *grand politics*.

Translated by A. Ludovici with modifications

Nachlass Fragments, 1887–1888

KSA 12 7[6] 1883–88 WP 287

My philosophy aims at a new order of rank: not at an individualistic morality. The spirit of the herd should rule within the herd – but not beyond it: the leaders of the herd require a fundamentally different valuation for their own actions, the same applies to the independent ones, or the 'beasts of prey', etc.

KSA 12 10[17] 1887–88 WP 866

The necessity to show *that a counter-movement is inevitably associated* with any increasingly economical use of men and mankind, with an ever more closely intertwined 'machinery' of interests and achievements. I call this counter-movement the *separation of the luxurious surplus of mankind:* by means of it a *stronger* type, a higher type, must come to light, which has other conditions for its origin and for its maintenance than the average man. My concept, my *parable* for this type is, as you know, the word 'Overman'.

Along the first road, which can now be completely surveyed, arose adaptation, flattening, the higher Chinese way, modesty in the instincts, satisfaction in the belittlement of man – a kind of *standstill at the level of man*. If ever we get that inevitably imminent general control of the economy of the earth, then mankind as machinery *can* find its best purpose in the service of it: as an enormous piece of clockwork consisting of ever smaller and ever more subtly adapted wheels; as an ever-growing superfluousness of all dominating and commanding elements; as a whole of enormous energy, whose individual factors represent *minimal strengths and values*. As opposed to this dwarfing and adaptation of men to a specialised kind of utility, a reverse movement is needed – the creation of the *synthetic, accumulating, justifying* man for whom the turning of mankind into a machine is a precondition of existence, as a lower frame on which he can devise his *higher mode* of existence ...

He is equally in need of the *enmity* of the masses, of those who are 'levelled down', he requires that feeling of distance from them; he stands upon them, he lives on them. This higher form of *aristocracy* is the form of the future. – To put it in a moral way, the collective machinery above described, that solidarity of all wheels, represents the most extreme example in the *exploitation of mankind:* but it presupposes the existence of those for whom such an exploitation would have some *meaning.* Otherwise it would signify, as a matter of fact, merely the general depreciation of the type man – a *retrograde phenomenon* on a grand scale.

Readers are beginning to see that I am combating *economic* optimism: as if the general welfare of everybody must necessarily increase with the growing self-sacrifice of everybody. The very reverse seems to me to be the case: *the self-sacrifice of everybody amounts to a collective loss*; man *is diminished*: – so that nobody knows anymore what end this monstrous purpose has served. A wherefore? A *new* wherefore? – this is what mankind requires …

KSA 12 10[31] 1887–88 WP 877

The Revolution made Napoleon possible: that is its justification. We ought to desire the anarchical collapse of the whole of our civilisation if such a reward were to be its result. Napoleon made nationalism possible: that is the latter's excuse. …

KSA 12 10[82] 1887–88 WP 784

Individualism is a modest and still unconscious form of 'will to power'; here, an individual seems to think it sufficient *to free himself* from the superiority of society (whether this superiority is that of the state or of the Church …) He does not set himself up in opposition as a *person*, but merely as an individual; he represents all individuals against the collectivity. That is to say: he instinctively places himself *on a level with every individual*; what he combats he does not combat as a person, but as individual against the collectivity.

Socialism is merely an *agitatory measure of the individualist*: he recognises the fact that in order to attain to something, men must organise themselves into a general movement, into a 'power'. But what he requires is not society as the object of the individual, but society *as a means of making many individuals possible*: – This is the instinct of socialists, though they frequently deceive themselves on this point (– apart from the fact that they, in order to make their kind prevail, often have to deceive others) Altruistic moral preaching in the service of individual egoism: one of the most common frauds of the *nineteenth* century.

Anarchism is also merely an *agitatory measure of socialism*; with it the socialist inspires fear, with fear he begins to fascinate and to terrorise: but what he does above all is to draw all courageous and reckless people to his side, even in spirit.

In spite of all this: *individualism* is the most modest stage of the will to power.

When one has reached a certain degree of independence, one always longs for more: *separation* occurs in proportion to the degree of force: the individual is no longer content to regard himself as equal to everybody, he actually *seeks for his peers* – he makes himself stand out from others. Individualism is followed by a development in *groups and organs*: correlative tendencies joining together and becoming active as a power, between these centres of power, friction, war, awareness of the forces on either side, reciprocity, rapprochement, the regulation of mutual services. Finally: an *order of rank*. NB.

1. the individuals emancipate themselves
2. they enter combat, and reach an agreement concerning 'equality of rights' (– justice – as an end).
3. once this is reached, the actual differences in degrees of power begin to make themselves felt, and to a greater extent than before (the reason being that on the whole peace is established, and innumerable small centres of power begin to create differences which formerly were scarcely noticeable). Now the individuals begin to form groups; these strive for privileges and preponderance The combat starts afresh in a milder form.

NB. One wants *freedom* only when one has no power. Once power is obtained, a preponderance thereof is the next thing one wants; if this is not achieved (owing to the fact that one is still too weak for it), then one wants *'justice'*, i.e. *'equal power'*.

KSA 12 10[135] 1887–88 WP 211

Christianity is possible as the *most private* form of life; it presupposes the existence of a narrow, isolated, absolutely unpolitical society – it belongs to the conventicle. On the other hand, a 'Christian state', 'Christian politics' – are only wishful prayers in the mouths of those who have *good reasons* to utter these wishful prayers. That they also speak of a 'God of legions' as a general chief of staff: they do not fool anybody with this. Even the Christian prince practises the politics of Machiavelli: provided namely that he does not practise bad politics.

KSA 12 10[188] 1887–88 WP 216

How even the 'masters' can become Christians. – It lies in the instinct of a *community* (clan, family, herd, commune) to regard all those conditions and aspirations, to which it owes its preservation, as in themselves *valuable*, for instance: obedience, mutual assistance, respect, moderation, pity – in order to *suppress* everything that happens to stand in the way of the above.

It lies likewise in the instinct of the *rulers* (whether they are individuals or classes) to patronise and applaud those virtues which make their subjects *amenable* and *submissive* (– *conditions* and passions which may be utterly different from their own).

The *instinct of the herd* and the *instinct of the rulers agree* in praising a certain number of qualities and conditions: but for different reasons, the first do so out of direct egoism, the second out of indirect egoism.

The submission on the part of master races to Christianity is essentially the result of the conviction that Christianity is a *religion for the herd*, that it teaches *obedience*: in short, that Christians are more easily ruled than non-Christians. With a hint of this nature, the Pope, even today, recommends Christian propaganda to the Emperor of China.

It should also be added that the seductive power of the Christian ideal works most strongly upon natures that love danger, adventure and contrasts, that love everything *that entails a risk*, while at the same time a *non plus ultra* of powerful feeling may be attained. In this respect, one has only to think of St Theresa, surrounded by the heroic instincts of her brothers: – Christianity appears in those circumstances as a form of excess of the will, of the strength of the will, as a sort of Quixotic heroism ...

KSA 13 11[31] 1887–88 WP 868

General aspect of the future European: the latter regarded as the most intelligent servile animal, very industrious, at bottom very modest, inquisitive to excess, multifarious, pampered, weak of will – a chaos of cosmopolitan passions and intelligences. How would it be possible for a *stronger* type to be bred from him? A type with classical taste? The classical taste: this is the will to simplicity, to reinforcement, to happiness made visible, the will to the terrible, the courage to psychological *nakedness* (– simplification is a consequence of the will to reinforcement; allowing happiness as well as nakedness to become visible is a consequence of the will to the terrible ...). In order to fight one's way out of that chaos and into this form, a certain constraint is necessary: one must have the choice between either going under or *prevailing*. A ruling race can only rise out of terrible and violent beginnings. Problem: where are the *barbarians* of the twentieth century? Obviously, they will only show themselves and consolidate themselves after enormous socialistic crises, – they will consist of those elements which are capable of the *greatest hardness towards themselves* and which can guarantee the *most enduring will* ...

KSA 13 11[54] 1887–88 WP 304

Concerning the dominion of virtue. How virtue is made to dominate
Ein tractatus politicus by Friedrich Nietzsche
Foreword
This political treatise is not for just anybody: it treats the *politics* of virtue, virtue's means and ways to *power*. For virtue to strive for dominion – who

would want to forbid it? But *how* it does it – ! One cannot believe it...Thus is this treatise not for just anybody. We wrote it for the use of all those who are interested, not so much in the process of becoming virtuous as in that of *making* others virtuous – in how virtue is made to dominate. I even intend to prove that in order to desire this one thing, the dominion of virtue, the other must be systematically avoided; that is to say, one must abstain from becoming virtuous. This sacrifice is great: but such an end is perhaps a sufficient reward for such a sacrifice. And even greater sacrifices!...And some of the most famous moralists have risked as much. For these, indeed, had already recognised and anticipated the truth which is to be revealed for the first time in this treatise: that the *dominion of virtue is virtually only attainable by the use of the same means* which are employed in the attainment of any other dominion, in any case not *by means* of virtue itself ...

As I have already said, this treatise deals with the politics of virtue: it postulates an ideal of these politics; it describes it as it ought to be, if anything at all can be perfect on this earth. Now, no philosopher can be in any doubt as to what the type of perfection is in politics; it is, of course, Machiavellianism. But Machiavellianism which is *pur, sans mélange, cru, vert, dans toute sa force, dans toute son âpreté*, is superhuman, divine, transcendental and can never be achieved by men – the most men can do is to approximate it...Even in this narrower kind of politics, in the politics of virtue, the ideal never seems to have been realised. Plato, too, only touched upon it. Granted that one has eyes for concealed things, one can discover, even in the most impartial and most conscious *moralists* (and this is indeed the name of these moral politicians, of any type of founders of newer moral forces), traces showing that they too paid their tribute to human weakness. *They all aspired to virtue* on their own account – at least in their moments of weariness: and this is the first and most capital error on the part of any moralist – whose duty it is to be an *immoralist in deeds*. That he *must* not *appear* to be the latter is another matter. Or rather it is *not* another matter: such a fundamental self-denial (or, expressed morally: dissimulation) belongs to the moralist's canon and to his own doctrine of duty: without it he can never attain his particular kind of perfection. Freedom from morality *and also from truth*, for the sake of that purpose which rewards every sacrifice: *dominion of morality* – that is the canon. Moralists are in need of the *attitude of virtue* and of the attitude of truth; their error begins when they *yield* to virtue, when they lose control of virtue, when they themselves become *moral* or *true*. A great moralist is, among other things, necessarily a great actor; his danger is that his pose may unconsciously become second nature, just like his ideal, which is to keep his *esse* and his *operari* apart in a divine way; everything he does must be done *sub specie boni* – a lofty, remote and exacting ideal! A *divine* ideal!...And, as a matter of fact, they say that the moralist thus imitates a model which is no less than God himself: God, the greatest Immoralist in deeds that exists, but who nevertheless understands how to remain what He *is*, the *good* God ...

KSA 13 11[127] 1887–88 WP 926

NB. Against *justice*... Against John Stuart Mill: I abhor the man's vulgarity, which says 'What is right for one man is right for another'; 'what you would not, etc., do not unto others'; which wishes to found the whole of human relationships upon *mutual services*, so that every action would appear to be a payment for something done to us. The hypothesis here is ignoble to the last degree: it is taken for granted that there is some sort of *equivalence in value between my actions and your actions*; the most personal value of an action is simply cancelled in this manner (that part of an action which has no equivalent and which cannot be remunerated –). 'Reciprocity' is a great vulgarity; the mere fact that what *I* do *cannot* and *may not* be done by another, that there is *no such thing* as *equivalence* – except in that *most select of sphere* of 'my equals', *inter pares* – ; that in a really profound sense a man never requites because he is something *unique* in himself and can only do *unique* things – this fundamental conviction contains the cause of aristocratic dissociation from the mob, because the latter believes in 'equality' and *consequently* in the feasibility of equivalence and 'reciprocity'.

KSA 13 11[140–42] 1887–88 WP 936

Herd animal ideals – at present culminating as the *highest* standard of value for 'society': Attempt to give them a cosmic, even metaphysical, value

I defend *aristocracy* against them.

A society which would in itself preserve a feeling of respect and *délicatesse* in regard to freedom, must consider itself as an exception, and have an opposing power from which it distinguishes itself, to which it is hostile, upon which it looks down

– the more rights I surrender and the more I level myself down to others, the more deeply do I fall under the dominion of the mediocre and ultimately of the greatest number

– the precondition which an aristocratic society must have in order to maintain a high degree of freedom among its members, is that extreme tension which arises from the presence of the *antagonistic* drive among its members: from the presence of the will to dominate...

if you wanted to do away with strong contrasts and differences of rank, you would also abolish strong love, lofty attitudes of the mind, and the feeling of being-for-itself.

Concerning the *actual* psychology of societies based upon freedom and equality:

what is it that tends to diminish in such a society?

the will to be *responsible for oneself* – a sign of the decline of autonomy

the *ability to defend and to attack*, even in spiritual matters – the power to command

the sense of reverence, of subservience, the ability to be silent

the *great passion*, the great task, tragedy and cheerfulness

KSA 13 11[152] 1887-88 WP 793

My 'future'

a severe polytechnic education

Military service: so that as a rule every man of the higher classes becomes an officer, whatever else he may be

KSA 13 11[235-36] 1887-88 WP 748

A little fresh air! This absurd condition of Europe must not last any longer! Is there a single idea behind this bovine nationalism? What possible value can there be in encouraging these gruff egos when everything today points to greater and common interests?...And that calls itself a 'Christian state'! And close to the higher circles, the court chaplain *canaille*!...And the 'new *Reich*' founded once again upon the most washed-out and despised of ideas, universal suffrage and equal rights for all ...

And *that*, at a moment when the *spiritual dependence* and denationalisation are obvious to all, and when the actual value and meaning of today's culture lies in a reciprocal rapprochement and fructification!

The economic unity of Europe must necessarily come – and with it, as a reaction, the *pacifist movement* ...

The struggling for advantage amidst a condition which is no good: this culture of big cities, of newspapers, of hurry and scurry, and of 'aimlessness'.

A *pacifist* party, free from all sentimentality, which forbids itself and its children to wage war; which forbids recourse to courts of justice; which forswears all fighting, all contradiction, all persecution; for a while the party of the oppressed; and very soon the *great* party. Opposed to everything in the shape of *revenge and resentment*.

A *war* party, proceeding in the opposite direction but with the same thoroughness and severity towards itself –

KSA 13 11[379] 1887-88 WP 209

The Nihilist

The gospel: the announcement that the road to happiness lies open for the lowly and the poor – that all one has to do is to emancipate oneself from all institutions, traditions and the tutelage of the higher classes: thus Christianity is no more than the *typical teaching of socialists*.

Property, acquisitions, fatherland, status and rank, tribunals, the police, the state, the Church, education, art, militarism: so many obstacles in the way of happiness, so many mistakes, snares, devil's artifices, on which the gospel passes sentence...All this is typical of the teaching of socialists.

Behind all this there is the outburst, the explosion of a dislike of the 'masters' that has been growing and growing, the instinct which discerns the happiness of freedom after such long oppression ...

Mostly a symptom of the fact that the inferior classes have been treated too humanely, that their tongues already savour a joy which is forbidden them ... It is not hunger that provokes revolutions, but the fact that the mob have contracted an appetite *en mangeant* ...

KSA 13 11[407] 1887–88 WP 729

...
The *maintenance of the military state* is the very last means of either adhering to the *great tradition* or holding on to it, in consideration of the *superior* or *strong* type of man. And all concepts which perpetuate enmity and distance of rank between states, may on that account seem justified ...
E.g. Nationalism, protective tariffs, – – –
the strong type, as the one who determines values, will be maintained ...

KSA 13 14[6] 1888 WP 51

Will to power as morality
The interrelation of all forms of corruption should be understood; and the Christian form not overlooked
Pascal as type
and also: the socialistic-communist corruption (a result of the Christian one)
the *highest* conception of society according to socialists is the *lowest* in the order of rank among societies the 'Beyond'-corruption: as though outside the real world of becoming there were a world of being

Here, there must be no *compromise*: here, man must eliminate, annihilate, wage war – the Christian-nihilistic standard of value must still be withdrawn from all things and attacked beneath every disguise. For instance, in modern *sociology*, music, pessimism (– all forms of the Christian ideal of values –)

Either one thing *or* the other is *true*: true – that is to say, tending to elevate the type man ...

The priest, the pastor, as objectionable forms of life all education to date, helpless, adrift, without ballast, afflicted with the contradiction of values –

KSA 13 14[29–30] 1888 WP 373

The origin of moral values.
Selfishness has as much value as the physiological value of him who possesses it.

Each individual represents the whole course of evolution (and he is not only, as morality teaches, something that begins at his birth): if he represents the ascent of the line of mankind, his value is, in fact, very great; and the concern about his preservation and the promoting of his growth may even be extreme. (It is the concern about the promise of the future in him which gives the well-constituted individual such an extraordinary right to egoism.) If he represents descending development, decay, chronic sickening: then he has little worth: and the greatest fairness would have him take as little room, strength and sunshine as possible from the well-constituted. In this case society's task is to *suppress egoism* (– for the latter may sometimes manifest itself in an absurd, morbid, and seditious manner –): whether it be a question of single individuals or of whole social classes, which are degenerating and withering away. A teaching and a religion of 'love', of the *suppression* of self-affirmation, of enduring, bearing, helping, of reciprocity in deeds and words may be of the highest value within the confines of such classes, even in the eyes of their rulers: for it restrains the feelings of rivalry, of *ressentiment*, of envy, feelings which are only too natural in the bungled and the botched – and it even deifies for them, under the ideal of humility and of obedience, the life of the slave, the controlled, the poor, the sick, the low. This explains why the ruling classes or races and individuals of all ages have always upheld the cult of unselfishness, the gospel of the lowly, the 'God on the cross'.

The preponderance of an altruistic way of valuing is the result of an instinct for being a failure. Upon examination, this point of view turns out to be: 'I am not worth much': simply a physiological valuation, more plainly still: it is the feeling of impotence, the lack of the great affirmative feelings of power (in muscles, nerves, and ganglia). This valuation gets translated, according to the particular culture of these classes, into a moral or religious judgement (– the ascendancy of religious or moral judgements is always a sign of low culture –): it tries to justify itself in spheres in which it recognises the concept 'value' in general. The interpretation by means of which the Christian sinner tries to understand himself is an attempt at *justifying* his lack of power and of self-confidence: he prefers to feel guilty rather than feel bad for nothing: it is in itself a symptom of decay to need interpretations of this sort. In some cases the bungled and the botched do not look for the reason for their unfortunate condition in their own 'guilt' (as the Christian does), but in society: the socialist, the anarchist, the nihilist, by feeling that his existence is something for which someone must be *guilty*, is the closest relative of the Christian, who also believes that he can more easily endure his ill ease and his wretched constitution when he has found someone whom he can hold *responsible* for it. The instinct of *revenge* and *ressentiment* appears in both cases here as a means of enduring life, as an instinct of self-preservation: just as the preference given to *altruistic* theory and practice. The *hatred of egoism*, whether it be one's own, as in the case of the Christian, or another's, as in the case of the socialist, thus appears as a valuation reached under the predominance of revenge; but also as a wise act of self-preservation on the part of the suffering, in the form of an increase of their feelings of co-operation and solidarity... At bottom, as I have already suggested, the discharge of *ressentiment* which takes place in the act of judging, rejecting, punishing egoism (one's own or another's) is yet another self-preservative instinct on the part of the bungled and the botched. In short: the cult of altruism is merely a particular form of egoism, which regularly appears under certain definite physiological circumstances.

When the socialist, with righteous indignation, calls for 'justice', 'rights', 'equal rights' it only shows that he is oppressed by his inadequate culture, which is unable to understand why he suffers: then again, he also finds pleasure in crying; if he were more at ease he would refrain from crying out in that way: in that case he would find his pleasure elsewhere. The same holds good of the Christian: he curses, condemns and slanders the 'world' – and does not even except himself. But that is no reason for taking his shouting seriously. In both cases we are in the presence of sick people who *feel better* for crying and who find relief in slander.

KSA 13 14[75] 1888 WP 40

The notion *'décadence'*

Decay, decline, waste are, *per se*, in no way open to objection: they are the necessary consequence of life, of vital growth. The phenomenon of *décadence* is just as necessary as any advance and progress in life is: we are not in a position which enables us to *suppress* it. On the contrary, reason *would have it retain its rights*...

It is disgraceful on the part of all socialist systematisers to argue that circumstances and social combinations could be devised which would put an end to all vice, illness, crime, prostitution and poverty... But that is tantamount to condemning *life*... A society is not at liberty to remain young. And even in its prime it must bring forth ordure and decaying matter. The more energetically and daringly it advances, the richer will it be in failures and in deformities, and the nearer it will be to its fall... Age is not done away with by means of institutions. Nor is illness. Nor is vice.

KSA 13 14[182] 1888 WP 864

Why the weak triumph

In short: the sick and the weak have more *sympathy*, are more 'humane' –: the sick and the weak have more *intellect*, are more changeable, more variegated, more entertaining, – more malicious: the sick alone invented *malice* (a morbid precocity is often to be observed among rickety, scrofulous, and tubercular people –)

esprit: the property of older races (Jews, Frenchmen, Chinese) The anti-Semites do not forgive the Jews for having both 'intellect' – and money: anti-Semitism, a name for the 'bungled and botched'

: the fool and the saint – the two most interesting kinds of men.... in close relation the 'genius' the great 'adventurers and criminals'

: the sick and the weak have always had *fascination* on their side, they are more *interesting* than the healthy

And all men, the most healthy in particular, have always been *sick* at certain periods of their lives: – great disturbances of the emotions, the passion for power, love, revenge, are all accompanied by very profound perturbations...

And, as for *décadence*: every man who does not die prematurely manifests it in almost every respect: – he therefore knows from experience the instincts which belong to it –
: for *half his life* nearly every man is décadent.

And finally: woman! *One-half of mankind* is weak, chronically sick, changeable, shifty – woman requires strength in order to cleave to it – she also requires a religion of the weak which glorifies weakness, love, and modesty as divine ... or, better still, she makes the strong weak – she *rules* when she succeeds in overcoming the strong... woman has always conspired with décadent types, the priests, against the 'mighty,' the 'strong,' *men* – woman put aside *children* for the cult of piety, pity, love: – the *mother* represents altruism *convincingly* ...

Finally: the increasing civilisation with its necessary correlatives, the increase of morbid elements, of the *neurotic-psychiatric* and of the *criminalistic* ... a sort of *intermediary species* arises, the *artist*, separated from the delinquency of deeds by a weak will and a fear of society, not yet ripe for the asylum, but reaching inquisitively with his antennas into both spheres: this specific plant of culture, the modern artist, painter, musician, above all novelist, who designates his kind with the very indefinite word 'naturalism' ...

Lunatics, criminals and 'naturalists' are on the increase: a sign of a growing culture plunging *forward* at headlong speed – that is to say, its waste, its decay, the rubbish that is shot from it every day, is beginning to acquire more importance, – the movement downward *is keeping up* ...

Finally: *the social mishmash,* which is the result of the revolution, of the establishment of equal rights, of the superstition called 'equal men'. At the same time, the bearers of the instincts of decline (of *ressentiment*, of discontent, of the lust for destruction, of anarchism and nihilism), including the instincts of slavery, of cowardice, of craftiness and *canaille*, which are inherent among those classes of society which have long been oppressed, are beginning to get infused into the blood of all ranks: two, three generations later, the race can no longer be recognised – everything has become *mob*. And thus there results a collective instinct against *selection*, against every kind of *privilege*; and this instinct operates with such power, certainty, hardness and cruelty that, as a matter of fact, in the end, even the *privileged classes* have to submit:
– all those who still wish to hold on to power flatter the mob, must have the mob on their side –
the 'geniuses' *above all*: they become the *heralds* of those feelings with which one inspires the mob – the expression of pity, of reverence even for all that suffers, that is low and despised, that has lived under persecution, becomes predominant (types: V. Hugo and R. Wagner).
The rise of the mob signifies once more the rise of the *old values*...

* * *

In the case of such an extreme movement, both in tempo and in means, as characterises our civilisation, the ballast of men shifts: of men whose worth is greatest, and whose mission, as it were, is to compensate for the very great danger of such a morbid movement; – such men become procrastinators *par excellence*, slow to accept anything, hesitant to let go of anything, relatively enduring in the midst of this vast mingling and changing of elements. In such circumstances stress is necessarily devolved upon the *mediocre*: *mediocrity*, as the trustee and bearer of the future, consolidates itself against the rule of the mob and of eccentrics (both of which are, in most cases, united). In this way a new antagonist grows for *exceptional men* – or in certain cases a new temptation. Provided that they do not adapt themselves to the mob and stand up for what satisfies the instincts of the 'disinherited,' they will find it necessary to be 'mediocre' and 'solid'. They know: *mediocritas* is also *aurea* – it alone even rules over money and gold (over all that *glitters* ...) ... And, once more, the old virtue and the whole *spent* world of ideals in general secure a gifted host of advocates ... Result: mediocrity acquires intellect, wit, genius, – it becomes entertaining, it seduces ...

* * *

Result. I will say one more thing about the third force. Trade, commerce, agriculture, science, a great part of art – all this can only stand upon a broad basis, upon a strongly and soundly consolidated mediocrity. In its service and assisted by it, *science* and even art do their work. Science could not wish for a better state of affairs: in its essence it belongs to an intermediary kind of man – among exceptions it is out of place – there is nothing aristocratic and still less anything anarchistic in its instincts. – The power of the middle is then upheld by means of commerce, but, above all, by means of money-dealing: the instinct of great financiers is opposed to everything extreme – on this account the Jews are, for the present, the *most conservative* power in our threatened and insecure Europe. They can have no use either for revolutions, for socialism, for militarism: if they want to have power and if they need to have power, even over the revolutionary party, then it is only the result of what I have already said, and it in no way contradicts it. Against other extreme movements they may occasionally require to excite terror – by showing *how much* power is in their hands. But their instinct itself is inveterately conservative – and 'mediocre' ... Wherever power exists, they know how to become mighty: but the application of their power always takes the same direction. The polite term for *mediocre*, as is well known, is the word *'liberal'*...

something, that is not funny and not even true ...

Reflexion. – It is all nonsense to suppose that this whole *victory of values* is anti-biological: one should try to explain it out of interest of life
the maintenance of the type 'man' even by means of this method of prevalence of the weak and the botched –
: if things were otherwise, would man not exist anymore?
Problem – – –

The *enhancement* of the type fatal to the *maintenance of the species?*
Why?
the experiences of history:
the strong races *decimate* each other *mutually*: war, lust for power, venturousness; their existence is a costly affair, in short, – they *annihilate* each other –
the strong emotions: *squandering* – strength is no longer *capitalised* ...
mental trouble, from excessive tension - periods of *profound slackness* and torpidity set in all great ages have to be *paid for* ...
the strong are, after all, weaker, more devoid of will, more absurd than the average weak ones
There are *squandering* races. –
'Permanence,' in itself, can have no value: one might prefer a shorter but more valuable existence for the species.
It would remain to be proved that even as things are, more value would be achieved than in the case of the shorter existence.
i.e. man, as a storehouse of power, attains to a much higher degree of dominion over things under the conditions which have existed hitherto ....
We are here face to face with a problem of economics – – –

KSA 13 15[42] 1888 WP 141

'Improvement'
A criticism of the holy lie
That a lie is allowed in pursuit of pious ends is a principle which belongs to the theory of all priestcraft – the object of this inquiry is to discover to what extent it belongs to its practice.

But philosophers, too, whenever they intend taking over the leadership of mankind, with the ulterior motives of priests in their minds, have never failed to arrogate to themselves the right to lie: Plato above all. The greatest of all is the double lie, developed by the typically Aryan philosophers of the Vedanta: two systems, contradicting each other in all their main points, but interchangeable, complementary and mutually expletory, when educational ends were in question. The lie of the one has to create a condition in which the truth of the other can alone become *audible* ...

How far does the pious lie of priests and philosophers go? – The question here is, what presuppositions do they advance in regard to education, and what are the dogmas they are compelled to *invent* in order to do justice to these presuppositions?

Firstly: they must have power, authority, absolute credibility on their side

Secondly: they must have the direction of the whole course of Nature in their hands, so that everything affecting the individual seems to be determined by their law

Thirdly: they must have a domain of power which extends further and whose control may escape the notice of those they subject: the sentence for the great beyond, the 'afterlife,' – and, of course, the means whereby the road to blessedness may be discovered

They have to put the notion of a natural course of things out of sight: but as they are intelligent and thoughtful people, they are able to *promise* a host of effects, which they naturally say are conditioned by prayers or by the strict observance of their law...they can, moreover, *prescribe* a large number of things which are exceedingly reasonable – only they must not point to experience or empiricism as the source of this wisdom, but to revelation or to the fruits of the 'most severe exercises of penance'

the *holy lie*, therefore, applies principally: to the *purpose* of an action (– the natural purpose, reason, is made to vanish, a moral purpose, the observance of some law, a service to God, seems to be the purpose

: to the *consequence* of an action (– the natural consequence is interpreted as something supernatural, and, in order to be more effective, other uncontrollable supernatural consequences are foretold.

in this way, a concept of *good* and *evil* is created, which seems quite divorced from the natural concept 'useful', 'harmful', 'life-promoting', 'life-reducing' – indeed, inasmuch as *another* life is imagined, the former concept may even be *antagonistic* to the natural concept of good and evil

in this way, the famous 'conscience' is created: an inner voice, which does not measure the worth of that action according to its results, but according to its intention and to the conformity of this intention with the 'Law'

The holy lie therefore invented

a *god* who *punishes* and *rewards*, who recognises and carefully observes the law-book of the priests, and who sends them into the world as his mouthpieces and representatives

an *afterlife*, in which, alone, the great penal machine is supposed to be active, – to this end the *immortality of the soul*

a *conscience* in man, understood as the knowledge that good and evil are permanent values, – that God himself speaks through it, whenever its counsels are in conformity with the priestly precept

Morality as the *denial* of all natural processes, as the reduction of all events to a morally necessary event, the moral effect (i.e. the idea of punishment and reward) as something which permeates the world, as only power, as creator of all transformations

Truth as given, revealed, coinciding with the teaching of the priests: as the condition to all salvation and happiness in this and the next world

In summa: what is the price paid for moral *improvement*?

Unhinging of *reason,* reduction of all motives to fear and hope (punishment and reward)

Dependence upon the tutelage of priests, and upon a formulary exactitude which is supposed to express a divine will

the implantation of a 'conscience' which establishes a false knowledge in the place of experience and experiment

: as though all one had to do or had not to do were predetermined – a kind of castration of the seeking and striving spirit
: in short, the worst *mutilation* of man that can be imagined passes for 'the good man'
Practically speaking, all reason, the whole heritage of intelligence, subtlety, caution, the precondition of the priestly canon, is arbitrarily reduced, when it is too late, to a simple *mechanical* process
conformity with the law already as purpose, as highest purpose, – *Life no longer has any problems* –
the whole conception of the world is soiled by the notion of *punishment* ...
Life itself, owing to the fact that the *priest's life* is upheld as the *non plus ultra* of perfection, is transformed into a denial and fouling of life ...
the concept 'God' represents a renunciation of life, a criticism of it, even a contempt for it...
truth is transformed into *the priestly* lie, the striving for truth into the *study of the Scriptures*, as a means to *become a theologian* ...

KSA 13 15[45] 1888 WP 142

A criticism of the Law-Book of Manu –
The whole book is founded upon the holy lie:
– was it the well-being of humanity that inspired the whole of this system? this type of man, who believes in the *interested nature* of every action, was he interested or not in the implementation of this system?
– the desire to improve mankind – what inspired this intention? From where is the concept of improvement taken?
– we find a type of man, the *sacerdotal*, who considers himself to be norm, the peak, the highest expression of the type 'man': he himself is the origin of the concept of 'improvement'
– he believes in his own superiority, he *wants* it too for that matter: the cause of the holy lie is the *will to power*....

* * *

Establishment of the dominion: to this end, ideas which place a *non plus ultra* of power with the priesthood are made to prevail
power by means of lying, as one recognises that one does not possess it in physical, in military form ...
lying as a supplement to power, – a new concept of 'truth'

* * *

It is a mistake to presuppose an *unconscious and naïve* development in this quarter, a sort of self-deception... Fanatics are not the discoverers of such exhaustive systems of oppression....
Cold-blooded prudence was at work here, the same sort of prudence which Plato showed when he worked out his 'state'

'One must desire the means when one desires the end' – this political insight was clear in the minds of all legislators

* * *

We possess the classical model as specifically *Aryan*: we can therefore hold the most gifted and most cool-headed type of man responsible for the most fundamental lie that has ever been told...Everywhere almost the lie was copied: the *Aryan influence* corrupted the whole world ...

KSA 13 15[44] 1888 WP 116

The reversal of the order of rank:
the pious counterfeiters, the priests are becoming Chandala in our midst:
– they occupy the position of charlatans, of quacks, of counterfeiters, of sorcerers: we regard them as corrupters of the will, as the great slanderers and vindictive enemies of life, as the *rebels* among the bungled and the botched

* * *

On the other hand, the Chandala of former times is paramount: at the head, the *blasphemers*, the *immoralists*, the independents of all kinds, the artists, the Jews, the minstrels – at bottom, all *disreputable* classes of men –
– we have elevated ourselves to *honourable* thoughts, even more, we *determine* what honour is on earth, 'nobility' ....
– all of us today are advocates of life –
– we *immoralists* are today the *strongest power*: the other great powers are in need of us... we recreate the world in our own image –
  We have transferred the label 'Chandala' to the *priests*, the *teachers of the beyond*, and to the *Christian society* which has grown crooked together with them, and in addition, to creatures of like origin, the pessimists, nihilists, romanticists of pity, criminals, and men of vicious habits, – the whole sphere in which the concept of 'God' appears as a *Saviour*...

* * *

We are proud of being no longer obliged to be liars, slanderers, detractors of life...
NB. Even if one would prove God to us, we would not know how to believe him.

KSA 13 22[1] 1888 WP 925

A marginal note to a niaiserie anglaise. – 'Do not unto others that which you would not that they should do unto you.' This passes for wisdom; this passes for cleverness; this passes for the very basis of morality – for 'a golden maxim.' John Stuart Mill believes in it – and what Englishman does not?... But the maxim does not bear the slightest investigation. The argument, 'Do not as you would not be done by,' forbids actions because of potentially harmful results: the thought behind this is that an action is invariably *requited*. What if someone came forward with the *'Principe'* in his hands, and said: 'It is precisely such actions that one *must* perform, to prevent others from performing them first – to deprive others of the chance to perform them on *us*?' – On the other hand, let us remember the Corsican whose honour demanded vendetta. He too does not desire to have a bullet through him; but the prospect of one, the probability of getting one, does *not* deter him from vindicating his honour... And in all *decent* actions are we not intentionally indifferent as to what result they will bring? To avoid an action which might have harmful results for ourselves – that would be tantamount to forbidding all decent actions in general ...

Apart from this, the above maxim is valuable because it betrays a certain *type of man*: it is the *instinct of the herd* which formulates itself through him, – we are equal, we regard each other as equal: as I am to you so are you to me – Here, one really believes in an *equivalence of actions,* which never manifests itself under any real circumstances. It is impossible to requite every action: among real individuals *equal actions do not exist*, consequently there can be no such thing as 'requital'... When I do anything, I am very far from thinking that any man is able to do anything at all like it: the action belongs *to me*... Nobody can pay me back for anything I do, the most that one would commit would be 'another' action –

Translated by A. Ludovici with modifications – Nathalie Lachance

Notes

Introduction

1. Curtis Cate, *Friedrich Nietzsche: A Biography* (London: Pimlico, 2003), p. 7.
2. R. Hinton Thomas, *Nietzsche in German Politics and Society: 1890–1918* (Manchester: Manchester University Press, 1983), p. 2.
3. An event which has been described as the 'cardinal point of reference in nineteenth-century political debates'. See Egon Flaig, 'Jacob Burckhardt, Greek Culture, and Modernity', *Out of Arcadia: Classics and Politics in Germany in the Age of Burckhardt, Nietzsche and Wilamowitz*, ed. Ingo Gildenhard and Martin Ruehl (London: Institute of Classical Studies, School of Advanced Study, University of London, 2003), p. 9.
4. Cited in *On the Genealogy of Morals and Ecce Homo*, trans. Walter Kaufmann (New York: Vintage Books, 1967), Appendix (d), p. 343.
5. See Ronald Hayman, *Nietzsche: A Critical Life* (New York: Penguin Books, 1980), p. 142.
6. See BGE 209; TI 'Germans' 4 and 'Skirmishes' 49.
7. See EH 'wise' 3, First version. These two meanings of the 'anti-political' are expressed, for example, in Thomas Mann, *Reflections of a Nonpolitical Man* (1918), trans. Walter D. Morris (New York: Frederick Ungar, 1983), esp. pp. 85, 191 and 303; and in Keith Ansell-Pearson, *An Introduction to Nietzsche as Political Thinker: The Perfect Nihilist* (Cambridge: Cambridge University Press, 1994), pp. 27–8. Norbert Elias writes that 'During the eighteenth and part of the nineteenth centuries, the anti-political bias of the middle-class concept of "culture" was directed against the politics of autocratic princes...At a later stage, this anti-political bias was turned against the parliamentary politics of a democratic state'. See Norbert Elias, *The Germans* (New York: Columbia University Press, 1996), pp. 126–7.
8. Wolfgang J. Mommsen, *Imperial Germany 1867–1918: Politics, Culture, and Society in an Authoritarian State*, trans. Richard Deveson (London: Arnold, 1995), p. 1.
9. Ibid., p. 5.
10. Hans-Ulrich Wehler, 'Bismarck's Imperialism, 1862–1890', *Imperial Germany*, ed. James J. Sheehan (New York: New Viewpoints, 1976), p. 183.
11. Lynn Abrams, *Bismarck and the German Empire: 1871–1918* (London: Routledge, 2006), p. 1.
12. Mommsen, *Imperial Germany 1867–1918*, p. 29.
13. Quoted in Hans-Ulrich Wehler, *The German Empire: 1871–1918*, trans. Kim Traynor (Providence, NH: Berg, 1985), p. 30.
14. See Abrams, *Bismarck and the German Empire*, p. 14.
15. Guenther Roth, *The Social Democrats in Imperial Germany: A Study in Working-Class Isolation and National Integration* (New Jersey: Bedminster Press, 1963), p. 69.
16. Duncan Large says Nietzsche's break with Bismarck occurred in 1888. He writes that Nietzsche could not 'continue indefinitely to maintain a positive image of Bismarck while condemning his creation, the *Reich*, and the distinction finally collapses'. Duncan Large, 'The Aristocratic Radical and the White Revolutionary', in *Das schwierige neunzehnte Jahrhundert. Germanistische Tagung zum 65. Geburtstag*

von Eda Sagarra im August 1998, ed. J. Barkhoff, G. Carr, and R. Paulin (Tübingen: Niemeyer, 2000), pp. 101–16, p. 13.
17. KSA 12 9[180] 1887 WP 884. A. J. P. Taylor agrees that Bismarck was constantly 'balancing between the various forces and playing one off against another; and he aimed to be the dominant partner in any association. He never became identified with any cause, whether monarchy or German nationalism or, later, conservatism'. A. J. P. Taylor, *Bismarck: The Man and Statesman* (London: Hamish Hamilton, 1965), p. 94.
18. Otto Pflanze, 'Bismarck's *Realpolitik*', *Imperial Germany*, ed. James J. Sheehan (New York: New Viewpoints, 1976), p. 159.
19. GS 357.
20. Peter Bergmann, *Nietzsche, 'the Last Antipolitical German'* (Bloomington, IN: Indiana University Press, 1987), p. 48.
21. In his book, *Grundsätzen der Realpolitik*.
22. Pflanze, 'Bismarck's *Realpolitik*', p. 156.
23. Ibid., p. 157.
24. In fact, Nietzsche often compared Bismarck to Napoleon Bonaparte. See Large, 'The Aristocratic Radical and the White Revolutionary', pp. 10–11.
25. As Lynn Abrams has described. Abrams, *Bismarck and the German Empire*, p. 28.
26. See Wehler's description of this ruling technique. Wehler, *The German Empire*, pp. 91–2. *Reichsfeinde* variously included throughout the Bismarckian era, Danes, Poles, Catholics, liberals, social democrats and Jews.
27. As Nietzsche writes, 'Even in the political realm, hostility has now become more spiritual.... Almost every party sees that its self-preservation is best served if its opposition does not lose its strength; and the same applies to grand politics. A new creation more particularly, such as the new *Reich*, has greater need of enemies than friends: only as a contrast does it begin to feel necessary, only as a contrast does it *become* necessary' (TI 'Morality' 3). In 1887 Bismarck had written, in the spirit of opposing the idea of the annihilation of the enemy, that 'France's continued existence as a great power is just as needful to us as that of any other of the great powers'. *Die grosse Politik der europäischen Kabinette*, VII, pp. 177–8. Quoted in Edward Mead Earle, 'Hitler: The Nazi Concept of War', *Makers of Modern Strategy: Military Thought from Machiavelli to Hitler*, ed. Edward Mead Earle (Princeton, NJ: Princeton University Press, 1943), p. 510.
28. Jan Rehmann, 'Re-Reading Nietzsche with Domenico Losurdo's Intellectual Biography'. *Historical Materialism* 15, 2007, pp. 1–60, p. 5.
29. BT 'Attempt at a Self-Criticism', 1886.
30. While Nietzsche considered Bismarck to be an anti-Semite (see, for example, KSA 12 2[98] 1886), Gordon Craig writes that 'Bismarck's attitude toward anti-Semitism was always ambivalent. His son Herbert once explained that the Chancellor opposed Stöcker because of his radical social views and because he was attacking the *wrong* Jews, the rich ones, who were committed to the *status quo*, rather than the propertyless Jews in the Parliament and the Press, who had nothing to lose and therefore joined every opposition movement'. Gordon A. Craig, *Germany, 1866–1945* (New York: Oxford University Press, 1978), p. 155, n. 42.
31. Taylor remarks that 'Bismarck disliked war, though not primarily for the suffering that it involved. War was for him a clumsy way of settling international disputes'. Taylor, *Bismarck: The Man and Statesman*, p. 79.
32. James N. Retallack, *Notables of the Right: The Conservative Party and Political Mobilization in Germany, 1876–1918* (Boston, MA: Unwin Hyman, 1988), p. 45.

33. Uriel Tal, *Christians and Jews in Germany: Religion, Politics, and Ideology in the Second Reich, 1870–1914*, trans. Noah Jonathan Jacobs (Ithaca, NY: Cornell University Press, 1975), p. 122.
34. See Craig, *Germany*, p. 63.
35. Vernon L. Lidtke, *The Outlawed Party: Social Democracy in Germany, 1878–1890* (Princeton, NJ: Princeton University Press, 1966), p. 53.
36. Roth, *The Social Democrats in Imperial Germany*, p. 51.
37. Lidtke comments that 'there were four fundamental reasons for [Bismarck's] desire to crush the SPD: in constitutional-political outlook, they were republican, and therefore a threat to monarchy; in foreign affairs, they were internationalists, which implied to Bismarck that they would be friends of Germany's enemies; in domestic affairs, they sought a fundamental transformation of the existing social and economic order, opposed to the Junker foundation of the society; and, in religious matters, they were atheists, and thus undermined the religious and moral norms of Christian society'. Lidtke, *The Outlawed Party*, p. 71.
38. Tal, *Christians and Jews in Germany*, p. 125.
39. Retallack, *Notables of the Right*, p. 45.
40. EH BT 4.
41. See Steven E. Aschheim, *The Nietzsche Legacy in Germany: 1890–1990* (Berkeley, CA: University of California Press, 1992), p. 85.
42. Letter to Franziska and Elisabeth Nietzsche, April 20, 1864, KSB 1:277.
43. Ibid.
44. Letter to Franziska and Elisabeth Nietzsche, end of June 1866, KSB 2:134–5 (cited as beginning of July). *Selected Letters of Friedrich Nietzsche*, ed. and trans. Christopher Middleton (Chicago and London: University of Chicago Press, 1969; repr. Indianapolis: Hackett, 1996), p. 14.
45. Letter to Gersdorff, end of August 1866, KSB 2:159. Middleton, *Selected Letters of Friedrich Nietzsche*, p. 17.
46. Ibid, p. 18, KSB 2:159.
47. Theodor Schieder, *The State and Society in Our Times*, trans. C. A. M. Sym (London: Thomas Nelson, 1962), p.25. Nietzsche appears to belatedly concur in a note from 1885 where he associates socialism's principal event as the Paris Commune even echoing Bebel's speech in the *Reichstag*: 'the coming century is likely to be convulsed in more than one spot, and the Paris Commune, which finds defenders and advocates even in Germany, will seem to have been but a slight indigestion compared with what is to come'. KSA 11 37[11] 1885 WP 125.
48. See Letter to Franziska and Elisabeth Nietzsche, December 12, 1870, KSB 3:163.
49. See Wehler, *The German Empire*, p. 150.
50. Letter to Gersdorff, November 7, 1870, KSB 3:155. See Middleton, *Selected Letters of Friedrich Nietzsche*, pp. 70–1, n. 43.
51. UM 'David Strauss', 1.
52. Gustav Freytag's *Grenzboten* responded to Nietzsche's arguments: 'When has Germany ever been greater, sounder, and more worthy of the name of a people of culture than today'? *Die Grenzboten*, xxxii, no. 4, 1873, p. 104ff. Quoted in Craig, *Germany*, p. 36.
53. See UW 26[16] 1873; UW 27[24] 1873; UW 27[60] 1873; UW 27[66] 1873 and UW 32[71] 1874.
54. UW 30[8] 1873–74.
55. Peter Bergmann writes, 'The Commune was, moreover, a profound shock that seemingly confirmed all his fears of the cultural barbarism of the lower classes'.

Bergmann, *Nietzsche, 'the Last Antipolitical German'*, p. 120. In particular, Nietzsche could not contain his anger towards the anarchist Bakunin, 'who out of hatred for the present wants to destroy history and the past. Now, to be sure, in order to eradicate the entire past it also would be necessary to eradicate human beings: but he only wants to destroy all prior *cultivation*, our intellectual inheritance in its entirety' (UW 26[14] 1873).

56. Letter to Gersdorff, June 21, 1871, KSB 3:204. Middleton, *Selected Letters of Friedrich Nietzsche*, pp. 80–1.
57. Ibid., KSB 3:203.
58. See KSA 1:767.
59. BT 18.
60. See Lionel Gossman, *Basel in the Age of Burckhardt: A Study in Unseasonable Ideas* (Chicago and London: University of Chicago Press, 2000), p. 430.
61. Abrams remarks that 'Despite classic liberal principles such as freedom of the individual the liberals supported the [illiberal] *Kulturkampf* by arguing that the repressive influence of the Catholic Church had to be dismantled if the German people were to be emancipated as individuals'. Abrams, *Bismarck and the German Empire*, p. 30.
62. See Tal, *Christians and Jews in Germany*, p. 84.
63. Ibid.
64. See Lionel Gossman, *Basel in the Age of Burckhardt*, p. 257.
65. UW 32[80] 1874.
66. Nietzsche's view of the Roman Catholic Church is expressed in a letter to Erwin Rohde dated February 28, 1875, KSB 5:27–8, where Nietzsche derides their friend Romundt's conversion to Roman Catholicism: 'do not fall off your chair when you hear that Romundt has plans to enter the Roman Catholic Church, and to become a priest in Germany... This wounds me inwardly... and sometimes I feel it is the most wicked thing that anyone could do to me'. Towards the end of the letter, he adds: '[I] am deeply ashamed when it is suspected of me that I have had anything to do with this utterly odious Catholic business'. Middleton, *Selected Letters of Friedrich Nietzsche*, pp. 131–2.
67. Prophetic because, by the time it ended, 'Not only had ecclesiastical power not been broken, but the Catholic Church had emerged from the struggle with its organisational edifice intact and its ideological buttresses stronger than ever before ...' See Helmut Walser Smith, *German Nationalism and Religious Conflict: Culture, Ideology, Politics, 1870–1914* (Princeton, NJ: Princeton University Press, 1995), pp. 50–1.
68. Quoted in James Sheehan, *German Liberalism in the Nineteenth Century* (Chicago: University of Chicago Press, 1978), p. 183.
69. Roth, *The Social Democrats in Imperial Germany*, p. 73.
70. Wehler, *The German Empire*, p. 95. Elsewhere Wehler writes, 'the anti-Socialist law, was intended as "a prophylactic measure" against social upheavals, completing his policy of taming the working classes'. Wehler, 'Bismarck's Imperialism, 1862–1890', p. 200.
71. Tal explains that '"Practical Christianity"... was coined by Bismarck at the beginning of the eighties to justify the regime's social policy and to seize the initiative from the Social Democrats by showing the social concern of an antisocialist imperial regime for improving the conditions of the workers by passing laws such as national insurance... [Bismarck:] to assert the political power of Christianity, and to contain the non-Christian forces of socialism and "Manchester" liberalism'. Tal, *Christians and Jews in Germany*, p. 133.

72. Lidtke, *The Outlawed Party*, p. 156.
73. Retallack, *Notables of the Right*, p. 48.
74. See Bergmann, *Nietzsche, 'the Last Antipolitical German'*, p. 32. The précis is dated January 13, 1862. See *Nietzsche Werke: Kritische Gesamtausgabe, Nachgelassene Aufzeichnungen*, Herbst 1858–Herbst 1862, de Gruyter, 2000, p. 357.
75. See Nietzsche's reference to the 'Schulze-Delitzsch model' in UW 29[66] 1873. The Liberal, Hermann Schulze-Delitzsch was the founder of the German credit and cooperative movement, which was committed to alleviating the material and spiritual plight of the working classes resulting from the decline of traditional society.
76. Quoted in Rehmann, 'Re-Reading Nietzsche with Domenico Losurdo's Intellectual Biography', p. 9. Nietzsche refers to the Imperial Message of November 17, 1881 in GS 188.
77. GS 188.
78. The *Kolonialgesellschaft* or *Kolonialverein* (Colonial Union) was established in Germany in 1882.
79. See Sheehan, *German Liberalism in the Nineteenth Century*, p. 201.
80. KSA 12 9[173] 1887 WP 315.
81. EH CW 3. It is interesting to note here that Catholic Germany, reintegrating itself into the *Reich* after the *Kulturkampf*, became involved in German colonialism. As Smith writes, 'Partly through the antislavery campaign, partly through the missionary activity of … [the] Jesuits, Catholic Germany became … involved in the new national state's "civilising mission" … for the goal of Christianising and cultivating the African natives'. Smith, *German Nationalism and Religious Conflict*, p. 76.
82. Erich Eyck, *Bismarck and the German Empire* (New York: Norton, 1968), p. 275.
83. KSA 11 37[9] 1885. Nietzsche writes, 'In order … that Europe may enter into the battle for the mastery of the world with good prospects of victory – it is easy to perceive against whom this battle will be waged – she must probably "come to an understanding" with England. The English colonies are needed for this struggle …'
84. Bergmann, *Nietzsche, 'the Last Antipolitical German'*, p. 163.
85. D 206.
86. One of the four broad conceptual areas that discussion of colonialism in Germany centred on. See *Bismarck, Europe, and Africa: The Berlin Conference 1884–1885 and the Onset of Partition*, eds. Stig Förster, Wolfgang J. Mommsen and Ronald Robinson (New York: Oxford University Press, 1988), p. 122.
87. WS 87.
88. BGE 208.
89. Letter to Franziska and Elisabeth Nietzsche, March 14, 1885, KSB 7:23. Middleton, *Selected Letters of Friedrich Nietzsche*, p. 238.
90. Quoted in Craig, *Germany*, p. 153.
91. See Tal, *Christians and Jews in Germany*, p. 146.
92. KSA 13 11[148] 1887–88 WP 30.
93. KSA 13 11[235–6] 1887–88 WP 748.
94. See Tal, *Christians and Jews in Germany*, p. 253.
95. Ibid.
96. Ibid. p. 227.
97. Ibid.
98. Letter to Franz Overbeck, March 24, 1887, KSB 8:48. Middleton, *Selected Letters of Friedrich Nietzsche*, p. 264.

99. GM III 26.
100. See GM II 11.
101. HH 475.
102. Like Nietzsche, Treitschke also 'interpreted the principle of integration as a complete ethnic-religious fusion in the sense of miscegenation'. Tal, *Christians and Jews in Germany*, p. 65.
103. BGE 251.
104. In a note from 1884, Nietzsche had already given the Jewish role in his new Europe some consideration: 'we require, too, the cleverest financiers, the Jews, in order to rule on earth'. See KSA 11 26[335] 1884.
105. See Letter to Georg Brandes, December 2, 1887, KSB 8:206. Middleton, *Selected Letters of Friedrich Nietzsche*, p. 279.
106. See Gossman, *Basel in the Age of Burckhardt*, pp. 288–9.
107. Roth, *The Social Democrats in Imperial Germany*, p. 28.
108. Sheehan, *German Liberalism in the Nineteenth Century*, pp. 154–5. Uriel Tal remarks that 'Treitschke expressed the fear felt by the "entire spiritual aristocracy of Germany" in the face of the rising lower social classes and the growing strength of the left, which aroused in his words "fears for the ideal cultural possessions that are imperiled by the brutish movement of the lower classes" ...' Tal, *Christians and Jews in Germany*, p. 67.
109. TI 'Skirmishes' 39.
110. Ibid. 38.
111. See, for example, 'The Greek State'; GS 377; TI 'Skirmishes', 38, 39; KSA 13[14]182 1888 WP 864.
112. Bismarck, *Gesammelten Werke*, XI, 611. Quoted in Theodor Schieder, 'Nietzsche and Bismarck', *The Historian* 29 (4), August, 1967, p. 591. For Nietzsche's reference to the Paris Commune and his echoing of the warning in Bebel's speech, see n. 47 above.
113. See Letter to Malwida von Meysenbug, September 24, 1886, KSB 7:257. Middleton, *Selected Letters of Friedrich Nietzsche*, p. 257.
114. See n. 17 above.

1 Schulpforta, 1862

1. The essay consists of two parts: a shorter introduction and a longer account of Napoleon III as president. The second and longer part plagiarises (with direct quotation and paraphrasing) Wolfgang Menzel's *Geschichte der letzten vierzig Jahre, 1816–1856*.

2 Agonistic Politics, 1871–1874

1. Letter to Franziska and Elisabeth Nietzsche, April 20, 1864, KSB 1:277.
2. Letter to Hermann Muschacke, August 30, 1865, KSB 2:80.
3. Letter to Franziska Nietzsche, June 1865, KSB 2:66.
4. Letter to Carl von Gersdorff, August 4, 1865, KSB 2:76.
5. Letter to Franziska and Elisabeth Nietzsche, beginning July 1866, KSB 2:136.
6. Ibid.
7. Letter to Carl von Gersdorff, end of August 1866, KSB 2:159.
8. Ibid.
9. Letter to Carl von Gersdorff, February 20, 1867, KSB 2:199.

10. Ibid.
11. Letter to Carl von Gersdorff, February 16, 1868, KSB 2:258.
12. Letter to Wilhelm Vischer (-Bilfinger), August 8, 1870, KSB 3:133.
13. Letter to Carl von Gersdorff, November 7, 1870, KSB 3:155.
14. Letter to Wilhelm Vischer (-Bilfinger), May 27, 1871, KSB 3:195.
15. Letter to Carl von Gersdorff, June 21, 1871, KSB 3:204.
16. Letter to Erwin Rohde, March 29, 1871, KSB 3:190.
17. Letter to Carl von Gersdorff, November 7, 1870, KSB 3:155.
18. UW 27[66]1873.
19. Ibid. 27[24]1873.
20. Ibid. 32[80]1874.
21. Letter to Erwin Rohde, November 23, 1870, KSB 3:160.
22. Letter to Carl von Gersdorff, June 21, 1871, KSB 3:203–4.
23. UW 32[63]1873.
    In this passage, Nietzsche is referring to the 'representational constitution' of the German *Reich* (1871), which was known as the Prusso-German constitution.

3 The Free Spirit, 1878–1880

1. HH 476.
2. HH 475.
3. EH HH 1.
4. WS 229 (not included in this volume).
5. See HH P 6.
6. WS 221.
7. EH HH 1.
8. HH 463.
9. HH 237.
10. HH 244.
11. HH 261.
12. The first volume of *Human, All Too Human* was published in May 1878.
13. HH 473.
14. As Bergmann observes. Peter Bergmann, *Nietzsche, 'the Last Antipolitical German'* (Bloomington, IN: Indiana University Press, 1987), p. 121.
15. HH 473.
16. WS 286.
17. HH 451.
18. HH 235.
19. HH 457.
20. MM 304.
21. Whether or not Nietzsche supported the anti-Socialist Laws is difficult to determine unequivocally. The only passage which explicitly refers to the 'exceptional rules' that have made 'enemies' – although 'welcome enemies' – of the socialist movement, and which thus sheds some light on Nietzsche's perception of these 'rules', is MM 316: 'The socialistic movements are today becoming more and more agreeable than terrifying to the dynastic governments, because by these movements they are provided with *a right and a weapon* for making exceptional rules, and can thus attack the figures that really fill them with terror, the democrats and anti-dynasts. – Towards all that such governments professedly detest they feel a secret cordiality and inclination ...' Nietzsche's position is that

dynastic governments (by which he means the Bismarckian/Wilhelmian *Reich*) introduced the anti-Socialist Laws ('exceptional rules') primarily to target the 'democrats and anti-dynasts' (by which he means the National Liberal and Progressive Liberal parties). This passage reveals that Nietzsche believed that Bismarck's measures were not really designed to undermine the power of the socialists, but of the liberals. Nietzsche's perception was partially correct as Bismarck's conservative goals required the weakening, or splitting, of the liberals in the *Reichstag* which debate over these Laws effectively achieved. Nevertheless, Nietzsche is wholly accurate in identifying a technique of political rule typically utilised by Bismarck, that is, governing through raising the threat of common enemies, yet Nietzsche appears to be grossly underestimating Bismarck's actual view of the socialists as a serious political threat to the *Reich*. Certainly, Nietzsche would have been aware of the extensive persecution of the socialist movement, the closing of their presses, the deportation and imprisonment of their leaders; these were not acts that betrayed a 'secret cordiality'. The question is: is Nietzsche supporting the democrats in this passage or is he suggesting that the government should have gone further and outlawed the socialist party completely (as the Laws permitted the parliamentary caucus of the SPD to continue to operate in the *Reichstag*)? The beginning of an answer may be found in Curtis Cate's remark that Nietzsche 'felt misgivings about the concessions the German Chancellor seemed prepared to make in not ruthlessly outlawing all communist and socialist movements'. See Curtis Cate, *Friedrich Nietzsche*: *A Biography* (London: Pimlico, 2003), p. 273.
22. MM 306.
23. WS 292.
24. HH 439.
25. HH 472.
26. See ibid.
27. WS 293.
28. See HH 450.
29. Ibid.
30. See HH 472.
31. He had, after all, assisted in the drafting of the Manifesto of the German Conservative Party in 1876, although it was the Free Conservative Party who were ultimately the Bismarckian Party.
32. HH 438.
33. Ibid.
34. WS 275.
35. Ibid.

4 The Campaign against Morality, 1881–1885

1. GS 188.
2. GS 24.
3. D 173.
4. EH D 2.
5. D 132.
6. Ibid.
7. D 206.
8. See D 534 and GS 10.

9. GS 40.
10. GS 42.
11. D 206.
12. D 190.
13. GS 283.
14. See GS 291 and KSA 10 7[26–27] 1883 WP 1026.
15. GS 23.
16. KSA 11 37[8] 1885 WP 957.
17. See, for example, D 188 and GS 236.
18. D 188.
19. Z 'On the new idol'. Zarathustra's speeches in Part One were given in a city called 'The Colourful Cow', which displays the same diversity belonging to the modern democratic city. It is also worth noting that Socrates referred to democracy as the most 'colourful' of regimes because it is home to all sorts of human beings and provides the most natural setting for the philosopher seeking initiates or companions (Plato, *Republic* 557c-d, 558a-b). See Laurence Lampert, *Nietzsche's Teaching: An Interpretation of* Thus Spoke Zarathustra (New Haven, CT and London: Yale University Press, 1986), p. 33.
20. Z 'On the rabble'.
21. Z 'On the tarantulas'.
22. Z 'On old and new tablets' 12.
23. Z 'On old and new tablets' 25.
24. Z 'Conversations with the kings' 1.
25. KSA 11 34[177] 1885 WP 753.
26. KSA 11 34[109] 1885.
27. KSA 11 26[9] 1884 WP 854.
28. KSA 11 25[174] 1884 WP 861.
29. See KSA 11 26[335] 1884.
30. KSA 11 37[9] 1885.
31. See KSA 11 26[335] 1884 and KSA 11 26[336] 1884.
32. KSA 11 37[9] 1885.
33. KSA 11 26[335] 1884.
34. KSA 11 37[9] 1885.
35. KSA 11 35[9] 1885 WP 132.
36. D 112.
37. KSA 11 37[9] 1885.
38. KSA 11 35[9] 1885 WP 132.

5 Aristocratic Radical, 1886–1887

1. EH BGE 2.
2. BGE 202.
3. BT 'Attempt at a Self-Criticism' 6 (not included in this volume).
4. BGE 203.
5. BGE 202 and KSA 12 10[5] 1887 WP 1017.
6. BGE 202.
7. GS 377.
8. BGE 251.
9. GS 377.
10. KSA 12 2[57] 1885–86 WP 960. See, also, BGE 61.

11. See, for example, BGE 258.
12. KSA 12 9[173] 1887 WP 315. Nietzsche would also express his disappointment that slavery ended in the United States after the Civil War. He refers to Harriet Beecher Stowe, the author of *Uncle Tom's Cabin* (1852), as a misguided disciple of Rousseau. See KSA 11 25[178] 1884 (not included in this volume).
13. BGE 239.
14. BGE 257.
15. Ibid.
16. BGE 203.
17. BGE 22.
18. GM II 11.
19. See BGE 257.
20. KSA 12 10[5] 1887 WP 1017.
21. See Lionel Gossman, *Basel in the Age of Burckhardt: A Study in Unseasonable Ideas* (Chicago: University of Chicago Press, 2002), p. 391. To Overbeck in 1882, Nietzsche writes: 'For me, the Renaissance remains the climax of this millennium, and what has happened since then is the grand reaction of all kinds of herd instincts against the "individualism" of that epoch'. *Selected Letters of Friedrich Nietzsche*, ed. and trans. Christopher Middleton (Chicago and London: University of Chicago Press, 1969; repr. Indianapolis: Hackett, 1996), p.195.
22. BGE 242.
23. KSA 12 9[153] 1887 WP 898.
24. GM I 16.
25. Ibid.
26. GS 362.
27. GM I 16.
28. BGE 46.
29. GM I 7.
30. See KSA 12 2[76] 1885–86 WP 660.
31. BGE 202.
32. GM I 5.
33. See GS 362.
34. Peter Bergmann, *Nietzsche, 'the Last Antipolitical German'* (Bloomington, IN: Indiana University Press, 1987), p. 162.
35. BGE 208.
36. See BGE 254.
37. BGE 241.
38. See GM II 11.
39. BGE 251.
40. Ibid.
41. GS 377.
42. GM I 7.
43. BGE 251.
44. Ibid.
45. BGE 208.
46. Uriel Tal, *Christians and Jews in Germany: Religion, Politics, and Ideology in the Second Reich, 1870–1914*, trans. Jonathan Jacobs (Ithaca, NY: Cornell University Press, 1975), p. 122.
47. See, for example, GS 358.
48. Tal, *Christians and Jews in Germany*, p. 132.

49. See BGE 256. In a letter to Malwida von Meysenbug, September 1886, Nietzsche observes, 'the whole Wagner business seems to be an unconscious approach to Rome, which is doing the same thing inwardly as Bismarck is doing outwardly'. See Middleton, *Selected Letters of Friedrich Nietzsche*, p. 256.
50. GS 358.
51. GS 377.
52. See KSA 12 10[117] 1887 WP 361.
53. GM II 24.

6 The Antichrist, 1888

1. Letter to Heinrich Köselitz, June 20, 1888, KSB 8:338–9.
2. The subtitle of *The Antichrist*.
3. See, for example, AC 57 and KSA 13 14[29–30] 1888 WP 373. Nietzsche's critique of these ideologies invariably revolves around the issues of equality, altruism, revolution and the 'social' or 'labour question'.
4. KSA 13 11[235] 1887–88 WP 748.
5. KSA 12 10[81] 1887 (not included in this volume).
6. EH CW 2.
7. Letter to Georg Brandes, October 20, 1888, KSB 8:456.
8. See KSA 13 25[18] 1888 (not included in this volume).
9. Letter to Heinrich Köselitz, October 30, 1888, KSB 8:462.
10. AC 43.
11. KSA 13 14[6] 1888 WP 51.
12. TI 'Morality' 3.
13. See KSA 12 10[135] 1887–88 WP 211.
14. See GS 357.
15. See Uriel Tal, *Christians and Jews in Germany: Religion, Politics, and Ideology in the Second Reich, 1870–1914*, trans. Jonathan Jacobs (Ithaca, NY: Cornell University Press, 1975), p. 133.
16. See, for example, KSA 13 11[148] 1887–1888 WP 30 (not included in this volume): 'The *Church* is still permitted to obtrude into all important experiences and main points of individual life... we still have the "Christian state"....' In *Twilight of the Idols*, Nietzsche writes, 'People forget that education, that *Bildung*, is itself an end – and *not* "the *Reich*"....' TI 'Improvers' 5.
17. TI 'Germans' 4.
18. EH 'wise' 3, First version.
19. Ibid.
20. TI 'Germans' 4.
21. KSA 13 11[235] 1887–88 WP 748.
22. See AC 62.
23. AC 43.
24. TI 'Skirmishes' 37.
25. AC 37.
26. TI 'Skirmishes' 39.
27. Ibid. 38.
28. Ibid.
29. Ibid. 39.
30. Ibid. 37.
31. EH CW 2.

32. See AC 61.
33. AC 2.
34. See EH 'good books' 1.
35. AC 57.
36. KSA 13 25[13] 1888 (not included in this volume).
37. A mutual security treaty between Germany, Austria-Hungary and Italy drafted in May 1882.
38. Letter to Helen Zimmern, December 8, 1888, KSB 8:512. For an account of this letter see Curtis Cate, *Friedrich Nietzsche: A Biography* (London: Pimlico, 2003), p. 544.
39. Letter to Kaiser Wilhelm II, beginning December 1888, KSB 8:503. Quoted in Cate, ibid., p. 547. For similar remarks, see EH 'destiny' 1. The spectre of global wars is intrinsic to Nietzsche's vision of *grand politics*.

Primary and Secondary Historical Works

Nietzsche in German

Gesammelte Werke (München: Musarion Verlag, 1922).
Sämtliche Briefe: Kritische Studienausgabe, ed. Giorgio Colli and Mazzino Montinari, 8 vols (Berlin and New York: de Gruyter; Munich: dtv, 1986).
Sämtliche Werke: Kritische Studienausgabe, ed. Giorgio Colli and Mazzino Montinari, 2nd edn, 15 vols (Berlin and New York: de Gruyter; Munich: dtv, 1988; CD-ROM 1995).
Werke: Kritische Gesamtausgabe, ed. Giorgio Colli, Mazzino Montinari, Wolfgang Müller-Lauter and Karl Pestalozzi, c. 40 vols (Berlin and New York: de Gruyter, 1967–).

Nietzsche in English

Collections

Basic Writings of Nietzsche, ed. and trans. Walter Kaufmann (New York: Modern Library, 1968).
The Complete Works of Friedrich Nietzsche, ed. Oscar Levy, 18 vols (Edinburgh and London: Foulis, 1909–13).
The Complete Works of Friedrich Nietzsche, ed. Ernst Behler and Bernd Magnus, 20 vols (Stanford, CA: Stanford University Press, 1995–).
The Nietzsche Reader, ed. Keith Ansell Pearson and Duncan Large (Oxford: Blackwell, 2006).
The Portable Nietzsche, ed. and trans. Walter Kaufmann (New York: Viking, 1954).

Individual published works

The Anti-Christ, Ecce Homo, Twilight of the Idols and Other Writings, ed. Aaron Ridley, trans. Judith Norman (Cambridge and New York: Cambridge University Press, 2005).
The Antichrist, trans. H. L. Mencken (New York: Alfred A. Knopf, 1918).
Beyond Good and Evil, trans. Walter Kaufmann (New York: Vintage Books, 1966).
Beyond Good and Evil, trans. R. J. Hollingdale (Harmondsworth: Penguin, 1973).
Beyond Good and Evil, trans. Marion Faber (Oxford and New York: Oxford University Press, 1998).
Beyond Good and Evil, ed. Rolf-Peter Horstmann and Judith Norman, trans. Judith Norman, (Cambridge and New York: Cambridge University Press, 2001).
The Birth of Tragedy and The Case of Wagner, trans. Walter Kaufmann (New York: Vintage Books, 1967).
The Birth of Tragedy, trans. Shaun Whiteside (Harmondsworth and New York: Penguin, 1993).

The Birth of Tragedy and Other Writings, ed. Raymond Geuss and Ronald Speirs, trans. Ronald Speirs (Cambridge and New York: Cambridge University Press, 1999).
The Birth of Tragedy, trans. Douglas Smith (Oxford and New York: Oxford University Press, 2000).
Daybreak, trans. R. J. Hollingdale (Cambridge and New York: Cambridge University Press, 1982).
Dithyrambs of Dionysus, trans. R. J. Hollingdale (Redding Ridge, CT: Black Swan Books, 1984; repr. London: Anvil Press, 2001).
Ecce Homo, trans. R. J. Hollingdale, 2nd edn (Harmondsworth and New York: Penguin, 1992).
Ecce Homo, trans. Duncan Large (Oxford and New York: Oxford University Press, 2006).
The Gay Science, trans. Walter Kaufmann (New York: Vintage Books, 1974).
The Gay Science, ed. Bernard Williams, trans. Josefine Nauckhoff and Adrian Del Caro (Cambridge and New York: Cambridge University Press, 2001).
Human, All Too Human: A Book for Free Spirits, vol. I, trans. Marion Faber, with Stephen Lehmann (Lincoln: University of Nebraska Press, 1984, 1986).
Human, All Too Human, trans. R. J. Hollingdale (Cambridge and New York: Cambridge University Press, 1986).
On the Genealogy of Morality, ed. Keith Ansell-Pearson, trans. Carol Diethe (Cambridge and New York: Cambridge University Press, 1994; 2nd rev. edn, 2006).
On the Genealogy of Morals, trans. Douglas Smith (Oxford and New York: Oxford University Press, 1996).
Thus Spoke Zarathustra, trans. R. J. Hollingdale (Harmondsworth and Baltimore, MD: Penguin, 1961).
Thus Spoke Zarathustra, trans. Graham Parkes (Oxford and New York: Oxford University Press, 2005).
Twilight of the Idols and The Anti-Christ, trans. R. J. Hollingdale (Harmondsworth and Baltimore, MD: Penguin, 1968).
Twilight of the Idols, trans. Duncan Large (Oxford and New York: Oxford University Press, 1998).
Untimely Meditations, trans. R. J. Hollingdale (Cambridge and New York: Cambridge University Press, 1983).

Individual unpublished works and notes (*Nachlass*)

Friedrich Nietzsche on Rhetoric and Language, ed. and trans. Sander L. Gilman, Carole Blair and David J. Parent (New York and Oxford: Oxford University Press, 1989).
Philosophy in the Tragic Age of the Greeks, trans. Marianne Cowan (Chicago: Refinery, 1962).
Philosophy and Truth: Selections from Nietzsche's Notebooks of the Early 1870s, ed. and trans. Daniel Breazeale (Atlantic Highlands, NJ: Humanities Press, 1979).
The Pre-Platonic Philosophers, trans. Greg Whitlock (Urbana and Chicago: University of Illinois Press, 2001).
Unpublished Writings from the Period of Unfashionable Observations, trans. Richard T. Gray (Stanford, CA: Stanford University Press, 1995).
The Will to Power, ed. Walter Kaufmann, trans. Walter Kaufmann and R. J. Hollingdale, (New York: Random House, 1967).
Writings from the Late Notebooks, ed. Rüdiger Bittner, trans. Kate Sturge (Cambridge and New York: Cambridge University Press, 2003).

Correspondence

Nietzsche: A Self-Portrait from his Letters, ed., trans. Peter Fuss and Henry Shapiro (Cambridge, MA: Harvard University Press, 1971).
Selected Letters of Friedrich Nietzsche, ed. Oscar Levy, trans. Anthony M. Ludovici (Garden City, NY and Toronto: Doubleday, Page, 1921).
Selected Letters of Friedrich Nietzsche, ed. and trans. Christopher Middleton (Chicago and London: University of Chicago Press, 1969; repr. Indianapolis: Hackett, 1996).

Secondary historical works

Abrams, Lynn. *Bismarck and the German Empire: 1871–1918* (London: Routledge, 2006).
Blackbourn, David and Eley, Geoff. *The Peculiarities of German History: Bourgeois Society and Politics in Nineteenth-Century Germany* (Oxford: Oxford University Press, 1984).
Bismarck, Europe, and Africa: The Berlin Conference 1884–1885 and the Onset of Partition, ed. Stig Förster, Wolfgang J. Mommsen and Ronald Robinson (New York: Oxford University Press, 1988).
Craig, Gordon A. *Germany, 1866–1945* (New York: Oxford University Press, 1978).
Earle, Edward Mead. 'Hitler: The Nazi Concept of War', *Makers of Modern Strategy: Military Thought from Machiavelli to Hitler*, ed. Edward Mead Earle (Princeton, NJ: Princeton University Press, 1943).
Eyck, Erich. *Bismarck and the German Empire* (New York: Norton, 1968).
Feuchtwanger, Edgar. *Imperial Germany 1850–1918* (New York: Routledge, 2001).
Flaig, Egon. 'Jacob Burckhardt, Greek Culture, and Modernity', *Out of Arcadia: Classics and Politics in Germany in the Age of Burckhardt, Nietzsche and Wilamowitz*, ed. Ingo Gildenhard and Martin Ruehl (London: Institute of Classical Studies, School of Advanced Study, University of London, 2003).
Gossmann, Lionel. *Basel in the Age of Burckhardt: A Study in Unseasonable Ideas* (Chicago and London: University of Chicago Press, 2000).
Lidtke, Vernon L. *The Outlawed Party: Social Democracy in Germany, 1878–1890* (Princeton, NJ: Princeton University Press, 1966).
Mann, Thomas. *Reflections of a Nonpolitical Man* (1918), trans. Walter D. Morris (New York: Frederick Ungar, 1983).
Mommsen, Wolfgang J. *Imperial Germany 1867–1918: Politics, Culture, and Society in an Authoritarian State*, trans. Richard Deveson (London: Arnold, 1995).
Pflanze, Otto. 'Bismarck's *Realpolitik*', *Imperial Germany*, ed. James J. Sheehan (New York: New Viewpoints, 1976).
Retallack, James N. *Notables of the Right: The Conservative Party and Political Mobilization in Germany, 1876–1918* (Boston, MA: Unwin Hyman, 1988).
Roth, Guenther. *The Social Democrats in Imperial Germany: A Study in Working-Class Isolation and National Integration* (New Jersey: Bedminster Press, 1963).
Sheehan, James. *German Liberalism in the Nineteenth Century* (Chicago: University of Chicago Press, 1978).
Schieder, Theodor. *The State and Society in Our Times*, trans. C. A. M. Sym (London: Thomas Nelson and Sons, 1962).
Smith, Helmut Walser. *German Nationalism and Religious Conflict: Culture, Ideology, Politics, 1870–1914* (Princeton, NJ: Princeton University Press, 1995).
Tal, Uriel. *Christians and Jews in Germany: Religion, Politics, and Ideology in the Second Reich, 1870–1914*, trans. Noah Jonathan Jacobs (Ithaca, NY: Cornell University Press, 1975).

Taylor, A. J. P. *Bismarck: The Man and Statesman* (London: Hamish Hamilton, 1965).
Wehler, Hans-Ulrich. 'Bismarck's Imperialism, 1862–1890', *Imperial Germany*, ed. James J. Sheehan (New York: New Viewpoints, 1976).
—— *The German Empire: 1871–1918*, trans. Kim Traynor (New Hampshire: Berg, 1985).
Williamson, George S. *The Longing for Myth in Germany: Religion and Aesthetic Culture from Romanticism to Nietzsche* (Chicago and London: University of Chicago Press, 2004).

Selected Bibliography

Books

Algermissen, Konrad. *Nietzsche und das Dritte Reich*. Celle: Verlag Joseph Giesel, 1947.

Ansell-Pearson, Keith. *An Introduction to Nietzsche as Political Thinker: The Perfect Nihilist*. Cambridge: Cambridge University Press, 1994.

———. *Nietzsche Contra Rousseau: A Study of Nietzsche's Moral and Political Thought*. Cambridge: Cambridge University Press, 1991.

Appel, Fredrick. *Nietzsche contra Democracy*. Ithaca, NY: Cornell University Press, 1999.

Aschheim, Steven E. *The Nietzsche Legacy in Germany: 1890–1990*. Berkeley, CA: University of California Press, 1992.

Backhaus, Jürgen G. and Drechsler, Wolfgang. Eds. *Friedrich Nietzsche (1844–1900): Economy and Society*. New York: Springer, 2006.

Barker, Ernest, Sir. *Nietzsche and Treitschke: The Worship of Power in Modern Germany*. London and Toronto: Oxford University Press, 1914.

Bauer, Karin. *Adorno's Nietzschean Narratives: Critiques of Ideology, Readings of Wagner*. New York: SUNY Press, 1999.

Bäumler, Alfred. *Nietzsche, der Philosoph und Politiker*. Leipzig: Reclam, 1931.

Benoist, Alain de. *Nietzsche: morale et grande politique*. Paris: 1973.

Bentley, Eric. *A Century of Hero-Worship*. Boston, MA: Beacon Press, 1957.

Bergmann, Peter. *Nietzsche, 'the Last Antipolitical German'*. Bloomington, IN: Indiana University Press, 1987.

Bünger, Peter. *Nietzsche als Kritiker des Sozialismus*. Aachen: Shaker Verlag, 1997.

Carroll, John. *Break-Out from the Crystal Palace: The Anarcho-psychological Critique: Stirner, Nietzsche, Dostoevsky*. London: Routledge & Kegan Paul, 1974.

Cate, Curtis. *Friedrich Nietzsche: A Biography*. London: Pimlico, 2003.

Conrad, M.G. *Der Übermensch in der Politik: Betrachtungen über die Reichzustände am Ende des Jahrhunderts*. Stuttgart: Robert Lutz, 1895.

Conway, Daniel W. *Nietzsche's Dangerous Game: Philosophy in the Twilight of the Idols*. Cambridge: Cambridge University Press, 1997.

———. *Nietzsche and the Political*. London: Routledge, 1997.

Detwiler, Bruce. *Nietzsche and the Politics of Aristocratic Radicalism*. Chicago: University of Chicago Press, 1990.

Dombowsky, Don. *Nietzsche's Machiavellian Politics*. Basingstoke: Palgrave Macmillan, 2004.

Dupuy, René-Jean. *Politique de Nietzsche*. Paris: Armand Colin, 1969.

East Europe Reads Nietzsche. Eds. Alice Freifeld, Peter Bergmann, and Bernice Glatzer Rosenthal. Boulder, CO: East European Monographs, 1998.

Eden, Robert. *Political Leadership and Nihilism: A Study of Weber and Nietzsche*. Tampa, FL: University Presses of Florida, 1983.

Elbe, Stefan. *Europe: A Nietzschean Perspective*. Advances in European Politics Series, London: Routledge, 2003.

Emden, Christian J. *Friedrich Nietzsche and the Politics of History.* Cambridge: Cambridge University Press, 2008.
Froese, Katrin. *Rousseau and Nietzsche: Toward an Aesthetic Modernity.* Lanham, MD: Lexington Books, 2001.
Galindo, Martha Zapata. *Triumph des Willens zur Macht: Zur Nietzsche-Rezeption im NS-Staat.* Hamburg: Argument Verlag, 1995.
Gawronsky, D. *Friedrich Nietzsche und das Dritte Reich.* Bern: Verlag Herbert Lang and Cie., 1935.
Gillespie, Michael Allen and Tracy B. Strong. Eds. *Nietzsche's New Seas: Explorations in Philosophy, Aesthetics, and Politics.* Chicago: University of Chicago Press, 1988.
Golomb, Jacob and Wistrich, Robert S. Eds. *Nietzsche, Godfather of Fascism? On the Uses and Abuses of a Philosophy.* Princeton, NJ: Princeton University Press, 2002.
Goodrich, Peter and Valverde, Mariana. Eds. *Nietzsche and Legal Theory: Half-Written Laws.* New York: Routledge, 2005.
Goyard-Fabre, Simone. *Nietzsche et la question politique.* Paris: Éditions Sirey, 1977.
Härtle, Heinrich. *Nietzsche und der Nationalsocialismus.* Munich: Zentralverlag der NSDAP, 1937.
Hatab, Lawrence J. *A Nietzschean Defense of Democracy: An Experiment in Postmodern Politics.* Chicago: Open Court, 1995.
Hayman, Ronald. *Nietzsche: A Critical Life.* New York: Penguin Books, 1980.
Heilke, Thomas. *Nietzsche's Tragic Regime: Culture, Aesthetics, and Political Education.* DeKalb, IL: Northern Illinois University Press, 1998.
Janz, Curt Paul. *Friedrich Nietzsche: Biographie.* 3 vols. Munich: Hanser, 1978–79.
Kazantzakis, Nikos. *Friedrich Nietzsche on the Philosophy of Right and the State.* Trans. Odysseus Makridis. Albany, NY: SUNY Press, 2006.
Kerger, Henry. *Autorität und Recht in Denken Nietzsches.* Berlin: Dunker und Humboldt, 1988.
Kiss, Endre. Ed. *Friedrich Nietzsche und die Globalen Probleme unserer Zeit.* Cuxhaven: Traude Junghans Verlag, 1997.
Kofman, Sarah. *Le mépris des Juifs: Nietzsche, les Juifs, l'antisémitisme.* Paris: Galilée, 1994.
Krulic, Brigitte. *Nietzsche Penseur de la Hiérarchie: Pour une lecture 'tocquevillienne' de Nietzsche.* Paris: L'Harmattan, 2002.
Kunnas, T. *Politik als Prostitution des Geistes. Eine Studie über das Politische in Nietzsches Werken.* München, 1982.
Landa, Ishay. *The Overman in the Marketplace: Nietzschean Heroism in Popular Culture.* Lanham, MD: Lexington Books, 2007.
Lampert, Laurence. *Leo Strauss and Nietzsche.* Chicago: University of Chicago Press, 1996.
Leroux, François. *Figures de la souveraineté: Nietzsche et la question politique.* Éditions Hurtubise, 1997.
Levenstein, Adolf. *Friedrich Nietzsche im Urteil der Arbeiterklasse.* Leipzig: F. Meiner, 1914.
Losurdo, Domenico. *Nietzsche, il ribelle aristocratico. Biografia intellettuale e bilancio critico.* Torino: Bollati Boringhieri, 2002.
Love, Nancy S. *Marx, Nietzsche and Modernity.* New York: Columbia University Press, 1986.
Macintyre, Ben. *Forgotten Fatherland: The Search for Elisabeth Nietzsche.* New York: Farrar Straus Giroux, 1992.
Mahon, Michael. *Foucault's Nietzschean Genealogy: Truth, Power and the Subject.* Albany, NY: SUNY Press, 1992.

Marti, Urs. *'Der grosse Pöbel- und Sklavenaufstand'*: *Nietzsches Auseinandersetzung mit Revolution und Demokratie*. Stuttgart: Verlag J. B. Metzler, 1993.
Martin, Alfred von. *Nietzsche und Burckhardt*. 2nd edn. Verlag Ernst Reinhardt in München, 1942.
McGrath, William J. *Dionysian Art and Populist Politics in Austria*. New Haven, CT: Yale University Press, 1974.
McIntyre, Alex. *The Sovereignty of Joy*: *Nietzsche's Vision of Grand Politics*. Toronto: University of Toronto Press, 1997.
Moore, Gregory. *Nietzsche, Biology and Metaphor*. Cambridge: Cambridge University Press, 2002.
Moore, John. Ed. *I Am Not A Man, I Am Dynamite!*: *Friedrich Nietzsche and the Anarchist Tradition*. Brooklyn: Autonomedia, 2004.
Nicolas, M. *De Nietzsche à Hitler*. Paris: 1938.
Nolte, Ernst. *Nietzsche und der Nietzscheanismus*. Berlin: Propylen, 1990.
Nolte, Josef. *Wir guten Europäer*: *Historisch-politische Versuche über uns selbst*. Tübingen: Narr, 1991.
Odouev, Stepan. *Par les sentiers de Zarathoustra*: *influence de la pensée de Nietzsche sur la philosophie bourgeoise allemande*. Trans. Catherine Emery. Moscow: Éditions du Progrès, 1980.
Okonta, Ike. *The Politics of Power*. New York: Peter Lang, 1992.
Oliver, K. and Pearsall, M. Eds. *Feminist Interpretations of Friedrich Nietzsche*. Pennsylvania: Pennsylvania State University Press, 1998.
Oppel, Frances Nesbitt. *Nietzsche on Gender*: *Beyond Man and Woman*. Charlottesville, VA: University of Virginia Press, 2005.
Ottmann, Henning. *Philosophie und Politik bei Nietzsche*. Berlin: Walter de Gruyter, 1987.
Owen, David. *Nietzsche, Politics and Modernity*: *A Critique of Liberal Reason*. London: SAGE Publications, 1995.
Picart, C. J. S. *Resentment and the 'Feminine' in Nietzsche's Politico-Aesthetics*. University Park, PA: Pennsylvania State University Press, 1999.
Prostka, N. *Nietzsches Machtbegriff in Bezeihung zu den Machiavellis*. Münster: 1989.
Pszczótkowski, Tomasz Grzegorz. *Zur Methodologie der Interpretation des Politischen bei Friedrich Nietzsche*. Frankfurt-am-Main: Peter Lang, 1996.
Rehmann, Jan. *Postmoderner Links-Nietzscheanismus. Deleuze und Foucault. Eine Dekonstruktion*. Hamburg: 2004.
Rosenthal, Alfred. *Nietzsches Euröpaisches Rasse-Problem* (*'Die Kampf um die Erdherrschaft'*). Leiden: E. J. Brill, 1935.
Rosenthal, Bernice Glatzer. *New Myth, New World*: *From Nietzsche to Stalinism*. Pennsylvania: Pennsylvania University Press, 2002.
———. *Nietzsche in Russia*. Princeton, NJ: Princeton University Press, 1986.
Santaniello, Weaver. *Nietzsche, God and the Jews*: *His Critique of Judeo-Christianity in Relation to the Nazi Myth*. Albany, NY: SUNY Press, 1994.
Sautet, Marc. *Nietzsche et la Commune*. Paris: Editions Le Sycomore, 1981.
Schank, Gerd. *'Rasse' und 'Züchtung' bei Nietzsche*. Berlin: Walter de Gruyter, 2000.
Schieder, Theodor. *Nietzsche und Bismarck*. Leiden: E. J. Brill, 1966.
Sedgwick. Peter R. *Nietzsche's Economy*: *Modernity, Normativity and Futurity*. Basingstoke: Palgrave Macmillan, 2007.
Seilliére, Ernest. *La Philosophie de l'impérialisme*: *vol. 2, Apollon ou Dionysos, étude critique sur Frédérick Nietzsche et l'utilitarisme impérialiste*. Paris: Plon-Nourrit, 1905.
Schrift, Alan D. Ed. *Why Nietzsche Still? Reflections on Drama, Culture, and Politics*. Berkeley, CA: University of California Press, 2000.

Shaw, Tamsin. *Nietzsche's Political Skepticism*. Princeton, NJ: Princeton University Press, 2007.
Siemens, H. and Roodt, V. Eds. *Nietzsche, Power and Politics: Rethinking Nietzsche's Legacy for Political Thought*. Berlin and New York: de Gruyter, 2008.
Solm-Laubach, Franz Graf zu. *Nietzsche and Early German Sociology*. Berlin: Walter de Gruyter, 2007.
Stell, Hans Dieter. *Machiavelli und Nietzsche*. München: 1987.
Stewart, Herbert Leslie. *Nietzsche and the Ideals of Modern Germany*. New York: Longman, Green, 1915.
Stewart, James D. *Nietzsche's Zarathustra and Political Thought. Studies in Social and Political Theory*. Vol. 29. New York: Edwin Mellen Press, 2002.
Strong, Tracy B. *Friedrich Nietzsche and the Politics of Transfiguration*. Berkeley, CA: University of California Press, 1975.
Taureck, Bernard H. F. *Nietzsche und der Faschismus: Eine Studie über Nietzsche politische Philosophie und ihre Folgen*. Hamburg: Junius Verlag, 1989.
Taylor, Seth. *Left-Wing Nietzscheans: The Politics of German Expressionism*. Berlin: Walter de Gruyter, 1990.
Thiele, Leslie Paul. *Nietzsche and the Politics of the Soul: A Study of Heroic Individualism*. Princeton, NJ: Princeton University Press, 1990.
Thomas, R. Hinton. *Nietzsche in German Politics and Society: 1890–1918*. Manchester: Manchester University Press, 1983.
Vacano, Diego A. von. *The Art of Power: Machiavelli, Nietzsche, and the Making of Aesthetic Political Theory*. Lanham, MD: Lexington Books, 2007.
Waite, Geoff. *Nietzsche's Corps/e: Aesthetics, Politics, Prophecy, or, The Spectacular Technoculture of Everyday Life*. Durham, NC and London: Duke University Press, 1996.
Warren, Mark. *Nietzsche and Political Thought*. Cambridge, MA: The MIT Press, 1988.

Articles and essays

Abbey, Ruth and Appel, Fredrick. 'Domesticating Nietzsche: A Response to Mark Warren'. *Political Theory*. 27(1), February 1999, 121–5.
———. 'Nietzsche and the Will to Politics'. *Review of Politics*. 60(1). Winter 1998, 83–114.
Acampora, Christa Davis. 'Demos Agonistes Redux. Reflections on the *Streit* of Political Agonism'. *Nietzsche-Studien*. 32, 2003, 374–90.
Acampora, Ralph, 'The Joyful Wisdom of Ecology'. *New Nietzsche Studies*. 5–3/4 and 6–1/2, Winter 2003 and Spring 2004, 22–34.
Ansell-Pearson, Keith. 'Nietzsche, Woman and Political Theory'. *Nietzsche, Feminism and Political Theory*. Ed. Paul Patton. London: Routledge, 1993.
———. 'The Significance of Michel Foucault's Reading of Nietzsche: Power, the Subject and Political Theory'. *Nietzsche-Studien*. 20, 1991, 267–83.
Balke, Friedrich. 'Die Figuren des Verbrechers in Nietzsches Biopolitik'. *Nietzsche-Studien*. 32, 2003, 171–205.
Barry, W. 'The Ideals of Anarchy: Friedrich Nietzsche'. *Quarterly Review*. clxxxiv, October, 1896, 299–328.
Bataille, Georges. 'Nietzsche and the Fascists' (1937). *Visions of Excess*. Ed. Allan Stoekl. Trans. Allan Stoekl, Carl R. Lovitt and Donald M. Leslie Jr. Minneapolis: University of Minnesota Press, 1985.
———. 'Nietzsche In Light of Marxism'. *Semiotext(e)*. Vol. 3, No. 1, 1978, 114–19.

Bäumler, Alfred. 'Nietzsche and National Socialism'. *Nazi Culture: Intellectual, Cultural and Social Life in the Third Reich*. Ed. George L. Mosse. Trans. Salvator Attanasio. New York: Grosset and Dunlop, 1966.
Behler, Ernst. 'Nietzsche in der marxistischen Kritik Osteuropas'. *Nietzsche-Studien*. 10/11, 1981/82, 34–58.
———. 'Nietzsche and Postfeminism'. *Nietzsche-Studien*. 22, 1993, 355–70.
———. 'Zur frühen sozialistischen Rezeption Nietzsches in Deutschland'. *Nietzsche-Studien*. 13, 1984, 503–20.
Bergmann, Peter. 'Nietzsche, Friedrich III and the Missing Generation in German History'. *Nietzsche-Studien*. 17, 1988, 195–217.
Bourne, Randolph. 'Denatured Nietzsche'. *The Dial*. October 1917, 389–91.
———. 'Trans-National America'. *Atlantic Monthly*. June 1917, 778–86.
Brobjer, Thomas H. 'The Absence of Political Ideals in Nietzsche's Writings. The Case of the Laws of Manu and the Associated Caste-Society'. *Nietzsche-Studien*. 27, 1998, 300–19.
———. 'Nietzsche's Knowledge of Marx and Marxism'. *Nietzsche-Studien*. 31, 2002, 298–313.
———. 'Nietzsche's Knowledge, Reading and Critique of Political Economy'. *The Journal of Nietzsche Studies*. 18, Fall 1999, 56–70.
———. 'Nietzsche as Political Thinker. A Response to D. Dombowsky'. *Nietzsche-Studien*. 30, 2001, 394–6.
Brose, K. 'Nietzsches Verhältnis zu John Stuart Mill. Eine geistewissenschaftliche Studie'. *Nietzsche-Studien*. 3, 1974, 152–74.
Bull, Malcolm. 'Where is the Anti-Nietzsche?' *New Left Review*. No. 3, May–June 2000, 121–45.
Cardozo Law Review. Nietzsche and Legal Theory. Vol. 24, No. 2, January 2003.
Caygill, Howard. 'The Return of Nietzsche and Marx'. *Nietzsche, Feminism and Political Theory*. Ed. Paul Patton. London: Routledge, 1993.
Clark, Maudemarie. 'Nietzsche's Antidemocratic Rhetoric'. *Southern Journal of Philosophy*. Vol. 37, 1999, 119–41.
Cohen, Jonathan R. 'Nietzsche's Elitism and the Cultural Division of Labor'. *Rending and Renewing the Social Order*. Eds. Hudson, Yeager. Lewiston, NY: Edwin Mellen Press, 1996.
Colman, John S. 'Nietzsche as Politique et Moraliste'. *Journal of the History of Ideas*. 27, October–December 1966, 549–74.
Conant, James. 'Nietzsche's Perfectionism: A Reading of *Schopenhauer as Educator*'. *Nietzsche's Postmoralism: Essays on Nietzsche's Prelude to Philosophy's Future*. Ed. Richard Schacht. Cambridge: Cambridge University Press, 2001.
Conway, Daniel W. 'Solving the Problem of Socrates: Nietzsche's *Zarathustra* as Political Irony'. *Political Theory*. 16, 1988, 257–80.
———. 'Nietzsche's Germano-mania'. *Nietzsche and the German Tradition*. Ed. Nicholas Martin. Bern: Peter Lang, 2003.
———. 'The Politics of Decadence'. *Southern Journal of Philosophy*. Vol. 37, 1999, 19–34.
Dannhauser, Werner J. 'Friedrich Nietzsche'. *History of Political Philosophy*. Eds. Leo Strauss, Joseph Cropsey. Chicago: University of Chicago Press, 1981.
D'Annunzio, Gabriele. 'The Beast Who Wills' (1892). *Stanford Italian Review*. Vol. 6, 1–2, 1986, 265–77.
Deleuze, Gilles. 'Pensée nomade'. *Nietzsche aujourd'hui*. Paris: Union Générale d'Editions, 1973.

Der Derian, James. 'The Value of Security: Hobbes, Marx, Nietzsche, and Baudrillard'. *The Political Subject of Violence*. Eds. David Campbell and Michael Dillon. Manchester: Manchester University Press, 1993.

Derrida, Jacques. 'Otiobiographies: The Teaching of Nietzsche and the Politics of the Proper Name'. *The Ear of the Other: Otiobiography Transference Translation*. Ed. Christie V. McDonald. Trans. Peggy Kamuf and Avital Ronell. New York: Schocken Books, 1985.

Diethe, Carol. 'Nietzsche and the Early German Feminists'. *Journal of Nietzsche Studies*. Issue 12, Autumn 1996.

———. 'Nietzsche and Nationalism'. *History of European Ideas*. Vol. 14, No. 2, 1992, 227–34.

Dombowsky, Don. '"Agitation anarchiste dans l'Empire"'. *Conjonctures*. No. 35, Automne 2002, 155–60.

———. 'A Response to Alan D. Schrift's "Nietzsche for Democracy?"' *Nietzsche-Studien*. 31, 2002, 278–90.

———. 'A Response to Thomas H. Brobjer's "The Absence of Political Ideals in Nietzsche's Writings"'. *Nietzsche-Studien*. 30, 2001, 387–93.

———. 'Remarks on Deleuze's "Pensée nomade": Politics, Tactics and the Philosophy of Law'. *Dogma: Revue électronique*, July 2006.

———. 'Nietzsche, Justice and the Critique of Liberal Democracy'. *Eidos*. Vol. XIV, No. 2, June 1997, 105–25.

———. 'Nietzsche and the Politics of Nationalism'. *The European Legacy: Journal of the International Society for the Study of European Ideas*. Vol. 4, No. 5, 1999, 23–36.

———. 'The Rhetoric of Legitimation: Nietzsche's "Doctrine" of Eternal Recurrence'. *Journal of Nietzsche Studies*. Issue 14, 1997, 26–45.

Drenthen, Martin. 'Nietzsche and the Paradox of Environmental Ethics.' *New Nietzsche Studies*. 5–1/2, Spring Summer 2002, 12–25.

Eden, Robert. 'The Rule of the Misfits: Ridicule in the Politics of Nietzsche and Machiavelli'. *World and I*. 1987, 589–99.

———. 'To What Extent Has the World of Concern to Contemporary Man Been Created by Nietzschean Politics?' *Nietzsche Heute*. Ed. Sigrid Bauschinger et al. Stuttgart: Francke, 1988.

Egyed, Béla. 'Nietzsche's Anti-democratic Liberalism'. *Kritika and Kontext*. Issue 2, 2007, 100–13.

Elbe, Stefan. 'Labyrinths of the Future: Nietzsche's Genealogy of Nationalism'. *Journal of Political Ideologies*. Vol. 7, No. 1, Spring 2002.

———. 'Of Seismographs and Earthquakes: Nietzsche, Nihilism and Genocide'. Bo Strath and James Kaye. Eds. *Enlightenment and Genocide: Contradictions of Modernity*. Brussels: Presses Interuniversitaires Europiennes, 2000.

Emden, Christian J. 'Toward a Critical Historicism: History and Politics in Nietzsche's Second "Untimely Meditation"'. *Modern Intellectual History*. 3, 1, 2006, 1–31.

Etter, A. 'Nietzsche und das Gesetzbuch des Manu'. *Nietzsche-Studien*. 16, 1987, 340–52.

Farrenkopf, John. 'Nietzsche, Spengler, and the Politics of Cultural Despair'. *Interpretation*. 20(2), Winter 1992–93, 165–85.

Fischer, K. R. 'Nazism as Nietzsche's "Experiment"'. *Nietzsche-Studien*. 6, 1977, 116–22.

Fowler, Mark. 'Nietzschean Perspectivism: "How Could Such a Philosophy – Dominate?"'. *Social Theory and Practice*. 16(2), Summer 1990, 119–62.

Gedö, András. 'Why Marx or Nietzsche?' *Nature, Society, and Thought*. Vol. 11, No. 3, 1998, 331–46.

Giroux, Dalie. 'L'Unité de la Forme et du Fond et la Grande Politique Nietzschéenne'. *Sociétés: Revue des Sciences Humaines et Sociales.* No. 81, 2003/3, 45–59.

Glenn, Paul F. 'Nietzsche's Napoleon: The Higher Man as Political Actor'. *Review of Politics.* 63(1), Winter 2001, 129–58.

Golomb, J. and Wistrich, R. 'Nietzsche, Politics, Fascism and the Jews'. *Nietzsche-Studien.* 30, 2001, 305–21.

Gröper, Richard. 'Nietzsche und der Krieg'. *Die Tat* 8/1, 1916, 25–38.

Guth, Alfred. 'Nietzsches "Neue Barbaren"'. *Nietzsche: Werk and Wirkungen.* Göttigen: Vandenhoeck and Ruprecht, 1974.

Haar, Michel. 'The Institution and Destitution of the Political According to Nietzsche'. *New Nietzsche Studies.* 2–/2, Fall/Winter 1997, 1–36.

Hatab, Lawrence J. 'Poststructuralism and Politics.' *New Nietzsche Studies.* 3–1/2, Winter/Spring 1999, 109–17.

———. 'Prospects for a Democratic Agon: Why We Can Still Be Nietzscheans'. *Journal of Nietzsche Studies.* Issue 24, Fall 2002, 132–47.

Helm, Barbara. 'Combating Misogyny? Responses to Nietzsche by Turn-of-the-Century German Feminists'. *Journal of Nietzsche Studies.* Issue 27, Spring 2004, 64–84.

Hillard, Derek. 'History as a Dual Process: Nietzsche on Exchange and Power'. *Nietzsche-Studien.* 31, 2002, 40–56.

Hodge, Joanna. 'Nietzsche, Heidegger, Europe: Five Remarks.' *Journal of Nietzsche Studies.* Issue 3, Spring 1992.

Hofmann, H. 'Jacob Burckhardt und Friedrich Nietzsche also Kritiker des Bismarckreiches'. *Der Staat* 10, 1971, 433–53.

Holub, Robert C. 'Nietzsche's Colonialist Imagination: Nueva Germania, Good Europeanism, and Great Politics.' *The Imperialist Imagination: German Colonialism and Its Legacy.* Ed. Sara Friedrichs-Meyer, Sara Lennox and Susanne Zantop. Ann Arbor, MI: University of Michigan Press, 1998, 33–49.

Honig, Bonnie. 'The Politics of Agonism: A Critical Response to "Beyond Good and Evil: Arendt, Nietzsche and the Aestheticization of Political Action" by Dana R. Villa'. *Political Theory.* 21(3), August 1993, 528–33.

Humble, Malcolm. 'Heinrich Mann and Arnold Zweig: Left-Wing Nietzscheans?'. *Nietzsche and the German Tradition.* Ed. Nicholas Martin. Bern: Peter Lang, 2003.

Hunt, Lester H. 'Politics and Anti-Politics: Nietzsche's View of the State'. *History of Philosophy Quarterly.* Vol. 2, No. 4, October 1985, 453–68.

Jung, W. 'Das Nietzsche-Bild von Georg Lukács. Zur Metakritik einer marxistischen Nietzsche-Deutung'. *Nietzsche-Studien.* 19, 1990, 419–30.

Kariel, Henry S. 'Nietzsche's Preface to Constitutionalism'. *Journal of Politics.* 25(2), May 1963, 211–25.

Kuenzli, Rudolph E. 'The Nazi Appropriation of Nietzsche'. *Nietzsche-Studien.*12, 1983, 428–35.

Lampert, Laurence. '"Peoples and Fatherlands": Nietzsche's Philosophical Politics'. *Southern Journal of Philosophy.* Vol. 37, 1999, 43–63.

Landa, Ishay. 'Nietzsche, the Chinese Worker's Friend'. *New Left Review.* No. 236, July/August 1999, 3–23.

Large, Duncan. 'The Aristocratic Radical and the White Revolutionary: Nietzsche's Bismarck'. *Das schwierige neunzehnte Jahrhundert. Germanistische Tagung zum 65. Gerburtstag von Eda Sagarra im August 1998.* Ed. J. Barkhoff, G. Carr and R. Paulin. Tubingen: Niemeyer, 2000, 101–16.

Levin, David Michael. 'Critical Comments on Hatab's Nietzschean Defense of Democracy'. *New Nietzsche Studies.* 2–1/2, Fall/Winter 1997, 123–32.

———. 'On Civilized Cruelty: Nietzsche on the Disciplinary Practices of Western Culture'. *New Nietzsche Studies.* 5–1/2, Spring Summer 2002, 72–94.

Lindsay, J. A. 'Eugenics and the Doctrine of the Super-Man'. *Eugenics Review.* VII, January, 1916, 247–62.

Lublinski, Samuel. 'Machiavelli und Nietzsche'. *Die Zukunft.* Jg. 9. Bd. 34, Berlin 1901, 73–82.

Ludovici, Anthony. 'Hitler and Nietzsche'. *English Review.* 64, January 1937, 44–52, and February 1937, 192–202.

Mara, Gerald M. and Dovi, Suzanne L. 'Mill, Nietzsche, and the Identity of Postmodern Liberalism'. *Journal of Politics.* 57(1), February 1995, 1–23.

Marti, Urs. 'Nietzsches Kritik der Französischen Revolution'. *Nietzsche-Studien.* 19, 1990, 312–35.

———. 'Der Plebejer in der Revolte – Ein Beitrag zur Genealogie des "Höheren Menschen"'. *Nietzsche-Studien.* 18, 1989, 550–72.

Martin, Nicholas. '"Fighting a Philosophy": The Figure of Nietzsche in British Propaganda of the First World War'. *The Modern Language Review.* Vol. 98, No. 2, April 2003, 367–80.

———. 'Nietzsche in the GDR: History of a Taboo'. *Nietzsche and the German Tradition.* Ed. Nicholas Martin. Bern: Peter Lang, 2003.

———. '"We good Europeans": Nietzsche's new Europe in Beyond Good and Evil. *History of European Ideas.* Vol. 20, Nos. 1–3, 1995, 141–4.

Maurer, Reinhart. 'Nietzsche und die Kritische Theorie'. *Nietzsche-Studien.* 10/11, 1981/82, 34–58.

McIntyre, Alex. '"Virtuosos of Contempt": An Investigation of Nietzsche's Political Philosophy through Certain Platonic Political Ideas'. *Nietzsche-Studien.* 21, 1992, 184–210.

Miller, James. 'Some Implications of Nietzsche's Thought for Marxism'. *Telos.* 37, Fall 1978, 22–41.

Neumann, H. 'Superman or Last Man? Nietzsche's Interpretation of Athens and Jerusalem'. *Nietzsche-Studien.* 5, 1976, 1–28.

Niemeyer, Christian. 'Nietzsches rhetorischer Antisemitismus'. *Nietzsche-Studien.* 26, 1997, 139–62.

Nussbaum, Martha. 'Is Nietzsche a Political Thinker?' *International Journal of Philosophical Studies.* Vol. 5, No. 1, 1997, 1–13.

Ohana, David. 'Nietzsche and Ernst Jünger: From Nihilism to Totalitarianism'. *History of European Ideas* 11, 1998, 751–8.

Ottmann, Henning. 'Anti-Lukács. Eine Kritik der Nietzsche-Kritik von Georg Lukács'. *Nietzsche-Studien.* 13, 1984, 570–86.

Outwaite, William. 'Nietzsche and Critical Theory'. *Nietzsche: A Critical Reader.* Ed. Peter R. Sedgwick. Oxford: Blackwell, 1995, 203–21.

Owen, David. 'Equality, Democracy, and Self-Respect: Reflections on Nietzsche's Agonal Perfectionism'. *Journal of Nietzsche Studies.* Issue 24, Fall 2002, 113–31.

Pangle, Thomas L. 'The Roots of Contemporary Nihilism and its Political Consequences According to Nietzsche'. *Review of Politics.* 45, 1, January 1983, 45–70.

———. 'The "Warrior Spirit" as an Inlet to the Political Philosophy of Nietzsche's Zarathustra'. *Nietzsche-Studien.* 15, 1986, 140–79.

Parkes, Graham. 'Wanderers in the Shadow of Nihilism: Nietzsche's Good Europeans'. *History of European Ideas.* Vol. 16, Nos. 4–6, 1993, 585–90.

Patton, Paul. 'Politics and the Concept of Power in Hobbes and Nietzsche'. *Nietzsche, Feminism and Political Theory*. Ed. Paul Patton. London: Routledge, 1993.

Polin, Raymond. 'Nietzsche und der Staat oder die Politik eines Einsamen'. *Nietzsche: Werk und Wirkungen*. Göttigen: Vandenhoeck and Ruprecht, 1974.

Pourgouris, M. C. 'Nietzsche contra Lukács: Politics of History and Epic Conceptions'. *Nietzsche-Studien*. 31, 2002, 241–52.

Pütz, P. 'Nietzsche und der Antisemitismus'. *Nietzsche-Studien*. 30, 2001, 295–304.

Rajchman, John. 'Nietzsche, Foucault and the Anarchism of Power'. *Semiotext(e)*. Vol. 3, No. 1, 1978, 96–107.

Read, James H. 'Nietzsche: Power as Oppression'. *Praxis International*. 9(1–2), April 1989, 72–87.

Redhead, Mark. 'Debate: Nietzsche and Liberal Democracy: A Relationship of Antagonistic Indebtedness?' *The Journal of Political Philosophy*. Vol. 5, No. 2, 1997, 183–93.

Rehmann, Jan. 'Re-Reading Nietzsche with Domenico Losurdo's Intellectual Biography'. *Historical Materialism*. 15, 2007, 1–60.

———. 'Towards a Deconstruction of Postmodernist Neo-Nietzscheanism: Deleuze and Foucault'. *Situations: Project of the Radical Imagination*. Vol. 2, No. 1, 2007, 7–16.

Reibnitz, B. v. 'Nietzsche's "Griechischer Staat" und das deutsche Kaiserreich'. *Der altsprachliche Unterricht*. III, 1987, 76–89.

Roche, Mark W. 'National Socialism and the Disintegration of Values: Reflections on Nietzsche, Rosenberg, and Broch.' *Journal of Value Inquiry*. 26(3), 1992, 367–80.

Ruehl, Martin. '*Politeia* 1871: Nietzsche *Contra* Wagner on the Greek State'. *Out of Arcadia: Classics and Politics in Germany in The Age of Burckhardt, Nietzsche and Wilamowitz*'. Eds. Ingo Gildenhard and Martin Ruehl. Institute of Classical Studies, School of Advanced Study, University of London, 2003, 61–86.

Sadler, Ted. 'The Postmodern Politicization of Nietzsche'. *Nietzsche, Feminism and Political Theory*. Ed. Paul Patton. London: Routledge, 1993.

Santaniello, Weaver. 'A Post-Holocaust Re-Examination of Nietzsche and the Jews: *Vis-à-vis* Christendom and Nazism'. *Nietzsche and Jewish Culture*. Ed. Jacob Golomb. London: Routledge, 1997.

Schank, Gerd. 'Race and Breeding in Nietzsche's Philosophy'. *Nietzsche and the German Tradition*. Ed. Nicholas Martin. Bern: Peter Lang, 2003.

Schieder, Theodor. 'Nietzsche and Bismarck'. Trans. Alexandra Hendee. *The Historian*. 29 (4), August 1967, 584–604.

Schrift, Alan D. 'Nietzsche *for* Democracy?' *Nietzsche-Studien*. 29, 2000, 220–33.

———. 'Response to Don Dombowsky'. *Nietzsche-Studien*. 31, 2002, 291–7.

Schutte, Ofelia. 'Nietzsche's Cultural Politics: A Critique'. *Southern Journal of Philosophy*. Vol. 37, 1999, 9–17.

Sedgwick, Peter. 'Violence, Economy and Temporality. Plotting the Political Terrain of *On the Genealogy of Morality*'. *Nietzsche-Studien*. 34, 2005, 163–85.

Serra, M. 'Goethe, Nietzsche et le sentiment national en France dans l'entre-deux guerres'. *Nietzsche-Studien*. 14, 1985, 337–56.

———. 'Nietzsche und die französischen Rechten 1930–1945'. *Nietzsche-Studien*. 13, 1984, 617–23.

Siemens, H. 'Agonal Communities of Taste: Law and Community in Nietzsche's Philosophy of Transvaluation'. *Journal of Nietzsche Studies*. Issue 24, Fall 2002, 83–112.

Smith, John H. 'Nietzsche's "Will to Power": Politics beyond (Hegelian) Recognition'. *New German Critique*. No. 73, Special Issue on Heiner Müller. Winter 1998, 133–63.

Sokel, W. H. 'Political Uses and Abuses of Nietzsche in Walter Kaufmann's Image of Nietzsche'. *Nietzsche-Studien.* 12, 1983, 436–42.
Spindel Conference 1998. *Nietzsche and Politics.* Ed. Jacqueline Scott. *The Southern Journal of Philosophy.* Vol. 37.
Stack, George J. 'Marx and Nietzsche: A Point of Affinity'. *Modern Schoolman.* 60, 1983, 247–63.
———. 'Nietzsche and the Laws of Manu'. *Sociology and Social Research.* 51, October 1966, 94–106.
Steilberg, Hays. 'Nietzsche and the Idea of National Identity: Randolph Bourne's "Transnational America"'. *German Life and Letters.* 48(4), October 1995, 487–98.
Strong, Tracy B. 'Nietzsche's Political Aesthetics'. *Nietzsche's New Seas.* Eds. Michael Allen Gillespie and T. B. Strong. Chicago: The University of Chicago Press, 1988.
———. 'Nietzsche's Political Misappropriation'. *The Cambridge Companion to Nietzsche.* Eds. Bernd Magnus and Kathleen M. Higgens. Cambridge: Cambridge University Press, 1996.
———. 'Nietzsche and Politics: Parables of the Shepherd and the Herd'. *Nietzsche: A Collection of Critical Essays.* Ed. Robert C. Solomon. Notre Dame, IN: University of Notre Dame Press, 1980.
———. 'Texts and Pretexts: Reflections on Perspectivism in Nietzsche'. *Political Theory.* 13(2), May 1985, 164–82.
Tanguay, Daniel. 'Strauss, Disciple de Nietzsche?' *Les Études philosophiques.* No. 1/2000, 105–32.
Taguieff, Pierre-André. 'The Traditional Paradigm – Horror of Modernity and Antiliberalism: Nietzsche in Reactionary Rhetoric'. *Why We Are Not Nietzscheans.* Eds. Luc Ferry and Alain Renaut. Trans. Robert de Loaiza. Chicago: University of Chicago Press, 1997.
Tapper, Marion. 'Ressentiment and Power: Some Reflections on Feminist Practices'. *Nietzsche, Feminism and Political Theory.* Ed. Paul Patton. London: Routledge, 1993.
Thiele, Leslie Paul. 'Nietzsche, Heidegger and Politics'. *Political Theory.* 22(3), August 1994, 468–90.
———. 'Nietzsche's Politics'. *Interpretation.* 17, Winter 1989–90, 275–90.
Tugendhat, Ernst. 'Macht und Antiegalitarismus bei Nietzsche und Hitler'. *Aufsätze 1992–2000.* Frankfurt-am-Main: Suhrkamp 2001.
Turner, Bryan. 'Nietzsche, Weber, and the Devaluation of Politics'. *Sociological Review.* 30, 1981, 367–91.
Trotsky, Leon. 'Some Words about the Philosophy of "the Superman"'. *Sochineniya.* Vol. 20, 1900.
Veyne, Paul. 'Ideology According to Marx and According to Nietzsche'. *Diogenes.* 99, 1977, 80–102.
Villa, Dana R. 'Beyond Good and Evil: Arendt, Nietzsche and the Aestheticization of Political Action'. *Political Theory.* 20, 1992, 274–308.
———. 'Democratizing the Agon'. *Why Nietzsche Still? Reflections on Drama, Culture and Politics.* Ed. Alan D. Schrift. Berkeley, CA: University of California Press, 2000.
———. 'Friedrich Nietzsche: Morality, Individualism, and Politics'. *Socratic Citizenship.* Princeton, NJ: Princeton University Press, 2001.
Voegelin, Eric. 'Nietzsche, the Crisis and the War'. *Journal of Politics.* Vol. 6, 1944, 177–211.
Waite, Geoff. 'Nietzsche's Baudelaire, or the Sublime Proleptic Spin of his Politico-Economic Thought'. *Representations.* No. 50, Spring 1995, 14–52.

———. The Politics of Reading Formations: The case of Nietzsche in Imperial Germany (1870–1919)'. *New German Critique*. 29, Spring/Summer 1983, 185–209.

———. 'Zarathustra or the Modern Prince: The Problem of Nietzschean Political Philosophy'. *Nietzsche Heute*. Ed. Sigrid Bauschinger et al. Stuttgart: Francke, 1988.

Ward, Janet. 'Nietzsche's Transvaluation of Jewish Parasitism'. *Journal of Nietzsche Studies*. Issue 24, Fall 2002, 54–82.

Warren, Mark. 'Nietzsche and the Political'. *New Nietzsche Studies*. 2–1/2, Fall/Winter 1997, 37–57.

———. 'Nietzsche and Political Philosophy'. *Political Theory*. 13, May 1985, 183–212.

———. 'The Politics of Nietzsche's Philosophy: Nihilism, Culture and Power'. *Political Studies*. 33, 1985, 418–38.

———. 'Reply to Ruth Abbey and Fredrick Appel'. *Political Theory*. 27(1), February 1999, 126–30.

Watson, James R. 'Nietzsche's Transnational Thinking'. *History of European Ideas*. Vol. 15, No. 1–3, 133–40.

Williams, H. 'Nietzsche and Fascism'. *History of European Ideas*. Vol. 11, 1989, 893–99.

Wilson, Peter Lamborn. 'A Nietzschean Coup d'État'. *Escape from the Nineteenth Century and Other Essays*. New York: Autonomedia, 1998.

Winchester, James. 'Nietzsche's Racial Profiling'. *Race and Racism in Modern Philosophy*. Ed. Andrew Valls. Ithaca, NY: Cornell University Press, 2005.

Zuckert, Catherine. 'Nietzsche's Rereading of Plato'. *Political Theory*. Vol. 13, No. 2, May 1985, 213–38.

Chapters

Abbey, Ruth. 'We Children of the Enlightenment'. *Nietzsche's Middle Period*. Oxford: Oxford University Press, 2000.

Barth, Hans. 'Nietzsche's Philosophy as the "Art of Mistrust"'. *Truth and Ideology*. Trans. Frederic Lilge. Berkeley, CA: University of California Press, 1992.

Bernstein, John Andrew. 'Foundations of Nietzschean Politics: The Ideals of Inequality' and 'Nietzsche and the Barbarians of the Twentieth Century'. *Nietzsche's Moral Philosophy*. Associated University Presses, 1987.

Brinton, Crane. 'Nietzsche and the Nazis'. *Nietzsche*. New York: Harper & Row, 1965.

Brown, Wendy. 'Postmodern Exposures, Feminist Hesitations' and 'Wounded Attachments'. *States of Injury: Power and Freedom in Late Modernity*. Princeton, NJ: Princeton University Press, 1995.

Cameron, Frank. 'Perfectionism and the Revaluation of All Values'. *Nietzsche and the 'Problem' of Morality*. New York: Peter Lang, 2002.

Camus, Albert. 'Nietzsche and Nihilism'. *The Rebel: An Essay on Man in Revolt*. New York: Vintage Books, 1956.

Cavell, Stanley. 'Aversive Thinking: Emersonian Representations in Heidegger and Nietzsche'. *Conditions Handsome and Unhandsome: The Constitution of Emersonian Perfectionism*. Chicago: University of Chicago Press, 1990.

Chytry, Josef. 'Nietzsche: Aesthetic Morals'. *The Aesthetic State: A Quest in Modern German Thought*. Berkeley, CA: University of California Press, 1989.

Connolly, William. 'Nietzsche: Politics and Homesickness'. *Political Theory and Modernity*. Ithaca, NY: Cornell University Press, 1988.

Foster, George Burman. 'Nietzsche and the State'. Nietzsche and Militarism'. 'Nietzsche and Democracy'. *Friedrich Nietzsche*. Ed. Curtis W. Reese. New York: Macmillan, 1931.
Gooding-Williams, Robert. 'Dionysus, the German Nation, and the Body'. *Zarathustra's Dionysian Modernism*. Stanford, CA: Stanford University Press, 2001.
Honig, Bonnie. 'Nietzsche and the Recovery of Responsibility'. *Political Theory and the Displacement of Politics*. Ithaca, NY: Cornell University Press, 1993.
Hunt, Lester H. 'Politics and Anti-Politics'. *Nietzsche and the Origin of Virtue*. London: Routledge, 1990.
Jacob, Alexander. 'German Aristocratic Doctrines: Treitschke, Nietzsche'. *Nobilitas: a Study of European Aristocratic Philosophy from Ancient Greece to the Early Twentieth Century*. Lanham, MD: University Press of America, 2001.
Jaspers, Karl. 'Great Politics'. *Nietzsche: An Introduction to the Understanding of His Philosophical Activity*. Trans. Charles F. Walraff and Frederick J. Schmitz. Tucson, AZ: University of Arizona Press, 1965.
Jünger, Friedrich Georg. 'Die Masse'. *Nietzsche*. Frankfurt Am Main: Vittorio Klostermann, 1949.
Kaufmann, Walter. '*Existenz* versus the State, Darwin and Rousseau'. *Nietzsche: Philosopher, Psychologist, Anti-Christ*. Princeton, NJ: Princeton University Press, 1950.
Kohn, Hans. 'Wagner and His Time'. *The Mind of Germany: The Education of a Nation*. New York: Charles Scribner's Sons, 1960.
Körber, Thomas. 'Politisierter Nietzsche'. *Nietzsche nach 1945*. Königshausen and Neumann, 2006.
Kroker, Arthur. 'In a Future that is Nietzsche'. *The Will to Technology and the Culture of Nihilism: Heidegger, Nietzsche and Marx*. Toronto: University of Toronto Press, 2004.
Lefebvre, Henri. 'Nietzsche et notre temps'. *Nietzsche*. Paris: Editions sociales internationales, 1939.
Lukács, Gyorgy. 'Nietzsche as Founder of Irrationalism in the Imperialist Period'. *The Destruction of Reason*. Trans. Peter Palmer. Atlantic Heights, NJ: Humanities Press, 1981.
Mencken, H. L. 'Government'. *Friedrich Nietzsche* (1913). New Brunswick: Transaction Publishers, 1993.
Nolte, Ernst. 'Fascism as a Metapolitical Phenomenon. Nietzsche: The Prebourgeois Soil of "Culture"'. *Three Faces of Fascism: Action Française, Italian Fascism, National Socialism*. London: Weidenfeld & Nicolson, 1965.
Richardson, John. 'Ethics-Politics'. *Nietzsche's New Darwinism*. New York: Oxford University Press, 2004.
Rosen, Stanley. 'Nietzsche's Revolution'. *The Ancients and the Moderns: Rethinking Modernity*. New Haven, CT: Yale University Press, 1989.
Schutte, Ofelia. 'Nietzsche's Politics'. *Beyond Nihilism: Nietzsche Without Masks*. Chicago: University of Chicago Press, 1984.
Smith, Douglas. '(De)nazifying Nietzsche: Appropriations and Counter-Appropriations' and 'Algerian Masquerade: Nietzsche and Decolonization'. *Transvaluations: Nietzsche in France 1872–1972*. Oxford: Clarendon Press, 1996.
Stone, Dan. 'Nietzsche and Eugenics'. *Breeding Superman: Nietzsche, Race and Eugenics in Edwardian and Interwar Britain*. Liverpool: Liverpool University Press, 2002, 62–93.
Taylor, Quentin P. 'Man and State'. *The Republic of Genius: A Reconstruction of Nietzsche's Early Thought*. Rochester, NY: University of Rochester Press, 1997.

Viereck, Peter. 'Treitschke, Nietzsche, and Bismarck'. *Metapolitics: The Roots of the Nazi Mind*. New York: Capricorn Books, 1961.

Welshon, Rex. 'Life, Virtue, Politics'. *The Philosophy of Nietzsche*. Montreal: McGill-Queen's University Press, 2004.

Williamson, George S. 'Nietzsche's *Kulturkampf*'. *The Longing for Myth in Germany: Religion and Aesthetic Culture from Romanticism to Nietzsche*. Chicago: University of Chicago Press, 2004.

Woods, Roger. 'Nietzsche as "Mentor"'. *The Conservative Revolution in the Weimar Republic*. Basingstoke: Macmillan, 1996.

Yack, Bernard. 'Nietzsche and Cultural Revolution'. *The Longing for Total Revolution: Philosophic Sources of Social Discontent from Rousseau to Marx and Nietzsche*. Princeton, NJ: Princeton University Press, 1986.

Index

absolutism 25
Achilles 36, 52, 56, 83
Aeschylus 83
agon 3, 10, 22, 36
agonism 37
Agrarian League 4
Alcaeus 144
Alcibiades 57, 181
Alexander (the Great) 52, 58, 272
altruism 250, 284, 286, 303 n. 3
Anacreon 39
anarchism 173, 197, 219, 240, 264, 277, 286
Anaximander 83
anti-political 2, 242, 246, 270, 293 n. 7
Antisemitische Correspondenz 19
anti-Semitism 1, 4, 6, 18–21, 72, 174, 200, 240, 285, 294 n. 30
anti-Socialist Laws 5, 6, 14, 22, 73, 74, 116, 299 n. 21
Apollo 44, 55
Archilochus 39, 144
Aristides 55
aristocracy 21, 44, 162, 205, 206, 233–5, 277, 281, 298 n. 108
Aristotle 54, 55, 84, 107
ascetic ideal 174, 214
asceticism 179, 263, 264
Austro-Prussian War 8
autocracy 2, 25, 118, 146, 161, 173

bad conscience 125, 151, 180, 190, 225, 227–9
Bakunin, M. 296
Balzac, H. 203
barbarism 11, 35, 43, 46, 48, 60, 63, 98, 204, 257, 295 n. 55
Barrau, T. H. 25
Battle of Sedan 9
Bebel, A. 5, 9, 11, 22, 35, 295 n. 47
Beecher Stowe, H. 302 n. 12
Beethoven, L. v. 145, 168, 203
bellum omnium contra omnes 43
Benedetti, Count 9
Bentham, J. 193

Bergmann, P. 3, 17, 295 n. 55, 299 n. 14
Berlin Conference 16, 17, 172
Bayreuth Festival (*Bayreuther Festspiele*) 72
Biedermann, K. 8
Bildung 247, 303 n. 16
Bismarck, H. 17, 294 n. 30
Bismarck, O. v. 1–17, 21, 22, 25, 31–3, 37, 72, 75, 88, 105, 116, 118, 119, 161, 164, 173, 174, 238, 241, 243, 246, 293 n. 16, 294 n. 17, n. 24, n. 27, n. 30, n. 31, 295 n. 37, 296 n. 71, 300 n. 21, 303 n. 49
Bizet, G. 202
Blanc, L. 27
Blanqui, L. A. 27
Bonaparte, L. (Napoleon III) 3, 7, 9, 24, 26, 27, 29, 298 n. 1
Bonaparte, N. (Napoleon I) 1, 22, 29, 92, 118, 119, 134–6, 141, 148, 161, 164, 166, 168, 172, 173, 180, 188, 195, 198, 203, 215, 216, 224, 232, 238, 242, 246, 253–5, 270, 275, 277, 294 n. 24
Borgia, C. 242, 248, 249, 268, 273
Brandes, G. 20
Buckle, T. 218, 254
Buddhism 165, 180, 184
Bugeaud, T. R. 27
Bund, Der 249, 272
Bundesrat 3, 13
Burckhardt, J. 21, 34, 172, 247
Byron, G. N. G., Lord 136

Caesar 141, 160–2, 235
Caesar, J. 28, 164, 181, 232, 251, 272
Caesarean 95, 172, 233
Caesarism 26
Callimachus 144
Caracalla 162
Carlyle, T. 136, 254, 273
Carrière, M. 62
Cate, C. 1, 300 n. 21
categorical imperative 138, 274

Catholic Centre Party 5, 6, 11–14, 37
Catholic Church 5, 12, 37, 72, 89, 97, 296 n. 61, n. 66, n. 67
Catholicism 96, 178, 296 n. 66
Cavaignac, L-E. 27, 28
Changarnier, N. 28
Christianity 19, 26, 40, 41, 63, 66, 72, 80–2, 97, 100, 120, 122, 123, 137, 161, 162, 171, 174, 178, 180, 214, 217, 238, 240–3, 256–62, 265–70, 274, 278, 279, 282, 296 n. 71
Christian Social Workers' Party 18
Christian state 1, 2, 5, 18, 24, 174, 240–2, 278, 282, 303 n. 16
civitas dei 18
colonialism 16, 17, 297 n. 81, n. 86
Comte, A. 123, 164
Confucius 166, 245
constitutionalism 2
Corneille, P. 144
Craig, G. 294 n. 30
Cromwell, O. 178

Darwinism 273
décadence 242, 250, 252, 253, 260, 275, 285, 286
Delacroix, E. 203
democracy 2–5, 13, 14, 74, 75, 94, 109, 111, 114, 115, 118, 162, 166, 171, 173, 194, 219, 233, 240, 242, 251, 260, 301 n. 19
Democritus 84
Demosthenes 83
Diogenes 90
Dionysus 255, 272
dissimulation 137, 150, 280
Dubois-Reymond, E. 67
Dühring, E. 19, 20, 225–7, 231, 240

Eckermann, J. P. 61
egalitarianism 171
egoism 41, 44, 63, 66, 77, 91, 113, 120, 149, 163, 193, 195, 211, 212, 227, 250, 258, 277, 279, 283, 284
Elias, N. 293 n. 7
Empedocles 83, 147
Enlightenment 34, 44, 72, 73, 82, 91, 109
Epicurean 66, 179, 181, 202
Epicurus 266

equality of rights, equal rights 21, 34, 39, 74, 88, 106, 118, 164, 166, 169–71, 175, 177, 185, 191, 193, 242, 248, 250, 258, 264, 278, 282, 285, 286
Eris 36, 54, 106
eudaemonism 191

Faust 104, 198
Fichte, J. 24, 198
Förster, B. 17, 18
Franconia 31
Franco-Prussian War 6, 9, 33, 36, 241
Frantz, K. 18
Free Conservative Party 4, 16, 300 n. 31
free spirit(s) 3, 72, 73, 75, 79, 80, 108, 130, 167, 176, 177, 179, 184, 190, 195, 268
freedom 250–3, 255
French Revolution 1, 2, 25, 44, 73, 117, 123, 173, 178, 194, 198, 215, 224, 242
Freytag, G. 8, 295 n. 52
Friedrich of Denmark 6, 7
Friedrich II (Holy Roman Emperor) 181, 268
Friedrich II (King of Prussia) 187, 188
Friedrich III (Crown Prince) 5, 16, 17, 240, 241
Friedrich Wilhelm IV 1, 24, 270
Fritsch, T. 19

Galiani, F. 163, 193
Geffcken, H. 241
General German Workers' Association 5
genius 24–7, 34–7, 42, 43, 45–8, 53, 55, 64, 65, 68–71, 75, 80, 82, 135, 136, 142, 146, 187, 188, 201–3, 211, 213, 223, 251, 253, 254, 266–8, 273, 275, 285–7
Gerlach, L. v. 4
German Confederation 7
German Conservative Party 4, 6, 18, 241, 300 n. 31
German Free Thought Party 5, 16
Germania 24, 26
German Wars of Liberation 1, 2, 25, 31, 198, 242, 246, 269, 275
Gersdorff, C. v. 10, 11, 33

Girardin, A. 27
Gobineau, J-A. 172
Goethe, J. W. 1, 61, 67, 104, 129, 145, 165, 168, 188, 198, 203, 228, 238, 246, 255, 270
good European(s) 17, 72, 96, 107, 108, 119, 165, 174, 196, 202, 217, 270
grand politics (*die grosse Politik*) 17, 22, 128, 173, 187, 196, 202, 241–3, 246, 276, 294 n. 27, 304 n. 39

Hamlet 185
Hammerstein, W. v. 6, 241
Händel, G. F. 238
Harms, F. 62
Hébert, J. R. 25
hedonism 191
Hegel, G. W. F. 52, 129, 190, 199, 201, 246
Hegelian philosophy 50
Heine, H. 168, 201, 203, 246
Helvetius, C-A. 193
Herder, J. G. 271
Hermodor 55
Hesiod 36, 53, 54, 106, 128
Hohenzollern (House of) 8, 9, 119, 163, 242, 243, 271
Homer 36, 43, 53, 55, 76, 128, 194
Horace 38, 120, 126, 144
Hugo, V. 28, 201, 286
humanisation 172, 237, 249
Humboldt, W. v. 129
Huss, J. 82

imperialism 5, 17, 35
Imperial Message 15, 297 n. 76
Imperium Romanum 145, 166, 178, 252, 257, 265, 267, 274
individualism 21, 22, 118, 169, 170, 277, 278, 302 n. 21
Inquisition 99
International, the 2, 15
Islam 267, 268

Jahn, O. 32
Jesuit Act 12
Jesuits 12, 56, 86, 297 n. 81
Jesuitism 170
Jesus Christ 25, 30, 81, 97, 164, 224
Jewish Question 18–20

Jews 18–20, 72, 96, 112, 119, 120, 131, 133, 146, 159, 160, 163, 170, 174, 200, 201, 220, 223, 224, 266, 268, 285, 287, 291, 294 n. 26, n. 30, 298 n. 104
Jörg, J. E. 33
Journal des Débats 273
Judaism 18, 19, 97, 174, 266
Junker(s) 2, 4, 6, 159, 273, 295 n. 37
justice 23, 40, 41, 43, 74, 76, 77, 87–90, 95, 105–7, 110, 112, 114, 118, 155, 156, 170, 171, 180, 182, 184, 210, 211, 216, 224–6, 231, 235, 248, 255, 278, 281, 282, 285

Kaiserreich 2, 15
Kant, I. 1, 75, 124, 164, 189, 190, 255, 269, 275
Klopstock, F. 24
Köselitz, H. (Peter Gast) 240
Kotzebue, A. F. v. 198
Krause, E. 270
Kreuzzeitung 6, 8, 174, 241, 273
Krug, G. 24
Kullman, H. 12
Kulturkampf 5, 6, 12, 13, 22, 37, 72, 174, 296 n. 61, 297 n. 81
Kulturstaat 12, 35, 36, 242

laissez-faire 5, 163
Lamartine, A. 27
Lamoricière, C. L. L. 28
Lange, F. 19
Large, D. 293 n. 16
Lassalle, F. 5
Law of Manu 244
Law-Book of Manu 242, 261–3, 290
Ledru-Rollin, A-A. 27
Leibniz, G. W. 238, 269, 275
Leo XIII 13
Leonardo da Vinci 181
Leopold (Prince) 9
Liebknecht, W. 5
liberalism 5, 6, 14, 18, 21, 22, 31, 34, 250
liberal revolutions 1
Livingstone, D. 135
London Protocol 7, 31
Louis-Philippe 27
Louis XIV 116, 130, 146, 148

Louis XV 25, 26
Louis XVI 25
Lucretius 266
Luther, M. 1, 5, 82, 135, 147, 161, 178, 214, 215, 261, 268, 269, 274

Machiavelli, N. 3, 79, 278
Machiavellian 3, 4, 8, 25, 73, 241
Machiavellianism 3, 235, 280
Manchester liberalism 5, 16, 296 n. 71
Machtpolitik 4
Manu 245, 263
March Brandenburg 20, 161
Marx, K. 2
Marr, W. 19
masses, the 21, 34, 35, 40, 41, 44, 45, 47, 51, 74, 75, 84, 91, 92, 95, 101, 118, 119, 128, 143, 145–7, 161, 166, 169, 173, 196, 204, 234, 257, 259, 261, 262, 275, 277
master morality 206, 208
Mazzini, G. 138
Mérimée, P. 89
Meyer, J. 62
Michelet, J. 188
militarism 25, 33, 34, 282, 287
Mill, J. S. 123, 281, 291
Miltiades 55, 57
Mirabeau, H. G. de Riqueti 89, 222
Mithras 266
Moltke, H. v. 10, 34
Mommsen, W. 2
monarchy 2, 6, 8, 10, 18, 26, 27, 33, 119, 162, 163, 294 n. 17, 295 n. 37
Montaigne, M. de 186
morality 24, 26, 58, 66, 75–80, 89, 105, 112, 113, 116, 118, 121–5, 127, 138, 141, 147, 165–7, 169–71, 178, 181–6, 190, 193, 206–8, 210, 211, 218, 220, 221, 223, 234, 237–9, 243–5, 248–50, 253, 254, 261, 273, 274, 276, 280, 283, 289, 291
Mundt, T. 15

nationalism 2, 4, 18, 22, 24, 72, 96, 98, 174, 217, 275, 277, 282, 283, 294 n. 17
National Liberal Party 5, 21

National Liberals 2, 5, 11–14, 16, 22, 37
Nationalzeitung 273
naturalism 286
natural law 4, 21, 172, 175, 263
Nero 162
new nobility 29, 118, 157
New Party of Life 6
Niebuhr, B. G. 161
Nietzsche, E. (Förster) 17
Nietzsche, L. 1, 270, 271
nihilism 229, 230, 286
North German Confederation 8, 9, 32, 33
Novalis, F. L. 24
Nueva Germania 17

Oehler, F. (Nietzsche) 270, 271
oligarchs of the spirit 73, 84
Oudinot, Marshal 27, 28
order of rank 15, 73, 117, 119, 162, 170, 172, 175, 193, 204, 206, 233, 236, 242, 264, 276, 278, 283, 291
Osiris 266
ostracism 55
Overman, the (*Übermensch*) 117, 152, 156, 237, 242, 248, 256, 273, 276

Paris Commune 3, 9, 10, 14, 15, 22, 34, 38, 73, 169, 295 n. 47, 298 n. 112
parliamentarianism 2, 3, 5, 21, 147, 189, 242, 246
Parmenides 83
Pascal, B. 178, 238, 283
pathos of distance 172, 204, 232, 242, 250, 259, 263
patriotism 8, 86, 196
Paul, J. 198
Pausanius 54
Pericles 55, 95, 194
pessimism 38, 185, 191, 201, 215, 246, 263, 283
Peter, C. 24
Phidias 39
Philetas 39, 144
philosopher-legislator(s) 2, 172
Pindar 56, 83
Pinder, W. 24
pity 34, 40, 41, 76, 77, 108, 118, 123, 124, 139, 146, 156, 157, 164, 166, 184, 191, 192, 195, 207, 208, 217,

pity – *continued*
    221, 230, 232, 235, 250, 256, 278, 286, 291
Plato 2, 21, 45, 46, 55, 56, 83, 95, 113, 245, 280, 288, 290
Plutarch 39
polis 34, 95, 96, 210
Polyklet 39
practical Christianity 14, 16, 22, 174, 241, 296 n. 71
press, the 18, 49, 103, 119, 165, 294 n. 30
Progressive Liberal Party 5, 6
Propertius 144
property 15, 36, 54, 66, 74, 85, 89, 101, 108, 112–14, 149, 169, 194, 237, 282
Protagoras 56
Protestantism 18, 269
Prussian May Laws 12, 37
public opinion 10, 58, 71, 84, 147, 180, 253
Pulpit Paragraph 11
puritanism 179
Pythagoras 83

race 1, 18, 20, 35, 62, 72, 76, 79, 96, 128, 129, 135, 138, 143, 149, 155, 163, 164, 166, 169, 174, 179, 181, 186, 193, 196–8, 200, 204, 205, 211, 217, 219, 220, 222, 227, 233, 236, 237, 244, 245, 256, 260, 270, 271, 274, 279, 284–6, 288
Ranke, L. v. 24, 164
Realpolitik 3, 4, 24, 32, 75, 241
Reformation 51, 63, 66, 81, 99, 147, 173, 174, 214, 215, 224, 242, 269, 274
Reich 2–6, 10–14, 17, 19, 22, 34, 36, 37, 58, 62, 116, 117, 135, 162, 171, 173, 240–3, 246, 247, 251, 252, 269, 270, 282, 293 n. 16, 294 n. 27, 297 n. 81, 299 n. 23, 300 n. 21, 303 n. 16
Reichsfeinde 4, 6, 37, 294 n. 26
Reichstag 3–5, 8, 9, 11, 13–16, 22, 32, 33, 171, 241, 295 n. 47, 300 n. 21
Reign of Terror 25
Reinsurance Treaty 174
religion 18, 19, 38, 40, 41, 62, 63, 92–4, 119, 138, 140, 147, 165, 166, 179, 183, 184, 217, 241, 243, 245, 259, 266, 274, 275, 279, 284, 286
Renaissance 1, 42, 73, 81, 82, 166, 167, 172, 173, 216, 224, 236, 238, 242, 249, 250, 254–6, 268, 269, 274, 302 n. 21
Renan, E. 164
ressentiment 20, 173, 174, 221–7, 231, 240, 259, 284, 286
revaluation of all values 23, 242, 270, 275
revenge 10, 57, 77, 78, 106, 108, 118, 120, 134, 139, 154–6, 178, 182, 208, 220, 225, 226, 231, 232, 248, 264, 266, 270, 282, 284
rights 3, 5, 6, 11, 23, 45, 52, 77, 87, 98, 107, 114, 121, 122, 140, 141, 147, 151, 162, 167, 173, 184, 194, 212, 224, 235, 245, 264, 281, 285
Ritschl, F. 32
Robespierre, M. de 261
Rochau, A. L. v. 3
Rohde, E. 37, 296 n. 66
Romundt, H. 296 n. 66
Roth, G. 21
Rousseau, J-J. 73, 91, 109, 235, 236, 238, 254, 261, 302 n. 12
Royal Proclamation 116

Saint-Just 25, 29
Saint-Simon 261
Sand, G. 198
sans-culottes 25, 30
Savonarola, G. 261
Schelling, F. 129
Schiller, F. 129
Schleiermacher, F. 129
Schleswig-Holstein crisis 1, 7
School Supervision Act 12
Schopenhauer, A. 33, 35, 61, 68, 71, 123, 124, 129, 201, 203, 238, 246, 250, 272
Schulze-Delitzsch, H. 297 n. 75
Schweinitz, General v. 17
Second French Republic 24
secularisation/secularism 2, 5, 12, 18, 24, 37
security 90, 107, 110, 116, 118, 125, 127, 142, 166, 177, 222, 264
Simonides 56

slave morality   25, 173, 206, 208, 221
slavery   17, 34, 36, 37, 39–41, 52, 74, 88, 90, 117, 133, 134, 143, 147, 172, 177, 195, 197, 204, 216, 233, 234, 237, 252, 261, 286, 302 n. 12
social contract   4, 18
Social Democratic Labour Party   5
Social Democratic Party (SPD)   5, 6, 13–15, 116, 295 n. 37, 300 n. 21
social insurance   5
socialism   3, 10, 14–16, 18, 38, 73, 74, 87, 95, 98, 100, 114, 116–19, 143, 164, 165, 168, 169, 171, 240, 277, 287, 295 n. 47, 296 n. 71
social question   6, 15, 19, 38, 117
social security   15, 22
Socrates   69, 83, 183, 186, 191, 301 n. 19
Solon   83
Spencer, H.   250
Spinoza, B.   97, 255
Spitteler, K.   272
St Augustine   181, 267
St Paul   224, 260, 266
St Theresa   279
state, the   3, 5, 10–13, 16, 21, 22, 33–5, 37, 41–5, 49–52, 55, 57, 62–4, 66, 68, 69, 71, 80, 81, 89, 92–5, 100, 103, 106, 107, 127, 134, 151, 152, 174, 215, 227, 238, 242, 246, 247, 251, 263, 277, 282
state socialism   5, 14, 22
Stein, H. v.   272
Stendhal (Henri Beyle)   165, 168, 172, 202, 203
Stephani, E.   32
Stöcker, A.   4, 6, 18, 19, 174, 240, 241, 294 n. 30
Stoicism   167, 177
Strauss, D. F.   36
Sue, E.   28
suffering   21, 40, 68, 85, 91, 92, 96, 124, 126, 132, 142, 177–9, 184, 192, 208, 220, 221, 228, 230, 231, 248, 275, 284, 294 n. 30
Sybel, H. v.   21, 31, 200
Syllabus of Errors   11

Taine, H.   201
Tal, U.   19, 296 n. 71, 298 n. 108
tariff law   14

Taylor, A. J. P.   294 n. 17, n. 31
terrorism   73, 95
Thales   84
Themistocles   55, 57
Theocritus   144
Theognis   219
Thiers, A.   9, 27, 28, 34
Third (French) Republic   9
Three Emperors' League   4, 174
Thucydides   55, 76, 83, 96, 107
Treaty of Frankfurt   9
Treaty of Vienna   7
Treitschke, H. v.   8, 21, 31, 32, 200, 240, 274, 298 n. 102, n. 108
tyranny   73, 83, 84, 125, 168, 175, 227, 231, 236, 237, 239, 251

Uhland, L.   104
universal rights of man   21
universal (male) suffrage (*suffrage universel*)   2, 3, 4, 18, 21, 31, 34, 44, 74, 75, 110, 115, 119, 161, 162, 164, 242, 282
utilitarianism   128, 191

Victoria (Princess)   16
Virchow, R.   12, 219
virtù   172, 173, 238, 242, 256
virtue   55, 78, 104, 108, 113, 128, 132–4, 139, 141, 152, 155, 160, 162, 164, 165, 169, 176, 180, 181, 186, 190–3, 195, 196, 200, 208, 210, 217, 231, 233, 234, 236–8, 245, 249–51, 253, 255, 256, 259, 279, 280, 287
Vischer, F. T.   274
Voltaire, F. M. A. de   72, 73, 85, 91, 123

Wächter, K. G. v.   32
Wagner, C.   271
Wagner, R.   33, 67, 68, 72, 174, 199, 201, 203, 204, 240, 246, 271, 286, 303 n. 49
war   4, 7–11, 14, 22, 23, 31–4, 36–8, 43–5, 51–4, 58, 59, 61, 67, 87, 89, 92, 97, 98, 103, 104, 111, 112, 114, 117, 126, 128, 134, 140, 142, 146, 148, 156, 161, 168, 174, 187, 188, 191, 215, 216, 219, 220, 223, 227, 229, 238, 239, 241, 243, 251,

war – *continued*
    256, 258, 266–8, 270, 276, 278, 282,
    283, 288, 294 n. 31, 304 n. 39
Wehler, H-U.   14, 294 n. 26, 296 n. 70
Widmann, V.   272, 273
Wilhelm I   2, 9, 10, 13–15, 24, 116
Wilhelm II   240, 241, 243
will to power   167, 172, 175, 177, 190,
    206, 228, 231, 234, 235, 240, 250,
    256, 278, 283, 290

workers   5, 14, 15, 75, 90, 110, 116, 117,
    134, 143, 148, 150, 174, 203, 235,
    296 n. 71
Würkert, L.   32
Wuttke, H.   32

Zarathustra   19, 117, 118, 152, 154, 156,
    159, 160, 260, 273, 301 n. 19
Zeno of Elea   56
Zimmern, H.   243